WHAT HAS
Jerusalem
TO DO WITH
Beijing?

WHAT HAS
Jerusalem
TO DO WITH
Beijing?

中 華

BIBLICAL INTERPRETATION

聖 經

FROM A CHINESE PERSPECTIVE

詮 釋

Yeo Khiok-khng (K.K.)

TRINITY PRESS INTERNATIONAL
Harrisburg, Pennsylvania

BS
476
.Y36
1998

Trinity Press International, P.O. Box 1321, Harrisburg, PA 17105
Trinity Press International is a division of the Morehouse Group

Library of Congress Cataloging-in-Publication Data
Yeo, Khiok-Khng.
    What has Jerusalem to do with Beijing : biblical interpretation
from a Chinese perspective / Yeo Khiok-khng (K.K.).
        p. cm.
    Includes bibliographical references and indexes.
    ISBN 1-56338-229-6 (alk. paper)
    1. Bible – Hermeneutics – Cross-cultural studies. 2. China –
Civilization. I. Title.
BS476.V36 1998
220.6′01 – dc21   98-13880
                                                             CIP

Printed in the United States of America

98   99   00   01   02   10   9   8   7   6   5   4   3   2   1

Contents

Part III
BIBLICAL MESSAGES FOR
THE CURRENT CHINESE SITUATION

Acknowledgments

Much appreciation is due to individuals and communities who have supported this writing project graciously. I especially appreciate the critique, affirmation, and sustaining prayer of Drs. Robert Jewett, Donald Alexander, David Himrod, Neal Fisher, Henry Young, Jack Seymour, John Hinkle, Philip Chia, Andrew Kwong, Wolfgang Roth, Phyllis Bird, Adolf Hansen, Yeow Choo Lak, Fernando Segovia, and the Yeo family (Kung-Siu, Timothy, Joseph, and Phoebe). Dr. Richard N. Soulen proofread the manuscript with careful and critical comments; his painstaking editing has made the monograph more readable. I am also grateful for the interest of Trinity Press International, especially Dr. Harold W. Rast's enthusiasm and Laura Barrett's leadership in publishing this work.

Credit is due to the following journals for allowing me to collect and revise the articles in this monograph:

"Amos (4:4–5) and Confucius: The Will (Ming) of God (T'ien)," *Asia Journal of Theology* 4 (October 1990): 472–88; appeared also in *Doing Theology with Asian Resources: Theology and Cultures*, vol. 2, edited by Yeow Choo Lak (Singapore: ATESEA, 1995), 85–102.

"The Meaning and Usage of 'REST' (*Katapausis* and *Sabbatismos*) in Hebrews 3:7–4:13," *Asia Journal of Theology* 5 (April 1991): 2–33.

"A Rhetorical Study of Acts 17:22–31: What Has Jerusalem to Do with Athens and Beijing?" *Jian Dao: A Journal of Bible and Theology* 1 (1994): 75–107.

"Revelation 5 in the Light of Pannenberg's Christology: Christ the End of History and the Hope of the Suffering," *Asia Journal of Theology* 8 (October 1994): 308–34.

"Isaiah 5:1–7 and 27:2–6: Let's Hear the Whole Song of Rejection and Restoration," *Jian Dao: A Journal of Bible and Theology* 3 (1995): 77–93.

"The 'Yin and Yang' of God (Ex 3:14) and Humanity (Gn 1:27)," *Zeitschrift für Religions- und Geistesgeschichte* 46, no. 4 (1994): 319–32.

"A Confucian Reading of Romans 7:14–25: Nomos (Law) and Li (Propriety)," *Jian Dao: A Journal of Bible and Theology* 5 (1996): 127–41.

A Chinese Introduction

This volume is a collection of ten essays on the Bible. It reflects the range of biblical reading I have preferred to do over the last seven years. Living in a multifaith, multitextual, and multicultural context, I cannot help but address the convention of reading employed here: a Chinese Christian reading of the biblical text from an Asian perspective.

I was born and reared as an atheist in Malaysia, but I respected the major traditions of Chinese philosophy and religion, the culture of which I was a part. At the age of eighteen, I came to appreciate and to worship the Messiah, who was born a Jew but died for all, including the Chinese. The Christ event is itself a transspatial and transtemporal event, which for this reason places on the followers of Christ the mandate of a cross-cultural hermeneutic. In my theological education I came to adore the apostle to the Gentiles, Paul, who remained a Jew but who zealously proclaimed the gospel of the Messiah to those without the law, the promise, and circumcision. His epistles, collected in the New Testament, became my favorite reading. The effort demonstrated in this monograph is my way of imitating Paul's cross-cultural hermeneutics. The first two chapters provide a biblical basis for clarifying the methodology of a cross-cultural reading. The first chapter is an attempt to consider various aspects of a cross-cultural reading which is biblical, theological, rhetorical, and contextual. The second chapter is more biblical as it reflects on Gal 3:1–20, a passage which supplies the needed resources for a cross-cultural hermeneutic.

The next eight chapters have to do with the ways I read the biblical text, always with one eye on the Asian context. To do a cross-cultural reading of the biblical text, I have divided the essays into two main categories: one group of essays dialogues with perennial themes in Chinese cultures. These essays seek to express biblical truth in the language of my own people. Nobody can communicate intelligibly in culture-free theological axioms; nor can Christian faith be meaningful in a cultural vacuum. Theological hermeneutics is the art and science of appropriating the eternal will of God (historically revealed in the Word of God in its Hebraic and Greco-Roman milieu) to the particular historical situation of people.[1] Since the task of the theological enterprise essentially is to interpret or construct truth in a way intelligible to people, the crucial need to speak the truth in the language of the people has been recognized ever since Creation. As such, every theological revelation and construction is contextual and indigenous. For theology not only addresses the needs of a particular people in a particular situation, it is also conveyed in and through the language of the people. The Scripture itself gives us the best example.[2] Chapters 3–7 seek to use the language of yin-yang philosophy and the Confucian understanding of *T'ien Ming* (mandate of Heaven) as well as *li* (law/propriety) and *jen* (love) to convey the biblical notions of God, humanity, rest, will of God, and so forth.

To express biblical truth contextually is to read intertextually; however, to minimize the possibility of eisegesis (reading into the text), I always begin from the biblical text rather than with the Confucian and yin-yang philosophical texts. Readers interested in the theoretical basis of intertextuality may wish to trace the

---

1. For more on hermeneutics, religions, and cultures see *Gospel and Culture: The Papers of a Consultation on the Gospel and Culture, Convened by the Lausanne Committee's Theology and Education Group,* ed. John Stott and Robert T. Coote (Pasadena, Calif.: William Carey Library, 1979); *Christianity and Other Religions, Selected Readings,* ed. John Hick and Brian Hebblethwaite (Philadelphia: Fortress, 1980); and Khiok-khng Yeo, *Rhetorical Interaction in 1 Corinthians 8 and 10: A Formal Analysis with Preliminary Suggestions for a Chinese Cross-Cultural Hermeneutic* (Leiden: E. J. Brill, 1995), chap. 3 ("Cross-Cultural and Rhetorical Hermeneutics").

2. Notice how the truth about and of God is revealed in the language of the Hebrews and the common Greeks. There seems not to be such a thing as "a pure holy language" about God which is untainted by the language of people. The incarnation of Christ speaks of the ultimate need for the truth to become flesh. Not only does God's revelation impinge on the lives of people, but the people's situation also cries out for God's response.

development of structuralism, poststructuralism, and intertextual reading.[3]

Chapters 3 to 6 employ intertextual theories of reading, such as structuralism. Structuralism and intertextual readings depend on semiotics as well as on culturally contingent factors of reading.[4] A system of semiotic codes is operative when both social conventions and transcendental symbols are interactive. But these codes are not autonomously universal; rather they are networks framed and conditioned by sociocultural factors.[5] As such, reading in a multi-faith, multitextual, and multicultural context cannot be a reading of the level of the textual code alone, but must include acknowledgment of and sensitivity to the readership as well as to textual contexts. The audience and textual contexts provide the network for and the possibility of reading.[6] This view is an extension of Julia Kristeva's notion of "intertextuality" and Bultmann's concept of "pre-understanding."[7] Culler speaks of the intelligibility of a text "in terms of a prior body of discourse."[8] He also notes the function

3. See Tzvetan Todorov, "Reading as Construction," in Susan R. Suleiman and Inge Crossman, eds., *The Reader in the Text: Essays on Audience Interpretation* (Princeton: Princeton University Press, 1980), 67–82; see also Spike Draisma, ed., *Intertextuality in Biblical Writings: Essays in Honour of Bas van Iersel* (Kempen: Kok, 1989). On intertextual reading of biblical texts, see Michael Worton and Judith Still, eds., *Intertextuality: Theories and Practices* (Manchester: Manchester University Press, 1990); Michael Fishbane, *Biblical Interpretation in Ancient Israel* (Oxford: Clarendon Press, 1985); Richard Hays, *Echoes of Scripture in the Letters of Paul* (New Haven: Yale University Press, 1989).

4. On poststructuralism, see Roland Barthes, "Theory of Text," in *Untying the Text: A Post-structuralist Reader,* ed. Robert Young (Boston: Routledge and Kegan Paul, 1981), 31–47; idem, *Elements of Semiology* (New York: Hill and Wang, 1964); idem, *The Pleasure of the Text* (New York: Hill and Wang, 1973).

5. Jonathan Culler mentions the readerly orientation of framing the sign in *Framing the Sign: Criticism and Its Institutions* (Oxford: Blackwell, 1988). Culler writes, "Framing the sign has several advantages over context: it reminds us that framing is something we do; it hints of the frame-up . . . a major use of context" (ix).

6. Consult Jonathan Culler's work on the possibility of reading in signs and semiotics, *The Pursuit of Signs: Semiotics, Literature, Deconstruction* (London: Routledge and Kegan Paul, 1981), 50; *Structuralist Poetics: Structuralism, Linguistics, and the Study of Literature* (London: Routledge and Kegan Paul, 1975), 30.

7. Julia Kristeva, *Revolution in Poetic Language* (New York: Columbia University Press, 1984), 60; Rudolf Bultmann, *Existence and Faith: Shorter Writings of Rudolf Bultmann* (London: Hodder and Stoughton, 1964), 342.

8. Culler, *The Pursuit of Signs,* 101.

of intertextuality as an allusion "to the paradoxical nature of discursive systems.... Everything in *la langue,* as Saussure says, must have first been in *parole.* But *parole* is made possible by *la langue,* and if one attempts to identify any utterance or text as a moment of origin one finds that they depend on prior codes."[9] Applying the insight of Culler, one may contend that Romans and the *Analects,* Hebrews and *Tao Te Ching,* exist intertextually in their *parole,* but their *langue* is made plain only in the reader's hermeneutics. While not following the postmodernists Riffaterre's and Kristeva's irreducible polyvalence and radical indeterminacy of intertextual boundaries,[10] the four essays do place artificial limits on the significations of *li* (law), *jen* (love in the Spirit), *T'ien Ming* (Will of God), and *Tai-Chi* (rest) in my reading of the *Analects* and the biblical passages.

To do a cross-cultural reading of biblical texts is also to let the biblical text respond to the particular context of the reader. Chapters 7–10 are examples of contextual readings of the biblical text for the current Chinese situation. In chapter 7, through the use of rhetorical criticism, Paul's preaching is heard as speaking not only to Athenian philosophers, but also to Chinese Taoists. In chapter 8, the message of hope found in the book of Revelation is heard as speaking to the Chinese Christians who lived through the Cultural Revolution. In chapter 9, Is 5:1–7 and 27:2–6 offer a political and social message of restoration to those who felt betrayed in the June Fourth event of national disgrace at Tienanmen Square. The chapter shows that these two pericopae (Is 5:2–7 and 27:2–6) form one unified song of judgment and restoration; it also argues that only in the vision and message of the whole, as conveyed in the song, can we find the coherent pattern of divine purpose in human history. Chapter 10 is an analysis of 1 Corinthians 11 and 14 in view of the Malaysian "Vision 2020" put out by the prime minister. It sug-

---

9. Culler, *The Pursuit of Signs,* 103.

10. Michael Riffaterre, *Semiotics of Poetry* (Bloomington: Indiana University Press, 1984); see also Julia Kristeva's understanding that a text will absorb the other texts in their intertextual space (*Revolution in Poetic Language;* idem, *Desire in Language: A Semiotic Approach to Literature and Art* [Oxford: Basil Blackwell, 1987]). See Culler's critique on the "undefined discursive space" intertextuality designates in *The Pursuit of Signs,* 109.

gests that the Pauline vision of mutuality between men and women is a better vision than that found in exclusively man or woman theologies which stop short of the wider transformation needed.

These experiments with cross-cultural hermeneutics hope to achieve the transformation of both biblical reading and the Chinese culture. To use the biblical text as a normative response to the Chinese and Malaysian contexts may neither be fair nor valid for a relativist if he/she assumes that the Bible is just one of the many sacred texts. I do not think that relativism *and* universalism are the answers to cross-cultural hermeneutics. On the one hand, the uniqueness of one's culture needs to be affirmed, while on the other hand, a culture needs the critique of another culture. If openness, even accepting criticism from others, is essential to cross-cultural hermeneutics, then the Chinese culture must be opened to the biblical text, though I acknowledge also that my reading of the Bible is influenced by my own cultural reading. A monocultural reading of the gospel can easily be idolatrous. We are always at the point of inventing systems of cultural symbols and creating communities of meaning, so that what we present through the culture is never absolute. So a cross-cultural reading is more objective than a monocultural reading of the biblical text.

Part I

The Methods of Cross-Cultural Hermeneutics

Chapter 1

Theological Methods and Chinese Contexts

The twentieth century, as it moves toward the twenty-first, can be characterized as the age of specialized technology, of an explosion of information, and of instantaneous communication. These hallmarks of our time do not necessarily indicate or guarantee that human culture is moving toward the eradication of conflict, the comprehension of the wholeness of life, or the mutual communality of diverse groups. On the contrary, humanity continues to face the crisis of alienation and the threat of annihilation as it uncritically accepts and glorifies twentieth-century technology. Satellite communication brings different parts of the world into our living rooms; but it does not necessarily help us to commune with one another. We may try to reach out to someone through the fiberglass line, but we seldom touch that person.[1] We use many words, but we do not always use them meaningfully. The explosion of knowledge has bred technological specialization, yet it has not enabled most of us to comprehend more of the totality of reality, as we would prefer. The result threatens to be disastrous, because we only know in part and not in whole; we do not see the interrelatedness of the parts.

The danger of specialization lies in the tunnel vision of the world and the fragmented lifestyle it creates. High technology cannot be a substitute for the human touch. Knowledge does not necessarily breed love. Particularity, while unavoidable, eventually boasts of

---

1. "Touch" is used in the sense that we recognize we are all internally related to each other; knowing that, we avoid being manipulative in rhetoric and avoid influencing each other ideologically.

itself and alienates all others. Universality seems too ideal and far removed; moreover, it has the danger of absorbing all particularities into a melting pot, obliterating one another's uniqueness. It has the further danger of giving a merely superficial sense of oneness. In short, the people of the earth face the crises of alienation, fragmentation, and annihilation more than ever before in the struggle to coexist on planet Earth.

The familiar theme of coexistence in Chinese stories (Confucian, Taoist, and the yin-yang schools) haunts me as I see similar characters and stories repeated in modern history. The issue of coexistence seems to be the basic problem underlying the human story. Are our stories fragmented by necessities of plot, by the tugs of beginning and end, by conflict and mistrust with our neighbors' stories, by ambiguity and meaninglessness? Is there any hope in this picture of gloom and doom? Of course there is. While I do not aim or claim to solve the world's problems, I do hope to address the issue of coexistence by way of a methodology that is cross-cultural and theological.

Content and Methodology of Theology

The essence and means of doing theology are distinct but related. Doing theology involves rational inquiry and theoretical formulation which point us to a more coherent and clearer disclosure of reality and ultimately of God. Theology is primarily a cognitive enterprise, an intellectual dimension of faith which concerns the whole structure and order of intelligibility in the universe. Theology can be a rational inquiry into the knowledge and creation of God, because God's revelation is either rational or suprarational but never irrational. There is an intelligible structure and order in the creation of God. Theology is, therefore, our attempt to love God with our minds, for faith seeks understanding. Faith has its subject matter, which is the subject of our theological enquiry. The experiment of cross-cultural reading of the biblical texts in this volume will show that the quest for meaning is the primary task of theology and that God is the primary subject matter of theology.

Theology has its *objective knowledge,* like any other discipline, where knowledge speaks with its own right, impinging on us with what it stands for. Theology is not merely a value-subjective, judgmental, alternative lifestyle, but a high calling of God to realize the objective, indicative, imperative, and subjunctive of God. This touches on the issues of the essence (content) and methodology of theology, that is, on ontology and epistemology.

Theological *methodology* is a rational inquiry into the knowledge of God. The difference between ontology (*what* we know about reality) and epistemology (*how* we know about reality) must be kept distinct, though they are mutually interactive. In methodology, ontology is faith prior to reason, while epistemology is reason prior to faith. In ontology, faith in God is based not on evidence but on the authority of God Himself through His revelation. But in epistemology, faith finds its logical support and evidence in reason, experience, and history.

In addition, theology is an interpretation of the essence of one's faith. The "essence" of theology is God, while the "form"[2] of theology is the expression or interpretation of our faith. Essence and content are different but related. "Human rational activity consists largely if not wholly in the discovery and creation of form."[3] No one can say that his/her formulation or conceptualization of God is absolute. However, despite one's finite interpretation, the essence of theology, which is God, is infinite. We experience God as the sure object of our trust despite the relative character of our interpretation or biblical reading. Of course, the task of hermeneutics is to get the form as close to the essence as possible. Therefore, theologizing is done not to "build walls" or to exclude others; rather, it is done to create dialogue, tolerance, and appreciation of one another's theology. This personal and communal understanding of theological inquiry is that only a community can do theology in mutual interaction, with tradition, and with postulations. While theologizing is mainly a cognitive enterprise, it becomes a great dynamic in one's spiritual formation, in practical ministry, and in social involvement and lifestyle. Theology needs to live and work

---

2. I might be using a highly Platonic term to set a nondualistic tone, as the reader will notice in my yin-yang framework.

3. Colin Gunton, "Review of Barth and God's Story," *Scottish Journal of Theology* 37 (1975): 375.

in the *dynamic tensions* which exist between the word of God and the community of believers, between biblical and systematic theologies, and between exegesis and homiletics.

In doing theology, the basic level is the theological and scientific, while the ultimate level is the evangelical and doxological. The climax of theology is not simply the construction of a coherent system (it *is* that, no doubt), but a new and fresh appreciation of the grace and love of God. The end of theology is always the beginning of doxology! Aristotle was probably the first to have a systematic view of theology as the first philosophy, wisdom, and as an *a priori* science: thus he calls it meta-physics. The scientific status of theology has had its renaissance in the Western world, making theology public and acceptable to the university world through the philosophical and scientific criteria employed.[4]

Theology is primarily a science and secondarily an art because it concerns itself first and foremost with matters of fact, causes and effects, relations of facts, and all that is entailed in the indicative mood of the "is." Only after dealing with the "is" can one address such issues as ethics and all that is entailed in the imperative mood of the "ought." Theology first deals with the First Cause, ontology, the why; and then it speaks to the how and what. The use of rhetorical criticism in biblical studies and hermeneutics is appropriate because rhetorical theory, like theology, is primarily a science and secondarily an art.[5]

In the theological method (as in scientific method), all theory and interpretation emerge as one reflects on one's experience, based on one's intuition and intellectual conviction concerning reality; then one makes an imaginative jump to postulate a new structural theory or reinterpretation which can be tested against one's experience of reality. This creative interaction of experience (heart) and theory (mind) makes the theological or scientific enterprise a dynamic ongoing process. Our openness to the truth is necessary

---

4. See W. Pannenberg, *Theology and the Philosophy of Science*, trans. Francis McDonagh (London: Darton, Longman & Todd, 1976), 14.

5. For more, see Lloyd F. Bitzer, "Central Problems in the Philosophy of Rhetoric," from *SCA Convention, November 88, Dimension Series Program:* "Intellectual Indebtedness in the Development of Speech Communication: The Influence of Other Disciplines."

so that our assumptions or fundamental ideas can be tested and reinterpreted.

Cross-Cultural Method as Particular, Universal, and Persuasive Truth

In the Newtonian physics, time and space are absolute and independent of mass and energy. In Einstein's general relativity theory, space and time form a continuum and are relational to mass and energy. If the incarnation of God's Son can be construed as God's way of relating to creation in space-time, then the potential of various contextual theologies to express the biblical message is also relative and conditioned. In other words, no particular theology is absolute. The task of biblical interpretation is to make the message of the incarnation visible, taking into account the contingencies of space and time.

Contextual theology is a particular and culturally oriented theology that acknowledges human beings as cultural beings. We can only interpret the world as we perceive it from a given situation. Contextual theology seeks to name the presence and love of God in a particular culture. Cross-cultural hermeneutics is related to universal, cosmic unity through diverse and ambiguous contexts.

In biblical reading, the role of culture is significant as a variant — the freedom of God's love and the contingency involved in the world. The two basic grids of culture are time and space, which make one culture different from all other cultures. Culture as an instrument of adaptation, the learned behaviors of persons, indicates the dynamic quality of cultural formation. Its interaction with theology is intimate and complex. In terms of space (i.e., ecologically speaking) religions or theologies of a survival culture such as that of Eskimos or desert people are different from theologies of a monsoon culture. All seem to seek God, yet the results are the wilderness religion, the meadow religion, the monsoon religion, and so forth.[6] In cross-cultural hermeneutics, therefore,

---

6. E.g., wilderness religions emphasize morality, the demand of the law; monsoon religions, such as in the Philippines, focus on social obligation: the rich are

the observational frames of reference keep changing, but at the same time the constant or invariant character of truth should not be ignored; in fact, it is this invariant that makes the hermeneutical bridge possible and makes the biblical message universally meaningful.

Working with biblical hermeneutics within the larger principle of cross-cultural hermeneutics, one needs to postulate the invisible means in order to explain the visible text. I would propose rhetorical studies as a means. Since "rhetoric is the oldest discipline of the discursive usage of language,"[7] it is proposed here that religious language and hermeneutics be seen under the fountainhead of rhetoric, which with dialectic is in turn under the umbrella of philosophy. In his *Rhetoric* and *Topics* Aristotle has rightly suggested this understanding. Unfortunately, Greco-Roman classical rhetorical theory tended to focus on the rhetor's persuasion of the audience more than on identification with the audience. K. Burke and C. Perelman have introduced the "New Rhetoric"[8] as a corrective lens to the classical practice. Perelman clarifies Aristotle's explanation of rhetoric:

> In analytical, or demonstrative, reasoning, the premises... are true and ultimate, or else derived from such premises, whereas in dialectical reasoning the premises consist of generally accepted opinion. The nature of reasoning in both cases was held to be the same, consisting in drawing conclusions from propositions posited as premises.[9]

---

luckier than the poor, thus obliged to help the poor; in China with its vast plain and many tribal groups, the religious concern is coexistence, therefore humanistic and ethical.

7. Paul Ricoeur, "Rhetoric-Poetics-Hermeneutics," in *From Metaphysics to Rhetoric,* ed. Michel Meyer (London: Kluwer Academic Publishers, 1986), 138.

8. See Chaïm Perelman, *The Realm of Rhetoric,* trans. William Kluback (Notre Dame, Ind.: University of Notre Dame Press, 1982); idem, *The New Rhetoric and the Humanities* (Dordrecht and Boston: D. Reidel, 1979); idem, *The New Rhetoric: A Treatise on Argumentation,* trans. John Wilkinson and Percell Weaver (Notre Dame, Ind.: University of Notre Dame Press, 1969); idem, *The New Rhetoric of Chaïm Perelman: Statement and Response,* ed. Ray D. Dearin (Lanham, Md.: University Press of America, 1989); K. Burke, *Rhetoric of Motives* (Berkeley: University of California Press, 1969); idem, *A Grammar of Motives* (New York: Prentice-Hall, 1952); and Martin Steinmann, *New Rhetorics* (New York: Scribner, 1967).

9. Perelman, *The New Rhetoric and the Humanities,* 26.

This is to say that rhetoric uses syllogisms, but it leaves some premises unexpressed, transforming them into enthymemes. Probably in reaction to Gorgias's and Isocrates' treatment of rhetoric as an art of political discourse only, Aristotle contends that rhetoric is a faculty (*dynameis*) and not just a substantive art of politics. He sees rhetoric as a practical art and an active means of communication in civic life. In reaction to Platonic epistemology of dialectic, Aristotle views *apodeixis* (demonstration) as an art of communication or means of persuasion, rather than a means of discovering the truth.[10] In Aristotle's philosophical system, the conceptualization of the practical and productive art of rhetoric is skillfully worked out in the *Rhetoric*.[11] The task of philosophy, especially first philosophy, is ideally to live a contemplative life which

> was essentially concerned with the pursuit, the comprehension, and the contemplation of the truth concerning the subject himself, the order and the nature of things, or divinity; starting from such comprehension, the wise man was supposed to be able to work out the rules of action, both public and private, as based on philosophical knowledge. Prudence and reasonable action flowed directly from knowledge.[12]

In other words, metaphysics involves the necessity of studying rhetoric and hermeneutics in relation to ontology (study of being) and epistemology (study of knowledge.) And rhetoric and hermeneutics involve the use of the deductive rhetorical "syllogism" of enthymeme and the inductive paradigm to express truth and meaning in order to persuade and inaugurate dialogue with the audience. The New Rhetoric conceives the rhetor and the audience as internally related and sees dialogue as necessary for truth.

The New Rhetoric advocates commonality and communability rather than mere persuasion and ideological change of an opponent. Chapters 3 to 6 seek to demonstrate a dialogical reading

---

10. *Rhetoric*, Bk. 1, chaps. 1 and 2.

11. According to the *Rhetoric* (1356a35–b4), just as there are two methods of argument for dialectic or scientific reasoning (i.e., deductive and inductive), there are also two forms of persuasion in rhetorical reasoning (i.e., the deductive rhetorical "syllogism" of enthymeme and the inductive paradigm).

12. Perelman, *The New Rhetoric and the Humanities*, 43. .

of the biblical texts with perennial themes in Chinese culture. Chapters 7–10 use the biblical message to address current Chinese issues. Both sections are committed to a dialogical reading, whereby it is hoped both Chinese culture and the biblical texts will be illumined through rhetorical criticism.

In chapters 7 and 8 rhetorical criticism is used as the interactive vehicle for conveying the message of Acts 17 and Revelation 5 to a Chinese audience. Rhetorical criticism is not a modern or postmodern methodology. Though there is a renaissance of interest in rhetorical criticism today, it is in fact the oldest form of exegesis. It seeks to explore the argumentative strategy and persuasive power of discourse within the social and political contexts of both the orator/author and audience/reader. As an integrative methodology, rhetorical criticism allows all other forms of exegesis to interact, with the aim of a more holistic understanding of the text at hand in its communicative purpose and effectiveness. The initial task of chapter 7 is to observe the rhetorical interaction of Paul's Areopagus speech with his philosophical audience. Although traditional historical criticism is used, the emphasis is on rhetorical analysis. It will be shown that the interaction between Paul and the audience is dialectical, between the Jewish Christian and Greco-Roman philosophical *topoi,* and that Paul's strategy throughout is to lead the audience from their awareness of the existence of God to an acceptance of the resurrection of and their salvation in Christ.

The intent of chapter 8 is to give the biblical and theological (not the psychological) reasons for the fact that the book of Revelation has such communicative and pastoral power for audiences both ancient and modern. This is achieved by a rhetorical analysis of Revelation 5. The theological position taken here, which focuses on this book's central christological imagery (lion/lamb), is indebted to Wolfhart Pannenberg's Christology as developed in his work *Jesus — God and Man.*

Biblical Reading and Chinese Contexts

Since the universe is a multileveled yet integrated whole, cross-cultural and interdisciplinary studies are required to make any inquiry adequately insightful and meaningful. An interdisciplinary study recognizes the necessity for the sciences and the humanities to have dialogue with each other. Interdisciplinary study is necessary, because the world and human experience are orderly and intrinsically intelligible; an integration of levels of understanding helps us to appreciate the orderliness and comprehensiveness of reality. Similarly, the unitary character of theological and scientific knowledge makes interdisciplinary studies possible. One can assume and hope that an interdisciplinary study will give correlation and coherence to the theological understanding of God's operations of revelation and salvation within our spatio-temporal existence. The conviction held here is that one of the main purposes for constructing a comprehensive and cross-cultural model of interpretation is for the sake of the unification or at least the reconciliation of nations and cultural groups in the world. Since I am writing from an Asian perspective in an Asian context, I will limit myself and speak only of diverse narrative theologies in Asia, mainly Chinese, to illustrate my point.

All the chapters in this monograph experiment with cross-cultural readings and interdisciplinary studies of the Bible. The task of this cross-cultural reading concerns the intricate relations between biblical narratives and the Chinese narratives. Biblical theology can be traced to the narrative theology of the Jews. Abraham is called to follow God, promised a land, and set apart to establish a covenantal people of God. The story of Moses continues the plot through God's deliverance of His people from Egypt, after which the desert experience portrays their wandering in hope of a promised land. The exiles, like their forebears, asked such existential questions as: "Who are we? . . . And why is there so much evil and suffering?" The answers emerge to these universal questions as people from every time and place retell their stories and traditions and relate them to the divine. The narrative theology of Christians of the first two centuries is told in the context of the Roman Empire. It was a context which forced Christians to question the meaning of their own existence. Their answers were derived from the traditions of different Jewish sects (Pharisees, Essenes, Zealots, etc.), and uniquely from Jesus, who began the new religious movement. Above all, the meaning of Christian existence was projected by its main actor, the Messiah himself, who envisioned the New Reign of God embodied in Abba Love.

The Chinese narrative begins with the coexistence of tribal groups who lived in the Yellow River Basin. Before the fifth century B.C.E. there was a period of relative peace and prosperity in China. Most schools of thought were developed in the fourth and fifth centuries B.C.E. to cope with matters of group coexistence and cultural deterioration. People were looking back to their ancestors for ways (Tao) to follow, for a philosophy of life, and a reclamation of serviceable traditions.

The yin-yang philosophy appeals to an understanding of the cosmos as one way to maintain the harmony humans can achieve between themselves and nature. Since chapters 3 and 4 use the yin-yang philosophical paradigm[13] as an overarching framework or principle for reading the biblical text, I wish to explain it in fuller detail here.[14] Some of the main presuppositions and tenets of yin-yang philosophy are:

1. Cosmology is more important than anthropology, because anthropology is a part of cosmology. If one wishes to know anthropology, one has to know its larger context, namely, cosmology.[15] A true understanding of the self is not attained merely by studying oneself, but requires studying the self in relation to the larger whole in which it exists. This approach assumes an organic, rather than an hierarchical, view of the self's relation to others. You and I are part of the purpose of God, who is the larger whole, or Ultimate Reality. Chapter 3 will illustrate my reading of two passages in Genesis and Exodus using this language.

---

13. Jung Young Lee, a contemporary philosopher, has used yin-yang philosophy as an interpretive paradigm for Christian theology. See Jung Young Lee, "Search for a Theological Paradigm: An Asian-American Journey," *Quarterly Review* (Spring 1989): 36–47; idem, *The I Ching and Modern Man: Metaphysical Implications of Change* (New York: University Books, 1974); idem, *The Principle of Changes: Understanding the I Ching* (New York: University Books, 1971); and idem, *The Theology of Change: A Christian Concept of God in an Eastern Perspective* (Maryknoll, N.Y.: Orbis Books, 1979).

14. For a historical perspective of this similar interpretive paradigm found in the Western world, see J. McKim Malville, *The Fermenting Universe: Myths of Eternal Change* (New York: Seabury Press, 1981), 9.

15. "The Book of Change contains the measure of Heaven and Earth, enabling us to comprehend the all-pervasive Tao and its order" (*Hsi tz'u chuan*, chap. 4).

2. Reality[16] is conceived ultimately as change,[17] rather than as being. Change is the absolute category or frame of reference. Change is an *a priori* category of existence.[18] Being is the manifestation of change; an unchanging being cannot exist in reality. Since change is responsible for the changing world,[19] it is the ultimate reality, which is also known as *T'ai chi* (the "Great Ultimate").[20] "The great ultimate is the change."[21] The great ultimate is the

---

16. The yin-yang approach is appropriate especially in reference to cosmology, anthropology, and the Great Ultimate (God or the divine reality).

17. The word "I," meaning change, has pictograms of sun and moon. Technically, yin means the shaded area, and yang means the sunlit slope of a mountain; see Lee, *Theology of Change*, 3–14. According to the *I Ching*, it is change, not process, that is the ultimate, noncontingent reality. This is where the *I Ching*'s understanding of change differs from Western process theology; see Lee, *Theology of Change*, for his critique and comparison, 14ff. "Whitehead then seems to separate God's primordial nature from his consequent nature; Whitehead fails to describe God in the most inclusive terms, the continuum of 'both-and' and 'this as well as that.' Whitehead also separates the world from the world. . . . If God is the ultimate reality, he must be ultimate both in actuality and in potentiality. . . . The *I Ching* concept of change as the ultimate reality must be understood in light of this inclusive way of thinking. In other words, change as the ultimate reality is always conceived in terms of simultaneous change and changelessness" (17–18).

18. In fact, it is not that substance or being changes to create process or becoming, but that change itself creates substance and being. It is change that changes all things, but the change itself is changeless. See Lee, "Search for a Theological Paradigm," 29.

19. "According to the *Classic (Ching) of Change (I)*, 'I' means chameleon; its metaphysical meaning is derived from the sun and the moon ('The yin and yang are correlated with the moon and the sun' [*Ta chuan*, sec. 1, chap. 6]) ever-changing relationship. According to the *I Ching* the sun changes night to day and the moon changes day to night. By the interchanging of days and nights, the four seasons are formed, and by the changing of the seasons all things change. When the sun reaches its zenith, it begins to decline. When the moon is full, it wanes again. Living things are born and grow, decay and die. From solar systems to electrons, everything in motion, everything changes. (Confucius says, 'Like the river, everything is flowing on ceaselessly, day and night' *Analects* 9:16.) . . . The universe is in constant flux, a continuously procreative organism. ('The process of production and reproduction is what is called change' [*Ta chuan*, sec. 1, chap. 5].) . . . In the systems of change, there is the Great Ultimate (*T'ai chi*), which generates the Two Modes (yin and yang). The Two Modes generate the Four Forms (major and minor yin and yang). The Four Forms generate the Eight Elements. The Eight Trigrams determine good and evil fortunes. And good and evil fortunes produce the great business of life" (Lee, *Theology of Change*, 2–3). See *I Ching*, "Hsi-tz'u," pt. 1, 11, for more details.

20. Lee, *Theology of Change*, 3.

21. *Ta chuan*, sec. 1, chap. 11.

changing changeless one.[22] That is, yin-yang is simultaneously inclusive of both the changing and the unchanging.[23] Yin and yang
are two fundamental components or two cardinal principles of
change.[24] In the fact of change, being and nonbeing are synthesized.[25] It is change that produces ontology, process that produces
existence with a purpose in dynamic time.[26]

3. Reality is always perceived as relatedness: "Change always
operates in the bipolar relationship known as yin-yang."[27] Because
it is relative it has a dipolar nature consisting of yin and yang. Yin
is the opposite but not the antagonist of yang, since the two poles
are mutually complementary. Because they are dipolar, one can-

---

22. *Tao Te Ching* says, "Essential nature is everchanging-changeless" (chap.
16). The *I Ching* says, "When it [change] is silent, it is immovable; when it moves,
it penetrates to all things in the universe."

23. Change is both changing and unchanging, being and becoming, because it
includes both yin and yang.

24. Nothing exists without them. Everything can be reduced to them. ("Creative
yang and the receptive yin are the gateway to change" [*Ta chuan,* sec. 1, chap. 16].)
If there is no yin and yang, there will be no change and thus nothing comes to being
and to process.

25. Reality is a continuous process of production and reproduction. This is possible because there is the interplay of yin (inactivity, decrease, nonbeing) and yang
(activity, increase, being).

26. I am not opting for the cyclic view of time (as was the ancient yin-yang
view) nor the linear view but a three dimensional view of *kairos,* qualitative time.
Chinese seldom talk about absolute time but time associated with events, dynamic
time. "The essence of time consists in change; the order of time proceeds with con-
catenation; the efficacy of time abides by durance. The rhythmic process of epochal
change is wheeling round into infinitude and perpetually dovetailing the old and
the new so as to issue into interpenetration which is continuant duration in creative
advance. This is the way in which time generates itself by its systematic entry into
a pervasive unity which constitutes the rational order of creative creativity. The dynamic sequence of time, ridding itself of the perished past and coming by the new
into present existence, really gains something over a loss. So, the change in time
is but a step to approaching eternity, which is perennial duration, whereby, before
the bygone is needed, the forefront of the succeeding has come into presence. And,
therefore there is here a linkage of being projecting itself into the prospect of eternity" (Thome H. Fang, "The World and the Individual in Chinese Metaphysics,"
in *The Chinese Mind: Essentials of Chinese Philosophy and Culture,* ed. Charles R.
Moore [Honolulu: University Press of Hawaii, 1971], 240). In the Confucian process of production and reproduction, time never comes to an end or repeats itself.
Every production has an element of novelty, since it requires a new relationship of
yin and yang.

27. Lee, "Search for a Theological Paradigm," 28.

not exist without the other. Yin is yin because of yang and yang is yang because of yin. Yin needs yang to be yin; neither can exist without the other. They are mutually inclusive[28] and relative.[29] Yin has part of yang, and yang has part of yin; or, yin is in yang and yang is in yin. They are two distinct aspects of the same and one reality, just as the symbols of yin (– –) and yang (—) illustrate. Lee explains that

> Yin is yang divided, and yang is yin united. The condition of separation makes yin possible, just as the condition of unity makes yang possible.... The distinctions between them are conditional and existential, not essential. Yin and yang are one in essence and two in existence.[30]

The yin-yang philosophy will be used in the chapters as a way of reading the biblical text. It will be shown that this approach is not only contextual in terms of a Chinese reading, but also creative in terms of understanding the biblical message from another cultural perspective.

The next Chinese tradition is that of Taoism, which began during the fourth and fifth centuries B.C.E., when Lao Tze and Chuang Tze attempted to solve the problem of cultural deterioration and conflict by saying that Truth or Tao is one, but that everyone has his/her own perspective and only sees part of the truth; as a result, each person has his/her own reading of reality which it is claimed reveals the truth. The solution to cultural conflict and claim of superiority is "nothingness," that is, the act of letting or of putting down one's own presupposition and bias. For even Truth comes from it (nothingness), and all shall return to it.

---

28. Inclusive: Since yin is relative to yang, it is a holistic category of "both/and" and not merely "either/or." Therefore, it denies absolutism (absolutism of dualism or monism) yet affirms absolutism (of both dualism or monism) simultaneously. (Lee, "Search for a Theological Paradigm," 30–31: "It is both one and two, for one is expressed in two and two is known in one.") As such, "both/and" thinking does not negate "either/or" thinking, but includes and deabsolutizes it.

29. "When the sun goes, the moon comes. When the moon goes, the sun comes. The alternation of sun and moon produces light. When cold goes, heat comes. When heat goes, cold comes. The alternation of cold and hot completes the year. What is going contracts. What is to come expands. The alternation of contraction and expansion produces progression" (*Ta chuan*, sec. 2, chap. 5).

30. Lee, *Theology of Change*, 4–5.

In *Tao Te Ching,* Lao Tze says "The Tao that can be told of is not the Eternal Tao...." " "The Speaker knows not; The Knower speaks not." Once one speaks of Tao with human language and concepts, he/she conditions and limits the Tao within his/her criteria and conditions, thus distorting the original Tao. The best way to know the Tao is to meditate and keep silent. Nevertheless, Lao Tze used five thousand words to write about the Tao. In a sense, this is because of the self-revealing Tao that invites speaking and interpretation. In chapter 25 of *Tao Te Ching,* Lao Tze says: "There is Something undifferentiated, and yet complete in Itself. Soundless and Formless; Independent and Unchanging; Pervasive and Inclusive. It can be regarded as the Mother of the Universe. I do not know Its name. I named It 'Tao.' Only I was forced to give It a name. I regard It simply the 'Great.' For in greatness, It produces. In producing, It expands. In expanding, It regenerates." So, to Lao Tze, Tao is the creative reality. The Chinese know that because of the great handiwork of God, exemplified in China by the mountains. Taoism stresses, therefore, the broadening of mind and lifestyle until one is harmonized with the cosmos, achieving a mystical, artistic way of life.

The story of Confucianism is traceable to Confucius (551–479 B.C.E.), who was born in a time of cultural and moral deterioration, the Spring-Autumn Period of Chinese history. Before that period, during the Chou Dynasty, the King of Chou employed two principles as common ground for unifying the people: music (as the harmony of emotion/feeling) and *li* (behavior expressed artistically; propriety or ritual) such as bowing — the nodding of the head (or bowing) is itself nothing, but it expresses respect. Confucius always looked back to the King of Chou because of the power of mutuality, harmony, and unity which he brought through music and *li.* Confucius thought about the existence of the Good. He argued that beauty and goodness are the foundations or the source of music and *li;* and that the potentiality of beauty and goodness resides in every person, but that it is up to each person to actualize, cultivate, and express that beauty and goodness.

Confucius taught that the *Tao* of *T'ien* ("the Heavenly Principle" or "the Heavenly Way") not only gives birth to people but continues to regenerate and sustain them. Confucius also regarded *jen* (love) as the fountainhead of all virtues. He exhorted all to actualize the mandate of *T'ien* by committing themselves to *jen*, because *jen* is what makes human beings human. In other words, the will of God for any community is to practice a lifestyle of love.

The narrative of Buddhism begins with Buddha's struggle with the problem of evil and suffering in the social context of racial diversity and polytheism. Its background is that of the Hindu concepts of caste and reincarnation. In a sense it is the story of the survival of the Indian people. Buddhism was founded by Siddartha Gautama in India (563–482 B.C.E.). The followers of Buddha (Buddhists) preceded the development of Buddhism. Buddha himself was a revolutionary figure, in many ways like Moses and Jesus; he cared for his people, envisioned the possibility of a promised land, conceived the possibilities of incarnation, and sought an existential understanding of the meaning of life. Naturally, his ideas were rejected by many traditionalists.[31]

Buddha believed that at the core of life lies *dukkha* (Sanskrit for "suffering"). Every Hindu is aware of *dukkha*. Death lies at the end of the road of every human life, and sooner or later this awareness surfaces; that is *dukkha*. The fundamental cause of *dukkha* is *tanha* (Sanskrit for "clinging"), sometimes translated as "desire." Reluctance to "let go" is the cause of *dukkha*.

Ultimate reality is conceived as *sunyata* ("emptiness"). *Sunyata* does not mean simply the absence of everything; rather it has the quite positive meaning of being the Ultimate Source of everything. Its very "nature" is that of unspecified relatedness in process. Emptiness is another name for the Buddhist doctrine of *Pratitya Samutpada*, Dependent Co-origination, which means that nothing exists in self-subsisting isolation; rather, everything is ultimately a web of relationships. This key Buddhist concept of "Dependent Co-origination" (*Pratitya Samutpada* in Sanskrit) means that all things are interrelated. Since nothing exists in isolation, all things exist as networks of interrelated connections and causes.[32] Conse-

---

31. I follow closely the exposition of Yagi and Swidler on Buddhism for the following three-paragraph summary. See Seiichi Yagi and Leonard Swidler, *A Bridge to Buddhist-Christian Dialogue* (New York: Paulist Press, 1990), 12–17, for an excellent narrative.

32. See Cromwell Crawford, "The Buddha's Thoughts on Thinking: Implica-

quently one seeks to be as cosmic as possible through selflessness, and to be always "becoming," because everything is in a state of flux.

Tanha (desire) can, in fact, be eliminated by following Gautama's Eightfold Path (cf. the Ten Commandments or Words in Hebrew Scripture). The Eightfold path is a series of ethical rules for thinking and acting. They are: Right Understanding, Right Thought, Right Speech, Right Action, Right Livelihood, Right Effort, Right Mindfulness, and Right Concentration. The vision or goal of following the Eightfold Path is Nirvana (Sanskrit for "blow out"; when a candle is blown out, it enters into a state of tranquillity). Nirvana basically means that *tanha* and the false self (*Atman,* self, in Sanskrit and *Ata* in Pali) have been "blown out" from the person, thus leading to the Buddhist doctrine of *An-atta,* or "no self."

In the respective narratives, each Asian story is unique and rich. At the same time each affirms the necessity and uniqueness of the normative biblical story which encompasses the intent of all stories in the whole world: God's revelation in Jesus the Messiah saves the human (individual and corporate) story (history) from "necessities of plot, from tugs of beginning (determinism) and ending (fatalism), from the Fall and the judgment."[33] And we can add: from conflict and mistrust, from ambiguity and meaninglessness, from alienation and loneliness, from evil and suffering, and from hubris and boasting.

---

tions for Ecumenical Dialogue," *Journal of Ecumenical Studies* 21 (Spring 1984), 242: "The Buddha saw things in their uniqueness, but this did not incur any fragmentation in his thinking. The part was part, but it was part of the whole.... This means that interrelationship belongs to the essential nature of things." Also, David Kalupahana, *Buddhist Philosophy* (Honolulu: University Press of Hawaii, 1976), 29; cf. Yagi and Swidler, *A Bridge to Buddhist-Christian Dialogue,* 8–9.

33. David Buttrick, *Homiletic: Moves and Structures* (Philadelphia: Fortress, 1987), 15.

Chapter 2

Galatians as a Resource for Christocentric Inclusivity

The concern for a viable approach to cross-cultural hermeneutics for constructing indigenous theology is a necessary and enduring one. Ever since Christianity received its commission to be the light and the salt of the world, the gospel of Jesus Christ has brought forth an audience, not only of Jews but also of Gentiles. Historically, we can trace this hermeneutical interest from Peter and Paul, Luke and John, Tertullian and Clement of Alexandria, Calvin and Luther, as well as from contemporary figures such as Richard Niebuhr and John Hick. All were concerned with cross-cultural hermeneutics.[1] One recurring issue in cross-cultural hermeneutics is the relationship between one's particular culture and the uniqueness of Christ. Is Christ particular? Is he universal? Is he inclusive? Is he exclusive? How are we to understand Christ in relation to the culture in which we live and to which we preach? The issue is all the more crucial when we consider our beliefs and our culture in relation to the beliefs and cultures of others. Are we to proselytize others? Can Christ serve as a unique, inclusive, and universal symbol?

Chapter 1 speaks of the comprehensive, cross-cultural, and interdisciplinary methodology that seems to be inclusive of all, but that does not mean that inclusivity has no boundary. When we speak of the uniqueness of Christ, does that mean that Christ can-

---

1. See *Gospel and Culture, The Papers of a Consultation on the Gospel and Culture, Convened by the Lausanne Committee's Theology and Education Group,* ed. John Stott and Robert T. Coote (Pasadena, Calif.: William Carey Library, 1979), 2–5.

not be inclusive in his uniqueness as well? This chapter examines Gal 2:15–16 to understand how Paul views Christ as the inclusive and all-sufficient symbol of the people of God — a people created out of diverse cultural and religious backgrounds. The conviction here is that Christ can serve as a sufficient identity symbol for all people. The chapter also examines both culture and Christ as identity symbols. How the old identity marker (culture) and the new identity marker (Christ) relate to each other is the hermeneutical question the chapter seeks to examine. It is also an attempt to take a new look at Paul's hermeneutics in Gal 3:1–20, which deals with Christ and Torah, the sacred tradition and cultural seedbed of the Jewish people.

The Galatian Debate concerning the "Full Gospel"

The occasion of Paul's letter to the churches of Galatia was a dispute over the place of the law in Christian faith and practice. The identity of Paul's opponents is disputed.[2] It is proposed here that they were conservative Jewish Christian missionaries from Jerusalem,[3] inspired by a zealously Pharisaic spirit (see Acts 15:1). They seriously challenged Paul's authority and required[4] (see Gal 6:12) the Gentile Christians of Galatia to be circumcised and to observe the Torah (that sacred element in their culture). Their argument was that in doing so the Gentile Christians would be fully accepted as the true people of God, belonging to the line of Abraham, and able to enjoy the benefits of the "full gospel" (see Gal 2:12). These missionaries had invaded the Galatian church with a "different gospel" (1:7) in order to perfect Paul's gospel. These intruders and the Judaizers from Jerusalem were probably related. Acts 15:1

---

2. For a brief survey of the "agitators" theories, see B. H. Brinsmead, *Galatians — Dialogical Response to Opponents* (Chico, Calif.: Scholars Press, 1982), 10–22.

3. After Paul's last visit to Galatian churches (Acts 18:23), the itinerant Jewish Christian missionaries arrived (see Gal 1:7, 4:17, 5:10, 6:12).

4. See Robert Jewett, "The Agitators and the Galatian Congregation," *New Testament Studies* 7 (1970–71), who says that *houtoi anagkazousin humas peritemnesthai* in Gal 6:12 "refers to the 'necessity' of circumcision" (200).

offers their challenge to the Gentile Christians, "Unless you are circumcised, according to the custom taught by Moses, you cannot be
saved." Evidence from Galatians also substantiates the view that
the opponents were Jewish Christians from Jerusalem. According
to Gal 2:4, those who opposed Paul were brethren who had been
secretly brought in from Jerusalem to spy out the freedom of Paul
and his companions. These Jewish Christians demanded that Gentile Christians adopt circumcision (5:2, 6:12f.) and obedience to
the Torah (3:2, 5:4). Paul saw these requirements as enslaving,
and he responded by charging his brethren with pursuing insin-
cere objectives (4:17, 6:12). The suggestion that the agitators were
Jewish Gnostics who obeyed the law for syncretistic reasons, as
Schmithals proposes, is to be rejected, but that the opponents had
an "orthodox, Pharisaic view of the law"[5] is obviously correct.

Why did these agitators attempt to pressure the Galatian Gentile
Christians into accepting circumcision? Paul offers a few reasons.
To begin with (6:12a), Paul says they want to make a good "showing in the flesh" (RSV). The Greek word *euprosōpēsai* ("showing
in the flesh") appears here, its only use in the New Testament. The
word means to have good manners as perceived by others[6] and
suggests that the agitators are more concerned with the symbol
of Jewish identity (i.e., circumcision and observance of the Torah)
than the reality to which the symbol points (i.e., the covenanted
love of God). Gal 6:13b ("to glorify in your flesh") shows that the
agitators want to use the Galatians as evidence of their religious
zeal, and to boast[7] of their tradition in the Torah. More important,
they want "to escape from persecution of the cross" (6:12b). The
agitators themselves may have been subject to persecution by non-
Christian Jews because of their subscription to Christianity, and
for this reason they sought to convince the Gentile Christians to

---

5. W. Schmithals, *Paul and the Gnostics* (Nashville: Abingdon, 1972), 13.

6. See E. Lohse, *Theological Dictionary of the New Testament*, ed. G. Kittel
and G. Friedrich, 9 vols., Eng. trans. by G. W. Bromiley (Grand Rapids, Mich.:
Eerdmans, 1964–76), 7:779 (hereafter cited as *TDNT*); J. B. Lightfoot, *The Epistle
of St. Paul to the Galatians* (repr., Grand Rapids, Mich., 1962), 222.

7. See R. A. Cole, *The Epistle of Paul to the Galatians*, Tyndale New Tes-
tament Commentaries (London: Tyndale, 1965), 181; J. J. Schoeps, *Paul: The
Theology of the Apostle in the Light of Jewish Religious History* (London:
Lutterworth, 1961), 77.

abide by their old traditions and thus to visibly belong to the true people of God. The non-Christian Jews would not have objected to their affiliation with the Cross, as long as they were loyal to the old traditions.

Galatians 2:15–16:
Christ the Inclusive Identity Symbol

The immediate context of 2:15–16 is an incident that had occurred in Antioch. Gentile Christians had been fully accepted into the circle of those Jews who believed that Jesus was God's Anointed. The pillars of Jerusalem had agreed that Gentiles need not be circumcised to be considered fellow believers and counted among the people of God (2:1–10). It was a normal custom for believers, Jews and Gentiles, to share fellowship meals together. But certain persons who had come from James caused Peter, Barnabas, and other Judean Jewish believers to withdraw from these fellowship meals with Gentile believers. The reason for their withdrawal was presumably to demonstrate their continued loyalty to their ancestral faith.[8]

Peter had been living[9] like a Gentile. His withdrawal from the fellowship meal was probably the result of pressure from the circumcision party.[10] Paul accused Peter of hypocrisy,[11] be-

---

8. See J. D. G. Dunn, "The New Perspective on Paul," *Bulletin of the John Rylands University Library* 65 (1982–83): 104.

9. The word "living" in Greek is present tense and suggests the basic principle of Peter's life, i.e., living like a Gentile. See Lightfoot, *The Epistle of St. Paul to the Galatians,* 114; E. W. Burton, *A Critical and Exegetical Commentary on the Epistle to the Galatians,* International Critical Commentary (Edinburgh: T. & T. Clark, 1968), 112; J. G. Machen, *The Origin of Paul's Religion* (London: Hodder & Stoughton, 1921), 123; and W. Bauer et al., *A Greek-English Lexicon of the New Testament* (University of Chicago Press, 1957), 336; hereafter cited as BAGD.

10. See E. E. Ellis, " 'Those of the Circumcision' and the Early Christian Mission," *Studia Evangelica* 4 (1968): 390.

11. The words "being hypocrite" in 2:13–14 do not denote a purposefully evil motive on Peter's part, but of masking his own real conviction. See BAGD, 845, 838; Lightfoot, *The Epistle of St. Paul to the Galatians,* 113; Burton, *A Critical and Exegetical Commentary on the Epistle to the Galatians,* 109; A. T. Robertson, *Word Pictures in the New Testament* (New York: Broadman, 1933), vol. 4, 287; K. S. Wuest, *Galatians in the Greek New Testament* (Grand Rapids: Eerdmans,

cause Peter did not follow his own convictions or the spirit of
the gospel (2:14). The conduct of Peter and other Judean Jewish
Christians had pressured the Gentile Christians to live like Jews
(*Ioudaizein*)[12] by observing food laws and circumcision. This pressure had placed the Gentile believers in unnecessary bondage; it
implied that Gentiles were still unclean and outside the community
of God's elect.

In 2:15–16, Paul echoes the argument rebuking Peter:

> We who are Jews by nature and not Gentile sinners, know
> that a man is not justified by works of law except through
> faith in Jesus Christ. And we have believed in Christ Jesus in
> order that we might be justified by faith in Christ and not
> by works of law, because by works of law shall no flesh be
> justified.[13]

The word "we" of 2:15 ("we who are Jews by birth and not Gentile sinners") refers to Paul, Peter, and other Jewish believers. This
Jewish self-definition[14] differentiates Jews from Gentiles. Betz says
succinctly that "Jewishness is determined by birth"[15] as the Jews
understand it. In other words, Gentiles are sinners precisely because they have no Torah and consequently observe no Torah.
Possession of Torah defines Jews religiously and ethnically.

1951), 72–73; and Machen's *Notes on Galatians*, ed. J. Skilton (Presbyterian and
Reformed, 1972), 138. My conclusion is that Peter's behavior contradicts his own
theological convictions, and for this reason, his behavior stood condemned (2:11).

12. *Ioudaizein* (2:14) occurs only here in the NT. It means to accept partially or
totally Judaistic customs (W. Gutbrod, "*Ioudaios,*" *TDNT* 3:383). H. N. Ridderbos, *Paul: An Outline of His Theology* (Grand Rapids, Mich.: Eerdmans, 1975),
284, points out that these laws and circumcision have the social and religious
function of distinguishing Jews from Gentiles.

13. This verse has been widely accepted as the most important one (only one
sentence in the Greek New Testament) in Galatians; e.g., T. W. Manson, *Studies in
the Gospels and Epistles*, ed. M. Black (Manchester: Manchester University Press,
1962), 188, says that this verse is the center theme and argument of Galatians.
H. D. Betz, *Galatians: A Commentary on Paul's Letter to the Churches in Galatia*,
Hermeneia (Philadelphia: Fortress, 1979), 115, says this verse is the beginning of
Paul's "propositio." Cf. G. S. Duncan, *The Epistle of Paul to the Galatians* (Hodder
and Stoughton, 1934), 64–65.

14. See Betz, *Galatians*, 115; E. Stauffer, "*Egō,*" *TDNT* 2:361–62; and Ronald
Y. K. Fung, *The Epistle to the Galatians* (Grand Rapids, Mich.: Eerdmans, 1988),
113.

15. Betz, *Galatians*, 115.

In order to respond to the exclusive mind-set of the Jewish Christians, Paul appeals first to the Jewish awareness of the concept of "being justified" (2:16),[16] which is not something interjected as part of the structure of "we who are Jews by birth." James Dunn claims that "being justified" is "evidently something Jewish."[17] He explains,

> This is covenant language...the language which stems from Israel's consciousness of election. The Gentiles are "sinners" precisely in so far as they neither know nor keep the law given by God to Israel. Paul's mention of "being justified" ...[has] a deliberate appeal to the standard Jewish belief,... that the Jews as a race are God's covenant people. Almost certainly then, his concept of righteousness...is thoroughly Jewish too, where God's righteousness is precisely God's covenant faithfulness, his saving power and love for his people Israel.[18]

Justification by faith in Christ is unprecedented in Judaism; "faith" in Gal 2:16 does not denote just any trust. Unfortunately, Dunn does not elaborate on this point. However, David Gordon in his article "The Problem at Galatia" shows that "faith" always refers to faith in Christ, so much so that Paul uses the two terms "faith" and "Christ" interchangeably to mean the same thing.[19] We can infer then that the "we" does not include Jews but only the Jewish Christians who have placed their trust in the Messiah. The use of the aorist "we believed" in Gal 2:16 can be used as an argument for this point: a new and decisive step is necessary for the Jews

---

16. "Being justified" appears three times as the same root word in Greek in Gal 2:16.

17. J. D. G. Dunn, "Paul and 'Covenantal Nomism,'" in *The Partings of the Ways between Christianity and Judaism and Their Significance for the Character of Christianity* (London: SCM; Philadelphia: Trinity Press International, 1991), 105. Cf. E. P. Sanders, who in *Paul and Palestinian Judaism* (Minneapolis: Fortress, 1977), 470–72, 501, 518 n. 5, 544, and *Paul, the Law, and the Jewish People* (Minneapolis: Fortress, 1983), 5–10, says that "being justified" is used by Paul primarily as a transfer term.

18. Dunn, "Paul and 'Covenantal Nomism,'" 105: "Concept of righteousness, both noun and verb, is almost certainly thoroughly Jewish with strong covenantal overtones."

19. T. D. Gordon, "The Problem at Galatia," *Interpretation* 41 (1987): 42–43.

when they place their trust in Christ. Here in his own cross-cultural hermeneutic, Paul has already taken a new step, using the concept not merely of trust but more specifically of trust in Christ as his hermeneutical key to refute the misunderstanding of the Jewish Christians and to propose a more inclusive symbol.

Paul then dismisses the idea of being justified "by works of the law" (appears three times in 2:16; cf. 3:2, 5, 10). Paul is not placing a proper understanding of the law in antithesis to a perverted view of the law or to the Mosaic or Abrahamic covenant which the law represents. Such an interpretation tends to see Judaism as a sort of perverted religion. And it also totally ignores the Jewish context and the situational character of the Galatian epistle. It assumes too quickly that the guilty conscience of individuals seeks salvation through a legalistic life. The Galatian debate is concerned not with individuals but with the people of God; more precisely, it is concerned not with the legalistic life of the individual but with the identity symbol of the people of God: "justification by faith in/of Christ" or by "works of law."

The phrase "faith in/of Christ" has its unique connotative meaning in Galatians. Reacting to traditional interpretations of "faith in/of Christ," Richard B. Hays contends that the phrase should always mean "the faithfulness of Jesus Christ."[20] Hays argues,

> Paul is not interested in "believing" as a mode of human activity that is somehow inherently salvific, nor does he give more than passing mention (2:16) to the idea that our faith is directed toward Jesus Christ as object. The emphasis of Paul's theological response to the Galatian crisis lies on Christ's activity for us. This activity of Christ is understood by the single word *pistis,* "faithfulness." This faithfulness of Jesus Christ is the efficient cause of the redemption/liberation of God's people.[21]

---

20. Richard B. Hays, *The Faith of Jesus Christ: An Investigation of the Narrative Substructure of Galatians 3:1–4:11* (Missoula, Mont.: Scholars Press, 1983), 139–90; idem, "Jesus' Faith and Ours: A Rereading of Galatians 3," in *Conflict and Context: Hermeneutics in the Americas* (Grand Rapids, Mich.: Eerdmans, 1986), 261–67.

21. Hays, "Jesus' Faith and Ours: A Rereading of Galatians 3," 267.

While the idea of the faithfulness of Jesus Christ cannot be dismissed, *pistis Iēsou Christou* should be exegeted as an objective genitive, "faith in Jesus Christ." In Gal 2:16, this idea of belief "in Jesus Christ" is underscored by the use of "in" (*en*) with the accusative: "we believed in Christ Jesus."[22]

An alternative interpretation would be to understand the immediate context of 2:16, that is, the debates at Jerusalem and Antioch, as focused on two issues, circumcision and Jewish food laws. Sanders, Dunn, Lohmeyer, and Tyson[23] see "works of the law" as nomistic service, that is, service of the law as covenantal work. These are works of "being in" the covenant and not works of "getting into" the covenant. Works of the law were not simply good works but observances of the law which characterize good Jews and set them apart from Gentiles. By doing the law, the good Jews showed they were within the covenant. That is, they were under the law. Circumcision and food laws particularly were understood as the objective markers for God's chosen people and signs of election. Paul himself used the terms "circumcised" and "uncircumcised" to designate respectively Jews and Gentiles.[24] Dunn substantiates this view by saying,

These observances (law and circumcision) were widely regarded as characteristically and distinctively Jewish. These identity markers...functioned as badges of covenant membership.

It would be virtually impossible to conceive of participation in God's covenant, and so in God's covenant righteousness, apart from these observances...these works of the law.[25]

---

22. See Fung's (*The Epistle to the Galatians,* 115 and n. 18) argument.

23. Sanders, *Paul, the Law, and the Jewish People,* 105, 147; J. D. G. Dunn, "Works of the Law and the Curse of the Law (Gal 3:10–14)," *New Testament Studies* 31, no. 4 (1985): 527; J. B. Tyson " 'Works of Law' in Galatians," *Journal of Biblical Literature* 92, no. 3 (1973): 423–31; Gordon, "The Problem at Galatia," 40. Cf. Ernst Lohmeyer, *Probleme Paulinischer Theologie* (Kohlhammer, n.d.), 31–74, for a careful analysis of the phrase "works of law."

24. See Gal 2:7–8; Gordon, "The Problem at Galatia," 39–41.

25. Dunn, "Paul and 'Covenantal Nomism,' " 107–8, 110. See Gn 17:9–14: "You shall be circumcised in the flesh of your foreskins, and it shall be a sign of the covenant...everlasting."

To be a Jew is to be a member of the covenant and to observe circumcision, food laws, and the Sabbath. In short, these observances were the cultural markers of the Jew. The phrase "works of the law" in Gal 2:16 is fairly restricted and precise,[26] referring to covenant works and not individual good works. In contrast to righteousness understood in terms of covenant works, Paul continues to speak of righteousness through faith in Jesus Christ. He resists emphasizing one particular cultural symbol as the identity marker of other people. On the one hand, Paul does not want to eliminate the cultural tradition for that particular group of people. On the other hand, he understands that a cultural symbol can never be totally inclusive. So the search for one inclusive symbol that affirms the uniqueness of all cultural symbols becomes necessary.

The new symbol is mentioned in 2:16: Only through faith[27] in Jesus Christ, even we have believed in Christ Jesus. This sentence speaks of the necessity of having faith in Jesus Christ. Christ is the object of faith, and not the subject of faith. But note it is not just "faith" that matters here. It is "Jesus Christ" that matters. Though justification by faith is a Jewish concept, justification in Christ Jesus is not. Given that in Jewish self-understanding covenantal nomism is not antithetical to faith, then at this point the only change or extension which the new movement, namely Christianity, asks for is that the traditional conservative Jewish faith be more precisely defined as faith in Jesus the Messiah.[28]

---

26. K. Haacker ("Paulus und das Judentum im Galaterbrief" ["Paul and Judaism in Galatians"], in *Gottes Augapfel*, ed. E. Brocke and J. Seim [Neukirchen-Vluyn: Neukirchener Verlag, 1986], 95–111) for example will probably argue for a more precise interpretation: zealous act of the Pharisee Jews who followed the Maccabean pattern of violent reaction against the Greco-Roman world.

27. There are various interpretations of "through faith": see T. W. Manson, *On Paul and John*, ed. M. Black (London: SCM, 1963), 62; Bauer, *"Pisteuō,"* BAGD, 660–65; Hays, *The Faith of Jesus Christ;* and Robinson Canon, "Faith of Jesus Christ," *Reformed Theological Review* 29 (September–December 1970): 71–81.

28. James Dunn is right in asserting that "in this verse (2:16) faith in Jesus Messiah begins to emerge not simply as a narrower definition of the elect of God, but as an alternative definition of the elect of God . . . faith in Jesus as Christ becomes the primary identity marker which renders the others (law and circumcision) superfluous" ("Paul and 'Covenantal Nomism,' " 112).

Galatians 3:1–20: Culture and Christ — Old and New Symbols

If Christ is the new, inclusive symbol for all people, how can one relate the old symbol to the new one? The response of Paul in Gal 3:1–20 addresses the relationship between Christ, the new marker of the people of God, and the law, the old marker of the people of God. In the preceding context (Galatians 2) Paul has argued that justification before God is accomplished not by doing nomistic service, but only (*ean mē*) through faith in Jesus Christ. Faith is not analogous to covenantal works. Justification is mediated through faith, and this faith has a distinct content: Jesus Christ. And this truth, namely, that justification comes by believing in Christ, is a foundational and common principle which both Jews and Gentiles must embrace. For this reason, Christ has become the new marker of the people of God. In Galatians 3, the question concerns the relationship between this new marker and the covenant of promise as seen in the salvation history.

Paul begins (chap. 3) by addressing his misguided audiences (vv. 2 and 5) with two rhetorical questions which contain the same antithesis: the notion of receiving the Spirit by works of the law or by hearing with faith.[29] The first question asks whether it was by works of the law or by hearing with faith that the Galatians began their Christian lives (i.e., "received the Spirit"; 3:2). The second question makes the same enquiry regarding their present experience of God's working among them (3:5). The expected answer to both questions is, "Not by works of the law but by hearing with faith." Though the answer is clear, Paul further proves his points by appealing to the authority of Scripture and the case of Abraham. The Abrahamic case is taken almost verbatim from the LXX of Gn 15:6.[30] It is interesting to note that the figure of Abraham is used in juxtaposition to the Mosaic tradition (later in the same chapter) in the parallel arguments of faith in God and works of law. Paul stresses the two main facts about Abraham: as the An-

---

29. Ronald Y. K. Fung, "Justification, Sonship, and the Gift of the Spirit," *China Graduate School of Theology Journal* 3 (July 1987): 74.

30. So Fung, "Justification, Sonship, and the Gift of the Spirit," 75.

cestor of the Jews, he demonstrates faith in God *and* his faith in God is counted to him as righteousness. Therefore, Abraham is reckoned righteous because of his faith in God.[31]

Paul contends that the true children of Abraham are exclusively persons of faith (*hoi ek pisteōs* in 3:7). Sonship to (or descent from) Abraham depends on a spiritual genealogy of faith which goes back to Abraham.[32] The distinguishing feature is no longer mere physical descent but spiritual descent. To state the case more precisely, it is faith and not circumcision or Torah that is the defining characteristic of Abraham's seed and of God's people. Paul proceeds to demonstrate this truth by explicating the implications of God's actions toward Abraham for the Gentiles (3:8). In verse 8, Paul cites God's promise to Abraham ("In you shall all the nations be blessed"). Paul's citation is a conflation of the LXX reading of Gn 12:3c ("be blessed in you"; cf. Gn 28:14b) and 22:18a ("all nations"; see Gn 18:18b; 26:4b). The words *panta ta ethnē* ("all nations") are substituted for the LXX's *pasai hai phylai* ("every race") in Gn 12:3 so as to bring in the word "nation," desired by Paul because of its current usage in the sense of "Gentiles." As such, the significance of this verse concerning the Gentiles should not be taken lightly; but already in Gn 12:3 and 18:18 the compound "be blessed" is designed to stress the fact that the blessing of Abraham embraces all races and peoples.[33]

The gospel that comes through Abraham to all Gentiles (nations) is a "beforehand gospel." The words "beforehand gospel" mean "preaching the gospel by anticipation" and not "preaching a preliminary gospel."[34] When the blessing comes to the Gentiles in Christ who is the seed of Abraham (Gn 13:16), the promise

---

31. G. Schrenk, *"Dikaiosynē," TDNT* 2:204.

32. See Cole, *The Epistle of Paul to the Galatians,* 92; Fung, "Justification, Sonship, and the Gift of the Spirit," 77.

33. This universalist promise was, however, scarcely taken up in the Jewish treatment of Abraham, said C. K. Barrett in *From First Adam to Last* (London: A. & C. Black, 1962), 34, 40. Perhaps this is Paul's radical interpretation in light of the Christ event.

34. A. T. Hanson, *Studies in Paul's Technique and Theology* (London: SPCK, 1974), 64. Cf. F. F. Bruce, "The Curse of the Law," in *Paul and Paulinism: Essays in Honour of C. K. Barrett,* ed. M. D. Hooker and S. G. Wilson (London: SPCK, 1982), 33.

is fulfilled. The prophecy that God would justify the nations by faith becomes a reality. And "the gospel beforehand" becomes the "gospel."[35] In other words, the old symbol of Abrahamic religion and ethnicity is linked to Christ and interpreted in light of the Christ event.

The relationship between the old people of God and the new people of God could be understood in terms of Abraham and Christ. C. H. Dodd observes that in the OT the *niph'al* form of "blessed" in Hebrew is properly reflexive, so that the meaning of "blessed" is "shall pray to be blessed as Abraham was blessed"[36] (cf. Gn 12:3c, 18:18a). It is more likely that the LXX translators understood the Hebrew verb in the passive sense and rendered it as unambiguously passive in the Greek: "be blessed." And it is in this sense that Paul understands the original promise and sees its fulfillment in the mission to the Gentiles.[37] Paul thus far (3:1–9) does not explicitly mention the role of Christ, but Abraham clearly serves as the forerunner of Christ. Paul points out the principle of justification by faith with Abraham as an example. This preaching (the gospel beforehand) to Abraham is a prediction that God will justify the Gentiles by means of faith (v. 8a) through Abraham's ("in you") faith. In other words, the promise that the Gentiles would be blessed through Abraham is grounded in, and explained by, the foreseen fact of their justification by faith after the pattern of his justification.[38] According to Paul, then, the promise to Abraham is a pre-announcement of the gospel that God would subsequently justify the Gentiles by faith. From all of this it follows ("as" in v. 9) that those persons who have faith in God are blessed as Abraham was blessed (for he has faith in God, too).

The salvific blessing of Jews and Gentiles through Abraham and Christ raises the question of order and condition of the people of God, old and new. T. L. Donaldson argues strongly that the

---

35. G. Friedrich, *"Proeungelizomai,"* TDNT 2:737.

36. C. H. Dodd, *According to the Scriptures* (London: Collins, 1965), 43; see Fung, *The Epistle to the Galatians,* 139. But neither the LXX nor the NT shows any trace of this interpretation. See Burton, *A Critical and Exegetical Commentary on the Epistle to the Galatians,* 160.

37. See F. F. Bruce, *The Epistle of Paul to the Galatians: A Commentary on the Greek Text* (Grand Rapids, Mich.: Eerdmans, 1982), 156.

38. Fung, "Justification, Sonship, and the Gift of the Spirit," 77.

pericope 3:1–4:7 dramatizes the eschatological[39] inclusion of the uncircumcised (Gentile believers) among the people of God by "representation and participation."[40] Donaldson interprets "us"[41] in 3:13 as the Jewish Christians exclusive of Gentile Christians.[42] Thus, he and many scholars[43] perceive the redemption of Israel as a prerequisite for (or a condition of) the blessing of the Gentiles. The reasons for this interpretation are first, that the emphatic placement of "us" (3:13) and "the nations" (3:14) at the beginning of the clauses suggests Paul's intention of contrasting the two groups of people; and second, that the context of 3:6–14 implies that Torah observers are subject to the curse as expressed by "us . . . all who rely on works of law."[44] Because the purpose of the law is to identify transgression, "those who rely on works of law" are transgressors. Hence Israel is under the curse of the law. All people are under the sway of the forces of the cosmos (4:3, 9), in opposition to God and hence under sin (3:22). Even Israel's possession of the law does not alter this fact. Israel's plight is a special form of the universal plight. While Gentiles are under the "elemental spirits," they are not under the law. To be "under the law" is a special way of being "under the cosmic elements" (4:3), which means that human beings are universally under the bondage of cos-

---

39. T. L. Donaldson, "The 'Curse of the Law' and the Inclusion of the Gentiles: Galatians 3:13–14," *New Testament Studies* 32 (1986): 110–11, writes, "The first century Judaism has a pattern of thinking about the Gentiles — the strand of eschatological expectation that anticipated a massive turning of the Gentiles to Yahweh as an consequence of the end-time redemption of Israel." For a similar argument, see Sanders, *Paul, the Law, and the Jewish People,* 171ff.; J. C. Beker, *Paul the Apostle: The Triumph of God in Life and Thought* (Philadelphia: Fortress, 1980), 331–37; G. von Rad, *Old Testament Theology,* trans. D. M. G. Stalker (London: Oliver and Boyd, 1965), 2:292–97.

40. Donaldson, "The 'Curse of the Law,'" 105. See Hays, *The Faith of Jesus Christ,* 193–235, and Betz, *Galatians,* 181.

41. Traditionally interpreted to mean the inclusive group of Jewish and Gentile Christians (e.g., Bruce, *The Epistle of Paul to the Galatians,* 166f; Sanders, *Paul, the Law, and the Jewish People,* 68f., 72, 81; D. Guthrie, *Galatians* [London: Nelson, 1969], 102–4; H. N. Ridderbos, *The Epistle of Paul to the Churches of Galatia,* New International Commentary on the New Testament [Grand Rapids, Mich.: Eerdmans, 1968], 125). If so, the redemption of Gentile and Jew happens at the same time that Christ becomes a curse for us all on the cross.

42. Donaldson, "The 'Curse of the Law,'" 105.

43. Hays, *Faith of Jesus Christ,* 86–92, 116–21.

44. Donaldson, "The 'Curse of the Law,'" 105.

mic principles.[45] Therefore, the purpose of the law is to clarify the universal human plight. Israel, the people of the law, serves as a representative sample of the whole of humankind under curse.

The order and condition of the spiritual blessings of the people of God are seen in the process of eschatological salvation.[46] This salvation is actualized by representation and participation with the following points.[47] First, Christ's death and resurrection comprise the eschatological crisis event in which the powers of this age are defeated and Christ himself makes the passage from this age to the age to come. Second, Christ as a representative[48] figure fully identifies with the sinful human condition (plight) even to the point of death (4:4), with the result that all can share in his resurrection, and thus be vindicated, justified, and given the life of the age to come (2:20). Finally, the way to receive these benefits is to be "in Christ" (2:17; 3:26, 28). To be "in Christ" is to participate with Christ in death and resurrection, a process in which faith plays a crucial part.

In Christ God's promise is now open to Jews and Gentiles. The law can no longer serve as a feature distinguishing Jews from Gentiles. Christ in his death has effectively abolished this restrictiveness and the zealous Jewish perception of God's righteousness of enculturation.[49] Israel and the law have a special place for establishing salvation for all people. "By creating a representative sample in which the human plight is clarified and concentrated, they set the stage for redemption."[50] Yet, Israel's culture, regardless how holy it is, cannot be used as an enculturating condition for other nations (Gentiles) to become the people of God. The shift from Torah

---

45. Donaldson, "The 'Curse of the Law,' " 103–4. See Beker, *Paul the Apostle,* 188, for the same idea.

46. On apocalyptic aspects of Paul's teaching, see Beker, *Paul the Apostle,* and S. Kim, *The Origin of Paul's Gospel* (Grand Rapids, Mich.: Eerdmans, 1981).

47. Donaldson, "The 'Curse of the Law,' " 105.

48. Note that Christ identifies not only with the human situation in general (Gal 4:4) but also with Israel in particular. As Israel's representative, Christ is the representative of all humankind; all can participate in Christ. See Donaldson, "The 'Curse of the Law,' " 106.

49. See Krister Stendahl, *Paul among Jews and Gentiles* (Philadelphia: Fortress, 1976), 78–96; W. D. Davies, *Jewish and Pauline Studies* (London: SPCK, 1984), 123–52.

50. Donaldson, "The 'Curse of the Law,' " 105.

to Christ precisely means that the cultural restriction and religious exclusivism must be abolished. Christ has extended the Abrahamic promise to the Gentiles. In this regard, J. C. Beker points out well that "the church of the Gentiles is an extension of the promises of God to Israel and not Israel's displacement."[51]

Paul's christological interpretation of the promises of God to the Gentiles is a radical one, which we will observe again in 3:15–17. In this pericope, justification is treated primarily with reference to the promise. In Gal 3:16 attention is drawn to a fact of biblical history, namely, that the promises were pronounced to Abraham "and his seed."[52] Paul understands "seed" as a reference to Christ. He is well aware of the collective sense of the word "seed" in the Genesis passage.[53] His identification here of the "seed" of promise as the Christ of history is not derived from a direct exegesis of the OT text, but rather is an interpretation of those texts in light of the Christ event.[54] Christ, according to Paul's reading of history, is the true heir of the promise, of the universal inheritance, and therefore Christ determines those who are to be fellow heirs.[55] All who are "in Christ Jesus" (3:26, 28), Jews or Gentiles, share in their status as seed in a derivative way (3:29). Or, as Donaldson expresses it, " 'In Christ' existence, rather than circumcision or Torah observance, is the defining characteristic of Abraham's seed."[56] Therefore, if Torah defines the people of God in the period of promise, Christ now defines the people of God in the period of fulfillment.[57] The identity symbol in the age of fulfillment is no longer that which separates Jews and Gentiles but the One in whom two are included.

In showing the historical function of the law, Paul takes up the figure of Abraham again in 3:15–18. The point regarding Abraham has to do with the covenant. In 3:15, Paul gives an analogy from daily life, a will, to illustrate the relationship between the law and

---

51. Beker, *Paul the Apostle,* 332.
52. Fung, "Justification, Sonship, and the Gift of the Spirit," 80.
53. Fung, "Justification, Sonship, and the Gift of the Spirit," 80.
54. Fung, "Justification, Sonship, and the Gift of the Spirit," 81.
55. J. Schneider and G. Friedrich, *"Epangellō," TDNT* 2:583.
56. Donaldson, "The 'Curse of the Law,' " 100.
57. Gordon, "The Problem at Galatia," 39.

the covenant of promise. Paul's point here is to show that once the arrangement is drawn up, settled, and enforced, then the will or testament cannot be changed. Likewise, law cannot set aside the covenant of promise already given 430 years prior to the giving of the law. The content of the promise is that covenant of promise. The promise to Abraham is the promise to fulfill the covenant. How? In Christ! For whom? For all people including Jews and Gentiles!

If primacy is to be placed on the Abrahamic covenant and its fulfillment in Christ, then why was the law given (3:19)? Paul does not explain why the Mosaic law is given at Mount Sinai in 3:19 and 20. Instead, he answers a more precise and significant question, that is, what is the status and purpose of the law in relation to the promise as seen in salvation history?[58] Paul gives the following answers:

1. "Because of transgressions" (3:19b). This phrase can be understood as "to restrain transgressions."[59] That is, the law is given to serve as a temporary expedient to reduce human evil until the Seed comes. A second interpretation is more plausible: to reveal transgression, to make sin manifest as sin.[60] That is, law is given to Israel, the people of God, to show the plight (curse) they are in. For in the absence of the law, sin, though real, is not visible; it is "not registered."[61] "Sin" is called "transgression"[62] after the giving of the law. The latter interpretation is not a Jewish understanding.[63]

---

58. As Manson, *On Paul and John,* 45, has observed.

59. View of J. C. O'Neill, *The Recovery of Paul's Letter to the Galatians* (London: SPCK, 1972), 52, 78. Cf. Ridderbos, *The Epistle of Paul to the Churches of Galatia,* 137.

60. Burton, *A Critical and Exegetical Commentary on the Epistle to the Galatians,* 188; Guthrie, *Galatians,* 108; W. Gunthen, *"Paraptōma,"* in *The New International Dictionary of New Testament Theology* (hereafter *NIDNTT*), 3:585; Bruce, *The Epistle of Paul to the Galatians,* 181–82; Beker, *Paul the Apostle,* 55, 243; Betz, *Galatians,* 165; and C. E. B. Cranfield, "St. Paul and the Law," in *New Testament Issues,* ed. R. Batey (London: SCM, 1970), 148.

61. Cranfield, "St. Paul and the Law," 148.

62. See J. Scheider, *"Parabasis,"* TDNT 5:739–40, on transgression. Donaldson, "The 'Curse of the Law,'" 104, says transgression is a special kind of sin (Gal 3:22), the violation of a specific divine commandment, the sin that is qualified by the law.

63. Betz, *Galatians,* 165; Schoeps, *Paul,* 194–95.

How Paul arrived at this radical non-Jewish, perhaps anti-Jewish position, is still an unresolved issue.

2. Law was added until the Seed had come (3:19b). That is, the negative function of the law as stated in (1) is limited in time[64] in salvation history because it is effective only till Christ comes. It operates as a parenthesis between the Abrahamic promise-covenant and Christ's coming. The phrase "was added" also tells us that it is a later addition (430 years later).

3. Law is inferior to Abrahamic covenant in that law is passed indirectly from God to man "by angels[65] through a mediator."[66] Since law is given through angels and declared by a mediator, then law is not only one step but two steps inferior to the promise of God to Abraham.[67]

4. The covenant is unconditional by nature: "A mediator does not represent just one party, but God is one" (3:20). This verse shows the mediator has two parties; one party is God, the other party is God's covenanted people.[68] That is, the effectiveness of the law depends on two parties. That is why covenantal works are required of the Jews. But "God is one"[69] means only that God is involved in offering the promise of inheritance, and only God can fulfill that promise in Christ.

5. The law has a temporary role in the history of redemption as a "custodian." That is, law has protected Israel from the idola-

---

64. See A. Oepke, *"Mesitēs," TDNT* 4:618; Betz, *Galatians,* 168.

65. Note here that this phrase does not mean that law is established, or created by angels, but that it is God's law given through angels, as most scholars will interpret (like Burton, *A Critical and Exegetical Commentary on the Epistle to the Galatians,* 189; Ridderbos, *The Epistle of Paul to the Churches of Galatia,* 139; Guthrie, *Galatians,* 109; Cranfield, "St. Paul and the Law," 163; Hanson, *Studies in Paul's Technique and Theology,* 214; M. J. Harris, "Appendix," *NIDNTT,* 3:1182.) Also see BAGD, 188; Betz, *Galatians,* 168–70. Hans Hübner, *Law in Paul's Thought* (Edinburgh: T. & T. Clark, 1984), 28ff., says angelic powers are hostile to humans in order to lure them into sin.

66. Betz, *Galatians,* 170; Lightfoot, *The Epistle of St. Paul to the Galatians,* 146; and Schoeps, *Paul,* 183, identify the mediator as Moses. They are right. See Ex 20:19; Dt 5:5, 23–27.

67. C. A. A. Scott, *Christianity according to St. Paul* (Cambridge: Cambridge University Press), 1966.

68. See Lightfoot, *The Epistle of St. Paul to the Galatians,* 146–47.

69. An important OT (Judaistic) concept of God as powerful, absolute. See Beker, *Paul the Apostle,* 341–47.

trous influences of the Gentiles until redemptive historical maturity is achieved, as explained in Gal 4:4: "When the time had fully come." Just as the "custodian" protects the child, leading him safely to school, and safely home again, so the law has protected Israel from the defiling influences of the Gentiles.[70] Christ has come; thus it is no longer necessary for Torah to protect Israel from the nations. The time has come also because Christ has lifted the curse of all, Jews and Gentiles.

Despite the fact that Paul was a Pharisee who must have had an exalted view of the law, we see that he offers some negative assessments of the law in light of the Christ event. Law in redemptive history is limited in effectiveness and conditional (dependent on two parties) in nature. However, the Abrahamic covenant of promise is one-party and unconditional.

Implications for Cross-Cultural Hermeneutics

The exegetical study above reveals the major issue between Paul and his opponents: defining the identity symbol for the people of God. That theme, as well as such subissues as the law as requirement and racial inclusiveness, are relevant issues in cross-cultural hermeneutics. How can Christ provide different cultural groups with a workable paradigm for living with one another? Are they, as ethnic and religious groups, so rigid in their religious and cultural traditions that these traditions have become for them a kind of law imposed on some and excluding others? The problem of ethnic diversity is even further complicated by the religious pluralism that flourishes in many parts of the world.

A cross-cultural hermeneutic which hinges on "faith in Christ" on the one hand and "cultural uniqueness" on the other has tremendous implications for the way we look at problems in the world today, such as those in former Yugoslavia (Orthodox versus Catholic), in Ireland (Protestant versus Catholic), or in

---

70. Gordon's ("The Problem at Galatia," 111) interpretation. For a different view, see David J. Lull, " 'The Law Was Our Pedagogue': A Study in Galatians 3:19–25," *Journal of Biblical Literature* 105 (1986): 481–98.

Malaysia (Muslim versus non-Muslim). The Malaysian context is the primary case study here.

The multicultural and religious diversity of Malaysia today gives rise to tensions which can easily spark conflict. With a population of about twenty million people, Malaysia is composed of Malays, Indians, Chinese, and more than a few dozen tribal groupings. Even the Chinese community is splintered by dialects and associations. Unfortunately, diversity does not often lead to admiration and respect for the unique beauty of others; instead, it often fuels envy and hatred.

Ethnic diversity is complicated by the religious pluralism which flourishes in Malaysia. Since the thirteenth century, following the introduction of Islam, most Malays have worshiped Allah.[71] Malays are constitutionally defined as Muslims, whether they are in fact or not. Such action on the part of the government tends to "formalize the boundaries of Malay ethnicity, so that its legal status vis-à-vis other ethnic groups can no longer be questioned. The boundaries of the non-Malay groups remain implied, meaning that they lack the legal means to regulate ethnic membership. Thus, the legitimation of selected cultural characteristics as ethnic identifiers is an important strategy in fortifying political interests and maintaining ethnic exclusiveness."[72] Malays are also constitutionally protected from being evangelized by other religious faiths. Some states within Malaysia have even declared that Islamic law is to be strictly observed by everyone. Most Chinese adhere to traditional Chinese religions, such as Buddhism, Confucianism, Taoism, ancestor worship, and various mythological gods. In recent years, many Chinese intellectuals have become agnostics or atheists, while some have become Christians. Most Indians are Hindus. All tribal groups have their own animistic religions.

---

71. Neither the Portuguese (1511) nor the Dutch (1641) nor the British (1784) who once colonized this region changed the religious and social lifestyle of the Malays. See S. Batumalai, "A Malaysian Neighbourology," *Asia Journal of Theology* 2 (October 1991): 350.

72. Raymond Lee, "Symbols of Separatism: Ethnicity and Status Politics in Contemporary Malaysia," in *Ethnicity and Ethnic Relations in Malaysia,* ed. Raymond Lee (De Kalb, Ill.: Center for Southeast Asian Studies, Northern Illinois University, 1986), 33.

The Malays perceived the threat posed by the economic and political achievement of non-Malays in the early years of the twentieth century.[73] Collin Abraham has shown how the British colonial government dominated and controlled the indigenous Malay *rakyat* (populace) politically and economically by strengthening the Malay ruling class, making them even more powerful.[74] In a similar fashion the colonial government tended to impose the *kapitan* (village chieftain) and *kangany* system on the Chinese and Indian peoples respectively.[75] This resulted in the situation described by Freedman:

> [T]he social map of Malaya was, so to speak, made up of a kaleidoscope of small culturally-defined units rearranging themselves in accordance with local conditions. "The Malays" did not interact with "the Chinese" and "the Indians."[76]

Malaysia is also dichotomized and disarrayed economically and politically. Non-Malays feel frustrated and victimized by various government economic plans (e.g., the New Economic Plan launched in early 1970) which grant privileges to the Malay, including preferential treatment regarding loans, student scholarships, housing, employment and business opportunities, as well as special legal protection. The politically conservative PAS (Parti Islam SeMalaysia), the liberal UMNO (United Malay National Organization), and various independent parties are controlled exclusively by Malays. Non-Malays have considered such domination to be unjust and undemocratic.

To the Malay, the word "Malaysia" means "the sacred homeland" to which they belong. The government claims that the Malays are "Bumiputras," or "princes of the soil," because they

---

73. See Khoo Kay Kim, "Sino-Malay Relations in Peninsular Malaysia before 1942," *Journal of Southeast Asian Studies* 12 (1981): 93–107.

74. Collin Abraham, "Manipulation and Management of Racial and Ethnic Groups in Colonial Malay: A Case Study of Ideological Domination and Control," in *Ethnicity and Ethnic Relations in Malaysia*, 1–3.

75. Abraham, "Manipulation and Management of Racial and Ethnic Groups in Colonial Malay," 3–4.

76. Maurice Freedman, "The Growth of a Plural Society in Malaya," *Pacific Affairs* 33 (1960): 167.

were the earliest settlers of the land. Other races, such as the Chinese, the Indians, and even the indigenous tribes, are considered "migrant races" — those who do not have the same rights and privileges as the Bumiputras. The notion of "Bumiputra" as applicable to one particular race runs head on against the understanding of the church (the body of Christ) as the inclusive people of God. The increasing polarization of Malay and non-Malay can only yield envy and conflict within Malaysia. Tensions in any religiously diverse community are real and difficult to resolve.[77] The race riot of 13 May 1969 is a perfect example. Another example was the insistence of the Universiti Teknologi Malaysia (UTM) in 1978 that all the graduands wear Malay/Islamic attire for the commencement exercises. Yet another: the rejection of the plan to build Merdeka University for other ethnic groups.[78]

Who or what is to define our identity as Malaysians? It would be unrealistic for me to suggest that Christ should be the identity symbol for Malaysians. But I believe that Christ does provide us with an identity symbol which not only cautions us not to exclude others but also calls us to find a symbol that would cause us to include others. In other words, Christ is that symbol which can generate for a multireligious community a more inclusive symbol. For example, though Malaysians are prone to face racial, cultural, and religious conflict, the sign of hope and the good news of salvation for Malaysia may be seen in agencies such as the National Alliance of Malaysia, the Malaysian Consultative Council of Buddhists, Christians, Hindus, and Sikhs (MCCBCHS). These are agencies which seek to overcome alienation by providing a medium for all the people to be identified with one another for the sake of cooperation. The MCCBCHS is by no means the Kingdom of Heaven, but it is to be hoped that this agency will be used by the Divine to accomplish His purposes, incorporating all into the plan of reconciliation and salvation. In Christ, God has provided us with a paradigm which we can look to as we seek to actualize the various aspects of our life together here in Malaysia. Since

---

77. In Malaysia, 53 percent are Muslim, 32 percent are Buddhist, 7 percent are Hindus, and 7 percent are Christians.

78. See Raymond Lee, "Symbols of Separatism," 36.

Christ is the only eternal identity symbol, we need to continue to let that Symbol generate more symbols of "life for others," before the eschaton comes.

Another implication which the Galatian passage has for cross-cultural hermeneutics pertains to the identity symbol of Christians today. What symbols are Christians to use in cross-cultural hermeneutics? Orthodox churches propose sacrament, liturgy, and right belief. Korean churches affirm prayer and fasting. Spanish churches want charismatic experiences. White churches are fond of logical formulations and sound dogma. Evangelical churches speak of personal conversion and devotion. Who is right? Everybody is, because each tradition or emphasis defines or characterizes that particular church or denomination. But the problems arise when one group or race perceives its traditions or emphasis as the only true one or, worse still, imposes it on others as essential to the gospel of Christ. To uphold or magnify one's absoluteness is to despise others' distinctiveness.

Paul did not renounce Judaism; he denounced the zealotry of the opponents who pressured the Gentile Christians in Galatia to conform to a particular standard in order for them to enjoy the full gospel. Such a superior mind-set and zealous spirit contradicted the principle of faith and the spirit of the Crucified Christ. Paul says to us today that the only essential identity symbol for Christians is faith in the Crucified Christ (Gal 2:20). Identification with Christ's crucifixion is the only essential Christians need to reinterpret all their traditions in light of the Christ event. Christ is absolute and the only necessary symbol. Christ is the common ground on which we can accept one another. Blacks or whites, beggars or bankers, Republicans or Democrats, all stand equal before God. All can participate in Christ. God fulfills the promise in Christ and offers a salvation beyond racial, sexual, or social identities and differences.

Again, it would be naive to suggest that Christ is the identity symbol for all religions. But I believe Christ does provide Christians an identity symbol that cautions them, not only to avoid excluding others, but to include others. In other words, Christ is the symbol that can be the most inclusive. Gal 2:15–16 gives us a clue; it does not give us a prescriptive answer. Reinterpretation of all the traditions and emphases in light of the Christ event is a viable Pauline hermeneutical principle. Christ is the only necessary symbol in this age of fulfillment.

Paul is making two adjustments to the understanding of the old symbol, Torah. First, Torah cannot continue to function as the identity symbol of the religion of Abraham because it excludes many of Abraham's heirs (3:6–9, 14, 28, etc.). Second, those dimensions of Torah which function to exclude Gentiles can no longer be observed, for example, circumcision and food laws. Such observances deny "the eschatological reality of the presence of the promise to Abraham."[79] And they enslave persons whom Christ has come to set free.

Paul believes that the Messiah has come in this New Age when all the messianic promises will be fulfilled. He has experienced the tension between the "now" and the "not yet" of eschatology, in which the law is abrogated in Christ, and yet also fulfilled in Christ. In Galatians 3 especially, Paul is pressed to state one side of the case to its limits because of the particular opposition from the Judaizers. In this New Age, the identity symbol of the people of God is to be reinterpreted in Christ. It is no longer the law. Membership of the true people of God is available by faith in the saving power of Christ's death and resurrection. And believers are partakers with Christ in this New Age (3:26, 27).

At various points in the epistle, Paul says, "So there is neither Jew nor Greek, there is neither slave nor free, there is neither male nor female; for you are all one in Christ Jesus. And if you are Christ's, then you are Abraham's offspring, heirs according to the promise" (3:28–29). Paul even affirms that he bears on his body, not the mark of circumcision, but the "marks of Jesus" (6:17). And he asserts that "neither circumcision counts for anything, nor uncircumcision, but a new creation" (6:15). Finally, he calls the Galatian believers "Israel of God" (6:16). Through this transposition of elements from two cultures, the Pauline cross-cultural hermeneutic elevates Christ as the universal, unifying identity symbol for all cultures.

---

79. Gordon, "The Problem at Galatia," 39.

Part II

Dialogue with Perennial Themes in Chinese Culture

Chapter 3

"Yin and Yang" in Genesis and Exodus

Since theologizing means interpreting and reincarnating the truth or the essence of our faith, what is attempted in this chapter is the use of "yin-yang" philosophy (see chap. 1 for its explication) as an alternate to classical, Western ways of thinking the truth about God and humanity. Rethinking classical, Western theology is crucial for me and my people because most (not all) Western biblical, historical, and systematic theology is seen through the Aristotelian, Hellenistic prisms of dualism and absolutism in their various forms. This is not to suggest that other paradigmatic and philosophical understandings of God and reality are wrong or inferior. There is nothing wrong in these perspectives for Westerners who can understand them, but they constitute a gulf needing to be bridged for Easterners.

The attempt here is to construct an indigenous theology which hopefully will bridge the gap between the thinking of the biblical worldview and the Chinese yin-yang worldview. This chapter merely attempts to speak the language with which the Chinese are comfortable. The approach taken here is biblical in that we begin with the biblical text as the primary (though not the only) witness to Christian truth. It is systematic in that we are imposing a certain principle (the yin-yang understanding) on the text. Nobody can approach the biblical text without any presuppositions, grids, or principles. The very fact that we use language to formulate and articulate a certain conceptualization indicates that we encounter texts with certain linguistic and cultural presuppositions. The problem is not that we are unable to come to the biblical text with a blank mind (which is in any case unnecessary), but that we are not conscious of the principles we bring to the texts. Therefore, I will be the first to acknowledge that the yin-yang understanding of God and humanity has its limitations and biases. Given the limitations, we will use the yin-yang thought language to interpret Ex 3:14 and Gn 1:26–27 as a way to construct a Chinese theology of God and humanity, with the hope that new insights might be achieved.

The Yin and Yang of God

Scripture does not contain syllogistic arguments for the existence of God;[1] rather, it assumes God exists.[2] The scriptural tradition presents evidence for the existence and nature of God as an encounter with the living God. This tradition is in harmony with Chinese theology, especially when adapted to the yin-yang model that speaks of the bipolar nature of things.

The bipolar nature of God is seen in God's hiddenness and revelation, transcendence, and immanence. God is both unknowable and distinct from the world; and yet, at the same time, God is knowable in His concern for the world through Jesus (the incarnated, crucified, and resurrected One) and through the Holy Spirit (the indwelling and transforming One). The locus classicus for God's transcendence is Ex 3:14. In Ex 3:14 God is revealed to Moses as "I am who I am" (or "I will be what I will be" or "I become what I become").[3] From that statement, three observations can be deduced:

First, the statement signifies the impossibility of defining or naming God in terms comprehensible to human minds. Words cannot

---

1. If it were possible to start from the premise that God exists and prove it by the process of syllogistic reasoning, the premise itself would always be larger than the conclusion.

2. E.g., Gn 1:1.

3. See W. R. Arnold, "The Divine Name in Exodus iii.14," *Journal of Biblical Literature* 24 (1905): 107–65; E. C. B. MacLaurin, "YHWH: The Origin of the Tetragrammaton," *Vetus Testamentum* 12 (1962): 439–63; R. de Vaux, "The Revelation of the Divine Name YHWH," *Proclamation and Presence*, ed. John I. Durham and J. R. Porter (Richmond: John Knox Press, 1970), 48–75; and John I. Durham, *Exodus*, Word Biblical Commentary (Waco, Tex.: Word, 1987), 34–41, for various interpretations and literature.

express God's reality, and to attempt to describe God in human language is to make God less than God. Thus, Barth, Kierkegaard, and R. Otto tried to differentiate qualitatively between God's attributes and humankind's. God is wholly other. I would add, God is the Wholly Other and the Immanent One. The name of God as "is-ness" is itself a nonsymbolic,[4] ineffable, primordial concept in the classical Judeo-Christian tradition. In other words, God is the Wholly Other, the Transcendent One. The Chinese classic *Tao Te Ching* evokes a similar claim: "The Tao that can be told is not the Tao; the Name that can be named is not the eternal Name."[5] This is the yin, the unknowable of God. We can have positive knowledge of God's existence but only negative knowledge of God's nature. We can contemplate God's attributes, but we cannot know the exact nature of these attributes. Our names for the attributes of God are all derivative words formed by a negative prefix such as infinitude, immutability, and so on. Each of these suggests the absence of a positive claim, for example, not finite, not mutable. Yet we cannot describe the exact positive characteristic which we have in mind, so words such as "omnipresence" and "omnipotence" are used. We know God is holy, yet when we ponder the meaning of holiness, as ascribed to God, we find that we do not know. But God has the yang aspect, which means God can be known, for "The Nameless is the origin of Heaven and Earth; The Named is the mother of all things."[6] This brings us to the next point.

Second, "I am who I am" in Hebrew is closely related to the tetragrammaton (YHWH), the most holy and personal Name of God. Both "I am" (*'ehyeh*) and the tetragrammaton seem to have

---

4. Similar to Tillich's notion of "Being itself." But Exodus here seems to stress the dynamic aspect of being, whereas Tillich seems to stress the ontological structural being: "God as being-itself is the ground of the ontological structure of being without being subject to this structure himself" (Paul Tillich, *Systematic Theology* [Chicago: University of Chicago Press, 1951], 1:239). Cf. 1:238. This name does not point beyond itself; it merely points to the existence of God and does not describe to us God's nature.

5. *Tao Te Ching*, chap. 1. See *The Way of Lao Tzu*, trans. Wing-tsit Chan (Indianapolis: Merrill, 1963), 97. See Chan's commentary on 97–101, and others: *The Way and Its Power*, trans. Arthur Waley (London: G. Allen & Unwin, 1942), 141–42; and *Lao Tzu Tao Te Ching* (n.p.: Penguin Books, 1963), 57.

6. *Tao Te Ching*, chap. 1.

derived from *hwh* ("being"), which can be translated as "to be," "to become," or even "is-ness."[7] The verbs are first-person Qal imperfects of the verb *hwh* ("be"), connoting continuing, unfinished action or reality. "I am" is a verb in the Hebrew and was rendered in the LXX with a participle functioning as a noun ("I am that being," *egō eimi ho ōn*), thus providing the basis for Philo, Origen, and others to conceive God essentially as Being.[8] But notice that the basic root word of "I am" (*'ehyeh*) and YHWH does not connote "substance," "pure being," or "essence" but a dynamic, active, living being of God thundering and acting in human affairs. According to van Leeuwen, "The name Yahweh, which is in origin Kenite or Ugaritic, takes us back to an indefinable power encountered in the lightning and thunder."[9] The verb *hayah*, when it refers to God, "expresses his personal, dynamic, active being vis-à-vis his people and his creation."[10] "Is" or "am" is seldom used in Hebrew, but when it is used, its verbal significance is stressed. It is correct, I think, that whenever "is" is used regarding the word of God, most English translations render it as "came to" or "happened."[11] "Yahweh" means "I make to be, whatever comes to be" in a causative sense.[12] That is, God is the Wholly Immanent, the most relative, personal One in the world.

---

7. See John Courtney Murray, *The Problem of God: Yesterday and Today* (New Haven: Yale University Press, 1964), 7; and Durham, *Exodus,* 39.

8. Andrio König, *Here Am I* (Grand Rapids, Mich.: Eerdmans, 1982), 67.

9. A. T. van Leeuwen, *Christianity in World History,* trans. H. H. Hoskins (New York: Charles Scribner's Sons, 1964), 48. Just like another name of God, El or Elohim, which expresses "life in its power" (Edmond Jacob, *Theology of the Old Testament,* trans. Arthur W. Heathcote and Philip J. Allcock [New York: Harper, 1958], 48) or meaning "to be strong," "to be mighty." (See Alan Richardson, *A Theological Word Book of the Bible* [New York: Macmillan, 1950], 91.)

10. Leeuwen, *Christianity in World History,* 47. See also Durham, *Exodus,* 39, and Thorleif Boman: "The *hayah* of God is to act as God, to deal as God, and to carry into effect as God.... The *hayah* of God is not given once for all in the great act of Exodus, but is only revealed in that act with particular clarity. Continuously he shows himself in manifestation of grace and mighty acts as the God of Israel" (*Hebrew Thought Compared with Greek,* trans. Jules L. Moreau [Philadelphia: Westminster Press, 1960], 47).

11. See Is 55:11, "so shall my word be," which goes on to state what it will do.

12. "With reference to the Lord the verb is used when he does something, when he acts" (König, *Here Am I,* 67).

The context of the passage also suggests this notion. Verses 6, 15, and 16 emphatically declare God to be the God of the past, of Abraham and Isaac and Jacob, and to be the God who acted for them. Verse 15 reads: "This [i.e., the God of Abraham, the God of Isaac, the God of Jacob] is my name forever, and thus I am to be remembered throughout all generations." In the immediate context of the declaration of his name as the "I am," the text elaborates in terms of historical links with, and care for, the patriarchs. The matter is emphasized again in verse 16: "The Lord, the God of your fathers, the God of Abraham, of Isaac, and of Jacob, has appeared to me, saying, 'I have observed you and what has been done to you in Egypt.' " In verses 12 and 14, God "answered Moses' protest of his own inadequacy with the assertion 'I AM with you.' "[13] In the words of Chinese philosophy, if the yin of God is God's mystery, God's unknowableness, then the yang of God is God's immanence and knowableness. God is both yin and yang. And we know of that yang of God only as God relates to the world in creation, preservation, direction, redemption, and so forth. Here, the passage speaks of the "I AM" God who is actively and continuously interacting with God's people.

Third, the interrelationship between the first and the second point can be linked by the faithfulness (ḥesed)[14] of God. That is, "I am" declares the unchangeable, constant faithfulness of God to live, to interact with, and to react to the people of God. Because God is actively interacting with history, God can change the form of divine interaction and the way of dealing with the people and the world. In this respect, God can change God's mind (repent), but only and always for the purpose of maintaining the divine faithfulness toward His people. The Greco-Roman mind tended to conceive of change as deterioration. The yin-yang mindset thinks of change as creativity, flexibility, and sensitivity. If God cannot change, God is insensitive to human needs and conditions.

---

13. Durham, Exodus, 39.

14. Or the NT understanding of God's love. If there is love, there is the wrath of God, because wrath is injured love (J. Moltmann, The Crucified God [London: SCM, 1974], 272). For this reason, the wrath of God is proclaimed most powerfully by the prophets of his love, such as Hosea (see 5:12, 14) and Jeremiah (see 13:12–14).

If God cannot change, God is merely an eternal principle or a programmed robot. But God in the Bible does change. In fact, God becomes an incarnated One, Jesus the Christ; that transformational process itself is change. God also changes God's mind (repents) in response to the repentance of humanity. That change does not terminate God's faithfulness; instead, it confirms it. In fact, it is always for the sake of that faithfulness (see Jonah 3; Jer 18:8), for the good of the people, that God changes. For God is the God of pathos[15] who is deeply engaged in the joys and sufferings of the people. Pathos means the willful and passionate involvement of God; God lives with his people and among them, their fate involves him, their love and obedience give him joy; and God suffers with them in their captivity and exile. Therefore, the unchanging and changing of God should not be seen as contradiction or absurdity, but should be seen as divine faithfulness.

Perhaps the extreme notions of God as Unchanging Being and God as the Absolute Becoming have to be discarded. "To be" is not in conflict with but is complementary to "being," just as yin and yang, though dipolar in essence, are not dualistic but rather complementary. Thus, "I am" means God is the acting God. "I am" implies and presupposes the being of God, but that must be understood as an active, totally concerned God immersed in history and the world.[16] Therefore, God is not just the absolute, eternal, unchangeable, sufficient-unto-himself being, but also the most sensitive, relative, and changing God.

These "both-and" aspects of God are clearly seen in the concept of the Triune God. God is both the yin and the yang. The Trinity is incomprehensible and will always remain a mystery. However, for the sake of a cognitive exercise, we can affirm that God the Father is God (Jn 6:27), God the Son is God (Heb 1:8), and God the Holy Spirit is God (Acts 5:3–4). There is one God, not three (Mt 28:19, Dt 6:4, Is 45:5, 1 Tm 2:5). They share the same essence (Jn 10:30), honor (Jn 5:23), and glory (Jn 17:5) to the extent they have perfect interaction in will, knowledge, com-

---

15. See A. J. Heschel, *The Prophets* (New York: Harper & Row, 1962), vol. 2, especially chaps. 1–3; and Moltmann, *The Crucified God*, 267–68.
16. See König, *Here Am I*, 67.

munion, and love (Mt 11:27; 1 Cor 2:10). Also, they are three; each has his own uniqueness. For example, (*a*) in the matter of personal relations the Father is viewed (if not strictly at least partly) from the perspective of begetting (or of paternity or maternity; see Eph 1:3, 3:14), the Son is viewed from the perspective of filiation, or being begotten (see Mt 3:17; Jn 19:7; Heb 1:2, 3), and the Spirit is viewed from the perspective of spiration (Ez 37:9, Jn 20:22). (*b*) The three persons of God have individual differences in some responsibilities and functions (Jn 16:14, Phil 2:6–11, 1 Cor 11:3), which are undertaken with voluntary dependence and subordination (an order of priority in work and not essence). Threeness in oneness will always be a mystery. But the term "Triune" seems to speak of their "is-ness:" distinctiveness and relatedness. Note that interrelatedness is not only evident among them, but also obvious between them and the world. Contemporary imagery tends to offer creative interpretation in portraying the mysterious, paradoxical nature of the Trinity, who is always in relation to or interaction with the world. For example, John Macquarrie prefers to speak of the Trinity in terms of Primordial Being (as the Father), Expressive Being (as the Son), and Unitive Being (as the Holy Spirit).[17] Lewis S. Ford, a process theologian, has also used the triadic structure within God as primordial for true possibilities for the world (the symbol of Father); as the "bodying forth of a new emergency in the creative advance of the world, one transcending human possibilities and so creating a new structure of existence" (the symbol Logos); and as God's "immanence within every creature in supplying to it initial aims for its particular creative possibilities" (the symbol Spirit).[18] This expression portrays the transcendent God who can be encountered through God's Word in Jesus and the movement of the Spirit among the people.[19]

---

17. John Macquarrie, *Principles of Christian Theology* (New York: Charles Scribner's Sons, 1966), 182–84.

18. Lewis S. Ford, "Process Trinitarianism," *Journal of the American Academy of Religion* 43, no. 2 (1975): 202.

19. See William J. Hill, *The Three-Personed God: The Trinity as a Mystery of Salvation* (Washington, D.C.: Catholic University of America Press, 1982), 204–7.

The Yin and Yang of Humanity

From the "is-ness" of God we will now turn to the "image of God," humanity. Traditional understanding of the "image of God" holds to the substantive interpretation; humanity is said to have or bear God's righteousness or holiness. But rather than the substantive, functional, and static views of the *imago Dei*,[20] a reconstruction of Karl Barth's relational interpretation is used here. The *imago Dei* refers both to, first, a vertical relationship (between God and person) and, second, a horizontal relationship (between persons).[21]

First, the image of God speaks of the vertical interrelationship between God and humanity. The first dimension of this *imago Dei* can be reflected in human encounters with, or in the human capacity to respond to, God, God's Words, or God's presence. In the Genesis narrative when Adam and Eve hear the Word of God, they are the only creatures who bear "the image and likeness of God" in their creaturely existence. Genesis 1–2 seems to suggest both that humanity needs to live beyond the fate of mere "managing" of the earth to the freedom and joy of participating in the Sabbath rest of their Creator God (1:28), and that humanity needs to trust in the creative Word of God that differentiates human creatureliness and grants human actualities and possibilities. One of the signs of differentiation is for humans to be aware of or to know God as the source and goal of life. In naming the other animals, Adam seems not to get a response even though both the humans and other animals share creatureliness. However, the differentiation God bestows on humans by God's creative Word gives humans the ability to respond to God, thus completing the two-way communication and communion between God and humanity. Humans depend on

20. For various interpretations on the *imago Dei* as (*a*) a supernatural distinction, (*b*) spiritual qualities or capacities, (*c*) the external form of humanity, (*d*) the functional role of humanity, and (*e*) the representative of God on earth, see Claus Westermann, *Genesis 1–11, a Commentary*, trans. John J. Scullion (Minneapolis: Augsburg Publishing House, 1984), 148–51.

21. See Karl Barth, *Church Dogmatics,* vol. 3, pt. 1 (Edinburgh: T. & T. Clark, 1958), 197–98. I am indebted to Ray S. Anderson (*On Being Human* [Grand Rapids, Mich.: Eerdmans, 1982], 69–87) for his insight on the discussion of the Barthian understanding of *imago Dei.*

the Creator God for freedom, life, hope, being, becoming, and all possibilities. So Barth argues,

> It [the *imago Dei*] does not consist in anything that man is or does. It consists as man himself consists as the creature of God. He would not be man if he were not the image of God. He is the image of God in the fact that he is man.[22]

It is that partnership, that ability to enter into a relationship with God, that makes humans creatures of God's image and likeness.

This first dimension of the *imago Dei* can be further supported by the form-critical analysis recently undertaken by Claus Westermann. Westermann contends that Gn 1:26–28 does not describe the qualitative distinctiveness of the *imago Dei,* but that the way and the process of narrating the creation of humanity (in contrast to the creation of all other creatures) speaks of the decision ("let us make") and specification ("in our image and in our likeness") that "the creator God decides to create something that is his own personal concern."[23] This text and its royal character suggest that

> what God decides to create must be something that has a relationship to him just as in the Sumerian and Babylonian texts people are related to the creator god as servants of the gods.... The sentence [Gn 1:27] means that the uniqueness of human beings consists in their being God's counterparts. The relationship to God is not something which is added to human existence; humans are created in such a way that their very existence is intended to be their relationship to God.[24]

What we wish to note here is that there is a relationship similar to the yin-yang relationship between God and humanity. Not only does Adam ("person" or "humanity"; or more literally "the earthly one") have personhood through the creative word of God in relationship to God, Adam ("human-being") is to live forever in responding to the word of God as the basis of his/her relationship

---

22. *Church Dogmatics,* vol. 3, pt. 1, 184.

23. Westermann, *Genesis 1–11,* 156.

24. Westermann, *Genesis 1–11,* 156–58. See S. Mowinckel, "Urmensch und 'Königsideologie,'" *Studia Theologica: Scandinavian Journal of Theology* 2 (1948): 71–89.

to God. Once "human-being" withdraws from the relationship, and doubts or disobeys God's creative word, "human-being" becomes less human — that is sinful. The "first sin" is therefore first and foremost religious and relational, not ethical or substantive. The so-called first commandment of God to Adam and Eve is not functionally an imperative, but a basis for human beings to find a constant relationship with God as they respond trustfully.

If God is the yang, humanity is the yin in interaction, in both relationship and partnership responding to God. The yin-yang paradigm is relevant to illustrate this vertical relationship, because the vertical relationship is highly organic and intimate. God and humanity are not the same; they are different from one another. For example, God is the Creator, while humanity is the creature of God; or God is infinite and humanity is finite. Yet the difference between God and humanity does not mean that God cannot relate to humanity, or vice versa. In fact, the yin-yang paradigm helps us to see that the yin and the yang, though different, are not opposite. Rather, the yin and the yang are always in complementary relationship to one another. In other words, God and humans, though different, can always be in relationship, a relationship which can culminate in the wholeness represented by the Great Ultimate circle of the *T'ai chi* emblem.

Two questions may be raised concerning this yin-yang understanding of the vertical relationship between God and humanity. The first concerns the mutual relationship between God and humans. Can we speak of God needing humans for relationship or for wholeness similar to that of the yin needing the yang or the yang needing the yin for the Great Ultimate? The second concerns the difference between God and humanity. Can we speak of God having a dot of humanity, and humanity having a dot of divinity just as yin has a dot of yang, and yang has a dot of yin in the *T'ai chi* emblem? According to yin-yang understanding, the answer to both questions is yes.

Second, the image of God speaks of a horizontal interrelationship. The creation account[25] does not mention any substantive or

---

25. Gn 1:26–27, 5:1–2. Cf. 9:6 and, in the Apocrypha, Wisdom 2:23 and Sirach 17:3.

ontological uniqueness concerning Adam ("human-being"). Notice that not only does the clause "male and female he created them" emphasize that both male and female are created "in our image" and "in our likeness," but it also explains "image" and "likeness" as the co-humanity of male and female relating and encountering each other.[26]

Because God exists through self-communion and self-encounter, the human bearing the image of God reflects this nature of God at two levels: the I-Thou[27] relationship with God, and the same relationship with fellow human beings.[28] The Genesis passage here uses plural pronouns for God[29] and humans in order to point out the correspondence between the intrinsic plurality of human beings as constituted male and female and the being of God, in which God encounters and relates to Himself. Genesis 2 clearly contends that for Adam to be alone is "not good," for Adam cannot differentiate and relate fully to himself without first encountering another. Then in Gn 2:23, this "man" (*'îsh*) has an I-Thou encounter with "woman" and vice versa. In a Chinese perspective, this is when the yin and the yang meet to become the whole. The male and the female are in mutuality, interdependence, reciprocity, interrelationship. This fusion not only gives rise to co-humanity, it also differentiates what is yin and what is yang. Furthermore, in and through that I-Thou encounter, the man and the woman both experience and become himself/herself as the distinct I-Self. In other words, the yin and the yang do not dissolve their uniqueness through that yin-yang encounter or interaction. For it is through that encounter with the yang that the yin knows and becomes the yin; and vice versa.

---

26. Barth, *Church Dogmatics*, vol. 3, pt. 1, 196–98. Therefore, the female and male relationship is "the only real principle of differentiation and relationship; as the original form not only of man's [or human's] confrontation of God and also of all [encounters] between man and man [or human and human], it is true *humanum* and therefore the true creaturely image of God" (*Church Dogmatics*, vol. 3, pt. 1, 186).

27. Barth's language here echoes Martin Buber's *I and Thou*, trans. Walter Kaufman (Edinburgh: T. & T. Clark), 1979.

28. Buber, *I and Thou*, 184.

29. Whether the "us" refers to the threefold God or the heavenly court or something else is impossible to determine. For preliminary discussion and literature, see Westermann, *Genesis 1–11*, 144–45.

In summary, the *imago Dei* ("male and female God created them") is not totally present in the form of individual humanity but is more complete as co-humanity. The yin and the yang do not exist for themselves but for the harmony of both. And through that interaction, the yin and the yang are differentiated. In other words, the *imago Dei* lies within the interpersonal relationship that exists among humans.

Despite the fact that the Genesis account takes its language from and speaks through a patriarchal culture, it does transcend that culture. We see that the nature and value of both male and female personhood are affirmed individually and corporately in the creation account. Both male and female are created in the *imago Dei*, one for the other. Specifically, the woman is *neged* ("helpmate" is a poor translation). That is, woman is "corresponding to" or "equal to" man.[30] Furthermore, the woman is the *'ēzer* ("divine help"), and if not superior, then at least is an equal "copartner," "co-helper," "coworker" or "enabler" of man, similar to Divine help to human being.[31] Similarly, in Chinese philosophy, yin is not inferior to yang; the two are simply different, just as the creation account affirms the equality between male and female. This does not mean equality in all responsibilities, without any subordination. But the value, personhood, dignity, and worth of the woman are equal to those of the man. If the yin-yang philosophy is correct, then the issue becomes one of establishing how both the woman and the man can relate to one another, rather than just focusing on the female or the male in isolation. For example, if there is any conflict between the yin and the yang, fixing problems of the yin alone will not create harmony; only by fixing problems of both the yin and the yang will any relationship, individual or interpersonal, be restored.

Another issue to be emphasized is not only that of co-humanity, but also that of the I-Self relationship. The I-Thou relationship between male and female does not eliminate, but enhances, the I-Self relationship. If the "I" seeks to find its identify and self-worth in

---

30. See Gn 2:18 and Francis Brown, S. R. Driver, and Charles A. Briggs, *Hebrew and English Lexicon of the Old Testament* (New York: Oxford University, 1955), 617.

31. See Ex 18:4; Dt 33:29; Pss 33:20; 70:5; 115:9, 10, 11, which use the same word for God as the divine helper of people.

itself, the "I" will never know and become that unique authentic self. But if the "I" seeks itself in the "we," the "I" has a better sense of the identity, meaning, and existence of itself and others. The encounter between the "I" and the "we" then does not threaten but builds up the I-Self identity and relationship.

Human existence is not intended to be just yin or just yang, but both yin and yang. The self needs another. One needs the yin to be the yang (and vice versa) to have the harmonious whole or the Great Ultimate. That interdependence does not eliminate individual uniqueness, just as the yin is not transformed into a lesser yin as it interacts with the yang. In fact, because of the presence of and interaction with the yang, the yin becomes all the more distinct yin. It should be remembered also that every yin has part of yang and every yang has a dot of yin, indicating that individuals are not without commonality with others. In other words, we are all different, but we also all share commonality — the communicability and communality as articulated in the yin-yang philosophy.

From the above, it can be understood why indigenous, traditional Chinese philosophy shapes its moral or ethical outlook, as it does its perception of reality, predominantly from yin-yang philosophy. No doubt, an understanding of the *imago Dei* has serious ramifications for ethics, too. For example, to hate or despise one another is to despise and hate that *imago Dei* within one's self and others. Murder is such an affront to both God and humanity because it is an affront to the *imago Dei,* which is embodied in humanity. To withhold the physical or spiritual needs of others is to destroy that interpersonal relationship which entails the *imago Dei,* and willfully to live as less than a person. Social justice is not just another divine imperative, because the created *imago Dei* of co-humanity presupposes all to be one's brother's and sister's and therefore one another's keepers. The human being is thus primarily a social being and only secondarily an unique individual person. No wonder that Jesus, the most human of human beings who is the very image of God, manifests that I-Thou relationship with God and people most perfectly.[32] Christ is fully human and he is the *imago Dei* (Col 1:15) who lives and gives his life not for himself

---

32. Barth, *Church Dogmatics,* vol. 3, pt. 2, 250–65. With regard to the em-

but totally for others and for God. In so doing, he has not lost but has encountered himself fully. Jesus has also known the dynamic and value of the *imago Dei.* As such, Jesus has come to preach the gospel, to heal the brokenhearted, to deliver the captives, and to set at liberty those who are bruised.

In bearing the *imago Dei,* the human being is essentially a social being. It is through interrelatedness, interdependence, mutuality, and reciprocity (just like the yin and yang) that all age, sexual, social, and ethnic groups are integrated, while at the same time all distinctiveness is affirmed and differentiated. Moreover, it is in that interrelatedness with God that all persons find their authentic selves and become fully human.

Conclusion

The above exposition of the biblical texts using the yin-yang paradigm represents an attempt to view the Christian notions of God and humanity through the lens of the Chinese mind-set. This new methodology does not assume or assert its superiority, validity, or comprehensiveness over traditional or contemporary methodologies of the West or the East. It seeks only to show the translatability of the Christian truth through the employment of the yin-yang philosophy. This methodology may help to enrich or critique other methodologies, though that task, while certainly vitally important, is beyond the scope of this chapter. What I have sought to accomplish here is to translate my understanding of the "is-ness" of God and the "image of God" within humanity into the indigenous philosophical language of the Chinese so that the Chinese reader can comprehend and embrace the biblical truth more easily and readily than by using a foreign philosophical language.

---

bodiment of God-Human Jesus, in Christ there is no male or female. This does not speak of unisexuality in Christ but equality of male and female.

Chapter 4

"Rest" in Hebrews and the Yin-Yang Worldview

The purpose of this chapter is threefold. First, it represents an attempt to discover the meaning of *katapausis* ("rest") and *sabbatismos* ("Sabbath rest") in the selected pericopae. The meaning of, and the relationships among, the Canaan rest, the Creation rest, the heavenly rest, and the Sabbath rest will be determined in light of the audience-author identity. Next I shall observe how the homilist uses Ps 95:7b–11 (LXX 94) and Gn 2:2 in Heb 3:7–4:13 in terms of his theology of "rest." One may ask, is the writer of Hebrews guilty of forcing an exegesis of the old promise as it is found in the Old Testament on New Testament believers? Or is the writer allegorizing the Canaan rest as a spiritual rest? What are the writer's hermeneutical presuppositions and principles? Finally, after determining what the passage meant to the first-century readers, we want to employ yin-yang philosophy as an interpretive paradigm to summarize the epistle's theology of rest, so as to make better sense of its message to both Western and Chinese readers.

Before the purpose of this chapter can be carried out, it is necessary (*a*) to delineate the historical situation of the audience and the author's purpose in writing; and, (*b*) to provide an historical-critical exegesis of the pericope in order to observe its context and content.

The Audience-Author Identity

It is fair to assume that all the New Testament epistles, including the Epistle to the Hebrews, were written to deal with specific polemic issues arising from the audiences' situations. Two closely interrelated factors to be considered, then, are the audience and the author. It is outside the scope and intention of this chapter to elaborate a solid theory of audience-author identity, but it will seek to offer a hypothesis to be tested in the exegetical section on 3:7–4:13.

There are at least four possible audience-author hypotheses. One theory stresses the Hellenistic-Judaistic influence on the audience. This theory is argued by Lala K. K. Dey and James W. Thompson, who propose that the author's "constant metaphysical dualism" in argument must be seen as a polemic against the Hellenistic Judaism which offered direct, mystical participation in the heavenly order over against the intermediary world of wisdom and angels.[1] The second theory postulates the audience as the conservative Jews of Qumran,[2] probably Essenes[3] or Zionists.[4] The audience is waiting for the end of the world in the midst of oppression. The audience has a low Christology, that is, it sees Christ as inferior to angels and Moses. The audience is on the brink of reverting to Judaism. The author is exhorting his readers to live a life of perseverance and to break with Judaism.

---

1. See Lala Kalyan Kumar Dey, *The Intermediary World and Patterns of Perfection in Philo and Hebrews* (Missoula, Mont.: Scholars Press, 1975); and James W. Thompson, "The *Katapausis* Motif in Hebrews," in *The Beginnings of Christian Philosophy: The Epistle to the Hebrews* (Washington, D.C.: Catholic Biblical Association of America, 1982).

2. See Yigael Yadin, "The Dead Sea Scrolls and the Epistle to the Hebrews," in *Scripta Hierosolymitana IV,* ed. C. Rabin and Y. Yadin (Jerusalem: Magnes Press, 1968), 36–55.

3. Kosmala says the author wrote to Essenes, urging them to become Christians. See H. Kosmala, *Hebräer-Essener-Christen* (Leiden: E. J. Brill, 1959).

4. This is the working hypothesis of G. W. Buchanan, *To the Hebrews: A New Translation with Introduction and Commentary* (Garden City, N.Y.: Doubleday, 1972), and Philip Edgcombe Hughes, *A Commentary on the Epistle to the Hebrews* (Grand Rapids, Mich.: Eerdmans, 1977). However, Hebrews seems to be closer to Philo than to Qumran, so Hugh Montefiore, *A Commentary on the Epistle to the Hebrews* (London: Adam & Charles Black, 1964), 18, and F. F. Bruce, *The Epistle to the Hebrews,* New International Commentary on the New Testament (Grand Rapids, Mich.: Eerdmans, 1978), 23. For an assessment of this theory, see F. F. Bruce, " 'To the Hebrews' or 'To the Essenes'?" *New Testament Studies* 9 (1963): 217–32; and Irvin W. Batdorf, "Hebrews and Qumran: Old Methods and New Directions," in *Festschrift to Honor F. Wilbur Gingrich* (Leiden: E. J. Brill, 1972), 20–25.

The third theory suggests that the audience is comprised of weary second-generation Christians who are caught in the dilemma of apocalypticism and their own severe life experiences. J. Moffatt and H. Attridge think that the audience of Hebrews is at the verge of falling away from the Living God due to various persecutions and tribulations they are facing (10:36; 12:13). Their leaders have died, probably as martyrs (see 13:7). This theory suspects the second generation became weary in their Christian faith. As such, the author is exhorting them not to give up their faith in Christ.[5] The fourth theory interprets the audience as first-generation Christians whose syncretistic background includes Roman and Jewish Merkabah mysticism,[6] even possibly gnostic influence. Williamson's studies show that the same words and same ideas are used by Philo and Hebrews but are used in very different ways. I agree with Williamson that Philo's and Hebrews' hermeneutics and philosophy are distinctively different. It is possible that the author is well trained also in Alexandrian Judaism, as was Philo.[7] All the above theories are possible reconstructions of the audience's situation, but the fourth hypothesis seems the most plausible, since it provides a broader platform for portraying the complex influence of the audience.

My positional thesis on the audience-author issue begins with the assertion that the author of Hebrews is steeped in the LXX, the Bible of the early church. The writer of Hebrews uses a lot of

5. Harold W. Attridge, *The Epistle to the Hebrews: A Commentary on the Epistle to the Hebrews* (Minneapolis: Fortress, 1989), 12. But James Moffatt, *A Critical and Exegetical Commentary on the Epistle to the Hebrews* (New York: Scribner's, 1924), xxi, says that 2:3–4, 10:32f., and 13:7 do not seem to suggest that the readers belonged to the second generation. But on page xxii, he theorizes that they are second-generation Christians.

6. Advocated by G. G. Scholem, *Major Trends in Jewish Mysticism* (Jerusalem, 1941), 43ff., who says that the Merkabah mystic perceives that "God's pre-existing throne is at once the goal and theme of his mystical vision" and therefore maintains interest in angels, the use of fire imagery, stressing the holiness and transcendence of God, and the journey through heavens to reach the heavenly sanctuary or God's throne. Cf. Ronald Williamson, "The Background of the Epistle to the Hebrews," *Expository Times* 87 (1975/76): 232–37.

7. It is a theory worked out by Williamson. See Ronald Williamson, *Philo and the Epistle to the Hebrews* (Leiden: E. J. Brill, 1970). Thus Williamson disagrees with S. G. Sowers, *The Hermeneutics of Philo and Hebrews* (Richmond: John Knox Press, 1965).

LXX quotations, which leads to the natural assumption that the author is a Diaspora rather than a Palestine Jew. The author redefines many Old Testament concepts in light of the person and work of Jesus which he places within the perceived tension between the present and the future, between the earthly and the heavenly, as captured in the terminology of "today" (an already *and* not-yet eschatology). He is probably combating the polemic situation faced by his syncretistic audience (Hellenistic Jewish Christians,[8] probably in Rome),[9] which is fearful of and hypnotized by Hellenistic philosophy, as well as the Philonic-Gnostic,[10] and the Merkabah mystical worldview of its time.[11] The audience is anxious about present and future life (see 2:3; 10:35–39); it is about to drift away from Christian faith and confession (3:1; 4:14; 10:23) because the expected heavenly Kingdom has apparently been postponed while they themselves endure ridicule, imprisonment, and persecution (10:32–34). The audience is in danger of losing its confidence and hope (3:6, 14; 6:11–12, 19; 10:35), of suffering from sclerosis (3:7–8, 13; 5:11), of drifting into worldly paganism (2:1–3; 3:12; 4:1; 6:4–6; 10:39), or of shrinking from faith in Jesus Christ (6:1–2; 13:9). The author is, therefore, not simply writing a letter but a serious "word of exhortation" (13:22) to exhort, encourage, and warn the audience.

The author skillfully uses the LXX by means of midrashic her-

---

8. See Bruce, *The Epistle to the Hebrews,* xxiii–xxx; Buchanan, *To the Hebrews,* 246–67; Hughes, *A Commentary on the Epistle to the Hebrews,* 26–51; and Simon Kistemaker, *The Psalm Citations in the Epistle to the Hebrews* (Amsterdam: Wed. G. Van Soest N.V., 1961), 186.

9. A view proposed by Merrill C. Tenney, "A New Approach to the Book of Hebrews," *Bibliotheca Sacra* 123 (1966): 230–36; Bruce, *The Epistle to the Hebrews,* xxiv–xxv; and Raymond E. Brown and John P. Meier, *Antioch and Rome* (New York: Paulist, 1983), 139–58.

10. See Walter Schmithals, *Neues Testament und Gnosis* (Darmstadt: Wissenschaftliche Buchgesellschaft, 1984), 138ff., who suggests that the audience is comprised of God-fearing Gentile Christians who have been driven out of the synagogue as a result of the reorganization at Jamnia following the fall of Jerusalem (80–100 C.E.) and have fallen under the pressure of persecution, from the side of the synagogue or from that of state authorities (so 10:32ff.) or a combination of both (12:1ff.; 13:3).

11. Williamson, "The Background of the Epistle to the Hebrews," 232–37, and Alan F. Segal, *Two Powers in Heaven: Early Rabbinic Reports about Christianity and Gnosticism* (Leiden: E. J. Brill, 1977).

meneutics to make his epistle accessible to the weary and oppressed community. He is trying to combat the erroneous worldview of the audience. It is very possible that the author is attacking an undue deference to angels (see Col 2:18) and the idea that the Son has been equated with one of the principalities and powers thought to govern and control the universe (see 1 Cor 15:24; Eph 3:10; etc.).[12] He may be using the words and concepts of Gnosticism and mysticism, but he certainly gives them a biblical twist with his own distinct interpretation, unlike that of his contemporaries. That is, the author is using the audience's own argument to argue against them. It would appear that the Gnostics, the mystics, and proponents of Philo's worldview may have, to a certain extent, brainwashed the audience, but certainly not the author.[13] For example, the preexistence of the redeemer (1:3), the descent of the redeemer through the heavenly worlds (9:11ff., 24f.), and the common origin of redeemer and the redeemed (2:11) — all dear to the author — are not gnostic or Hellenistic ideas in the incarnational form found in the epistle.

Before turning to Heb 3:7–4:13 to observe the meaning and usage of "rest," let us first look at the context of the pericope itself.

An Exegetical Study of Hebrews 3:7–4:13

The Literary Context

The preceding context (3:1–6) of the pericope (3:7–4:13) emphasizes the identity of the readers as the "holy brethren," the

---

12. This position is held by Montefiore, *A Commentary on the Epistle to the Hebrews,* 39ff.; and Robert Jewett, *Letter to Pilgrims: A Commentary on the Epistle to the Hebrews* (New York: Pilgrim Press, 1981), 5–8. As Jewett suggests, "It appears that the Christian congregations . . . interpreted the intermittent harassment and persecution they had experienced as proof that hostile cosmic forces were still in control of history and nature. . . . Salvation was therefore in part a matter of gaining power over the hostile cosmic forces" (11).

13. See Williamson, *Philo and the Epistle to the Hebrews;* idem, "The Background of the Epistle to the Hebrews," 232–37; and Sowers, *The Hermeneutics of Philo and Hebrews* (I disagree with Sowers's contention that the epistle is an anti-Judaic one). E. Käsemann suggests that the author himself is influenced by the gnostic worldview and by Philo. See *Das Wandernde Gottesvolk* (Göttingen: Vandenhoeck & Ruprecht, 1959), 21–70.

"partakers of heavenly call" (3:1),[14] and the "house of God" (3:6).[15] Notice also that the high priestly virtue of faithfulness exemplified in Jesus has already been established in 3:1–5. Now the writer's point is to link the relationship of the readers, who are the members of God's household (or, to be more precise, are "the house of God" where God dwells), with Jesus, the Son in God's household.[16] Taking a step further, the writer links the relationship between the readers and Christ in the complex paraenesis of 3:7–4:13: the readers must be faithful and must persevere to the end, just as Christ did.[17] *Metochoi* ("share") is a special term used to identify both Jesus' earthly suffering with the people, and the church with its transcendent heavenly calling (3:1).[18] The conditional clause of 3:6b, "if we hold fast our confidence," then serves as a springboard for the writer to cite Psalm 95 and Gn 2:2 to expand the faithfulness theme of his exhortation more fully.

---

14. Or to render the verse as a triple vocative, "brethren, saints, partakers of a heavenly call," if one punctuates with a comma between "brethren" and "saints." See Hughes, *A Commentary on the Epistle to the Hebrews,* 125.

15. It is rendered in Greek as "we ourselves are the household." See *The Greek New Testament,* 3d edition, ed. Kurt Aland et al. (New York: United Bible Societies, 1975), 751; William L. Lane, *Hebrews 1:1–9:28,* Word Biblical Commentary 47A (Waco, Tex.: Word, 1991), 71, note c.

16. See Alan Mugridge, " 'Warnings in the Epistle to the Hebrews': An Exegetical and Theological Study," *Reformed Theological Review* 46 (September–December 1987): 75; Thomas Kem Oberholtzer, "The Warning Passages in Hebrews, Part 2 (of 5 Parts): The Kingdom Rest in Hebrews 3:1–4:13," *Bibliotheca Sacra* 145 (April–June 1988): 187; Kistemaker, *The Psalm Citations in the Epistle to the Hebrews,* 108; and Lane, *Hebrews 1:1–9:28,* 71.

17. The "faith" theme is prevalent in this passage. The perseverance theme also persists in the same passage, e.g., "if we hold fast our confidence and pride in our hope" (3:6; similar passage in 3:14). See variant readings in *The Greek New Testament* and Bruce M. Metzger, *A Textual Commentary on the Greek New Testament,* Companion Volume to the United Bible Societies' Greek New Testament (New York: United Bible Societies, 1971), 665; and Marvin R. Vincent, *Word Studies in the New Testament* (New York: Charles Scribner's Sons, 1902), 4:414.

18. See Thompson, "The *Katapausis* Motif in Hebrews," 94; H. Hanse, *"Metechō,"* Theological Dictionary of the New Testament (hereafter *TDNT*), ed. G. Kittel and G. Friedrich, 9 vols. (Grand Rapids, Mich.: Eerdmans, 1964–76), 2:830.

The Problems in the Use of the Old Testament

The abundance of citations of the Old Testament in the Epistle to the Hebrews is obvious. The often debated and most controversial issue of New Testament theology is the hermeneutical justification and intelligibility of the use of the Old Testament in the New.[19] One of the thornier problems is the use of Ps 95:7b–11 (LXX Psalm 94) and Gn 2:2 in Heb 3:7–4:13. The writer of Hebrews introduces Psalm 95 (LXX 94) in Heb 3:7 with the phrase, "the Holy Spirit says."[20] Psalm 95 is a Psalm of David most probably quoted by the writer according to the Septuagint (thus it is Psalm 94) and not the MT.[21] It is the *Venite* ("O Come"), a call-to-worship psalm,[22] composed probably "for the Feast of Tabernacles, when God's people relived, in token, their time of encampment in the

---

19. For preliminary understanding on this issue of citations and textual variations, see Bruce, *The Epistle to the Hebrews,* xlvii–lii; John C. McCullough, "The Old Testament Quotations in Hebrews," *New Testament Studies* 26 (April 1979): 363–75; H. J. B. Combrink, "Some Thoughts on the Old Testament Citations in the Epistle to the Hebrews," *Neotestamentica* 5 (1971); George Howard, "Hebrews and the Old Testament Quotations," *Novum Testamentum* 10 (1968): 208–16; and Kistemaker, *The Psalm Citations in the Epistle to the Hebrews,* 108–16.

20. Interestingly enough, none of the usual "introductory formulas" of Paul, like "it is written" or "the Scripture says," is used, but phrases like "God says" or "Christ says" or "the Spirit says," as observed by R. v. G. Tasker, *The Old Testament in the New Testament* (Philadelphia: Westminster Press, n.d.), 115. Thus, the OT is God's Word to the author, and he is faithful to his original insight in Heb 1:1 that God has spoken. See Juliana Casey, *Hebrews* (Wilmington, Del.: Michael Glazier, 1980), 23.

21. Psalm 95 is anonymous in the Masoretic Text (see *Biblia Hebraica Stuttgartensia* [Stuttgart: Deutsche Bibelgesellschaft, 1984], 1177), but the LXX assigns it to David (see *The Septuagint with Apocrypha: Greek and English,* ed. Sir Lancelot C. L. Brenton [Grand Rapids, Mich.: Regency Reference Library, 1986], 755). The author's phrase in 4:7, "in David," may simply mean he is quoting from the LXX rather than the MT. See Bruce, *The Epistle to the Hebrews,* 75; Thomas Hewitt, *The Epistle to the Hebrews* (Grand Rapids, Mich.: Eerdmans, 1960), 87; and W. C. Kaiser, Jr., *The Uses of the Old Testament in the New* (Chicago: Moody Press, 1985), 166, n. 30; George Howard, in a detailed analysis, disagrees; see Howard, "Hebrews," 208–15.

22. Ancient Mishnah tradition regarded this psalm as a New Year psalm and a liturgy of the autumn festival, in which Yahweh is revealed as the Creator and Lord of the universe. Early Christian churches widely used this psalm as a call to worship, too. See Derek Kidner, *Psalms 73–150, a Commentary,* Tyndale Old Testament Commentaries (Downers Grove, Ill.: InterVarsity Press, 1975), 343; and Artur Weiser, *The Psalms: A Commentary* (Philadelphia: Westminster Press, 1962), 625.

wilderness."[23] The voice of God breaks in in verses 8 to 11 to challenge and to warn Israel to be faithful to its covenantal God, who is being depicted in the first seven verses of the psalm.[24] It is against this same thrust and theme that the writer of Hebrews wishes to impress his point on his audience. Just as the psalmist uses the wilderness experience of Israel under Moses[25] to warn and exhort his people against unbelief and disobedience at the time of the psalmist, so the homilist applies the psalmist's warning to the recipients of this epistle.

However, the homilist's use of the psalm is not without problems. Besides the three insignificant variations of spelling and verbal forms of "they saw," "forty," and "I said,"[26] attention needs to be focused on the following three divergences (from either MT or LXX) which affect the interpretation of the passage.

First is the change of the verbal form "they tested" in the LXX to a noun form in the prepositional phrase "in the test" (Heb 3:9). Though a few manuscripts of the epistle have "they tested" or even "they tested me," "in the test" is most probably the original reading in the epistle.[27] H. J. B. Combrink suggests that the preferred noun form conveys the better theological meaning of "people tested by God," rather than the active meaning of the verb — "people are testing God."[28] If the LXX verbal form were theologically unacceptable, one wonders why it was not rejected or altered by the copyist before the time of the homilist of the

---

23. Kidner, *Psalms 73–150,* 343.

24. See Kidner, *Psalms 73–150,* 343; Weiser, *The Psalms: A Commentary,* 625.

25. That is, Israel's rebellion at Meribah and Massah and elsewhere throughout the forty years in the wilderness; see Ex 17:1–7; Nm 20:1–13; and Nm 14:1–45.

26. See Heb 3:9–10 and McCullough, "The Old Testament," 369–70. McCullough is not sure if the homilist changed the form or "simply copied his Vorlage" (370). For more, see Attridge, *The Epistle to the Hebrews,* 113–21.

27. 𝔓13.46, ℵ* A B C D* P have "in the test"; thus, there is strong evidence for this reading. For detailed textual variants and evidence, see *Novum Testamentum Graece,* 566; McCullough, "The Old Testament," 369–71; W. Bauer et al., *A Greek-English Lexicon of the New Testament* (Chicago: University of Chicago Press, 1957), 202; Bruce, *The Epistle to the Hebrews,* 60; Attridge, *The Epistle to the Hebrews,* 113–21; and Lane, *Hebrews 1:1–9:28,* 82.

28. Combrink, "Some Thoughts on the Old Testament Citations in the Epistle to the Hebrews," 30.

epistle.[29] Attridge simply explains that this change is the result of textual corruption.[30] It is more likely that "in the test" is used to keep the place name "in Meribah" of the MT, or at least to remind the readers of the incident at Meribah in which the Israelites were tempting or "striving against" God.[31] McCullough explains that this change

> came about to avoid a harsh repetition in the original sentence, where *epeipasan* is followed closely by *edokimasan*. . . . In the MT there is a clear reference to the story of Meribah in Exodus 17. In the LXX, however, Meribah is translated by the general term meaning "provocation." Thus the whole period of wandering in the desert is looked on as a time of God's testing, and God's loathing of the Israelites . . . is simultaneous with that. Both, therefore, continue forty years in the LXX.[32]

The change here then would be stylistic, avoiding "harsh repetition." At the same time the author is still able to maintain the theological significance of depicting the Israelites' testing of God over forty years.[33]

Second, the author changes "that" in the LXX to "this" in the epistle.[34] Most biblical scholars reason that the homilist's pur-

---

29. See McCullough, "The Old Testament," 370.

30. Attridge, *The Epistle to the Hebrews*, 115.

31. The root for Meribah is *ryb,* which means "to contend," "to find fault," or "to strive," as it is translated in the LXX (Ex 17:2–7 and Nm 20:13). A similar translational phenomenon appears in Dt 33:8 (and 8:2), where *bmsh* ("in Massah" means "tempting") is translated in the LXX as *en peira* ("in trial"). See Attridge, *The Epistle to the Hebrews*, 115, and *Biblia Hebraica Stuttgartensia,* 1177.

32. McCullough, "The Old Testament," 371. See Kistemaker, *The Psalm Citations in the Epistle to the Hebrews,* 35.

33. For other theories on this change, see F. Rendall, *The Epistle to the Hebrews* (London, 1883), 31; C. J. Vaughan, *The Epistle to the Hebrews* (London, 1890), 66; E. C. Wickham, *The Epistle to the Hebrews* (London, 1910), 22f.

34. 𝔓13.46 A B C D* have "this," strong evidence for this reading. See *Novum Testamentum Graece,* 567; Brooke Foss Westcott, *The Epistle to the Hebrews, the Greek Text with Notes and Essays* (Grand Rapids, Mich.: Eerdmans, 1974), 154; and Lane, *Hebrews 1:1–9:28,* 82.

pose for changing this word is to apply the exhortation to his present congregation with an added note of urgency.[35] The problem with this explanation is that the main verb "I was provoked" in the clause is past tense, and not present tense. That is, God *was* angry with "that" generation rather than "this" one. Strictly speaking also, the application of the wilderness theme begins only in 3:12. Therefore, it is better to explain this divergence as a stylistic change, because " 'that' is a *hapax legomenon* in the New Testament while 'this' is common. The author of Hebrews or a previous copyist merely substituted a common expression for an uncommon one."[36]

The third and the most difficult variant is the presence and position of "therefore" in 3:10 in all manuscripts.[37] The word "therefore" is not present in the LXX or MT. Since it is placed after "forty years," it begins the next clause. As such, the forty years in the LXX refer to God's being angry, whereas the forty years in the epistle refer to the Israelites' testing God and seeing God's works.[38] The homilist's purpose in using "therefore" is intentional and vital to his argument. That is, the Israelites had tested and seen God's works for forty years in 3:9, whereas in 3:17 the homilist states clearly that God was angry for forty years with the Israelites. Therefore, the period of testing is parallel to and simultaneous with the period of God's wrath.[39] This reasoning is substantiated by the position of "therefore," which is being inserted in between the two phrases "they saw my works" and "I was provoked with this generation." Why it is placed there? The reason seems to be mere stylistic alteration. McCullough observes that

---

35. E.g., Bruce, *The Epistle to the Hebrews*, 60; Hughes, *A Commentary on the Epistle to the Hebrews*, 145; Jewett, *Letter to Pilgrims*, 54.

36. McCullough, "The Old Testament," 371.

37. *Novum Testamentum Graece*, 566.

38. McCullough, "The Old Testament," 371; Vincent, *Word Studies in the New Testament*, 4:416; Graham Hughes, *Hebrews and Hermeneutics* (Cambridge: Cambridge University Press, 1979), 162, n. 57. Attridge (*The Epistle to the Hebrews*, 115) says the forty years in Hebrews refer to the Israelites' testing God only.

39. Or as McCullough says, "In the author's view, therefore, the testing and anger were simultaneous, and lasted for 40 years" ("The Old Testament," 371). See also Combrink, "Some Thoughts on the Old Testament Citations in the Epistle to the Hebrews," 30.

The LXX follows the Semitic asyndetical construction, with three clauses "put me to the test," "saw my works" and "I was provoked" placed side by side. The author of Hebrews, however, with his Greek background, shows the relationship between the clauses by adding a "therefore." Since the MT and LXX both had an "and" between the first two clauses, the natural place for the "Therefore" was between the second and third clauses.[40]

In other words, the author wishes to apply the forty-year period to all three clauses. The Exodus generation going through the forty-year experience becomes the central motif in the author's theological reflection in the present pericope.

The Meaning of the Exodus Generation

The psalmist used the experience of Israel under Moses to warn the Israelites of his day against unbelief and disobedience. In a similar way the author of Hebrews applies the psalmist's warning to the recipients of his epistle. The writer appeals to the readers to listen to (obey) the voice of God and to exhort one another daily as the household of God, as partakers of Christ. Notice how the author here, by citing Psalm 95 (94) in the light of Numbers 14, uses the experience of the Israelite Exodus generation to warn against the audience's disobedience. By citing Psalm 95 the author also draws on Exodus typology to illustrate how the wandering people of God (old or new) are to move (i.e., a pilgrimage motif) and draw near to the divine goal (i.e., "Rest").

It is possible that the writer is thinking of the death of Christ as the second "exodus" and links the forty years' wandering with the forty years since Jesus has accomplished his "exodus" on the cross.[41] However, it is more likely that, when the homilist looks back at Israel's history, he notices that the Israelites had been graciously elected and delivered but had not been faithful to God. That is, the Israelites had seen God's works ("and they saw my

---

40. McCullough, "The Old Testament," 371–72.

41. If the epistle is written shortly after 70 C.E. See Bruce, *The Epistle to the Hebrews*, 65, for some evidence from Qumran literature.

works," 3:9), yet they had tempted and tried God ("they put . . . in
the test," 3:9),[42] and provoked (3:16) God for forty years. Therefore, God was displeased to the extreme,[43] or was grieved utterly.
So God swore, "They shall not enter into my rest" (3:11).[44] This
disobedience and God's oath are correlated by the preposition "as"
in 3:11.[45] The seriousness of their disobedience is seen in the sever-
ity of the common Hebraistic oath-formula: "God is speaking as
'May I not be Jehovah if (the ellipsis) they shall enter into my
rest.'"[46]

The reason that the Israelites (and Christians too) were unable
to enter God's rest is described variously. First, it is because of their
"evil heart of unbelief" (3:12, 19, and 4:6, 11) and "hardening of
heart" (3:15). In other words, an evil heart is a hardening or a
refusal to believe, trust, and respond to God (or God's word, or
God's presence). *Apistias,* which should be translated as "disbelief," specifies that in which the more general evil heart consists.[47]
Therefore, an evil heart is a disbelieving or faithless heart. A. T.
Robertson rightly asserts that, "*Apistias* is more than mere unbelief, here rather disbelief, refusal to believe, genitive case describing
the evil heart marked by disbelief."[48] Notice the literal reading of
the clause "lest any one of you should be hardened." The aorist

---

42. Trying one to the extent of seeing how far one can go. See 1 Cor 10:9 and
Vincent, *Word Studies in the New Testament,* 4:416.

43. First aorist active of the Greek word "displeased," meaning extreme anger
and disgust. See A. T. Robertson, *Word Pictures in the New Testament* (New York:
Ray Long & Richard R. Smith, Inc., 1932), 5:357; and BAGD, 351.

44. The concept of rest will be discussed in the next section.

45. See Vincent, *Word Studies in the New Testament,* 4:416; Robertson, *Word
Pictures in the New Testament,* 5:357; Hewitt, *The Epistle to the Hebrews,* 82; and
Lane, *Hebrews 1:1–9:28,* 86.

46. Vincent, *Word Studies in the New Testament,* 4:417. Attridge (*The Epistle
to the Hebrews,* 116, n. 36) rightly observes that the LXX translates the Hebrew
oath-formula with wooden literalness: "The Hebrew formula consists of the pro-
tasis of a conditional sentence ('if they enter'), where the apodosis is suppressed.
The LXX simply translates the conditional without regard to its function ('if they
enter')." And Hewitt is right in observing that "If they shall enter into my rest" (AV)
is a literal translation of the Greek, which is simply an idiomatic use of a strong
negative and, therefore, should be translated as the RSV does — "They shall never
enter my rest." Cf. Hewitt, *The Epistle to the Hebrews,* 87; and Lane, *Hebrews
1:1–9:28,* 87.

47. Vincent, *Word Studies in the New Testament,* 4:417–18.

48. Robertson, *Word Pictures in the New Testament,* 5:357. So Kistemaker, *The*

subjunctive "be hardened" would seem to imply that hardening had not yet taken place on the part of the readers.[49]

The second reason that the Israelites were unable to enter God's rest is because of their "departing[50] from the Living God" (3:12; cf. 9:14; 10:31; 12:22). That is, disbelief is an apostasy or separation from the God of Life. Unbelief is thus understood in terms of once having known, encountered, experienced, and believed God, and then having turned away from the Living God.[51] Worse still, an unbelieving or an evil heart is an overt action of "open defiance to God, [thus] the sin of tempting God (3:8f. and 3:17)."[52] Therefore, an unbelieving heart may result in apostasy. "Heart" is obviously an anthropological term designating the totality of a person or one's existence. "Departing from the Living God" (3:12) then describes a person not only refusing to respond to the presence of God, but also wanting to depart from that very God of Life.

The final reason is because of the Israelites' "rebellion" (3:16), "sin" (3:17), and "disobedience"[53] (3:18). Disbelief or faithlessness is expressed in terms of "deliberate, rebellious secession"[54] or disobedience.

Psalm Citations in the Epistle to the Hebrews, 111; Attridge, *The Epistle to the Hebrews,* 116.

49. See Hughes, *A Commentary on the Epistle to the Hebrews,* 148.

50. Oberholtzer contends that, "Since the sense is not temporal, no antecedent action may be inferred from the tense of the infinitive; only the aspect is in view. The intent in this passage is not to display a persistence, a nature, but an event." See Oberholtzer, "The Warning Passages in Hebrews," 188.

51. R. C. H. Lenski, *The Interpretation of the Epistle to the Hebrews and of the Epistle of James* (Columbus, Ohio: Lutheran Book Concern, 1938), 118.

52. Lenski, *The Interpretation of the Epistle to the Hebrews and of the Epistle of James,* 118, and Kistemaker, *The Psalm Citations in the Epistle to the Hebrews,* 111.

53. The reading is "faithlessness/disbelieve" in $\mathfrak{P}^{46}$ lat (*Novum Testamentum Graece,* 567) instead of "disobedience," a variant which is an allusion to the failure of the desert generation in Heb 4:6, 11. The substitution of "faithlessness" for "disobedience" is most likely a simplifying correction, under the influence of 3:19 and 4:2. Cf. 4:6, 11; 11:31. Of course, lack of faith is very closely related to disobedience. See Bruce, *The Epistle to the Hebrews,* 61, n. 34; and Harold W. Attridge, " 'Let Us Strive to Enter That Rest': The Logic of Hebrews 4:1–11," *Harvard Theological Review* 73 (January–April 1980): 280–81.

54. Hughes, *A Commentary on the Epistle to the Hebrews,* 145. Also, Mugridge, " 'Warnings in the Epistle to the Hebrews': An Exegetical and Theological Study," 75; Lane, *Hebrews 1:1–9:28,* 88.

The three reasons given here speak of a person's "ir-response-ability" toward, or deliberative "response-ability" against, God's voice, God's presence, or even God Himself. Just cause for one to be unable to enter into God's rest.

The Calling of the Living God to the Believing Community

After considering these reasons for those desert generations being "unable to enter because of unbelief" (3:19), it becomes clear that faithlessness is not a lack of obedience or lack of faith, but willful, deliberate rejection of the gracious act (3:9, "God's works") or revelation ("voice" in 3:7, 15; 4:7; and cf. 4:12–13) from the Living God. For such persons have "good tidings proclaimed" (4:2) to them, yet they "did not meet with[55] faith in the hearers" (4:2), that is, they do not respond to the good news. The comparison of the warnings to the Israelites and to the present readers is made here. That is, all have the same privilege and the same resulting penalty if they disbelieve or become unfaithful.

All these negative behaviors of unbelief stand in sharp contrast to the faithfulness of Christ, the Son of God, and to the high calling of steadfastness given to all Christians, the sons and daughters of God. As Oberholtzer puts it, "The 'falling away' then was a willful withdrawal from service as believers-priests and . . . [from] worship in the priestly house of 3:1–6."[56] In spite of the stern warning and the terrible oath from the Living God, the homilist has not failed to let the readers know about, and to invite them to, the eternal calling of that same Living God[57] — which is to enter into God's rest. The failure of the unbelieving Israelites did not nullify the promise of God's rest for God's people. The homilist skillfully makes use of

---

55. Problematic textual variation on the Greek word of "did not meet with"; see Hewitt, *The Epistle to the Hebrews,* 86–87, and Robertson, *Word Pictures in the New Testament,* 5:361.

56. Oberholtzer, "The Warning Passages in Hebrews," 189. For a similar idea, see Westcott, *Epistle to the Hebrews,* 83; and Kistemaker, *The Psalm Citations in the Epistle to the Hebrews,* 111.

57. Jewett says, "[T]he author . . . wishes to warn his congregation about the requirements of dialogue without contributing to their anxiety that the rest is barred by divine wrath" (*Letter to Pilgrims,* 55).

the key word "today" (3:7, 13, 15; 4:7) in the psalm. Luke Timothy Johnson explains that "the 'today' of the psalm must...be an eternal call of God. Therefore, the word of Scripture addresses his present hearers directly. They are not to harden their hearts as the people did in the desert.... if God can still speak of a 'today,' his promise too must remain: 'Therefore the promise of his rest remains' (4:1)."[58]

The precise meaning of "rest" will be discussed extensively in the next section. Now we need to observe how the homilist exhorts his readers to be faithful. First, he assures them of their status in, and relationship to, God: that they have already become (*gegonamen*, perfect tense)[59] partakers of Christ (3:14). The gnostic interpretation of participating in the divinity or the aeons in the universe is misleading.[60] Robert Jewett convincingly refutes the gnostic interpretation when he argues, "The basis for this striking claim [participants with Christ] is not the divine nature of the gnostic-self, but rather Christ's participation in the limited human nature of flesh and blood [2:14]."[61] Indeed, the indicative nature of this claim is based on the finished work of Christ, his faithfulness to God, his obedience perfected through suffering, and his supreme consummated revelation of God to human beings.[62] The indicative carries with it the imperative of "partakers[63] of Christ" (3:6) which is given specifically and concretely so that they might enter into God's rest. The imperative carries three basic exhortations. First, they are to "hold fast [their] confidence and pride in hope" (3:6; cf. 3:14).[64] That is, they are to maintain fearless confession and

---

58. Luke Timothy Johnson, *The Writings of the New Testament: An Interpretation* (Philadelphia: Fortress, 1986), 423.

59. For the "realized" dimension of Hebrews' eschatology, see 6:4; 12:28.

60. Jewett, *Letter to Pilgrims*, 59–60.

61. Jewett, *Letter to Pilgrims*, 59–60.

62. These seem to be the main subthemes of the epistle. Or to express this participation in another way: "partakers of a heavenly calling" (3:1), "partakers of Christ" (3:14), "partakers of the Holy Spirit" (6:4), "partakers of chastening" (12:8), "anointed...beyond the partakers of God" (1:9).

63. See H. Hanse, "*Metechō*," *TDNT* 2:830; Thompson, "The *Katapausis* Motif in Hebrews," 93–95.

64. The phrase "firm unto the end" is probably an insertion influenced by 3:14. See *Novum Testamentum Graece*, 566; Bruce, *The Epistle to the Hebrews*, 54; Metzger, *Textual Commentary*, 281; Lane, *Hebrews 1:1–9:28*, 88.

joyful hope to be faithful partakers of Christ. As F. F. Bruce writes, "Christians live by faith and not by sight; but while their hope is in things unseen, it is something to exult in, not to be ashamed of."[65]

Hebrews 3:14 also introduces a second exhortation: " ... holding fast [their] first confidence firm to the end." That is, they are to persevere to the end, to be faithful and to faithfully endure. Pilgrimage life for the wandering people of God finds its test of faithfulness in each day. "To the end" points to the limit of faithfulness required, but "today" speaks of the concreteness of "end" and the time frame of faithfulness expected.[66] Thus, the moment-to-moment encounter with God is important for one to be faithful to God. In fact, that indicative relationship which each person has with God gives rise to the constant imperative to maintain that relationship with God. That is why Christian life is a pilgrimage of faith, constantly responding appropriately to the Living God. Genuine faith proves itself by persevering to the end. But this task of perseverance, or keeping on believing, is obviously too massive for any to carry alone. Therefore, individual believers are reminded to exhort, to encourage, and to care for one another as a community of believers (3:14; see "cloud of witness ... innumerable angels ... assembly of the first born ... spirits of just men made perfect ... Jesus the mediator of a new covenant," 12:1–24) on that pilgrimage (i.e., past, present, and future) of faith.

Finally, they are to be responsive to God's voice and word every day (3:7, 15; 4:7; cf. 4:2). As Jewett expounds, "Their salvation was inaugurated by the gospel (1:1–2; 2:3–4), and now they are to recognize that it addresses them day by day.... From the moment it encounters them, their present and future are determined by their response to it. To turn away from it is to forfeit life, but to accept it in faith is to enter his rest."[67]

The indicatives and the imperatives analyzed above are held in tension by the writer because of the tension within the "already-

---

65. Bruce, *The Epistle to the Hebrews,* 59.

66. Jewett explains, "[T]he participation with Christ has a historical horizon, because the relationship with which we started is to be kept firm to the end. There is a strong sense of the exigencies of time in this expression, for the relationship enjoyed today must be renewed tomorrow or be lost" (*Letter to Pilgrims,* 60).

67. Jewett, *Letter to Pilgrims,* 60, 63.

and-not-yet" eschatological age in which he and his audience live. C. K. Barrett observes that "their life is one of hope and struggle, in which they are sustained by the fact that that for which they strive has already been achieved for them, and that they have already begun to enjoy it."[68] The epistle maintains both aspects of this tension very well. Lincoln substantiates this point when he writes,

> [I]n 2:5–3:6 the predominant mood is one of certainty because of the solidarity between Jesus and His brothers, while in...[3:7–4:13] the emphasis is one of fear lest there be exclusion from the consummation of salvation on account of apostasy....Believers are part of Christ's eschatological edifice *but only if* [emphasis mine] they hold fast their confidence and pride in their hope.[69]

All these three points are positive exhortations for one to be a faithful partaker of Christ. These exhortations stand in contrast with the characteristics of an "unbelieving heart." No wonder the writer throughout the epistle appeals to the readers to listen to God's voice (2:1, 3:8) and to appropriate it by faith (3:12, 4:3) through endurance, drawing near to God (4:16), and encouraging one another daily (3:7, 13, 15; 4:7; 9:8; 10:24, while it is called "today"), so that they may enter into God's rest.

The Meaning of *Katapausis* and *Sabbatismos*

So far, we have seen how the writer of Hebrews uses Psalm 95 in the first segment (Heb 3:7–19) to establish the availability of rest and the necessity of persevering faith in order for one to enter into God's rest. We have also seen how the writer creates

68. C. K. Barrett, "The Eschatology of the Epistle to the Hebrews," in *The Background of the New Testament and Its Eschatology, in Honour of Charles Harold Dodd,* ed. W. D. Davies and D. Daube (Cambridge: Cambridge University Press, 1956), 365.

69. A. T. Lincoln, "Sabbath, Rest, and Eschatology in the New Testament," in *From Sabbath to Lord's Day: A Biblical, Historical, and Theological Investigation,* ed. D. A. Carson (Grand Rapids, Mich.: Zondervan, 1982), 206.

a sense of urgency about the possibility of losing rest. In the second segment (4:1–5), the author uses the last verse of Psalm 95 to interpret again the availability of God's rest. He then uses another text (Gn 2:2) to further elaborate his point by mentioning the Creation-Sabbath rest.

It is the thesis of this chapter that Heb 3:7–4:13 is a midrash on Ps 95:7–11 and Gn 2:2, based on the rabbinic *gezera shawa* interpretative principle (i.e., *midrash-pesher* method of exposition).[70] The author uses the *katapausis* ("rest") and *sabbatismos* ("Sabbath rest") motifs to exhort the readers to participate constantly and fully in the single yet multiple aspects of God's rest. This he argues can be achieved by claiming and striving to encounter the presence of God, now and forevermore, in the tension of the "already-and-not-yet" eschatological "today."

To establish that thesis, we shall first look at different interpretations of the "rest" motif in the passage. We will also survey the use of "rest" in some biblical and extrabiblical sources, and then expound an alternative interpretation. Finally, we will deduce the hermeneutical principles of the homilist's interpretation of the OT in this pericope.

Different Interpretations of the "Rest" Motif

There are at least four main interpretations of the theology of "rest." The first is the gnostic orientation, which employs the biblical term *anapausis* ("rest") as a major gnostic category and associates it with "hope," "love," "rest," and "faith."[71] The word *anapausis* is even used to refer to God, to Christ, or to the highest aeon of the heavenly world, the original home of the Gnostic.[72] As

---

70. See sec. 2 ("An Exegetical Study of Hebrews 3:7–4:13") for the writer's method of using OT passages in Hebrews. On the rabbinic *gezera shawa* methodology, see Hermann Strack, *Introduction to Talmud and Midrash* (Philadelphia: Jewish Publication Society, 1931), 94.

71. See Thompson, "The *Katapausis* Motif in Hebrews," 88. Käsemann, in *Das Wandernde Gottesvolk,* is the main advocate of this interpretation of the author of Hebrews. See the critique given by Hofius Otfried, *Katapausis: Die Vorstellung vom Endzeitlichen Ruheort im Hebräerbrief* (Tübingen: Mohr, 1970).

72. "According to the Valentinians, God is...known in the *Gos. Truth* 42:22 as the 'one who rests.' Christ is described as 'rest' (*Act. Th.* 177. 10–12). God is fre-

such, the Gnostics' purpose in life is to seek *anapausis,* which is mediated by the redeemer.[73] This interpretation fits well with the Gnostics' belief in the Melchizedek tradition and their pursuit of heavenly *katapausis.*[74]

The writer of Hebrews, however, uses non-gnostic concepts (i.e., a holistic, not dualistic, understanding of "heart"), categories (i.e., "evil" is not in one's origin or destiny, but in "rebellious" action), and emphasis (i.e., "rest" is not obtainable by possessing "knowledge" but by obedience and perseverance).[75] Refuting the gnostic understanding of "rest," of course, is not to say that the writer of Hebrews does not believe in heavenly *katapausis.*

The second orientation is one which emphasizes the Greek metaphysical understanding of *anapausis* ("rest") and *hebdomas* ("seven"). James Thompson observes that Philo and Clement skillfully exegeted the biblical texts which contain *anapausis, katapausis,* and "Noah" to mean the immutability of God.[76] He notes as well that Philo and Clement saw the Pythagorean number "7," deemed the most peaceful number, as describing God alone.[77] They suggested that the seventh day of Hebrew Sabbath rest was a

---

quently addressed in prayer as *anapausis.* . . . According to *Soph. Jes. Chr.* 110:5–7, 'The first aeon is called Unity and Rest (*anapausis*)' " (Thompson, "The *Katapausis* Motif in Hebrews," 88).

73. "The Gnostic texts frequently speak of the goal of finding rest. Redemption consists in a return to the *plērōma,* or rest, of the father" (see *Gos. Thom.* 60; Thompson, "The *Katapausis* Motif in Hebrews," 88).

74. See H. A. Lombard, "*Katapausis* in the Letter to the Hebrews," *Neotestamentica* 5 (1971): 60; Gerd Theissen, *Untersuchungen zum Hebräerbrief* (Gütersloh: Gütersloher Verlagshaus, Gerd Mohn, 1969), 2:115–45; Käsemann, *Das Wandernde Gottesvolk,* 41.

75. See Jewett, *Letter to Pilgrims,* 56–57, and Lincoln, "Sabbath, Rest, and Eschatology in the New Testament," 180, for their sharp critique of gnostic interpretation; see also Otfried, *Katapausis,* and Williamson, *Philo and the Epistle to the Hebrews.*

76. See Thompson, "The *Katapausis* Motif in Hebrews," 82–88, for details. Another advocate of this view is C. Spicq, whose view is extensively refuted by R. Williamson. Most recently, Robert Thurston has tried to link Hebrews with Philo in "Philo and the Epistle to the Hebrews," *Evangelical Quarterly* 58 (1986): 133–43.

77. Thompson explains, "*Anapausis* is thus related to the number symbolism which was known also to Philo and to the Pythagoreans. The identification of rest with the number seven . . . has developed from the influence of Pythagoreanism on Platonic thought" (*"Katapausis,"* 87).

symbol of resting in God, of transcending this creation, and of obtaining the stable and immutable nature of God. The weakness of this hermeneutical posture (of Philo and Clement) is its highly dualistic understanding of the relation between Creation and God. Worse still, the use of a highly allegorical interpretation does not allow the text and the context to speak for themselves. Instead, the symbolisms and metaphysics have overwhelmed and choked the basic meaning and message of the text.

The third orientation is one which understands the "rest" in Hebrews 3–4 as the apocalyptic, materialistic, and futuristic expectation of a new Jerusalem exclusively realized in the second advent of Christ.[78] W. C. Kaiser and Oberholtzer, for example, suggest that Psalm 95 (LXX 94) is in a series of psalms (93–100) with eschatological overtones depicting the millennial king reigning over all. Kaiser argues that the "rest" of God in Psalm 95 is tied up with the events of the second advent.[79] F. F. Bruce refutes the AV's rendering *eiserchometha* (4:3) as "do enter." As he explains, "It [rest] lies ahead as something yet to be attained."[80] Robertson also supports Bruce's view: " 'Do enter' [is] emphatic futuristic present middle indicative..., i.e., we are sure to enter in, we who believe."[81]

While not denying the futuristic nature of God's rest, the present reality of entering cannot be overemphasized. The relationship between the present and the future must be kept in perspective. The

---

78. See Barrett, "The Eschatology of the Epistle to the Hebrews," 363–93; Bruce, *The Epistle to the Hebrews,* 321; Kaiser, *The Uses of the Old Testament in the New,* 169–70; Walter C. Kaiser, Jr. "The Promise Theme and Theology of Rest," *Bibliotheca Sacra* 130 (April–June 1973): 142–50; Oberholtzer, "The Warning Passages in Hebrews," 185–96; Stanley D. Toussaint, "The Eschatology of the Warning Passages in the Book of Hebrews," *Grace Theological Journal* 3 (Spring 1982): 71–80; Buchanan, *To the Hebrews,* 6; Käsemann, *Das Wandernde Gottesvolk,* 68; and E. Lohse, *"Sabbaton," TDNT* 7:34, for more on this orientation.

79. Kaiser, *The Uses of the Old Testament in the New,* 163, and Oberholtzer, "The Warning Passages in Hebrews," 185–87; Kaiser, in "The Promise" (142–43), says, "[T]he generation of the wilderness could have participated in this future kingdom or rest of God to some extent, but they refused to do so in unbelief. Therefore, they were twice the losers, temporally and spiritually, in that historic moment and in the second advent." (Cf. Lane, *Hebrews 1:1–9:28, 95.*)

80. Bruce, *The Epistle to the Hebrews,* 73, n. 17.

81. Robertson, *Word Pictures in the New Testament,* 5:361.

writer's view of eschatology in relation to the consummated salvation must be given due note. The writer saw the community of believers as "living in a time of fulfillment inaugurated by Christ 'at the end of these days' (1:2), 'at the end of the ages' (9:26); but this was yet to be consummated by His return (9:28) and His complete rule in the world to come (2:5ff.)."[82] Hence, the "today" is the meantime in which they feel the tension between hope and struggle, between the indicatives in Christ and the imperatives to be in Christ, and between already entering rest (4:3) and the striving needed to enter that rest (4:11). This interpretation can be construed slightly differently in deriving the apocalyptic nature of "rest" from the Merkabah mysticism tradition.[83]

The fourth interpretation is that of Käsemann, who says that the author of Hebrews does not derive the *katapausis* motif from the Old Testament. Käsemann sees the *katapausis* as an exclusively futuristic heavenly rest. He also argues that the author is heavily influenced by Alexandrian Gnosticism.[84] Therefore, Käsemann incorporates all the three interpretations stated above. Despite my rejection of Käsemann's proposal on the author's orientation, I suspect that what is true for the author might possibly be true for the audience. Thus, while the author does not accept the argument of the audience, he does use their mind-set and understanding to argue against them.

An Alternative Interpretation

We will consider the theology of "rest" in light of the Old Testament usage before an alternative interpretation is given. The writer of Hebrews never tells us what "rest" means; he assumes the reader knows. We can determine the locale; it is at least the Canaan rest, the earthly settlement on the promised land of Canaan conquered

---

82. Lincoln, "Sabbath, Rest, and Eschatology in the New Testament," 205–6; cf. Lane, *Hebrews 1:1–9:28*, 95.

83. Consult Ithamar Gruenwald, *Apocalyptic and Merkavah Mysticism* (Leiden: E. J. Brill, 1980); Johann Maier, *Von Kultus zur Gnosis: Bundeslade, Gottesthron und Märkabah* (Salzburg: Otto Müller, 1964); and David J. Halperin, *The Merkabah in Rabbinic Literature* (New Haven: American Oriental Society, 1980).

84. Käsemann, *Das Wandernde Gottesvolk*, 74–75.

under the leadership of Joshua and Caleb.[85] But it is not merely
the rest in earthly Canaan, because the promise of entering the rest
"was offered again in the Psalm, even when the Israelites were in
possession of the land."[86]

The writer turns to Ps 95:11 for his use of the phrase "my rest."
The Septuagint term is *katapausis* ("rest," 3:11, 18; 4:1, 3 [used
twice], 5, 10, 11; *katapauein* is used in the intransitive in 4:4,
10, and in the transitive in 4:8). *Katapausis* occurs ten times in
the LXX, meaning either "a state of rest" or "a resting place."[87]
Katapausis in the LXX is a translation of three Hebrew words:
(*a*) *'ăḥuzāh* (e.g., Lv 25:28), meaning "possession by right of inheritance";[88] (*b*) *shabāṯ* (e.g., Ex 34:21), which is a technical term for
rest on the seventh day;[89] and (*c*) *nûaḥ* (e.g., Ex 35:2), which in
its *hiphil* stem usually assumes a technical status of a resting place
granted by God, either from all enemies or as a cessation of sorrow
and labor.[90] Both *katapausis* of the LXX and *nûaḥ* of the MT, in
Psalm 94 and 95, respectively, clearly have a local meaning, that

---

85. Vincent, *Word Studies in the New Testament,* 4:417, and Robertson, *Word Pictures in the New Testament,* 5:357, argue for this primarily, and only secondarily the heavenly rest.

86. Hewitt, *The Epistle to the Hebrews,* 87, so argues, supported by Bruce, *The Epistle to the Hebrews,* 72, and Kaiser, "The Promise Theme and Theology of Rest," 148.

87. Käsemann, *Das Wandernde Gottesvolk,* 208, points this out: the meaning "rest" occurs in Ex 35:2, 2 Mc 15:1, Nm 10:35, and 1 Kgs 8:56; "resting place" in Dt 12:9, Ps 131:14, 1 Chr 6:31, 2 Chr 6:41, Is 66:1, and Jdt 9:8.

88. Francis Brown, S. R. Driver, and Charles A. Briggs, eds., *A Hebrew and English Lexicon of the Old Testament with an Appendix Containing the Biblical Aramaic* [BDB], based on the lexicon of William Gesenius as translated by Edward Robinson (Oxford: Clarendon Press, n.d.), 28.

89. BDB, 991–92; Lombard, "*Katapausis* in the Letter to the Hebrews," 64; Lane, *Hebrews 1:1–9:28,* 97–105. See Gn 2:2f., 8:22; Ex 5:5, 31:17, 34:21; Dt 32:26; Neh 4:5, 6:3, Hos 1:4; Lam 5:14; Ez 30:13; Dn 9:27.

90. BDB, 628; Kaiser, *The Uses of the Old Testament in the New,* 120; Leonard J. Coppes, "*Nûaḥ,* rest, settle down," *Theological Wordbook of the Old Testament,* ed. R. Laird Harris (Chicago: Moody Press, 1980), 2:562–63; R. Hensel and C. Brown, "Rest," *The New International Dictionary of New Testament Theology* (hereafter *NIDNTT*), ed. Lothar Coenen, Erich Beyreuther, and Hans Bietenhard, Eng. trans. by Colin Brown (Grand Rapids, Mich.: Regency Reference Library, 1971), 3:256; Jewett, *Letter to Pilgrims,* 55. See Ex 33:14; Dt 3:20; 12:10; 25:19; Jos 1:13, 15; 21:44; 22:4; 23:1; 2 Chr 14:5; 2 Sm 7:1, 11; 1 Kgs 5:18; 1 Chr 22:9, 18; 23:25; 2 Chr 14:6; 15:15; 20:30; 32:22; Is 14:3; 28:12.

is, a reference to the promised land of Canaan. Kaiser, however, maintains,

> In spite of all emphasis on the promised land as the rest of God for Israel, the spiritual element also is prominent in this noun form. This finds expression whenever this rest is connected with the themes of the ark of God or the temple.[91]

For example, the word *nûaḥ* is used both for God's resting place in the promised land (Dt 12:9) and for God's sanctuary (Ps 132:8, 14).[92] In other Old Testament passages, the resting place of the people and that of God are combined so that the resting place of God is also the resting place of the people (Dt 12:9, 11; 1 Chr 23:25; 2 Chr 6:4).[93] My conclusion is that the fundamental or underlying idea of "rest" that appears through the Old Testament seems to indicate that it refers primarily to *the presence of God*.[94] It is the presence of God that makes a place "rest-ful," and that same presence delivers Israelites from their enemies (rest in Canaan or the promised land).

The first meaning of rest as the *presence of God* makes sense, especially when one considers the following context of this pericope. Heb 3:7–4:13 is to be seen not as an appendix of the epistle but as a capstone that allows the writer to build on the theme of the priestly work of Christ (3:14–10:25), who is to bring the presence of God by the perfect sacrifice of body and blood. When the believers come to the throne of grace through Christ's work,

---

91. Kaiser, "The Promise Theme and Theology of Rest," 140.

92. It appears with the same meaning and same root/stem but different form in 1 Chr 6:16 and 2 Chr 6:41. See Lincoln, "Sabbath, Rest, and Eschatology in the New Testament," 208; Lane, *Hebrews 1:1–9:28*, 101.

93. Lincoln, "Sabbath, Rest, and Eschatology in the New Testament," 208.

94. Not only does the OT usage of *katapausis* and *sabbatismos* support my conclusion, but the author of Hebrews seems to have that idea too. The verse immediately following 4:7–13 speaks of the person and works of Christ as "the Great High Priest who passed through heaven" (4:14). That means that the purpose of Christ's work is to bring the believers to God and God to them. Heb 4:15 elaborates the availability and qualities of that Great High Priest, who is now able to sympathize with them. Then in 4:16 the exhortation is given to "draw near the throne of grace"; this definitely speaks of the presence of God, which is now available to the believers (with the meaning of a gracious, and not a repulsive or fearful, presence).

they encounter the presence of God, and are said to have entered God's rest.

Second, since "rest" is where the presence of God dwells, it is not mere idleness, inertia, or passivity; it is a "perfect activity"[95] of *communing with or of worshiping God.*[96] As Kaiser notes,

> God's rest is the gracious gift of the land promised to the pa-
> triarchs with its attendant blessings such as the cessation of
> all hostile enemy action (Deut 12:10), or sorrow (Isa 14:3)
> and labor (Isa 28:12). It is also the place where the presence
> of the Lord dwells (Ps 132:8). [Thus], possession, inheritance
> and rest function almost as synonymous ideas here.[97]

This second aspect of "rest" is supported by the thrust of LXX Psalm 94 — a liturgical call-to-worship psalm used in temple festivals.

Third, the author uses the term "rest" in this pericope most probably under the influence of rabbinic exegesis and Jewish apocalyptic literature, which understood Ps 95:11 to mean an eschatological resting place associated with the heavenly promised land, the heavenly Jerusalem, and the heavenly sanctuary.[98] It is *heavenly rest* because heaven (which according to the author is not just a future reality but a present one; see 12:22) is the eternal place where God dwells and reigns with his people forever.[99] The psalmist (Ps 95:7, 8) also spoke of Israel's resting place as yet

---

95. Tasker, *The Old Testament in the New Testament,* 118.

96. Or as Lombard says, "We must...consider the rest of God and his people in a strictly existential-personal and primary-soteriological perspective and context" ("*Katapausis* in the Letter to the Hebrews," 69).

97. Kaiser, *The Uses of the Old Testament in the New,* 158.

98. Probably by the end of the first century, Ps 95:11 is linked with Dt 12:9 and Ps 132:14 to mean future world (see *Tos. Sanh.* 13:10; *B. Sanh.* 110b; *j. Sanh.* X, 29c, 5; *Aboth de R. Nathan* 36). In addition some rabbis call the new Jerusalem God's resting place (see *Sifre Deut.* 1; *Midr. Cant.* 7:5; *Pesik* 20, 143a.) See Lincoln, "Sabbath, Rest, and Eschatology in the New Testament," 209, for details. Further, George W. MacRae, "Heavenly Temple and Eschatology in the Letter to the Hebrews," *Semeia* 12 (1978): 179–99, shows that the writer of Hebrews has the realized, Alexandrian eschatology while his audience has the futurist, apocalyptic eschatology.

99. R. H. Gundry, *A Survey of the New Testament* (Grand Rapids, Mich.: Zondervan, 1970), 318; and Tasker, *The Old Testament in the New Testament,* 118, seem to suggest that also.

to be entered. In the perspective of salvation history, the promise of rest is eventually fulfilled soteriologically by Jesus Christ. Lombard links the soteriological nature and the futuristic aspect of this "rest" well when he states, "By the power of the grace of God in Jesus Christ, this reality of consummated form of 'rest' converges at the Eschaton and is solely realizable in the closest communion with God here and also hereafter" (i.e., the present and the future-present).[100]

Fourth, the eschatological nature of "my rest" is not just that but is part and parcel of the *Creation rest (sabbatismos)*. By linking Ps 95:11 with Gn 2:2 in Heb 4:3, the writer is suggesting that the heavenly rest is part of God's Creation rest, just as the Canaan rest is a part of the divine rest. Moreover, by linking *katapausis* from Psalm 95 with the verb *katapausen* in Genesis 2, the writer is suggesting that the Canaan rest and the heavenly rest are the same rest which God himself entered on the first Sabbath. Attridge explicates the relationship between these two terms, *katapausis* and *sabbatismos*:

> This suggestion is made explicit in v. 9, "Therefore a *sabbatismos* is left for the people of God." It seems clear then that the author's argument...hinges upon the equation of *katapausis* and *sabbatismos*, that is, upon the redefinition of the first term by means of the second.[101]

The term *sabbatismos* occurs in the New Testament only in Heb 4:9.[102] The writer deliberately substitutes *katapausis* and *sabbatismos* in 4:9 because he has already connected *katapausis* with God's Creation rest on the seventh day in 4:3, and because the word *katapausis* is used in the LXX (Ex 35:2; 2 Mc 15:1) to mean Sabbath rest also.[103] This clarification of *katapausis* in terms

---

100. Lombard, "*Katapausis* in the Letter to the Hebrews," 67.

101. Attridge, " 'Let Us Strive to Enter That Rest': The Logic of Hebrews 4:1–11," 282. Also suggested by O. Bauernfeind, "*Katapauō*," *TDNT* 3:627–28; Lane, *Hebrews 1:1–9:28*, 101.

102. See Victor P. Hamilton, "*shabat*, cease, desist, rest," *Theological Wordbook*, 2:902–3; E. Lohse, "*Sabbaton*," *TDNT* 7:34; see N. E. Andreasen, *Old Testament Sabbath*, 100–173, for extensive etymological understanding of *shabat* and variants.

103. Lincoln, "Sabbath, Rest, and Eschatology in the New Testament," 213.

of *sabbatismos* shows that all the many aspects or stages of attaining "rest" (whether in Canaan or in heaven, whether political or apocalyptical) are really one and the same "Sabbath rest" of God Himself, which the psalmist referred to as "my rest"[104] (i.e., God's rest). The common thread underlying and interlinking all these aspects of "rest" is participation in God's eternal sabbatical repose,[105] or enjoying the presence of God, the Source of life. Therefore, to enter into God's rest is to enter into Canaan, but it is more than that; it is also to experience the whole extent of other spiritual aspects of the promise of rest. Above all, it is to enter and enjoy the Sabbath rest of God. Kaiser summarizes, "One can...view this 'rest of God' in a way that involves a corporate solidarity of the whole rest [God's Sabbath rest] with all its parts or as a collective single program which purposely embraces several related aspects realized in marked and progressive stages."[106]

It is in this sense also that the writer of Hebrews can speak of "the claim that the achievement of that rest remains a possibility"[107] in 4:9: "So then there remains a Sabbath rest (*sabbatismos*) for the people of God." Therefore, the Sabbath rest which the New Testament people of God must observe is to enter God's rest (*katapausis* again in 4:10) and thereby to cease from one's works (4:10a). Entering into God's rest is analogous to God's ceasing to work on His creation (4:4 and 10b).

The "rest" spoken of here does not have a local or physical reference but a relational-redemptive connotation. The *analogy* of 4:10b ("ceases from his labors as God did from his") is not be-

---

104. See "My/thy" sabbath(s)" in OT (Ex 31:13; Lv 19:3, 30; Is 56:4; 58:13; Ez 20:12 and passim; 22:26; 23:38; 44:24; Neh 9:14). The interpretation here is supported by Andreasen, *OT Sabbath*, 207, as well as by Attridge, *The Epistle to the Hebrews*, 128, who also seems to suggest this soteriological interpretation of rest. Andreasen also argues for the distinctiveness of Yahweh's holiness and presence being manifested on the day of rest: "In fact, the holiness of the day, which was recognized by the abstention from work on it, depended on the recognition of the real presence of Yahweh on that day" (207).

105. Therefore, it is possible to enter the land and not attain the rest that is God's life (4:8). See Johnson, *The Writings of the New Testament: An Interpretation*, 423; Attridge, *The Epistle to the Hebrews*, 126.

106. Kaiser, "The Promise Theme and Theology of Rest," 148.

107. Attridge, *The Epistle to the Hebrews*, 281. Attridge argues that this is the point the writer wants to make in 4:3–5.

tween "works" of God and one who enters rest, but between the *rest* of God and the *rest* of the participants, as the OT understanding implies (i.e., cessation of sorrow, insecurity, and also sense of oneness with God as one encounters God's presence).[108]

Whether the author understands the creation Sabbath in terms of the divine *otiositas* motif,[109] or in terms of the cultic emphasis[110] of the Priestly source of the exilic period, is difficult to determine. However, in the light of our proposed audience hypothesis, it is likely that the author has the divine *otiositas* motif in mind. That is, the author is implying by the term "God's rest" the concept of stability or order in the cosmos.[111] The author's concern may be stated thus: If Yahweh is at rest in Zion, then national and

---

108. Refer to the section where I survey the concept of rest as used in the OT.

109. *Otiositas* is used here to describe the inactivity and rest of God after struggling to bring creation out of the chaos as depicted in most Near Eastern creation myths. See R. Pettazzoni, "Myths of Beginning and Creation-Myths," in *Essays on the History of Religion,* trans. H. T. Rose (Leiden: E. J. Brill, 1954), 24–36. It is very possible that the author has this motif in mind when writing Hebrews because of the nature of the struggle, persecution, and alienation the audience is facing.

110. Andreasen's analysis of Gn 2:1–4a; Ex 16:4–5, 22–30; 31:12–17; 35:2–3; Lv 16:31; 19:3, 30; 23:3, 11, 15, 16, 32, 38; 24:8; 25:1–7; 26:2, 34–35, 43; Nm 15:32–36; and 28:9–10 seems to suggest that the P writer during the exilic or postexilic period was composing and using the Genesis text (2:1–4) to justify the institution of Sabbath as a weekly worship day, a holy day. Thus, Andreasen doubts that the creation story in Genesis is in any way influenced by Mesopotamian or Babylonian creation myths, because the Priestly writer is a nationalistic writer in time of captivity or return from exile; furthermore, after a lengthy discussion, Andreasen concludes, "Gn 2:1–3 is not portraying a divine *otiositas.* . . . The creation account does thus not originate as a literary composition [to justify Sabbath institution]. . . . the main concern of Gn 1:1–2:4 is with creation, and not with the Sabbath" (186–93). See Andreasen, *OT Sabbath,* 62–92, 117, 186–87.

111. Andreasen, however, would perhaps not agree with my speculation, for he sees the Genesis creation "rest" motif as distinctively different from that of the extrabiblical *otiositas* motif: "Now there is no evidence of divine Sabbath keeping in extrabiblical myths, and so the creation Sabbath could easily be considered a unique feature of the Old Testament. It is curious, however, that precisely the Old Testament should make Yahweh rest and even refresh himself after his creative work, for Yahweh is not a God who would tire or retire in the face of new and extraordinarily heavy activities, or before other aggressive powers, nor is the world's stability assured by his inactivity, but on the contrary by his activity within creation" ("OT Sabbath," 183). I agree with Andreasen, except that here I am arguing that the author of Hebrews is aware of extrabiblical *otiositas,* especially in the mind of his audience; thus the author is able to use this concept and make it intelligible to them in relation to the divine *otiositas* of God.

political security is established. "My rest" in Ps 95:11, therefore, refers to the security Israelites have from disturbance by their enemies.[112] There is rest in God's rest. "He rested from his own works" describes or explains the essential nature of "rest" of "the one who enters" in 4:10a. The author clarifies the nature of "rest" by making the analogy of God resting from his works (4:10b). God never stops working, but there is a real sense in which God's self-communion within the Godhead on the seventh day is unlike that on the other six days of creation. And that self-communion is the climax of creation: God stops creating and enjoys God's presence before the whole creation.

Is God's rest a motionless, static rest? By no means! God's rest is a dynamic rest in the context of creation. That is, dynamic rest is experienced in the midst of movement. For rest only makes sense in the midst of unrest. Rest becomes real in a life which is in constant movement. Rest becomes unique and precious and all the more necessary in the life of a pilgrim. God's rest is to become our rest. That is God's intention. Also, as one enters God's rest, one is no doubt overwhelmed by God's presence. In other words, one finds security in the midst of persecution, stability in the midst of change (or seeming chaos), peace in the midst of suffering. This redemptive rest is the "re-creation" rest which God originally intended all to share with God in the Creation rest (i.e., God's rest). Redemptive rest is a present spiritual rest of constant response to the voice of God, and of participation in the presence of God. This faithful, trusting relationship with God is the basic starting point for Hebrews' interpretation of salvation and perfection.

The continuing invitation of Ps 95:7–8 shows that Israel's entrance into Canaan under Joshua was a partial and temporary entering into God's rest. That Canaan rest is only the beginning of entering. The full meaning of rest cannot be limited to space (Canaan or heaven) or time (past or present or future), but must be inclusive of a series of fulfillments to the promise of rest. Entrance into God's rest is response to God's voice through faith (or

---

112. For details of this argument, see Gerhard von Rad, "There Remains Still a Rest for the People of God: An Investigation of a Biblical Conception," in *The Problem of the Hexateuch and Other Essays,* trans. E. W. Trueman Dicken (New York: McGraw-Hill, 1966), 94–102.

faithfully). It may also mean ceasing both from disbelieving in God and from manipulating life. There is no evidence as yet for Jewett's argument that God's rest carries within it the connotation of cessation from self-righteous works.[113] The word "works" in this pericope is more fully developed by the author later in 6:1 ("repentance from dead works") and 9:14 ("from dead works") as dead works[114] or a futile, self-manipulative kind of pseudosalvation.

We can summarize the above discussion by saying that the writer deliberately takes a word or a concept which is closely related to the physical inheritance of the land of Canaan and uses it to embody both a physical and a deeply relational and spiritual concept. As Kaiser has written, "The rest which God gives is at once historical (Canaan), soteriological (salvation), and eschatological (the Kingdom and our reign with Christ)."[115] Which is to say that the writer seems to conceive many facets (Sabbath rest, Canaan rest, heavenly rest, eschatological rest, redemptive rest) of a single rest (Creation-Sabbath-Divine rest) which God intended for mankind.[116] The Creation rest is the commencement of the divine rest which the Creator entered and in which the Creator intended all to share.

---

113. See Jewett, *Letter to Pilgrims,* 64–69. The antithesis within the pericope is not between faith and self-justifying works but between faith and disbelief. Readers are asked to "strive" and to "hold fast," which denote hard, persevering work required on the part of the readers. The comparison between God's cessation of works and the cessation of work by those who enter God's rest focuses not on works but on rest, because God's work does not consist of "self-justifying" works.

114. Several commentators make the same point: John Calvin, *Commentaries on the Epistle of Paul the Apostle to the Hebrews,* translated from the original Latin and edited by Rev. John Owen (Edinburgh: T. Constable, n.d.), 48; Lombard, "*Katapausis* in the Letter to the Hebrews," 65–66: "The obedient people shall receive from God the rest [that releases them] from God's holy wrath and from privations, enemy attacks and sinful activities. Thereby they will enter a life of rest, being the pleasurable activity of complete and devoted service to God"; Bruce, *The Epistle to the Hebrews,* 72; Lincoln, "Sabbath, Rest, and Eschatology in the New Testament," 213; Hewitt, *The Epistle to the Hebrews,* 91; Combrink, "Some Thoughts on the Old Testament Citations in the Epistle to the Hebrews," 60.

115. Kaiser, "The Promise Theme and Theology of Rest," 138.

116. Among the many commentators, Peters, Kaiser, and Toussaint have explicitly stated the multiplicity of the single rest of God. Most commentators do not see this relationship. See G. N. H. Peters, *The Theocratic Kingdom* (New York and London, 1884), 2:441–42; Kaiser, "The Promise Theme and Theology of Rest," 138; and Toussaint, "Eschatology," 71.

The Hermeneutical Principles of the Homilist

Let us now sum up our understanding of "God's rest" and deduce the hermeneutical principles the writer of Hebrews uses in Hebrews 3–4.

First, the writer uses the midrash-pesher method to exposit the OT in his theology.[117] He begins with the major arguments of the Psalm (3:7–12) to reveal the heart of the matter (3:13–14). Often major points are repeated (3:15). Then he explains in detail the important concepts pertaining to his argument (3:16–4:10). Finally, he concludes with a summary exhorting the readers (4:11–13).[118] While the writer of Hebrews does not use the OT out of context, at the same time he is not bound by the text.[119] He has the freedom to link important concepts or words to make his point. Likewise, he plays on words (e.g., "today") to serve his purpose. All these techniques are employed only after he has considered the historical setting and facts of Psalm 95 and Genesis 2.

Second, the writer makes use of midrash, with its typological interpretation, to warn and exhort the readers to hold fast (unwavering, steadfast). Just as 3:6 contains both an indicative clause ("we are the house") and an imperative clause ("if . . . hold fast"), so 3:12–4:2 contains both a warning from the psalm and an assurance of encouragement (4:3–11).[120] The indicative "we are the house" of 3:6 "presupposes the correspondence between the old and new people of God,"[121] both of whom have heard the word of

---

117. Kistemaker, *The Psalm Citations in the Epistle to the Hebrews*, 111; Lincoln, "Sabbath, Rest, and Eschatology in the New Testament," 149; Combrink, "Some Thoughts on the Old Testament Citations in the Epistle to the Hebrews," 30; Casey, *Hebrews*, 18; and Lane, *Hebrews 1:1–9:28*, 95.

118. Lawrence Wills ("The Form of the Sermon in Hellenistic Judaism and Early Christianity," *Harvard Theological Review* 77, no. 3–4 [1984]: 277–99) identifies this form of "word of exhortation" as a common form of the Hellenistic Jewish and early Christian sermon, characterized by three parts of authoritative exempla, conclusion, and exhortation.

119. See Johnson, *The Writings of the New Testament: An Interpretation*, 422. He unconvincingly argues that the writer of Hebrews exploits and alters the text. See sec. 2 of this chapter on the skillful and legitimate use of OT citations from Psalms and Genesis in Hebrews 3–4.

120. Thompson, "The *Katapausis* Motif in Hebrews," 92.

121. Thompson, "The *Katapausis* Motif in Hebrews," 92.

promise and of good tidings (4:11–12). As Thompson points out, there is more than a typological correspondence present here:

> In 3:6a, "house" refers to God's heavenly residence, of which the readers have become "partakers" (3:1). Through the work of Christ, access to the heavenly world has been granted. Thus the church is God's house as a result of the exaltation of Christ. Christ is the "brother" who has participated in human existence (2:10–17); the church now shares in his heavenly calling.... "Partakers of Christ" is both formally and substantively parallel to "we are the house" (3:6) and to "partakers of heavenly call" (3:1).[122]

Through this midrash, the author's purpose is twofold: to affirm and to assure the readers of their status in, and relationship with, God, which is a blessed, heavenly, exalted, and stable existence; and, to warn, promise, and encourage the readers to hold fast and to enter into God's rest.

Third, the writer traces the single purpose or promise of the divine rest (namely, the Genesis Creation rest, in which God invited all to participate) — as manifested and fulfilled in multiple disjoined forms[123] (historical in Canaan, redemptive in Christ, and consummated in heaven) — throughout history as a series of divine promises. As such, the possessing of Canaan *is* the rest, but the rest *is more* than that, and certainly includes relational and spiritual aspects as well.[124] Though "things combined in the promise were disjoined in the fulfillment,"[125] the writer is able to see "this rest of God in a way that involves a corporate solidarity of the whole rest with all its parts.... [It] embraces several related aspects realized in marked and progressive stages...all one piece; a single divine rest with related aspects."[126]

Fourth, with salvation history in perspective, the writer intricately and paradoxically mingles the future and the present into the

---

122. Thompson, "The *Katapausis* Motif in Hebrews," 92, 94.
123. Bauernfeind, *"Katapauō,"* TDNT 3:627; Franz Delitzsch, *Commentary on the Epistle to the Hebrews*, trans. Thomas L. Kingsbury (Edinburgh, 1886), 1:195.
124. See Kaiser, *The Uses of the Old Testament in the New,* 166.
125. Delitzsch, *Commentary on the Epistle to the Hebrews,* 1:195.
126. Kaiser, "The Promise Theme and Theology of Rest," 149.

"today" by exhorting the readers to live a life of pilgrimage and faith as the new people of God. Lincoln clarifies the redemptive purpose:

> After the Fall, God's original intentions for humanity's enjoyment of the promised consummation rest are now worked out through God's acts of redemption among His people. The resting place in the promised land, in Jerusalem, and in the sanctuary all point forward to the fulfillment of God's redemptive purpose. Now in Hebrews ... the consummation rest is pictured in terms of a heavenly resting place, the antitype of the resting place in the promised land referred to in Ps 95:11.[127]

But the crucial question is: When do we attain God's rest? "Today" or in a future in heaven?[128] There are at least two points in Heb 4:3 which will help us determine that issue. Heb 4:3 says that "we who have believed enter the rest." First, "enter" in Greek is truly a present tense rather than Robertson's so called "emphatic future present."[129] By putting "enter" first, the writer emphasizes that the readers "are already ... entering" God's rest.[130] Second, "believed" (aorist participle) is not merely an awaiting of a future reality or awaiting fulfillment in a participation in God's rest; rather, it is the key to grasping the whole of invisible truth or heavenly reality now and here. Lincoln suggests that "faith makes real in the present that which is future, unseen, or heavenly [Hebrews

---

127. Lincoln, "Sabbath, Rest, and Eschatology in the New Testament," 210.

128. The author conceives that the everlasting city or new Jerusalem is already present in heaven (13:14, 12:22), though it is still to come. In Hebrews the heavenly Jerusalem (12:22) has both spatial and temporal connotations. It does not stand for the eternal in the sense of that which is ideal and timeless, but rather signifies that the future is already present in heaven and, therefore, available now.

129. Robertson, *Word Pictures in the New Testament,* 5:361. My interpretation is congruent with that of many scholars such as Lincoln ("Sabbath, Rest, and Eschatology in the New Testament," 211–12); Westcott, *Epistle to the Hebrews,* 94–95; Barrett, "The Eschatology of the Epistle to the Hebrews," 372; and Kistemaker, *The Psalm Citations in the Epistle to the Hebrews,* 109.

130. Montefiore, *A Commentary on the Epistle to the Hebrews,* 83. So also Attridge (*The Epistle to the Hebrews,* 126), who says "enter" is "a reference to the complex process in which 'believers' are even now engaged, although this process will certainly have an eschatological consummation."

11]. This is why those who have believed can be said to enter the rest already."[131]

The readers of Hebrews have heard the word and the promise of God in Jesus Christ, especially in "these last days" (1:1, 2), that is, "today" (3:7, 13, 15; 4:7). In other words, "today" brackets the period of the "already" and the "not yet" of the end time. In "today," God's rest is both a reality and a promise.[132] All who believe have already entered it, and all are urged to continue to strive to enter it.[133] God's people are exhorted to enter now the promise of God's rest, made available to them by faith,[134] and to continue to enter God's rest moment by moment in the pilgrimage of life. Those who do are called "the partakers of Christ" (3:14). At the same time, they are exhorted to hold firm (3:6) until the end; they are said to enter into God's rest (4:3) and at the same time (3:14) they are exhorted to strive to enter that rest (4:11) constantly. It is a paradoxical truth of Christian life.

A Chinese Hermeneutical Reading

Hebrews and Yin-Yang

The author of Hebrews assumes that the aeons in the cosmos[135] are in constant flux or movement. Not only does he eschew denying change and the resultant chaos, he even accepts this truth and takes the further step of describing the life of faith as a life of pilgrimage,

---

131. Lincoln, "Sabbath, Rest, and Eschatology in the New Testament," 215.

132. Bauernfeind (*"Katapauō," TDNT* 3:627) says, "The distinctive LXX use of the term is the normative linguistic instrument by which to describe the way from the OT via the today of the NT to the final ends of God." So Lombard, *"Katapausis* in the Letter to the Hebrews," 67.

133. Barrett ("The Eschatology of the Epistle to the Hebrews," 372) makes this point.

134. Or as Jewett puts it so well, "An important feature about the opening lines of this argument is the promise provides the basis for the demand. The indicative precedes the imperative, for the rest lies open in an unconditional fashion, not requiring the fulfillment of a demand before entering into it" (*Letter to Pilgrims,* 62).

135. For a preliminary understanding of cosmology in Hebrews, see Paul Ellingworth, "Jesus and the Universe in Hebrews," *Evangelical Quarterly* 58, no. 4 (1986): 337–50, and the bibliography therein.

that is, a life of process and change, with seemingly endless challenges on the way. This understanding of cosmology and human experience is quite similar to yin-yang philosophy. In *I Ching* (the *Book of Changes*) and *Tao Te Ching*, the earliest books of cosmology, the concept of change is depicted as the essence of the cosmic process.[136] The *T'ai chi* (Great Ultimate) emblem,

which represents ultimate reality, finds expression in the yin-yang symbol, which in turn represents the process of change: yin and yang respectively signify rest and movement, being and becoming, responsiveness and creativity, and so forth. Ultimate reality is to be understood in terms of change, rather than merely as a static, deterministic state. It is change that produces ontology, pilgrimage that produces rest, process that produces existence, and suffering that produces perfection. It is change that produces creativity through the process of becoming.

The *Tao Te Ching* says, "Essential nature is everchanging-changeless."[137] In other words, change, or even chaos, is not to be disliked, manipulated, or feared. Change produces a life of pilgrimage. It is in that change and pilgrimage that one finds his being, the meaning of existence,[138] just as the pioneer of faith and salvation,

---

136. The audience of Hebrews seeks to manipulate the change and chaos of the cosmos by worshiping angels; ancient Chinese, however, seek to know the *ming* or *tien-ming* (heavenly will) of God in this flux so that they are able to do the will of God. See Helmut Wilhelm, *Heaven, Earth, and Man in the Book of Changes* (Seattle and London: University of Washington Press, 1977), 53: "[D]ivine commands can determine the events through which positive or negative guidelines are set for man. If such guidelines seem contrary, one must nevertheless submit.... Whenever possible, one must follow the will of heaven devotedly."

137. Chap. 16. The *I Ching* says, "When it [change] is silent, it is immovable; when it moves, it penetrates to all things in the universe." Change is both changing and unchanging, because it is both yin, rest, and yang, movement.

138. Wilhelm, *Heaven, Earth, and Man in the Book of Changes,* 77, states, "Meaning appears in every given change,... in the Way that leads from every given hexagram to every one of the others."

who is the "everchanging-changeless," did. According to the author the preexistent Jesus brought forth the cosmos and controls it (Heb 1:2–3, 2:8b), yet he partakes of our human nature in flesh and blood (Heb 2:9–10) and shares obediently our suffering and death (Heb 2:10–11). In the midst of change, chaos, and entropy, Christ has expiated human sin, accomplished atonement, been exalted to glory and honor, and has become the Great High Priest (2:17–18; 4:14–15). Thus, the yin-yang nature of the cosmos and life is to be accepted.[139] That is, one has to accept change and chaos as edifying components of the whole cosmos, as designed by God.

The writer of Hebrews views the cosmos and Jesus in the context of change rather than static state or being. Because cosmology and Christology are understood in terms of "changelogy," "changelogy" is to be understood in terms of relationship. This is where the concept of yin-yang can also shed some light on our understanding of anthropology as a part of cosmology. Yin cannot be yin by itself. Yin is yin because of yang. Yin and yang, therefore, are mutually interdependent and inclusive. Yin has a part of yang within it, and yang has a part of yin within it. They are reciprocal in this intimate interpersonal relationship.

The yin-yang understanding of cosmology may be unfamiliar to modern thinking. For Western readers,[140] an illustration from Planck's quantum physics and Einstein's relativity theory might help here.[141] Quantum-relative physics stresses the interrelation-

---

139. Note that the yin-yang nature of the cosmos does not necessarily accept the second law of thermodynamics, entropy, to be the inclusive law of nature. Yin-yang philosophy would include both entropy and evolution.

140. In the philosophy of *I Ching,* all of yin and yang are but moments in the fluctuating fire of change. Each is necessary to the meaning and existing of its opposite. In 500 B.C.E. Heraclitus saw water and earth as but transient aspects of the ceaseless metamorphosis of flame: "You cannot step twice into the same river for other waters are ever flowing on to you." "The Heraclitean viewpoint is found in modern quantum mechanics in which the things of the world are described as changing probability functions and in relativity theory in which objects become nothing more than tubes through which flow smaller tubes and smaller tubes, *ad infinitum*" (J. McKim Malville, *The Fermenting Universe: Myths of Eternal Change* [New York: The Seabury Press, 1981], 9).

141. See R. P. Feynman, *QED: The Strange Theory of Light and Matter* (Princeton: Princeton University Press, 1985); Tony Hey and Patrick Walters, *The Quantum Universe* (Cambridge: Cambridge University Press, 1987); J. C. Polkinghorne, *The Quantum World* (London: Longman Press, 1984), chap. 5.

ships of space and time, of velocity and position, and of all electromagnetic fields, which are a basic makeup of the entire microcosm and macrocosm. It also stresses the interrelatedness and inclusiveness of many aspects (e.g., light as particles and wave; mass and energy as one reality, etc.) as one totality.[142] Quantum-relative physics outwits conventional Newtonian physics because it has discovered, contrary to Newton, that both atoms and the cosmos are changing and in constant motion. Since quantum-relative physics has the precision to measure the changing motion by means of atomic clocks or in units of light years, it is more valid than Newtonian physics in the understanding of space, time, and velocity.[143]

The principles of inclusiveness and mutuality in yin-yang philosophy and quantum-relative physics grant us scientific "hermeneutical tools" to perceive Hebrews and ourselves in a new way. Reality and cosmology are neither yin or yang, but both. Matter is not merely a spatial element but also a temporal one. Light is both wavelike and corpuscular. In the duck/rabbit illustration below,[144] the duck and the rabbit are one harmonious reality.

They are one in essence but two in existence, and they exist in mutual relationship.

---

142. According to the theory of relativity the universe is constantly in the process of becoming. Time and space are not independent of each other but dependent and inclusive.

143. This does not eliminate the contribution and mystery of traditional physics. In fact, if the speed of an object is equal to zero, Newtonian physics holds true. For a scholarly evaluation of the traditional physics, see David K. Himrod, "Secrecy in Modern Science," in *Secrecy in Religions,* ed. Kees W. Bolle (Leiden: E. J. Brill, 1987), 103–50.

144. J. C. Polkinghorne, *One World: The Interaction of Science and Theology* (Princeton: Princeton University Press, 1986), 9–10.

Turning back now to the text before us, we see that the author of Hebrews never seeks to eliminate the changing and chaotic aspects of the original cosmos. Change and chaos threaten human existence and give rise to feelings of ambivalence. They seem to undermine God's sovereignty. But the author affirms change and chaos as the design of the aeons within the cosmos. As Malville writes, "Etched deeply into the face of the cosmos is eternal change. It penetrates so thoroughly the matter and energy of the universe that perhaps the ultimate meaning of our lives may be perceived in the promise of change. Change is indeed a blessing for in change one finds rest; it is weariness to be always toiling at the same things and always beginning afresh."[145] The idea of pilgrimage, so prevalent in Hebrews, gives an indication of becoming in the process of change, and the concept "rest" speaks of meaningful existence, stability, peace, confidence, and contentment in the midst of change and process. As Jewett has observed, "Hebrews interprets adversity as an inevitable and unresolvable aspect of the created order as designed by God. Insecurity is built in, so to speak, as the 'discipline' intended by the 'Father' of all."[146]

The writer of Hebrews also stresses the interrelational aspect between change and rest in the pilgrimage, between the indicative and the imperative of salvation, between the faithfulness of Christ and the faithfulness of the pilgrims, and between "already" and "not-yet" eschatology. Pain and joy, suffering and perfection, chaos and rest, change and stability, uncertainty and confidence are actually dual aspects of one and the same reality. As the yin and the yang are not mutually exclusive, but complementary, so also can be the uncertainty we face on the one hand and the rest of God that we experience on the other.[147]

---

145. Malville, *The Fermenting Universe: Myths of Eternal Change,* viii, 8.
146. Jewett, *Letter to Pilgrims,* 12.
147. As *Tao Te Ching* says:

> The Tao that can be told of is not the eternal Tao;
> The name that can be named is not the eternal name.
> The Nameless is the origin of Heaven and Earth;
> The Named is the mother of all things.
> Therefore let there always be nonbeing, so we may see the subtlety,
> And let there always be being, so we may see their outcome.
> The two are the same,

The author of Hebrews is convinced that the locus of meaning is found only in the lives of pilgrims, as they struggle within the community of faith to live faithfully with the word of God. Meaning and existence find their loci in interpersonal relationships. Interpersonal relationships constitute an intricate and delicate art and science, but they need to be achieved to make the pilgrimage itself meaningful and restful. Christians are the cultic community on the move. They are joined together in this pilgrimage now and forevermore, as yin and yang are joined together for harmony and oneness in the eternal cosmic process of change.[148] "The way to the 'I' of each is the 'You' of the others."[149]

---

but after they are produced, they have different names.
They both may be called deep and profound.
Deeper and more profound,
The door to all subtleties!
When the people of the world all know beauty as beauty,
There arises the recognition of ugliness.
When they all know the good as good,
There arises the recognition of evil.
Therefore, Being and nonbeing produce each other;
Difficult and easy complete each other;
High and low distinguish each other;
Sound and voice harmonize each other;
Front and behind accompany each other.

The Way of Lao Tzu, trans. Wing-tsit Chan (Indianapolis: Bobbs-Merrill, 1963), 97.

148. Yin has part of yang and yang has part of yin. They are reciprocal in that intimate interpersonal relationship, as *Book of Changes* (*I Ching*) says:

The Changes is a book
From which one cannot hold aloof.
Its Tao
Is forever changing,
Alteration, movement . . .
Flowing . . .
Rising and sinking without fixed law,
Firm and yielding transform each other.
They cannot be confined within a rule;
It is only change that is at work here.

See *The I Ching or Book of Changes,* the Richard Wilhelm translation rendered in English by Cary F. Baynes, 3d ed. (Princeton: Princeton University Press, 1967), 348.

149. Francisco Bravo, *Christ in the Thought of Teilhard de Chardin* (South Bend, Ind.: University of Notre Dame Press, 1967), 22.

Finally, the author seems to have a consciousness of time similar to that found in yin-yang philosophy, an awareness of an event as oriented to the present, occurring at a particular point of time to bring meaning to life. This is not to suggest that neither the author of Hebrews nor yin-yang philosophy has a concept of future time, because both have a present-time orientation on the past-present-future time line. Both Hebrews and yin-yang philosophy are conscious of linear or procedural time and of three-dimensional time, but the emphasis is on the "now," with both the past and the future providing instruction on how to live now. Such an approach does not cause one to conceive of a tension between the "now" and the "not yet."[150] The only incompatibility between Hebrews and yin-yang philosophy with regard to time is the cyclical or spiral nature of time within yin-yang philosophy. Perhaps we can modify the spiral time line as recurring or overlapping on the three-dimensional time line (past, present, future); that is, we can acknowledge that there is a beginning and ending of events or history, but in the nowness of time, recurring change, flux, and events bring challenges and meaning to life.

Unrest, Restlessness, and Rest

After two thousand years of explosive growth in knowledge and technology, human beings in the modern world have not appeased the cosmic forces in their lives any better than the Christians of the Hebrews audience. The world and the universe at large actually seem more alien and more threatening than ever before. People frequently feel dehumanized and despiritualized, a feeling which only brings nervous breakdowns, sleeping pills, and so forth.

Cosmic forces seem to overwhelm the human spirit: the greenhouse effect, the fate of the Hong Kong Chinese in the year 1997, the struggle of the Chinese in China for freedom and responsible government, the perceived threat of UFOs and outer-space

---

150. Bruce J. Malina argues convincingly that the first century had a Mediterranean time-perception of present orientation, rather than a modern, Swiss time-perception of future orientation. See Bruce J. Malina, "Christ and Time: Swiss or Mediterranean?" *Catholic Biblical Quarterly* 51 (1989): 1–31. Malina works his model out of Kluckhohn's and Strodtbeck's value-orientation models.

aliens, environmental pollution, nuclear waste, oil spills, terrorist hijackings, contaminated fruit and vegetables, nuclear war, chemical weapons, AIDS, computer viruses, savings and loan crises, political unrest in different parts of the world — all raise the level of anxiety. No feature of the universe has been discovered which is not undergoing some form of metamorphosis. We are fearful and uncertain of change, the future, and personal fate. The human spirit is caught in a changing world, with the attendant horror of having nothing permanent to cling to; thus many still "worship the angels and cosmic forces" of the day. The masses turn to horoscopes, read stars, pursue knowledge, and have faith in extra-celestial beings — those gnostic revealers of the day like Bo and Peep, Guinea and Pig.[151] Many believe those who preach a gospel of prosperity, miraculous healing, faith healing, or the message of satanic cults. Some put total trust in scientific technology, government institutions, national defense, financial principles, Wall Street, status, and materialism, hoping to find certainty, confidence, and peace of mind. But such misplaced trust is only to be caught in the tragic-ironic drama of life.

The message of Hebrews speaks just as loudly and clearly to this restless and uncertain generation as it did to the first. The universe is made by God (1:10), by God's creative word (11:3), through Christ (1:2). It is subjected to God (see 12:26). Jesus, as the exalted Son, rules over both the present age/old world (Heb 9:9), which seems to pass away, and the future age/heavenly world (2:5), which lies before a redeemed humanity as the goal of its pilgrimage.[152] One is only to know that change and chaos, insecurity

---

151. See Ted Peters, *UFOs — God's Chariots? Flying Saucers in Politics, Science, and Religion* (Atlanta: John Knox Press, 1977), 131ff. Marshall Herff Applewhite and Bonnie Trusdale Nettles of Houston called themselves by code names such as Him and Her, He and She, Bo and Peep, Guinea and Pig, who claimed to be the two witnesses of Revelation 11. They preached a UFO theology of HIM (Human Individual Metamorphosis), saying that they were terrestrially reincarnated heavenly beings, requiring followers to do as Jesus required the rich young ruler to do: to sell what you have, to give all your money to the poor, and to find treasure in heaven. Then, they said, a UFO would come and take you to a heavenly home.

152. The plural form of aeons seems to conjure up both the present age/old world and new age/heavenly world. See J. P. Meier, "Structure and Theology in Heb 1:1–14," *Biblica* 66 (1985): 178–83.

and uncertainty are built into the cosmic system and will not be eradicated. The good news is that we can enter into God's rest in the midst of anxiety, ambiguity, and uncertainty. Today, right here and now, all can enter into God's rest. God's rest is not only in the future and in heaven; more importantly, it is here and now. None has to wait for a scenic retirement home to enter God's rest; all can enter God's rest when they commune with God here and now. Since God's rest is given in promise in its multidimensional aspects, and since God's rest is more than one of those aspects, yet all in unity, it is necessary always to enter into God's rest every-day. Let readers not forget that they have a pioneer and perfecter of faith, a leader for the pilgrimage who is preexistent, the creator and controller of the cosmos. This Jesus has redeemed the pilgrim community by sharing human nature and the conditions of pilgrimage: weakness, perplexity, uncertainty, suffering, and death.

The author declares: Jesus the Leader has gone before all. Jesus, the pioneer and perfecter of faith, their pathfinder, their forerunner has suffered, endured persecution, and tasted death for the pilgrims' sake (see 2:10–13, 12:3–13). Now he is the Great High Priest who leads them to God and God to them (Hebrews 4–6; 7:26, 9:4). So the rest pilgrims can have in this restless world is the moment-to-moment encounter with God's very presence in their daily lives here and now. For those who believe are entering into God's rest where God's presence meets them where they are. It is with every step to the mountaintop and down into the valley of darkness that pilgrims encounter God, one another, and themselves. Rest is not inactivity, but instead the untiring activity of that constant encounter with the presence of God. As pilgrims respond accordingly, faithful to the voice of God, along with brothers and sisters, they not only walk where God leads them, but they also find God's rest despite the wandering; they find peace despite the persecution; they find contentment despite uncertainty.

Chapter 5

The Ming of T'ien (Will of God) in Amos and Confucius

The purpose of this chapter is twofold: first, to analyze the selected pericope (Am 4:4–5) in order to observe emerging themes or emphases therein, and to synthesize these themes with the immediate context of the pericope and with the message of the whole book (especially 5:4–24); and second, to compare the concepts that are most prominent in this pericope with similar concepts in Confucius's classics, so that both texts can be brought into a cross-cultural dialogue with one another. Let us first examine briefly the biblical text in terms of form and literary criticism.

Satirical Poetry

The first task is to establish the limits and form of the pericope itself. Walter Brueggemann understands 4:1–13 as a unified speech.[1] H. W. Wolff, however, observes that in the oracle formula of verse 5b, "sharply defined prosody and the change of theme mark a major literary break"[2] at verse 5. For our purposes, we shall consider 4:4–5 as one of the three units of 4:4–13 (with the other two vv. 6–12 and 13) and understand 4:4–5 as a continuation of the ironic indictment on the cultic life at Bethel mentioned in 3:14 and on the social injustice of the "cows of Bashan" mentioned in 4:1–3.

---

1. W. Brueggemann, "Amos 4:4–13 and Israel's Covenant Worship," *Vetus Testamentum* 15 (1965): 9.

2. Hans Walter Wolff, *Joel and Amos: A Commentary on the Books of the Prophets Joel and Amos,* trans. Waldermar Janzen (Philadelphia: Fortress, 1984), 211.

In terms of literary criticism, Am 4:4–5 by itself is composed of three bicola (A, B, C) of 3–3 meter, and another bicolon (D) of 2–2 meter:

A. 4. "Come to Bethel, and transgress;
      to Gilgal, and multiply transgression;

B. bring your sacrifices every morning,
      your tithes every three days;

C. 5. offer a sacrifice of thanksgiving of that which is leavened,
      and proclaim freewill offerings, publish them;

D. for so you love to do,
      O people of Israel!"
    says the Lord God. (RSV)

In the three regular three-stress bicola, the second member of each bicolon intensifies its preceding parallel in meaning. Then the last sentence with its two-stress bicolon creates the familiar staccato effect.[3] Note also that the last bicolon of 2–2 meter is a "run-on" line without the internal parallelism of the first three lines. Thus, the poetry ends with climactic changes of structure and meter so as to attract the attention of the audience or readers to the indictments placed. Finally, the seriousness of the indictment is reinforced by the ending words, "the oracle of the Lord." Throughout the poetry, the author's skillful use of words that rhyme (such as the sounds *b, u, km, l, q*) provides emphasis to the contrast between the actions of the first audience and Yahweh's perception of their cultic activities.

The Priestly Call-to-Worship and Prophetic Indictments

The hermeneutical analysis and assumptions above will help us to "crack" open the pericope. One of the assumptions of the present writer is that, since this pericope is satirical poetry without explicit

---

3. Wolff, *Joel and Amos*, 212.

indictment, the meaning and interpretation of the pericope need to be supplied from elsewhere in the book.

Worshiping or Transgressing Yahweh

The pericope begins with "Come to Bethel," which is the official priestly opening call-to-worship or priestly instruction.[4] "Come" or "enter" connotes the entrance of the pilgrims into the sanctuary[5] with the purpose of worshiping Yahweh and with the goal of obtaining the life the Torah promises.[6] In this case, the author acts like a "priest" who addresses the people speaking in first person with plural imperatives of come, transgress, multiply, bring, offer, and proclaim. The author's intent presumably is to instruct the audience concerning the cultic ritual to be performed at the shrines.[7] Yet the author does not instruct; instead, he adds a second imperative, "transgress," in verse 4a, which is a command to sin or rebel. The same intensified form of command is repeated by "to transgress more."

"Rebel" or "transgress" is used in Amos more than "sin" (5:12; 9:8, 10) or "iniquity" (3:2). "Rebel" is used in Amos elsewhere in noun form with reference to crime against individuals or their property. It is used only here (in Amos) in its verbal form meaning "to break with Yahweh"[8] or "to rebel against Yahweh"[9] (see 5:4–5, 14–15). We have here in the beginning of the pericope not a genuine call to worship but the prophet's satirical caricature of priestly calls to worship.[10] Cultic zeal and piety can only then be

---

4. John H. Hayes, *Amos: The Eighth-Century Prophet: His Times and His Preaching* (Nashville: Abingdon, 1988), 142; Wolff, *Joel and Amos,* 218. Wolff says, "[T]he oracle [is] . . . a 'parody of a priestly torah.' [That is, the Torah teachings] were cultic instructions addressed in the imperative plural and, secondly, an evaluative concluding statement which could be introduced by *ky* (for, because)" (211).

5. See Am 5:5; Pss 95:6; 96:8; 100:2, 4; Hos 4:15; Is 1:12; and Jl 1:13 for the same idea in the imperative masculine plural; BDB, 97–98.

6. Wolff, *Joel and Amos,* 218.

7. See James Luther Mays, *Amos: A Commentary* (Philadelphia: Westminster Press, 1969), 74.

8. Wolff's meaning (*Joel and Amos,* 219).

9. BDB, 213.

10. Hayes, *Amos,* 142; J. Alberto Soggin, *The Prophet Amos* (London: SCM Press, 1982), 71–72; and Mays, *Amos,* 74.

understood in the negative sense of the words. The satire is therefore directed against the religious and expected activities of the
people. Those who come to the sanctuary end up by sinning in
the very pious and zealous activities they are doing. "Rebel" or
"transgress" may have been Amos's sarcastic invitational word to
Israelite priests and/or Levites to rebel in transgression against Yahweh.[11] Since Amos-B, the Deuteronomistic redactor,[12] is pressing
charges against the upper and ruling class and the religious leaders,
we may assume that the audience the author has in mind does not
include the laity — especially the poor, the afflicted, and the lowly
ones who are being trampled on (see 2:7). His message of indictment to the ruling class thus becomes simultaneously a message of
comfort and hope to the lower class; the sentence of death to the
oppressors becomes a message of liberation to the oppressed.

Whether the author is saying that merely attending the sanctuaries constitutes transgression, or that the incorrect practice
of the cult constitutes transgression, or both, as the word "and
transgress" indicates, needs to be carefully examined later in this
chapter. It is sufficient here to note that the same parody and
judgment are intensified and repeated in the words "and multiply
transgression/rebellion."

Because of the repeated use of judgment terminology, many
scholars understand this pericope as a *ryb*-pattern ("lawsuit")
against the "fertility cult"; the author turned the "fertility-cult
clause" into the form of cultic instruction.[13] However, Brueggemann understands the pericope as a specific indictment against
abuse of the cultic act of covenant making, not against cultic ac-

---

11. Proposed by Douglas Stuart, *Hosea-Jonah,* Word Biblical Commentary
(Waco, Tex.: Word, 1987), 337.

12. Amos-A is the prophet who appealed to the northerners not to go to Bethel,
and Amos-B is the Deuteronomistic historian.

13. Wolff, *Joel and Amos,* 211–12; M. O. Boyle, "The Covenant Lawsuit of the
Prophet Amos 3:1–4:13," *Vetus Testamentum* 21 (1971): 349–51. Boyle proposes
that Am 5:21 is also a "fertility-cult clause" (351). Boyle mentions that the OT
covenant lawsuit as well as the extrabiblical lawsuit proceeding from the epic of
Tukulti-Ninurtal expresses the uselessness of recourse to ritual sacrifice as a result
of legal prosecution (Is 1:13–15; Mi 6:6–7; Ps 1:8–13; Jer 2:2–28; Dt 32:16–17,
etc.). He would interpret 4:4–5 as collective Israel sinning against the first Sinaitic
commandment and sees the law at issue as apodictic rather than casuistic. Boyle,
"The Covenant Lawsuit of the Prophet Amos 3:1–4:13," 349–51.

tivities in general.[14] Unlike other scholars, Brueggemann argues that 4:4–13 is a liturgy of covenant renewal; verses 4–5 are to him a "denunciation of false covenant-making which adheres to covenant places, covenant times, and covenant actions... without meaningful covenant relation." He substantiates his point by observing that: (*a*) the shrines of Bethel and Gilgal are commonly acknowledged as sites of covenant renewal; (*b*) the satirical language employed in verses 4–13 "refers to the perversion of the Sinai covenant tradition in the linguistic shift from 'the third morning on the third day' (Ex 19:11, 16; 24:2, 4) to 'every morning and every three days' (Amos 4:4)"; (*c*) the "sacrifice" (Am 4:4) used here is the covenant sacrifice par excellence of Ex 24:5. Thus, he sees the purpose of the unit verses 4–13 as "not destruction but renewed covenant."[15]

However, it is difficult to substantiate Brueggemann's points because there are no examples in the book of Amos of a discussion of covenant renewal and, most importantly, because the context of the pericope suggests no invitation to repentance but instead implies that the divine judgment is imminent and inescapable (see 4:6–13). Wolff is certainly right in his analysis of the language and style of the pericope, and in his analysis of the relation between 4:4–5 and 4:6–11. He concludes that Amos is not celebrating the liturgy of a covenant renewal as Reventlow and Brueggemann would argue.[16] Surely, the goal of the satirical priestly instruction here is condemnation instead of the life that the Torah promises.

Bethel and Gilgal: Religious Schism

Why is it that Bethel and Gilgal are mentioned and turned into puns? The historical and theological significance of Bethel and Gilgal may provide an answer.[17] Bethel, about 18 kilometers (11

---

14. Brueggemann, "Amos 4:4–13 and Israel's Covenant Worship," 9.

15. Brueggemann, "Amos 4:4–13 and Israel's Covenant Worship," 9.

16. Wolff, *Joel and Amos*, 214.

17. Hans M. Barstad, *The Religious Polemics of Amos* (Leiden: E. J. Brill, 1984), 49–54; Stuart, *Hosea-Jonah*, 337; Wolff, *Joel and Amos*, 219; Hayes, *Amos*, 142–43; Erling Hammershaimb, *The Book of Amos: A Commentary*, trans. John Sturdy (Oxford: Basil Blackwell, 1970), 68; Hans-Joachim Kraus, *Worship in Is-*

miles) north of Jerusalem,[18] was inaugurated as a sanctuary by Jacob (Gn 28:10–22), though Abraham earlier had first pitched a
tent and built an altar there (Gn 12:8). It remained a worship center after the conquest (Jgs 20:18). Samuel judged there (1 Sm 7:16).
With the breakup of the Solomonic state, Bethel was made the chief
sanctuary of the northern kingdom by Jeroboam I when the north
declared its independence from Jerusalem and the Davidic family
(1 Kgs 12:26–33). Under Jeroboam I, it became a rival of Jerusalem, as implied in Am 7:13; its priest Amaziah named it "the king's
sanctuary . . . and the temple of the kingdom."[19]

Gilgal, 30 kilometers (20 miles) east southeast of Bethel on the
edge of Jericho, was the first place the Israelites pitched camp
after the crossing of the Jordan (see Jos 4:19–5:15; Gilgal literally
means "stone circle"). It was the site of Saul's anointment as king
(1 Samuel 11). By the eighth century, it apparently had replaced
Dan as a northern pilgrimage site of sanctuary (see Am 5:5; Hos
4:15; 9:15; 12:11).

Clearly, one could not name two more hallowed and venerable
places for worship of Yahweh than Bethel and Gilgal. The often
suggested idea that the author is accusing Israel of participating
in the syncretistic cult of the Canaanites at Bethel and Gilgal has
no support in the book of Amos, including the pericope at hand.
Our greatest task in exegeting this pericope, then, is to determine
whether the author is attacking the illegitimate, local, and rival
cult at Bethel and Gilgal, or whether he is just attacking the improper manner and motives of the cultic activities at the legitimate
shrines at Bethel and Gilgal. Auld says that Bethel and Gilgal have
no significance except for their accessibility to wordplay:

---

rael: A Cultic History of the Old Testament, trans. Geoffrey Buswell (Richmond:
John Knox Press, 1966), 146–65.

18. Bethel is 40 kilometers (25 miles) south of Samaria. The old sanctuary lay
east of the town at Burj Beitin. See Wolff, Joel and Amos, 219; Philip J. King, Amos,
Hosea, Micah: An Archaeological Commentary (Philadelphia: Westminster Press,
1988), 40–41.

19. "The other royally designated national shrine in Israel was at Dan far to
the north at the headwaters of the Jordan River. In Amos's day, Dan was probably
already in Syrian hands" (Hayes, Amos, 143).

It was simple to suggest a mischievous connection between *glgl* and the Hebrew verb *glh,* "to be exiled." Then Bethel was either a near neighbour to or an alternative name for a place called Beth-On; and the Hebrew spelling of that name *'wn* could be misunderstood for the noun *'awen* meaning "trouble."[20]

That explanation seems unlikely. Most scholars say the author is accusing Israel's cult of worshiping at the wrong place, in a wrong manner, and for wrong motives. Coote offers the best explanation in terms of literary-composition theory,[21] for there is more in the naming of Bethel and Gilgal than Auld has offered. Coote persuasively argues that Amos, the stage-A prophet, could not have appealed to northerners not to go to Bethel. Coote contends that Am 4:4–5 has been recomposed by a Deuteronomistic historian (i.e., Amos-B) who takes Josiah's destruction of the altar at Bethel to be the ultimate vindication of the altar in Jerusalem. Thus, the Deuteronomistic writer opposes the counter "house of God" (Beth-el) revived during the schism (see 1 Kgs 12:32–13:3; 2 Kgs 23:15–16) when he mentions Bethel. Josiah's reform not only purified the cult at Bethel but also centralized the cult at Jerusalem. The Torah document he found had stipulated that the one single people of God were to worship one single God at one single place (Dt 12:5).[22] In other words, in Amos-B's period Bethel and Gilgal represent the strife which existed between support for Jeroboam II at Bethel and Pekah at Gilgal.[23] This opposition between Jerusalem and Bethel is a seventh-century issue, as the Deuteronomistic history makes clear. As Coote states, in the view of Amos-B "Yahweh's cult in Jerusalem precludes the cult of Bethel." Such exclusion "is akin to the deuteronomistic view that

---

20. A. Graeme Auld, *Amos* (Sheffield: JSOT Press, 1986), 64.

21. Soggin, *Amos,* 72; Stuart, *Hosea-Jonah,* 337–38.

22. See Robert B. Coote, *Amos among the Prophets: Composition and Theology* (Philadelphia: Fortress Press, 1981), 50–51; Bernhard Lang, *Monotheism and the Prophetic Minority: An Essay in Biblical History and Sociology* (Sheffield: Almond Press, 1983), 23, 31, on monotheism or Yahwism.

23. See *Israelite and Judaean History,* ed. John H. Hayes and J. Maxwell Miller (Philadelphia: Westminster Press, 1977), 425–30.

Yahweh is to be worshiped in Jerusalem alone, and that it does not come directly from the prophet Amos."[24]

The first charge of Amos we can infer from this pericope, therefore, is that the cult active at Bethel and Gilgal, in the mind of Amos-B, represents the religious division and strife imposed on the Israelite society by the ruling class.

Sacrifice and Offering: Religious Indulgence

The first accusation is to be seen in the overzealousness and excessiveness of sacrifices the worshipers bring to Bethel and Gilgal. Wolff argues that the *hiphil* form of "to bring" (*bw'*) designates the process of sacrifice and offering as a whole.[25] In verse 4b, Amos commands the people to bring their sacrifices in the morning and their tithes on the third day. Stuart, Soggin, Mays, Brueggemann, and the RSV suggest that "morning" and "third day" should be read with a distributive sense, to be translated as "every morning" and "every third day," respectively.[26] If that is so, we can explain the accusation in any of the following three ways: (*a*) the author exaggerates the situation in order to magnify the parody (see 1 Sm 1:3, 7, 21, which speak of a sacrifice once a year, while according to Dt 26:12 the tithes were presented only in the third year, the year of the tithes); (*b*) the author places another charge against the worshipers because they pervert the covenant tradition or requirement; and, (*c*) despite the intense and zealous sacrifice, the worship of the people is still not acceptable by Yahweh. The translations of BDB, Hayes, Hammershaimb, and Wolff — "in the morning" and "on the third day" — are more plausible,[27] for the reasons that: (*a*) the singular form of "morning" in Hebrew is used to mean "on the morning" while the plural form is used always to mean "every morning" (see Is 33:2; Pss 73:14; 101:8; and Lam 3:23); (*b*) the usual custom of pilgrimage is to offer sacrifice the day after the ar-

---

24. Coote, *Amos,* 53.

25. Wolff, *Joel and Amos,* 219. See BDB, 99, which does not explain explicitly.

26. Stuart, *Hosea-Jonah,* 338; Soggin, *Amos,* 71; Brueggemann, "Amos 4:4–13 and Israel's Covenant Worship," 9; Mays, *Amos,* 75.

27. BDB, 134, 400 (the Hebrew preposition *l* means "on" or "at"); Hayes, *Amos,* 143; Hammershaimb, *Amos,* 69; Wolff, *Joel and Amos,* 219; (*b*) the

rival in the early morning and to pay the tithe on the third day, which is two days after the arrival; and, (c) the irony is fostered more by a seemingly perfect, normal routine of sacrifice than by an explicitly stated perversion of sacrificing.

"Sacrifice" (*zibḥēykem* is a slaughtered sacrifice. It could be a peace offering (Leviticus 3; 7:11ff.) in which part of the offering is eaten as a sacred meal of communion with the deity.[28] It could also be a thanksgiving freewill offering for well-being, or in fulfillment of a vow (Lv 7:11–18). Either way, such an occasion is usually a time of conspicuous bacchanalian expression of the worshipers' well-being. The priests often receive the breast and right thigh of the sacrifice and only the fat is burned on the altar (Lv 7:28–36); the remainder of the sacrifice is returned to the worshipers for their consumption within a few days of the slaughtering.[29]

The reference to bringing of tithes[30] on the third day could imply that this is the special day for their presentation. In the book of the covenant (Exodus 21–23) there is no prescription about tithes, but Deuteronomy (12:6f., 17f.; 14:22f.; 26:12ff.) contains detailed rules. The tithe, which has an ancient connection with the shrine of Bethel (Gn 28:22),[31] was a tenth of the annual yield of the land, which the Israelite was to bring to a sanctuary and use in the festival meals before the Lord (Dt 14:22–29; see 1 Sm 8:15, 17).[32] It was probably the Deuteronomic (see 14:22–29) kind of tithe which was consumed by the worshipers in Amos's time (except in the third year when it went to the Levites and the poor).

The next ritual is "offering." Here the Hebrew word (*wĕqattēr*) is *piel* infinitive absolute, which is used as a finite verb and has the same meaning as the other surrounding imperatives. Verse 5a is an elaboration of the same sacrificial system stated in verse 4. "Of-

---

28. Mays, *Amos*, 75; BDB, 257–58. For extensive and recent writings on sacrifices and offerings, see Gary Anderson, *Sacrifices and Offerings in Ancient Israel* (Missoula, Mont.: Scholars Press, 1987).

29. Hayes, *Amos*, 144.

30. BDB, 798.

31. A legend about Jacob was told to justify the giving of tithes at Bethel (see Gn 28:18–22). Nothing is said in this story, however, about the time for bringing the tithes.

32. Mays, *Amos*, 75; see J. Petersen, *Israel*, vols. 3–4 (London and Copenhagen, 1940), 307ff., and Hammershaimb, *Amos*, 69.

fering" is a technical term which refers to any offering by fire,[33] sometimes parallel to "sacrifice" (e.g., Hos 4:13; see Lv 17:5, 6). But here the *piel* stem is used to indicate its derogatory usage, since the *hiphil* stem is normally used for legitimate offering. Amos associates *qtr* explicitly to offerings "from that which is leavened" (see Ex 23:18).[34] Stuart argues that the grammar of verse 5a makes "leaven" the object of "burn," to imply that the worshipers violated the sacrificial law of Lv 2:11 (see 6:14–17).[35] It would then seem that *mḥmṣ* must mean "without unleavened bread" with a privative sense — but that is unlikely. Hammershaimb may offer a better explanation:

> "[A] sacrifice of praise" or "a thank-offering" is, as appears from the name, a sacrifice that is offered in thankfulness. Lev 7:11f. prescribes that if one brings a peace offering as a thanksgiving, one should offer apart from the sacrificial animal unleavened cakes, etc. This is corroborated by the prohibition of leaven in Lev 2:11, see Ex 23:18. On the other hand Lev 7:13 and 23:17 speak of leavened bread. The passage in Amos shows that at this time the use of leavened bread in connection with the sacrificial animal was regarded as the best manner of making a sacrifice.... Also, unleavened bread is of course an older custom than leavened bread. At the time of Amos, however, the new and more refined custom of using leavened bread had gained admittance to the cult. The contradictory provisions in the laws come therefore from different times.[36]

This suggests that the thanksgiving offering is not a different kind of sacrifice, but the use of the sacrifice of peace offering to

---

33. See *qtr,* meaning "the smell of sacrifice" or "incense." See Soggin, *Amos,* 71; Hammershaimb, *Amos,* 70.

34. LXX has a different reading: "They read the law openly, publicly," probably arising from a wrong reading of the Hebrew, not a different original. The expression fits well and should not be corrected to "unleavened bread" (*Gesenius' Hebrew Grammar,* ed. E. Kautzsch, trans. A. E. Cowley [hereafter GKC], 119y) as Snaith (*Amos,* 2 vols. [London, 1945–46]) would prefer. See Soggin, *Amos,* 71.

35. Leavened bread was part of the peace offering (Lv 7:13), but it was not to be burned. See Stuart, *Hosea-Jonah,* 338; Mays, *Amos,* 75.

36. Hammershaimb, *Amos,* 70.

praise God for blessings (Lv 7:12–15; 22:29–30). The freewill offering, like the thanksgiving offering, is a voluntary sacrifice and a peace offering which the worshipers made on their own initiative to express devotion.[37] The Israelites "proclaim loud and clear...and love (to do these rituals)." The publicizing of freewill offerings refers to making known such offerings, and inviting others to participate in the "gala barbecue"[38] rituals, which only satisfied their own desire and were not congruent with God's will. No wonder the author says those sacrifices and tithes are not God's but theirs. Such offerings are not pleasing to God. As Hayes points out, those rituals are so despicable before Yahweh and the prophet because

> The sacrifices Amos mentions were sacrifices primarily consumed by the worshipers.... The context indicates that the sacrifices were condemned as another example of the self-indulgence of the ruling establishment (see 3:15; 4:1).[39]

The God of Israel reproaches not only a schismatic cult but, more importantly, also the cultic participants who seek their own love or pleasure in the name of religion.[40] They think that religion will save them, but they are wrong, because their cultic activities themselves are transgressions in the eyes of God. "For so you love to do, O people of Israel!" points out the shocking reality of their love. In the usual priestly Torah the imperatives would be followed by a "for" clause of promise based on the person and will of

---

37. Mays, *Amos*, 75; and Stuart, *Hosea-Jonah*, 338; BDB, 621.

38. Hayes, *Amos*, 144.

39. Hayes, *Amos*, 144–45. Hayes explains: "We can infer that the lower classes of Israelite society were probably incapable of such sacrificial extravagance because of the expense involved, particularly if they were already under heavy taxation" (145).

40. This is to disagree with James M. Ward (*Amos and Isaiah: Prophets of the Word of God* [Nashville: Abingdon, 1969], 139), who argues that what Amos attacks here is the Palestinian cultic system. "Worship at the Palestinian sanctuaries during the period of the Israelite monarchy was an amalgam of customs derived from ancient tribal religion, the cults of local Canaanite deities, and the covenantal traditions of the Israelite confederacy. The basic system of daily and monthly sacrifices, which were supported out of temple revenues and royal subsidies, and of occasional private sacrifices was not distinctively Yahwistic. Everything cultic that Amos repudiated is attributable to this sacrificial system."

Yahweh. Here, the "for" clause is an ugly revelation of YHWH's rejection and judgment.

Succoth and Love: Social Injustice and Moral Indifference

Is Amos-B speaking of general religious activity or the special fall Succoth celebration? One cannot know with certainty, but Coote and Hayes identify the pilgrimage sacrificial celebration as the fall pilgrimage festival Succoth (Tabernacles or Booths)/Ingatherings or Asiph (see Ex 23:16, 34:22).[41] These three names refer to one of Israel's great annual festivals, celebrated with joy in autumn at the completion of the agricultural year, to recall Israel's wilderness pilgrimage and, apparently, as a renewal of the covenant.[42] This fall festival was a seven-day affair (see Ex 19:10–16; Hos 6:1–2) which was observed from the fifteenth to the twenty-second of the seventh month, Tishri (1 Kgs 12:32–33). The first day of the seventh month of the festival was the "day of the king" and the beginning of a new year.[43]

> [I]t was during succoth that Solomon transferred the ark to the newly built sanctuary of Yahweh in Jerusalem (1 Kings 8:2, 65). Likewise it was during succoth that Jeroboam I sought to dedicate the reinstituted cult at his revived sanctuary at Bethel (1 Kings 12:32–33). Since succoth commemorates the dedication of both rival sanctuaries, there is

---

41. Many commentators suspect vv. 4–5 must have been a speech delivered during a festival assembly (Mays, *Amos,* 74; Hayes, *Amos,* 142; Hammershaimb, *Amos,* 68; Ward, *Amos and Isaiah,* 140). But Coote and Hayes identify 4:4–5 as B-stage, which concerns Bethel and religio-political opposition between Bethel and Jerusalem as cult sanctuaries, and which addressed the far wider range of people who participated in the Succoth festival (Coote, *Amos,* 48, and Hayes, *Amos,* 38, 145, 174). See Kraus, *Worship in Israel,* 60–70, 108, 141–45.

42. It is both a pilgrimage festival to commemorate the wandering of Israel and a harvest festival. Whether originally it was an agricultural feast borrowed from the Canaanites (so Wellhausen)/Babylon (so Auerbach, "Die Feste im alten Israel," *Vetus Testamentum* 8 [1958]: 1ff.), or from the beginning an Israelite cultic practice (so Kraus, *Worship in Israel*) is debatable.

43. Hayes, *Amos,* 143–44; and Coote, *Amos,* 53. If Amos had this day in mind, he would have been referring to the fall festival of 750, according to Hayes's historical reconstruction.

no better moment to represent the conflict between them. Succoth symbolizes the opposition of Jerusalem and Bethel.[44]

Hayes's historical construction shows that Amos was preaching at the time of the fall festival in the year 750–749 B.C.E., "which witnessed the coronation of Pekah as a rival king to Jeroboam II."[45] If so, then, Am 4:4–5 condemns the two competitive observances of the same festival, which contribute to the further polarization and disintegration of Israelite society (5:18–27 also suggests that). The term "Israel" in this pericope would then be referring to the whole nation Israel and not just the northern kingdom. The religious, moral, and social corruption and divisiveness of the whole nation stand under condemnation by the prophet Amos (4:4–5).

Succoth also provided the occasion for celebrating the culmination of the entire agricultural year with new wine and crops. It was a time to celebrate harvest. Perhaps the author is accusing the Israelites of delighting in abundant sacrifices and failing to turn truly to Yahweh (4:6–11). James M. Ward contends that "in the context of the book as a whole this failure must be interpreted as social injustice and moral indifference."[46] And that is the *third* accusation of the author, perhaps the most pivotal point of this pericope and of the whole book. For what is described in this pericope is an expected and required form of worshiping Yahweh. Yahweh wants the worshipers to be more concerned about social justice than about worship.

This third accusation must be understood also in the covenantal term "love" which Amos uses. By using this term, Amos reveals that Israel's supposed love is not true love for Yahweh or true ethical responsibility as required by the covenantal relationship, but is merely compliance with the sacrificial system.[47] Israel is guilty of taking bribes (Am 5:11b, 12), committing adultery (Am 2:7b; 2:1, 5; 5:7), "turning justice into bitterness" (Am 5:7, 6:12a), per-

---

44. Coote, *Amos*, 57. Hayes also points out, "Worship at Bethel and Gilgal at this particular time would have had strong political implications in a country bordering on civil war" (144).

45. Hayes, *Amos*, 38. Though I do not accept Hayes's literary composition of the book, his historical construction of Amos's preaching at 750 may be correct.

46. Ward, *Amos and Isaiah*, 138.

47. See Stuart, *Hosea-Jonah*, 338.

secuting the righteous (Am 5:7, 6:12), and distorting the truth (Am 5:10b). Consequently, the leaders have brought "a reign of terror" (Am 6:3) to the land, the innocent are deprived of justice (Am 5:12b), the poor are treated like dust (Am 2:7a) and forced to give up their basic needs such as grain (Am 5:11, 4:1), and the helpless are swindled (Am 5:11). The prophet also condemns the rich women and greedy landowners who are living in complacency and vanity (Am 4:1; 6:1–7). They have secured magnificent homes, comfortable beds, abundant treasure, and feastly food (Am 6:4), but they forget the poor and the needy (Am 6:6–7). The moral injustice shown by the immediate context and the message of the whole book is clear. The rich ritual and sacrificial system cannot substitute for the requirement to do social justice to the oppressed, the poor, and the innocent. God is concerned not with sacrifice but with justice and righteousness (5:21–24). God requires the Israelites to do the covenantal deeds of goodness, mercy, justice, and righteousness for the society.

The Will of Yahweh and Indictments of the Prophet

The conclusion in verse 5b implies that the ritual arises not from the will of Yahweh but from worshipers' self-love. Not that rituals and sacrifices themselves are not pleasing to God, but that the Israelites are using the guise of a rich ritualistic cult to cover their transgressions of social injustice and divisiveness. If social justice prevailed in the land, the rich rituals and sacrifices would indeed be pleasing in the eyes of Yahweh. But those perfectly required and acceptable acts of worship are rejected and condemned because of the social injustices that wrecked the whole society (as 5:21–24 explicitly states). Wolff contends that what Amos "has in mind here is probably the substitution of cultic offerings for justice towards the oppressed (cf. 5:21–24 and the oracles immediately preceding ours in 3:9–4:3!)"[48] No wonder that Yahweh says, "Seek me and

---

48. Wolff, *Amos*, 219. So Auld (*Amos*, 60) sees social and religious indictment interrelated in passages as follows: 4:1–3 — vv. 4–5; 5:7 — vv. 4–6; and 5:10–13 — vv. 14–15. Coote explains the emerging of the religious theme as stage B and the social theme as stage A.

live; but do not seek Bethel, and do not enter into Gilgal . . . for Gilgal shall surely go into exile, and Bethel shall come to nought" (Am 5:5). But what is "seek me"? To seek Yahweh is to hate evil and to seek and do good (5:14). Apparently, there is nothing wrong with the cultic activities per se, but the message of the book in 3:14; 5:5–15, 21–24; and 7:12 seems to imply that the author (at least Amos-B) is condemning not only the disunified cult at Bethel and Gilgal, but also more seriously (and here especially Amos-A) the social injustice which the ruling class and religious leaders have perpetrated in the guise of sacrifice and offerings. In 5:21–24, which has similar but more explicit accusations regarding feasts, assemblies, sacrifices, offerings, and religious songs, Amos states what instead is required of the people: "But[49] let justice roll along[50] like the waters and righteousness like never-failing streams."[51]

Judgment and indictment are given by the prophet. But they also belong to Yahweh, as the oracle formula "says the Lord God" indicates.[52] Am 4:4–5 indicts Israel for its cultic practices at the wrong places, in the wrong manner, and from the wrong perspective. Israel has not honored the Oneness of God. Israel has profaned the Name of God by religious and social strife and division. Israel is guilty also of the excessive celebration of Succoth which ends in self-indulgence and self-love. Israel is charged with the crime of

---

49. A sharp contrast: rather than the sacrifices, feasts, and music, something altogether different must be there. Here is an explicit requirement of the people, unlike the pericope in 4:4–5.

50. Hayes contends that Amos is attacking the cultic activities at Bethel and Gilgal which represent both the "polarization and disintegration of Israelite society" and the neglect of social justice. Thus Yahweh is demanding justice and righteousness for proper order in society (*Amos*, 174).

51. The two metaphors employed to describe the desire for justice and righteousness draw on imagery associated with water; a central motif of the fall festival was the coming of the autumn rains and the renewal of streams (Hayes, *Amos*, 174).

52. The formula occurs a total of twenty-one times in Amos, thirteen times as a concluding formula (2:11, 16; 3:15; 4:3, 5, 6, 8, 9, 10, 11; 9:7, 8, 12), three times in a medial position (3:10; 6:14; 8:3), and five times with other formulas as part of an oracular introduction (3:13; 6:8; 8:9, 11; 9:13). The last eight usages are later redactions; the first thirteen are genuine usages of Amos's old oracles. The formula is not frequently attested elsewhere prior to Jeremiah (169 times) and Ezekiel (85 times). Even if it is attested, it is not as Israelite cultic proclamation but is associated with human speakers (Nm 24:3–4, 15–16, and 2 Sm 23:1, etc.) (Wolff, *Amos*, 143.)

loving the sacrificial systems and their details without loving the covenantal relationship and the ethical requirement of the covenant. Israel has received the oracle of judgment; it is the oracle of the Lord. There is no chance of repentance and return given in this pericope. It is an oracle of judgment and indictment only.

Amos and Confucius

Am 4:4–5, as we have seen, is a satirical indictment against a divided Israelite society which has masked social injustice in the guise of a rich Yahwist cult. Reading Am 4:4–5 along with Am 5:21–24, God's requirements for the leaders and society are explicitly clear. The basis of social justice and order is theocentric and human-oriented. The prophetic view of and concern for social justice and social order stem from the prophets' pious devotion to God and their caring love for people. In other words, religion pleasing to Yahweh is not congruent with our popular understanding of worship as "attending church," but a more radical expectation of social righteousness and order. The question we are interested in is: Has the theocentricity of Amos's message any parallel in Confucius's "anthropocentric" teaching?

First, we note that Confucius was deeply concerned with humanity in the ceremony of li ("propriety")[53] and jen ("love"), and not the ceremony of force or injustice. And that social mandate, according to Confucius, is that of Heaven.[54] Traditionally, Confucius's thought has been interpreted as totally optimistic humanism without any reference to divinity or spirituality. In this chapter, a different position will be taken, one akin to Herbert Fingarette's thesis in his book called Confucius — The Secular as Sacred. Fingarette argues not only that Confucius's teaching originated from the concept of Heaven, but also that his notion of holiness of life

---

53. Li is "the specifically humanizing form of the dynamic relation of man-to-man" (Herbert Fingarette, Confucius — The Secular as Sacred [New York: Harper & Row, 1972], 7.

54. For Confucius, "Heaven" means the purposeful Supreme Being. See Fung Yu-lan, History of Chinese Philosophy, 2d ed., trans. Derk Bodde (Princeton: Princeton University Press, 1952), 1:57, 31ff.

teaches that the secular is the place where the sacred is manifested. Suggesting that the concept of *T'ien* or Heaven is analogous to the Jewish/Christian concept of Yahweh is, to say the least, an enormous task. But it is not difficult at this point to see both Amos's and Confucius's appeal for social order and righteousness as being God or Heaven-oriented.

In studying the *Four Books* of Confucius, one can also see that Confucius's line of thought moves from the Doctrine of the Mean (*Chung-yung*), to the Great Learning, to the *Analects,* and then to other writings, for what is said in the later works presupposes ideas found in the Doctrine of the Mean. That suggests that Confucius's chief concern regarding human relationships builds on his understanding of what it means to know and to actualize mandates of Heaven. What Confucius teaches about interpersonal relationships is implied by his understanding of actualizing the decree of heaven in human nature and personhood.[55]

Confucius assumes human-relatedness is mandated by Heaven, given by God. That is, the distinctive human quality is endowed by Heaven. Milton Chiu explains, "While Heaven is the metaphysical source and basis of the moral quality of human beings, epistemologically, human beings know Heaven through the morality and rationality in human nature."[56] This idea is parallel to the prophet Amos's belief and emphasis on the need for righteousness and justice.

The prophet Amos believed that the personal God was unique in God's very essence — goodness, justice, and righteousness. This can be inferred from Amos's belief that God requires justice and righteousness from the people (5:24) and that God asks the people to seek God and live (5:6), that is, to seek good and not evil (5:14) and to establish justice. As such, God desires a land of justice and righteousness (Am 5:24). God hates robbery and iniquity, and God wills to give justice to the orphan, the weak, the afflicted,

---

55. *Chung-yung* (The Doctrine of the Mean) says, "What Heaven has conferred is called the nature; an accordance with this nature is called the path of duty; the regulation of this path is called instruction." See James Legge's translation and notes: *The Four Books* (Taipei: Culture Book Co., 1975), 43.

56. Milton M. Chiu, *The Tao of Chinese Religion* (Lanham, Md.: University Press of America, 1984), 184.

the destitute, and the needy. Consequently, the prophet would not prophesy on behalf of the Lord, the God of righteousness, and then stand aloof when the defenseless, the lowly, and the poor were ill-treated (Am 6:1, 3–7; 2:6–7). Note that "righteous" and "justice" are placed in synonymous parallelism in Am 5:24, showing that the prophets viewed "being righteous" as "doing justice." God condemns the self-complacency and sordid selfishness of the rich ("cows of Bashan") who trample the poor and the lowly like dust.

Since Yahweh was Israel's Maker (especially in the sense of the covenant promise), Israel must identify with the nature of Yah-weh's righteousness and justice in their lives (Am 4:4–5; 5:24). As God had shown God's justice and infinite mercy to God's people, so the people were to respond to God as a nation (Am 3:2) by be-ing righteous. God's mandate to the people is to "let justice roll like the water, and righteousness like a never-failing stream" (5:23–24). In the language of Confucius, God expects human beings who are endowed with the nature of *jen* ("love") to be *jen jen* ("a loving person"); that is the mandate of Heaven.

Second, Confucius believed that the ruling class, especially the king or the emperor, not only should know but should model that mandate of Heaven for all the people. Confucianism teaches that Heaven has endowed humankind with a nature containing the "basic stuff" of goodness, but human beings are unable to do good by themselves. Human nature must be strengthened by the will of Heaven and reinforced by the principles of Heaven in order to do good.[57] The monarchy or kingship is established to promote such good conduct as the people's model. This is one of Heaven's pur-poses. The kings, being entrusted by Heaven with the task of ruling the people, hold a lofty position and a heavy responsibility. The ancient sages invented the writing of the word "king" by drawing three horizontal lines, which were connected through the center by a vertical stroke. The three horizontal lines signify the realms of Heaven, Earth, and humanity, and the central vertical line signifies

---

57. See Chiu, *The Tao of Chinese Religion*, 189. See Chun-chiu Fan-lu, 11.1; and Chien Han Shu, 56.16: "He who does not understand the Decree of Heaven cannot become a superior man."

the interrelationship of the three realms.[58] The king is to model and actualize the mandate of Heaven by committing himself to love.[59]

The warnings and indictments of Amos were geared toward the rich and the ruling class. They had obviously departed from the will of the LORD and not committed themselves to love. What they loved was superficial and outward. They loved to burn sacrifices, but they did not love the common people. Both the prophets of Yahweh and Confucius pinpointed the greatest danger facing religious people: it is possible to profess to love God and yet not love people; both the prophet and Confucius emphasized social justice and proper interpersonal relationships.

Third, morality seems to be more important to Amos and Confucius than one's religiosity. Amos says that God desires our justice and righteousness toward the lowly and the poor more than our worship and sacrifices to God himself (Am 4:4–5). What 4:4–5 describes is a rich and pure Yahwist cult and the expected worship and sacrifice of the people. Why did the prophet condemn that cult? The answer is found in 5:21–24, which implies that the worship of Yahweh should not take precedence over social justice. A similar concern is found in Confucius and his followers. Morality is so crucial to human beings, says Mencius (372–289 B.C.E.), the most distinguished Confucian philosopher next to Confucius himself, that it (moral conduct) is the very thing that differentiates humans from beasts and birds.[60] Morality is the concrete and the best expression of human spirituality.

Rather than ruling with command, threat, or punishment, Confucius proposed ruling with *li* (propriety or ritual), the cultured yet natural pattern of interpersonal relationships that "works through spontaneous coordination rooted in reverent dignity."[61] Holiness in human existence is crucial in life. Confucius sees *te* ("moral") as that which is realized in public when one interacts with others in

---

58. See Chen Li Fu, *The Confucian Way: A New and Systematic Study of The Four Books*, translated from the Chinese by Shih Shun Liu (London: KPI Limited, 1986), 450. Chen says, "He who appreciates the Way of Heaven and Earth in their love of life, he who governs with a view to common existence — he is an advocate of the Kingly Way, of benevolent government" (450).

59. Chiu, *The Tao of Chinese Religion*, 191f.; see Chun-chiu Fan-lu, 11.9.

60. Mencius, 4b, 19.

61. Fingarette, *Confucius*, 8. See *Analects* 2:3, 13:3.

the patterns of *li* ("propriety"), such as reciprocal loyalty, sincerity, and respect. Here, the public is spiritual; the secular is sacred.[62] Fingarette is correct in his observation that "the virtues that Confucius stresses are indeed all dynamic and social. For example, *shu* (mutuality in human relations), *chung* (loyalty) and *hsin* (good trust toward others) — all inherently involve a dynamic relation to other persons. On the other hand, such static and inner virtues as purity or innocence play no role in the *Analects*."[63]

Fourth, both Amos and Confucius see love as the basis of interpersonal relationships and for living out just and righteous lives. Confucius states that what makes human beings human is *jen*, similar to the biblical concept of love. The word *jen* in Chinese is composed of two radicals: "human being" and "two." It connotes all the moral qualities which govern the relationships between two human beings. Etymologically, it is to be translated simply as human-relatedness, but philosophically, human-relatedness should be defined specifically as morality or love. As such, it is the cardinal principle of human relationships.[64]

When "worship and religion" mislead us into believing that we can please God through them and that our iniquities can be overlooked, then worship becomes hypocritical, or — to use Amos's term — it becomes transgression (see Am 4:4–5). From a Chinese perspective we could also say that we have not understood Confucius's teachings of *jen* (love), *li* (propriety), and *te* (moral). We have also not internalized what Fingarette called "the secular as sacred":

> The image of Holy Rite [*li*] as a metaphor of human existence brings foremost to our attention the dimension of the holy in man's existence. There are several dimensions of Holy Rite which culminate in its holiness. Rite brings out forcefully not only the harmony and beauty of social forms, the inherent and ultimate dignity of human intercourse; it brings out also the moral perfection implicit in achieving one's ends by dealing with others as beings of equal dignity, as free co-participants in *li*. Furthermore, to act by ceremony is to be

---

62. Fingarette, *Confucius*, 42–47.
63. Fingarette, *Confucius*, 55.
64. Fung, *History of Chinese Philosophy*, 69–73.

completely open to the other; for ceremony is public, shared, transparent; to act otherwise is to be secret, obscure and devious, or merely tyrannically coercive.[65]

In other words, to be a *jen jen* ("a loving person") is to express oneself in loving action and to participate in the holy as the dimension of all truly human existence. "Human life in its entirety finally appears as one vast, spontaneous and Holy Rite: the community of [hu]man."[66] Faith in God should always find its expression in one's relationship with others in the society. The individual cannot hide from or neglect the social responsibility to care for the poor, the oppressed, widows, and the young. God wants the response of worship. However, justice and righteousness within society must be one's concern prior to worship. Righteousness is not a duty of religion, it is a way of knowing and serving God. To be a *jen jen* ("a loving person") is to be courteous, diligent, loyal, brave, and kind (*Analects* 13:19, 14:5, 17:6) as actualized in public life.

Jen means to love our fellow beings;[67] *jen* means to be conscientious (*chung*) and altruistic (*shu*).[68] *Chung* means literally both "honest to oneself" and "faithful to others." Confucius advised that "desiring to maintain oneself, one should sustain others; desiring to develop oneself, one should develop others." *Shu* means "having a heart like others would have." Confucius taught, "Do not do to others what you do not like yourself." Both *chung* and *shu* are to express the mutuality of practices of *jen*. According to Confucius, *jen* means "to be able to carry five things into practice wherever one goes." These five things are "respect, tolerance, faithfulness, earnestness and gracefulness. With respect you will avoid insult; with tolerance you will win over everyone; with faithfulness men will trust you; with earnestness you will have achievement;

---

65. Fingarette, *Confucius*, 16.

66. Fingarette, *Confucius*, 17. See *Analects* 3:17, 4:5, 6, 8. For a different interpretation of *jen* and *li* in Confucius's thought, see Fingarette, *Confucius*; Fung, *History of Chinese Philosophy*, 72–72, 94; and Tu Wei-ming, *Confucian Thought: Selfhood as Creative Transformation* (New York: State University Press, 1985), 81–92.

67. *Analects* 12:22.

68. *Analects* 4:15.

and with gracefulness you will be fitted to command others."[69] Strictly speaking, *jen,* the way to be human, is neither theocentric nor anthropocentric, but a mutuality of human and Heaven.[70] As such, human responsibility has its transcendent anchorage in God; at the same time, that transcendent anchorage always seeks its expression in the immanent reality of human affairs. The discussion on the connection between Amos's and Confucius's understanding of love and *jen,* respectively, does not mean that they are the same. Amos thinks out of a very personal concept of God/Yahweh, while Confucius thinks out of a rather impersonal concept of *T'ien.* My reading does not intend to employ an easy and slippery move of taking either "love" or "Yahweh" out of their biblical and linguistic settings and applying them elsewhere. My intertextual reading here is to point out similarities in differences and differences in similarities.

Perhaps, through the above comparative study of Amos's message and Confucius's teaching, we have come to perceive words like love and *jen* not as psychological terms or ontological aspects of a human being, but as words which refer to an inclusive virtue or spiritual condition.[71] Mencius says, "Human-heartedness (*jen*) is the mind of human beings; righteousness is the path of human conduct."[72]

In summary, we have noted that according to Amos, Yahweh desires peace and order, not strife and divisiveness, within society. This courageous author not only charges the Israelites with social injustice and excessive ritualistic worship, but he also charges the Israelites with political and religious schism (the latter is the focus of Amos-B). The true and faithful society is one where human beings treat each other as human (*jen*), or, to be more specific, one in which life is lived according to the obligations and privileges of *li,* out of the love and loyalty (*chung*) and respect (*shu*) called for by the human relationships which each has with the other.[73] "Virtue does not exist in isolation; there must be neighbors," says Con-

---

69. Mencius 2a, 6. See Chiu, *The Tao of Chinese Religion,* 181ff.
70. Fingarette, *Confucius,* 60.
71. Fingarette, *Confucius,* 37–38.
72. Mencius, 6a, 11.
73. See Fingarette, *Confucius,* 77–78.

fucius.[74] In the first instance, this link is to the general reciprocal good faith and respect among men (*shu* and *chung*); in the second instance this reciprocal good faith is given a specific content: it is that set of specific social relationships articulated in detail by *li*. In short, where reciprocal good faith and respect are expressed through the specific forms defined in *li*, there is *jen*'s way. Humanity is transformed by participation with others in ceremony which is communal. And that is the mandate of Heaven (or the will of Yahweh), that all may live in righteousness and orderliness in relation to others as a sacred society.

---

74. *Analects* 4:25. See Fingarette, *Confucius*, 42.

_____

Chapter 6

Li and Jen (Torah and Spirit) in Romans

Since Christian faith cannot be meaningful in a cultural vacuum, making every theological revelation and construction an indigenous and a contextual enterprise, this chapter is an attempt to "translate" intelligibly the meaning of Rom 7:14–25 into the Confucian "language" — specifically "for the sake of my brethren, my kinsmen by race," to whom belong not the sonship, the glory, the covenants, the giving of the Torah, but the Christ (see 9:3–4)! In order to construct an indigenous Chinese Christian theology, this chapter will first give a brief survey and critique of interpretations of the pericope. I will then propose an alternative view and grapple with pertinent issues in the pericope to expound and support that view. Finally I will suggest how Confucius's understanding of *T'ien* ("heaven") and cultivating selfhood — especially in terms of *li* (propriety) and *jen* (love) — correspond to the complex Pauline understanding of *nomos* (Torah) and *pneuma* (Spirit) in Romans.

The Purpose of Romans

There are basically two ways of approaching the nature and purpose of the Epistle to the Romans, as Karl P. Donfried has shown; one is to understand Romans as a theological treatise or dissertation in the form of a circular letter, while the other is to perceive Romans as a situational letter addressing a specific audience.[1] This

---

1. Karl P. Donfried, in the book *The Romans Debate* (Minneapolis: Augsburg Publishing House, 1977), has edited and collected essays which represent these two

chapter approximates the view of J. Christiaan Beker who artic-
ulates an alternative interpretation. Beker suggests that Pauline
theology is both "coherent and contingent"; therefore, there is
a "convergence of motivations" in Romans to elicit support for
Paul's mission to Spain *and* to explain the meaning of his gospel
as a way of bridging conflict between the Jews and the Gentiles.[2]
Romans is not Paul's theological treatise, or last will, though Paul
writes systematically and theologically. Rather, it is addressed to a
specific situation within the Roman house churches.

An analysis of the situation behind Romans reveals manifold
purposes. The purpose of Paul's writing surely lies not just in
the Spanish mission. For clearly it is written to address also the
polemical situation in the Roman churches. Paul wrote Romans
approximately in 57 C.E. (probably at Corinth), partly in preparation to visit Jerusalem (Rom 15:25, 30–32; see Acts 21:1–16)
for the offering,[3] but mainly to seek the Roman churches' unity
in support of his gospel mission. The Roman house churches,
which Paul probably knew quite well,[4] were not then unified (see
15:7–13). Relationships within these ethnically, ideologically, and
religiously mixed congregations had produced conflict. Rom 14:1–
15:13[5] suggests that the conflict was between "the weak," the

camps; the former has been argued by T. W. Manson, Günther Bornkamm, and
Robert J. Karris, and the latter by Jacob Jervell, Wolfgang Wiefel, and Donfried
himself.

2. "Paul's thought is geared to a specific situation and...his arguments cannot be divorced from the need of the moment" (*Paul the Apostle: The Triumph of
God in Life and Thought* [Philadelphia: Fortress, 1980], 25; see also 71–74). Recently, A. J. M. Wedderburn has argued in a more inclusive manner than the above
that Paul's writing of Romans has multiple reasons and "a cluster of different interlocking factors" (*The Reasons for Romans* [Edinburgh: T. & T. Clark, 1988],
142).

3. The situation in Jerusalem is not the primary reason why Paul wrote Romans. Rome itself is a dominant factor. The objections to the latter theory are
answered by Joel Marcus successfully in "The Circumcision and the Uncircumcision
in Rome," *New Testament Studies* 35 (1989): 70–71.

4. In chap. 16, Paul greets most of the thirty individuals by name, which
enables Paul to write to their local, specific situation. However, T. W. Manson disagrees and suggests that chap. 16 is an addendum to a letter originally sent to the
church of Ephesus; K. P. Donfried and R. E. Brown have successfully given a rebuttal to Manson's argument. See T. W. Manson, "St. Paul's Letter to the Romans —
and Others," in *The Romans Debate*, 1–16.

5. For a discussion on the literary problem proposed by R. J. Karris on these

Law-observant Jewish Christians, and "the strong," the Law-free Gentile Christians. While the "weak" might have included a few Gentile Christians who practiced the law, and the "strong" might have included a few Jewish Christians who felt freedom from the law because of the advent of the Messiah,[6] the generalization is still applicable. Rom 15:1–6 and 7–13 show that "Gentile" and "Jewish" are not only ethnic, but also Law-contingent terms. That is, most of the Jewish Christians at Rome[7] laid emphasis on the traditional observances of their ancestral faith;[8] most of the Gentile Christians felt it unnecessary to subscribe to the Torah because they were now in Christ.

The ugliness of this conflict is seen in the name-calling between Jewish and Gentile Christians. The Jewish Christians used the "circumcision/uncircumcision" terminology, while the Gentile Christians used the "weak/strong" terminology.[9] Fourteen of the thirty-five instances of "circumcision" and eleven of the twenty uses of "uncircumcision" in the New Testament appear in Romans. Marcus surveys these two terms against the rabbinic usage of *mîlâ* (circumcised penis) and *'orlâ* (foreskin) and concludes that "circumcision/uncircumcision" should be translated concretely as "circumcised penis (glans)/foreskin," rather than with the stative abstractions "state of being circumcised/uncircumcised."[10] These "circumcision/uncircumcision" terms are epithets designating groups of people in Romans (2:26–27; 3:30; 4:9; 15:8) for a dual purpose, both to insult others and to lift up one's own pride.[11]

---

passages and Marcus's rebuttal, see R. J. Karris, "The Occasion of Romans," in *The Romans Debate*, 75–99; and Marcus, "The Circumcision," 70–71.

6. As suggested by U. Wilckens, *Der Brief an die Römer* (Zurich: Benziger. 1978–82), 3:111–15. See also R. E. Brown, "Not Jewish Christianity," *Catholic Biblical Quarterly* 45 (1983): 74–79; and J. P. Meier, *Antioch and Rome: New Testament Cradles of Catholic Christianity* (New York: Paulist, 1983), 1–9.

7. The Jewish Community at Rome began to emerge not long after the accession of Claudius.

8. For example, some Roman writers tell us so (Suetonius, *Augustus* 76.2).

9. For detailed analysis, see Marcus, "The Circumcision," 73–81.

10. Marcus, "The Circumcision," 75. See M. Jastrow, *A Dictionary of the Targumim, the Talmud Babli and Yerushalmi, and the Midrashic Literature*, 2 vols. (New York: Judaica, 1982), 1:774.

11. Marcus, "The Circumcision," 75; and Wilckens, *Römer*, 1:155, n. 398. Cf. K. L. Schmidt, "*Akrobystia*," TDNT 1:225–26.

Notice also that the use of "circumcision" in Rom 2:25–27 is preceded by a citation of Is 52:5 in Rom 2:24, "which speaks of the
name of God being *blasphemed* among the Gentiles because of
the Jews."[12] The basic problem in the Roman congregations was
therefore one group's assertion of superiority over the other.

The dominant issue Paul deals with in this epistle is this Jewish-
Gentile Christian relationship of superiority (see 1:16; 2:25–29;
1:7; 8:33; 9:6–13; 11:5–7, 28–32), which he addresses by talking
about the righteousness of God. When Paul writes that both Jews
and Gentiles need the righteousness of God he is not talking about
the individual's status before God. As a pastoral theologian working in the concreteness of a missionary situation, he exhorts the
Roman Christians to live and cooperate for the sake of the Spanish mission and in order for both Jews and Gentiles (11:17–24)
to eventually worship God together (15:8–12). Indeed, God is the
God of Jews and Gentiles (see Rom 3:29).

Current Debate regarding the Interpretation of Romans 7:14–25

It is logical to assume that Rom 7:14–25 is part of the larger response of Paul — "righteousness of God" — to the Jewish-Gentile
Christians in Rome. It is "the most discussed and fought over
part"[13] of Romans. The following views represent only some of
the major scholarly interpretations in the debate.

The first interpretation views the pericope as describing the
pre-conversion or the non-Christian experience of humanity living
under law and struggling with sin and law. Scholars holding this
view vary in their interpretations.[14] Within this view are those who

---

12. Marcus, "The Circumcision," 79.

13. Anders Nygren, *Commentary on Romans*, trans. Carl C. Rasmussen (Philadelphia: Muhlenberg Press, 1949), 284.

14. Scholars who suggest this view are C. H. Dodd, *The Epistle of Paul to the
Romans* (New York: Harper, 1970), 125–26; W. G. Kümmel, *Man in the New Testament* (London: Epworth, 1963), 49ff.; Karl Kertelge, "Exegetische Überlegungen
zum Verständnis der paulinischen Anthropologie nach Römer 7," *Zeitschrift für
die Neutestamentliche Wissenschaft und die Kunde der älteren Kirche* 62 (1971):
112; and J. A. Ziesler ("The Role of the Tenth Commandment in Romans 7,"

interpret the pericope as the non-Christian experience of the pre-converted Paul who was unable to break through the power of sin and flesh to fulfill God's requirements.[15] Others contend that Paul here is describing the universal human experience under law, sin, and death before one's conversion and as seen from the vantage of one's new existence in Christ.[16]

However, it is unlikely that the autobiographical Paul seeks to represent all unconverted persons in this pericope; for that Paul would have used his favorite Adam figure. Furthermore, the understanding that the pre-conversion Paul was incapable of fulfilling the law has been refuted in current research. Philippians 3 for example clearly describes Paul prior to conversion as faultless before the law.[17]

The second interpretation sees the pericope as describing the normative Christian experience of the flesh-spirit conflict between two aeons or two existences within the process of salvation history. The conflict itself is seen as an inescapable reality. Scholars holding to this view[18] see the tension described by Paul in verses 14–25 as

---

Journal for the Study of the New Testament 33 [1988]: 41–56), who argues from the understanding of the Tenth Commandment as the "law" Paul talks about in Romans 7.

15. For example, B. L. Martin, "Some Reflections on the Identity of *EGŌ* in Romans 7:14–25," *Scottish Journal of Theology* 1 (1981): 39–47.

16. Note the extreme position of Kümmel that the "I" is not autobiographical of Paul, i.e., not even the personal experience of Paul before his conversion, because the "I" is merely a rhetorical device (W. G. Kümmel, *Römer 7 und die Bekehrung des Paulus* [1929; reprint, Munich: Kaiser, 1974], 112).

17. For more, see Jewett, *Romans,* Basic Bible Commentary (Nashville: Graded Press, 1986), 86–87, on the Lutheran misunderstanding of this passage that tends to have distorted understanding of first-century Judaism and has "imposed on Paul a kind of introspective conscience that was not characteristic of him." See F. F. Bruce (*Paul: Apostle of the Free Spirit* [Exeter: Paternoster, 1977], 196), who doubts that Paul had an introspective conscience.

18. E. Stauffer, "*Egō,*" *Theological Dictionary of the New Testament* (hereafter *TDNT*) 2:343–62; Nygren, *Commentary on Romans,* 284–96; C. K. Barrett, *The Epistle to the Romans* (London: A. & C. Black, 1973), 151–53; J. Murray, *The Epistle to the Romans* (Grand Rapids, Mich.: Eerdmans, 1968), 1:257–59; F. F. Bruce, *The Epistle of Paul to the Romans,* New International Commentary on the New Testament (Grand Rapids, Mich.: Eerdmans, 1963), 150–53; C. E. B. Cranfield, *A Critical and Exegetical Commentary on the Epistle to the Romans,* 6th ed. (Edinburgh: T. & T. Clark, 1975–79), 1:344–47, 356–58; David N. Steele and Curtis C. Thomas, *Romans: An Interpretive Outline* (Philadelphia: Presbyte-

not that of an unbeliever but the Christian's realistic, two-aeon experience of conflict between the forces of the flesh and the spirit. That is, the two natures (old and new) of a Christian, or the spiritual self and the sinful self, are at war with each other.[19] These scholars choose Gal 5:16–18 as their favorite cross-reference text to support their argument concerning the continuous tension between the flesh and the spirit, which are perceived as diametrically opposed to each other in every Christian life, as evidenced in this pericope as well as Gal 5:17.[20]

However, this view fails to discern the assured victory and reality that Christians can experience in bondage-free lives (see Romans 6–8). Dunn may be right in seeing the movement of salvation history from Judaism's law to Christianity's Christ, but he misses the intimate relation of Paul with the Torah, his ancestral faith.[21] Furthermore, the use of Gal 5:17 as a cross-reference text is invalid at least on two counts: first, Spirit is not present in Rom 7:14–25; and second, Paul's view of Christian life in Galatians 5

rian and Reformed Publishing Co., 1963), 56–61; Anthony A. Hoekema, "The Struggle between Old and New Natures in the Converted Man," *Evangelical Theological Society Journal* 5 (1962): 42–50; David Wenham, "The Christian Life: A Life of Tension? A Consideration of the Nature of Christian Experience in Paul," in *Pauline Studies,* Festschrift to F. F. Bruce, ed. D. A. Hagner and M. J. Harris (Exeter: Paternoster, 1980), 84; W. D. Davies, "Free from the Law," *Interpretation* 7 (1953): 160–62; Herman Ridderbos, *Paul: An Outline of His Theology* (Grand Rapids, Mich.: Eerdmans, 1975), 127; D. H. Campbell, "The Identity of *egō* in Romans 7:7–25," *Studia Biblica III,* ed. E. A. Livingstone, Papers on Paul and Other New Testament Authors, Sixth International Congress on Biblical Studies (Sheffield, 1978), 57–64; and Mark A. Seifrid, "The Subject of Rom 7:14–25," *Novum Testamentum* 34, no. 4 (1992): 333.

19. See especially the arguments of Hoekema ("The Struggle between Old and New Natures in the Converted Man," 42–50); Wenham ("The Christian Life: A Life of Tension?" 84); Davies ("Free from the Law," 160–62); and R. N. Longenecker (*Paul: Apostle of Liberty* [New York: Harper & Row, 1964], 115).

20. See however Ronald Y. K. Fung ("The Impotence of the Laws: Towards a Fresh Understanding of Romans 7:14–25," in *Scripture, Tradition, and Interpretation,* Festschrift for F. Harrison, ed. W. W. Gasque and W. S. LaSor [Grand Rapids, Mich.: Eerdmans, 1978], 36–37) and Donald L. Alexander ("Sanctification Reconsidered: Spiritual Conflict in Romans 7:14–25," *His Dominion* 13 [Spring 1987]: 6–8) for a forceful and convincing argument against those scholars who use Gal 5:16–18 as a text with which to interpret this pericope along the line of flesh-spirit conflict.

21. For a sharp critique of Dunn's view, see Wenham, "The Christian Life: A Life of Tension?" 80–84.

is not of moral frustration and failure but of sure victory, whereas in Romans 7 the view is of moral frustration. In short, what Paul describes in Romans 7 is not a normative Christian experience of unresolved tension.

The third interpretation is that of D. M. Lloyd-Jones, who understands this pericope as referring to neither the regenerated nor ungenerated person exclusively, but to the person caught somewhere in between. This person, termed the "mediocre," is the "I" who is convicted of sin as he/she sees both the holiness of the law and that he/she is not yet at the point of conversion.[22] The weakness of this view lies in its hermeneutical suspicion and in its theological "fumbling" in understanding the identity of the "I." The interpretation is as weak as the "I" within it. There is no solid evidence in the passage even to suggest the experience of a "mediocre." Lloyd-Jones is doing a contemporary eisegesis of the passage.

The fourth interpretation is that of C. L. Mitton, who views the "I" as an earnest moral person, perhaps a nominal or backsliding Christian who seeks to obey the commandment of God but who ends up in distress.[23] Unfortunately, he has not sufficiently developed this view. Ronald Y. K. Fung and Donald L. Alexander have expanded Mitton's view by interpreting the "I" as the renewed nature or regenerated Christian who not only acknowledges the law as spiritual and good, but as one who even seeks to use the law to overcome his indwelling sin; yet this Christian labors in vain and despair because the believer here ignores the work of the Spirit.[24] In short, the law is impotent to deliver the Christian from indwelling

---

22. David Martyn Lloyd-Jones, *Romans: An Exposition of Chapter 7:1–8:4: The Law, Its Functions and Limits* (London: Banner of Truth Trust, 1973), 255–56, 261–62.

23. C. L. Mitton, "Romans 7 Reconsidered," *Expository Times* 65 (1953–54): 133. Mitton also mentions the possibility of a "converted Christian who has slipped back … into a legalistic attitude to God and to righteousness." Fung ("The Impotence of the Laws," 34–45) and Alexander ("Sanctification Reconsidered," 2–15) reconstruct their own view by using Mitton's suggestion here.

24. Fung, "The Impotence of the Laws," 40, states: "[T]he dilemma and the spiritual conflict of Romans 7:14–25 emerge directly from the impotence of the law to deliver from the bondage of indwelling sin or to make the believer holy." See also Alexander, "Sanctification Reconsidered," 8–10.

sin or to make the believer holy. Alexander even presupposes that "the heart of Paul's teaching even in the life of the believer is to intensify his sinful nature."[25] This view is not plausible, because Fung and Alexander fail to define the law and sin in relationship to Paul the Jew. Paul is seen here as a universal Christian, who pursues holiness in his/her spiritual life. The concrete background out of which the passage arises is erased altogether. These scholars have not articulated how Paul's Jewish and Pharisaic background play a part in this pericope.

The fifth interpretation is that of Robert H. Gundry, who understands this pericope as Paul's bar mitzvah experience in conflict with the Jewish law and its prohibition against lust: "the very sin in its sexual sense is dead prior to puberty but springs to life in a lad about the time he becomes bar mitzvah and therefore legally and morally responsible."[26] He takes the word "covetousness" to apply exclusively to sexual lust and then sees verse 9 ("I was once alive apart from the law") as referring to Paul's bar mitzvah. The contextual evidence of the pericope makes this view almost untenable, let alone convincing.[27] Gundry never mentions or explains verse 8b, "wrought in me all covetousness." He implies that "covetousness" in verse 8b means "sexual lust." Neither Ex 20:17 nor Dt 5:21 limits "covetousness" to sexual desire. Ziesler also counterargues that "throughout the NT and LXX the word 'covetousness' [in Greek] lacks a specifically sexual reference."[28]

The sixth interpretation is that of Robert Jewett, who contends that Rom 7:1–12 describes not the problem of the law per se, but Paul's desire to conform to the expectation of the law "for the purpose of prideful control [as, for example, is evidenced] in the

---

25. Alexander, "Sanctification Reconsidered," 9.

26. Robert H. Gundry, "The Moral Frustration of Paul before His Conversion: Sexual Lust in Romans 7:7–25," in *Pauline Studies: Essays Presented to F. F. Bruce,* ed. Donald A. Hagner and Murray J. Harris (Grand Rapids, Mich.: Eerdmans, 1980), 228–45. See W. D. Davies, *Paul and Rabbinic Judaism,* 2d ed. (London, 1955), 24–26, 30–31, who contends that the largely sexual evil impulse battles with the good impulse at the age of thirteen, according to rabbinic traditions.

27. See a critique of Gundry's view by J. A. Ziesler, "The Role of the Tenth Commandment in Romans 7," *Journal for the Study of the New Testament* 33 (1988): 41–56.

28. Ziesler, "Tenth Commandment in Romans 7," 45.

Roman house church situations."[29] Rom 7:14–25 then describes "the profound dilemma of [Paul's] former life. He had sought to do the will of God and had passionately devoted himself to conformity to the law but found that he ended up in hostile reaction against God."[30] This view is quite plausible except that the present tense and the issue of verses 14–25 in contrast to verses 2–13 seem to reveal more than Paul's past struggle with the Jewish law as a Pharisaic Jew. Perhaps the present tense needs to be seen not only as the past action of Paul but the present action of the readers who share Paul's action.[31] The identity of the "I" as a powerful rhetorical device deserves further clarification.

An Alternative Interpretation

Over against the view that Romans 7:14–25 is a "digressive excursus,"[32] the pericope should be seen as an important one in which Paul intends to demonstrate, by the personal example of a Pharisee, how one should view the righteousness of God, not by means of the tradition of the Torah but by the "law" (or Torah) of the Spirit. Paul the Pharisee seeks to obey the Torah with zeal, but finds in light of the present "in-Christ" experience that his blamelessness before the Torah does not necessarily indicate his righteousness

---

29. Robert Jewett, *Romans,* Genesis to Revelation Series (Nashville: Graded Press, 1986), 74; and his *Romans* in the Basic Bible Commentary series, 84–89. Paul Achtemeier has a similar but more general view than Jewett. Achtemeier (*Romans* [Atlanta: John Knox Press, 1985], 120–26) contends that the passage describes Paul's experience as a persecutor of the Christian church and possibly includes also those who are trapped under the Law.

30. Jewett, *Romans,* Genesis to Revelation Series, 75; and *Romans,* Basic Bible Commentary Series, 87.

31. After I finished writing this article, I found that Seifrid's research came to a similar conclusion; see his "The Subject of Rom 7:14–25," 317–18, and Stanley E. Porter, *Verbal Aspect in the Greek of the New Testament with Reference to Tense and Mood,* Studies in Biblical Greek 1 (New York: Peter Lang, 1989), 75–109.

32. See scholars' view of this pericope as a "digressive excursus" (J. C. Beker, *Paul the Apostle: The Triumph of God in Life and Thought* [Philadelphia: Fortress, 1980], 83); or as a "foreign body," an "independent tract" (Walter Schmithals, *Die theologische Anthropologie des Paulus: Auslegung von Röm 7, 17–8,39* [Stuttgart: Kohlhammer, 1980], 18–20).

before God and people.[33] The truth of the matter is, his strict conformity to the Torah only resulted in his hatred for the church
of God.

Conflicting Experience without the Spirit

Paul's experience of wanting to love the Torah but instead persecuting the Christian church, of wanting to do good but doing
evil, is implied in verse 18. What Paul means by "nothing good"
in verse 18 is that Paul the believer knows "at hand"[34] ("I can
will...at hand"; 7:18) that that which is required of him is to do
good; but the good is not "at hand" ("but I cannot do the right";
7:18). He wanted all to become people of God through obedience
to the Torah (which was good), but his action turned out to be
persecution of the church (which was bad).

Paul's strong desire, will, intention, or zeal to conform to the
Torah as a Pharisee is at odds with his performance (see v. 15). The
tension between the desire and the performance reminds us of the
Tenth Commandment quoted in verses 7–8. According to Ziesler,
the Tenth Commandment is used here mainly "because in some
Jewish tradition covetousness, or wrong desire, was held to be the
sin from which all others flow."[35] The reason for the tension is not

---

33. In verses 7–13 the subject is that of sin and Torah in the past experience of
humankind under Adam's sin; in verses 14–25 the same theme is discussed from the
writer's present perspective (i.e., in view of Christ) on his past Pharisaic experience.
Paul begins with "we know," which is an indirect appeal to "a commonly acknowledged truth" that Paul shares with his correspondents. The word *gar* ("for," which
the NIV omits) implies the change of perspective (Bruce M. Metzger, *Textual Commentary on the Greek New Testament,* Companion Volume to the United Bible
Societies' Greek New Testament [New York: United Bible Societies, 1971], 515).
Lenski prefers to divide *oidamen* into *oida men,* which would agree with the singular throughout the passage, but there is nothing to elicit the *men.* See Seifrid,
"The Subject of Rom 7:14–25," 320–23, on Paul's use of the confessing "I" of
early Judaism in Rom 7:14–25. See the parallel Qumran material Seifrid gives on
pp. 322–23.

34. F. Büchsel, *"Parakeimai,"* TDNT 3:656, says "lie ready, at disposal."

35. See Philo, *Spec. Leg.* IV, 84–94; *De Dec.* 142, 150, 173; *Apoc. Mos.* 19:3;
Apoc. Abr. 24:10; *Targum Neofiti I* Ex 20:17 and Dt 5:18; Ex 20:17 *Mekilta;*
Ziesler, "Tenth Commandment in Romans 7," 47; G. Theissen, *Psychological As-
pects of Pauline Theology,* trans. J. P. Calvin (Philadelphia: Fortress, 1987), 207;
Käsemann, *Romans,* 194.

"the Law's inability to deliver what it demands" as Ziesler argues, but the indwelling sin in Paul. Thus, despite the conflict, Paul is quick to put things in perspective. First, in verse 16 he affirms the goodness of the Torah, despite the fact that it is being used by sin to create frustration within him. Second, in verse 17, he pinpoints the cause of his frustration as indwelling sin and not the Torah.

This concept of indwelling sin means not that somewhere in Paul's flesh or body is a "not-yet redeemed" entity, but rather that his frustration lies precisely in missing the work of the Divine Spirit, that is, in his fleshly weakness. The phrase "because of your fleshly weakness" (6:19) refers to the Christian experience. That phrase may be related to "the flesh" in chapter 7, and it links with 8:26, where the Spirit is said to aid our "weakness."[36] Paul's use of *sarx* ("flesh") is perhaps best understood in the restrictive sense[37] of "in me:" the totality of a person apart from the directive or influence of the Holy Spirit. And the Spirit is totally absent here. Since the Holy Spirit is not mentioned in this pericope, the predicament of Paul's frustration can be attributed to his failure to recognize and appropriate the way of the Spirit.

Paul reiterates his conflicting experience with sin and the Torah in verses 19–21 (see also vv. 14–18). It is obvious that verse 20 repeats almost word for word verses 16a and 17 concerning the controlling power of indwelling sin. Also, the last two clauses of verse 21 are a compressed form of verses 18b–19.[38] Paul again reiterates his view in verse 22 that the Torah itself is good and that his innermost being rejoices in it. But it is precisely that which is good, spiritual, and loved by Paul (i.e., the Jewish Torah) which wars with another "law" of his mind and makes him prisoner to the "law" of sin. Despite Paul's delight in the Torah (v. 22), his approval (v. 23) of it as good (v. 16b), and his willingness to keep it (vv. 18b, 19, 21), the victor is the "law" of sin. The

36. Cranfield, *Commentary on the Epistle to the Romans*, 1:326.

37. Suggested by Fung, "The Impotence of the Laws," 43; W. Sanday and A. C. Headlam, *A Critical and Exegetical Commentary on the Epistle to the Romans* (New York: Scribner, 1962), 182.

38. J. D. G. Dunn, *Romans 1–8*, Word Biblical Commentary (Dallas: Word, 1988), 392.

word "wretched" ("miserable," or "distressed"[39]) indicates that Paul therefore despairs.[40] This is neither an anthropological tension, nor a tension between one's new faith in Christ and one's former faith or tradition. It is the despair of Paul the Pharisee, who had misunderstood the will of God for Jews and Gentiles.

The Good Torah Captivated by Sin

The fact of Paul's conflicting experience, that Paul has not done what he wants to do, shows that he is not opposing the Torah per se. He is for it and agrees that it is good. "The Torah is spiritual" is an affirmation of the divine origin and authority of the Torah which is the "fundamental dogma of Judaism."[41] Torah is the embodiment of the whole Jewish cultural and religious tradition. As such, only a Jew, especially a Pharisee, can make this affirmation.

If the Torah is so "spiritual"[42] (holy and just and good also), what is the problem with the Torah here? There is no flaw in the Torah per se; the problem is with sin. Paul saw himself as "sold under sin" because of the "law" of sin that dwells in him (see v. 17: "the sin that dwells within me"). He claims to be "carnal" because he walks "according to humanity" (7:22) and not "according to the Spirit" (8:5), in the new way of life.[43] In short, sin in this pericope should be understood from the specific perspective of a Pharisee who has asserted his own understanding of Torah; it is a righteousness seen as absolute superiority over others, to the point of persecuting those who do not accept his point of view.

Paul's frustration with the Torah does not reveal that the fault is the Torah's. On the contrary, he affirms the holiness and goodness of the Torah and attributes his frustration to sin and his own "sinfulness." That it was sin and not the Torah which brought about death in a person "under the Torah" (i.e., a Jew) is shown in verses 7–13. In verse 14 Paul continues to show how the Torah is used

---

39. Appears here and in Rv 3:17 in the NT.

40. See Wis 3:11; 13:10; Dunn, *Romans 1–8*, 396.

41. Cranfield, *Commentary on the Epistle to the Romans*, 1:355.

42. An adjective Paul uses 24 times out of its 26 NT occurrences. See Leon Morris, *The Epistle to the Romans* (Grand Rapids, Mich.: Eerdmans, 1988), 290.

43. Fung, "The Impotence of the Laws," 43; see 1 Cor 3:1, 3, where the same word *sarkinos* is used in opposition to *pneuma*.

by sin to cause death even among Jewish Christians in the Roman house churches, because they seek to fight for the Torah, that is, to gain the righteousness of the Torah.

The frustration with Torah and sin reveals the essence of human predicament, including both Gentile and Jewish Christians. The clause ("on the one hand with my mind I serve the law of God, but on the other with my flesh the law of sin") recalls the language of verses 22–23 ("I delight in the law of God" [v. 22], and "the law of my mind" [v. 23a]) and 6:17–23 ("slave to God"), which speaks of the universality of sin in humanity. All human beings are sinners (Romans 3), in bondage to sin (Romans 6), and they validate the bondage by their own evil acts (Rom 1:18–32, 6:23; cf. 5:12f.). They are above all victims "sold under sin" (7:14). Sin is perceived here as a personified ruling power. Sin is portrayed elsewhere in the image of a tyrant lord-ruler (*basileuō* in 5:21 and 6:12; *kyrieusei* in 6:14) who makes all human beings "captives,"[44] who enslaves all (*douleuein* in 6:6; *douloi* in 6:17, 20), and who pays all the wages of death (1:32; 5:12–21; 6:16, 21, 23; 7:5, 10, 13, 24). Here "sold by sin" is the imagery of a slave market.[45] The perfect-passive participle "sold" points to the continuing state of the "I" carried off by sin. The ruinous Adamite condition of the human race is depicted forcefully in the phrase "sold under sin." It is the condition exemplified by Paul's previous experience arising from perfect observance of the Torah, but on reflection from the point of view of his life now in Christ, he is made aware of his sinfulness in Adam. The Gentile Christians' behavior is also sinful in the sense that, though the Gentiles do not have the Torah, they do have "law" revealed to them in their conscience (inner conviction).

The "Spirit" Answer and the Two Laws

Paul poses a question in the latter part of verse 24 in pursuit of his frustration with Torah and sin: who will deliver him "from the

---

44. Dunn, *Romans 1–8*, 388.
45. Morris, *The Epistle to the Romans*, 291.

body of this death"?; that is, from indwelling sin.[46] His past devotion to the Torah, his own cultural and religious tradition, has
blinded him to the new act of the righteousness of God in Christ,
who is the savior of the Gentile world.[47] The answer to the victory comes in verse 25: "through[48] Jesus Christ our Lord." We can
identify that point with Paul's conversion experience. It is not until
Rom 8:1 that Paul discusses his ultimate help in the Spirit and advances his theological answer to his frustration in 7:14–25. Paul
is aware both of his existence as not entirely *sarx* ("flesh") and of
his new life in Christ, in the power of the Holy Spirit.[49] Paul eventually realizes his error and begins to view the Torah of the Spirit
as a new Torah. Paul finds the victory over his dilemma in 8:2,
"the Torah of the Spirit of life in Christ Jesus." The new Torah of
the Spirit of life in Christ Jesus is more inclusive than the tradition
of Torah and is essential for the coexistence and salvation of both
Jews and Gentiles (i.e., all people).

The issue at stake in the pericope is how to affirm the holiness
and the goodness of the Torah, and at the same time to deny the
Pharisaic interpretation that Gentiles should keep the Torah for salvation. The "I" in the pericope is Paul the Pharisee whose behavior
is representative of the Jewish and Gentile Christians in Rome. This
pericope therefore serves to remind Jewish Christians not to abuse
the law (as Paul once did) but to live in the Spirit before God with
Gentile Christians. It also reminds Gentile Christians not to take
pride in their own traditions and to consider themselves strong
and others weak. For both Jewish and Gentile believers are now
in Christ Jesus (8:1). For the law of the Spirit has led both the Jewish and Gentile Christians into victory over sin and death (8:2–13)
and into the confession that they are all children of God (8:14).

---

46. "The body of this death" is a further variation on "body of sin" (6:6), "this
mortal body" (6:12), "my flesh" (7:18), "my constituent parts" (7:23). See Dunn,
Romans 1–8, 397.

47. Lloyd Gaston, *Paul and the Torah* (Vancouver: University of British Columbia Press, 1987), 33.

48. Dunn (*Romans 1–8*, 397) says "the *dia* may do double service: to stress
Christ's mediatorial role in prayer to God; and to imply his mediatorial role as
God's agent of the final deliverance."

49. Fung, "The Impotence of the Laws," 43.

Those who are in Christ (7:25) in the Spirit (8:2) do not abrogate but fulfill the Torah (8:4).

The comparison and contrast of the two laws, Torah and Spirit (the new Torah), in 7:14–25 and 8:1–11 respectively, is most significant. It expresses Paul's realization that as a Pharisaic Christian he should now move from the Pharisaic view of the law to the law of the Spirit. It is noteworthy that the Spirit is mentioned over a dozen times in the beginning of Romans 8 alone. Paul declares that "the law of the Spirit of life in Christ Jesus has set him free from the law of sin and death" (8:2). Paul considers himself among the "us" who "walk not according to the flesh, but according to the Spirit" (8:4). Those who walk according to the Spirit fulfill "the commandment of the Torah" (8:4). Life in the Spirit is primarily communal and ethical, only secondarily individual and ritual. In other words, the way of the Spirit is practiced not in terms of zealous conformity to religious rites required by the Torah, but in terms of the commitment of the whole person, whose renewed relationship with God then becomes expressed in the encounter with one's neighbor in and through the Spirit.

Theological Significance

After offering an interpretation of the pericope and before giving a Pauline-Confucian intertextual reading, I will summarize the theological significance of the pericope in the following four points.

1. A *New View of Past Experience from the Christ Event*

Paul reaches a new understanding of his past experience with the Torah, with his own zeal and righteousness, when he encounters Christ. The Torah had been Paul's first love and pride, for he was a zealous Pharisee (see Gal 1:13–14, Phil 3:4–6, 1 Cor 15:9), one who believed that the function of the Torah was to maintain the Jews as the elected people of God. As a Pharisaic Jew Paul was proud of his perfection in fulfilling the Torah and its obligations.[50] Paul was proud of his previous conformity to the Torah because he believed he had been able to maintain the same covenantal relationship with God that most first-century Jews sought.[51] Dieter Lührmann is right in saying that "the three terms Law, zeal, and righteousness obviously belong together. Since the times of the Maccabees zeal meant to fight for the Law; righteousness meant to live according to the Law."[52]

In this passage Torah represents a cultural and a religious code which embodied the heart of Paul's ancestral faith, the Pharisaic faith which could be traced back to the Mosaic Torah. Westerholm has appropriately rendered Torah as "a collection which spells out Israel's covenantal obligations."[53] This Torah or set of covenantal obligations has its basis in Deuteronomy (4:8; 30:10; 32:46).[54] J. D. Dunn and B. Martin agree with Westerholm that the Pauline understanding of *nomos* ("law") is that it sums up "Israel's obligations as set out by Moses and is fully in line with Hebrew usage of torah."[55] In short, Torah to Paul is a cultural and religious code

---

50. This kind of attitude is common among the Pharisees; see W. G. Kümmel, *Römer 7 und die Bekehrung des Paulus*, 111–17; Cranfield, *Commentary on the Epistle to the Romans*, 1:344.

51. See Dunn, *Romans 1–8*, lxiii–lxxii; E. P. Sanders, *Paul, the Law, and the Jewish People* (Minneapolis: Fortress, 1983), 544; Gaston, *Paul and the Torah*, 48–54; Francis Watson, *Paul, Judaism, and the Gentiles: A Sociological Approach* (Cambridge, New York: Cambridge University Press, 1986), 2–18. For a contrary view, see Ridderbos, *Paul*, 130–35.

52. D. Lührmann, "Paul and the Pharisaic Tradition," *Journal for the Study of the New Testament* 34 (1989): 75.

53. S. Westerholm, *Israel's Law and the Church's Faith: Paul and His Recent Interpreters* (Grand Rapids, Mich.: Eerdmans, 1988), 330–31.

54. In the book of Deuteronomy, obedience to the law is required as Israel's response to the divine grace and act, which forms a distinct part of the covenantal theology. The term "covenantal nomism" is popularly used to mean the same thing. Note for example that throughout Deuteronomy 5–28, statues, ordinances, and instructions are set out as God's covenant with Israel, and the promise within the Torah is resoundingly clear: "Do this and live" (2:13; 4:1, 10, 40; 5:29–33; 6:1–2, 18, 24; 7:12–13, 10:5). See Dunn, *Romans 1–8*, lxviii, for a reinforcement of the idea that upholding the Torah was requisite to Jewish self-identity under Ezra, and especially during the Maccabean crisis.

55. Dunn, *Romans 1–8*, lxvii–lxviii; cf. Rom 2:12, 17–18; 7:12; 10:5, with 1 Kgs 2:3; Ezr 7:6, 10, 12, 14, 26; Neh 8:14; 9:14, 34; and Jer 32:23.

which identifies him as a Jew,[56] more particularly as a Pharisee (see Acts 23:6, 26:5, 22:3, 5:34).

As a loyal Pharisaic Jew, Paul was concerned with how Gentiles could come into the full citizenship of the people of God — by adopting the Torah of Israel. In the Jewish tradition, the Gentiles are sinners par excellence, as Lührmann reminds us.[57] Gaston has provided valuable research for a background understanding of Torah as used in this pericope. He shows that in some of the writings of Paul's rabbinic contemporaries the view is expressed that both Jews and Gentiles will have a relationship with God, especially in the end time,[58] only through the Torah — directly or indirectly.[59] *Test. Naph.* 8:3 says that God intends to "save the nation of Israel and to gather together the righteous from amongst the nations." E. P. Sanders has rightly presented the point that "in the entire body of Palestinian Jewish literature between Ben Sirach and the redaction of the Mishnah, with only the exception of 4 Ezra, membership in the covenant is considered salvation."[60] Both Jews and Gentiles can achieve and maintain their status in the membership of God only by observing the Torah. And that is the conviction of Paul as a Jew before he knew Christ. Many rabbinic sources believe that God did offer the Torah to both Jews and Gentiles, but only the Jews accepted it; therefore, the Torah gives life to the Jews and it brings death to the Gentiles. To the Jews therefore, the Torah is a gracious covenant from God.[61] Paul's previous

---

56. Dunn, *Romans 1–8*, lxix; Wayne A. Meeks, *The First Urban Christians: The Social World of the Apostle Paul* (New Haven and London: Yale University Press, 1983), 97.

57. Lührmann, "Paul and the Pharisaic Tradition," 87.

58. For example, *m. Sanh.* 10:1 says, "All Israel has a share in the world to come," and R. Joshua speaks in *t. Sanh.* 13:2 of "righteous among the nations of the world who have a share in the world to come."

59. For example, Gutbrod, "*Nomos,*" *TDNT* 4:1055, says, "Man has his relationship with God only in his relationship with the Torah," or as Maimonides says, "Everyone who accepts the seven [Noahic] commandments and observes them carefully is one of the righteous of the nations of the world and has a share in the world to come. But he must accept and observe them [the Torah] . . . " (*M. T. Melakhim*, 8, 11).

60. E. P. Sanders, "The Covenant as a Soteriological Category and the Nature of Salvation in Palestinian and Hellenistic Judaism," in *Jews, Greeks, and Christians*, ed. R. Hamerton-Kelly and R. Scroggs (Leiden: E. J. Brill, 1976), 15.

61. Gaston, *Paul and the Torah*, 26.

zeal for the Torah in persecuting the church should be seen in this light. Paul was concerned for Gentiles to be members of the people of God; hence, as a Pharisaic Jew, most probably of the House of Shammai,[62] Paul was zealous to see that his cultural and religious tradition (i.e., the Torah) be accepted by all so that they could be saved.[63] For Paul the Torah is Israel's great privilege (Rom 2:17–20; 3:1–2; 9:4–5), but it should be understood as a covenantal relationship leading to obedience in a life of faith. The Mishnah (*Ber.* 2:2) says that the Israelite "first takes upon himself the yoke of the Kingdom of Heaven and afterwards takes upon himself the yoke of the commandments." Only Paul the former Pharisee could articulate, "I delight in the law of God, in my inmost self" (v. 22). This is why Paul was known for his "strictness" (or "exactness") in observing the law (see Gal 1:14).[64]

But viewing his past actions from his subsequent Christian perspective, Paul saw that his love for the Torah did not necessarily mean he was pleasing God. In fact, the opposite occurred, for Paul's zeal for the law caused him to persecute the church all the more (see Galatians 1 and Philippians 3). Seen in the light of the Christ event, Paul now understood that his righteous zeal for the Torah was in fact a self-righteousness that repudiated and rejected God's righteousness. His devotion for the Torah had been used by indwelling sin to exert prideful control over himself and others. Worse still, his loyalty to the Torah as the absolute standard for inclusion among God's people had resulted in his persecution of the disciples and followers of Christ. The death of Christ had revealed to him that God's righteousness was available to all according to the principle of faith (trust) rather than to strict conformity to a cultural or religious value system. The death of Christ also revealed to Paul that Christ had died precisely to obviate rigid conformity

---

62. Davies, *Paul and Rabbinic Judaism*, 66; J. T. Townsend, "I Corinthians 3:15 and the School of Shammai," *Harvard Theological Review* 61 (1968): 500–504; and H. Hübner, "Gal 3:10 und die Herkunft des Paulus," *Kerygma und Dogma* 19 (1973): 215–31.

63. Gaston has shown that the Shammaites "were less open than some to compromise on matters of the law in relationship to proselytes, their pessimism concerning Gentiles, and in general their greater zeal for the law" (*Paul and the Torah*, 28).

64. Dunn, *Romans 1–8*, xl, lxviii.

to the Jewish faith and Torah. Christ died as a "lawbreaker," not because he was antinomian but because meeting people's needs took precedence over obedience to the Torah. Love supersedes conformity. Christ had been crucified by the idolatrous and absolute belief system of the Torah. But Christ's resurrection indicated the eschatological reality of truth: it is open-ended and will always emerge in the end time.

2. The Identity and Function of "I"

The first-person singular in Rom 7:9–25 is used to depict the experience of a typical Pharisee. Literally the "I" is Paul the Pharisee; rhetorically the "I" represents the Jewish Christians and the Gentile Christians at Rome.

The six emphatic uses of "I" (7:9, 10, 14, 17, [20,] 24, 25) are to be interpreted as autobiographical, though not focusing exclusively on Paul.[65] That is, Paul is not talking as a representative non-Christian or Christian. The "I" is a powerful rhetorical device[66] which Paul uses to confess his own great sin of the past as a Pharisaic Jew[67] and to identify the sin common to both the Jewish Christians and the Gentile Christians at Rome. "I" can refer to all

---

65. So Dodd, *The Epistle of Paul to the Romans,* 107; Kertelge, "Exegetische Überlegungen zum Verständnis der paulinischen Anthropologie nach Römer 7," 107–8; J. D. G. Dunn, "Rom 7:14–25 in the Theology of Paul," *Theologische Zeitschrift* 5 (1975): 260–61; Beker, *Paul the Apostle,* 240–43; Theissen, *Psychological Aspects of Pauline Theology,* 190–208. See 1 Cor 10:29–30 and Gal 2:18–20, where the "I" form is also autobiographical. For history of interpretation on "I," see Otto Kuss, *Der Römerbrief* (Regensburg: F. Pustet, 1963–78), 462–85, and Cranfield, *Commentary on the Epistle to the Romans,* 1:342–44.

66. Many scholars disagree with Kümmel that the "I" is merely a rhetorical device and argue that it is Paul's own anguish and pathetic cry and confession. See Mitton, "Romans 7," 78; J. I. Packer, "The 'Wretched Man' of Romans 7," *Studia Evangelica* (1964): 621–27; J. Lambrecht, "Man before and without Christ: Rom 7 and Pauline Anthropology," *Louvain Studies* 5 (1974): 31–32; Gundry, "The Moral Frustration of Paul before His Conversion," 229; Dunn, "Rom 7:14–25 in the Theology of Paul," 260–61.

67. Seifrid's structural analysis of Rom 7:14–25 comes to a similar conclusion. He argues that Paul's proof takes three forms: first is 7:14–17 whereby Jewish traditional and confessional language is used; second is 7:18–20 whereby the "I" becomes Paul the example for the audience; and third is 7:21–25 whereby the narration is given as a model to the audience. See Seifrid, "The Subject of Rom 7:14–25," 326–27.

humanity, including Paul himself. A similar rhetorical use of "I" is found in 1 Corinthians 13, except that Romans 7 has a greater element of personal vividness and specificity in order to make the identification work effectively.

In any case, that the experience of the "I" is Paul's cannot be refuted. Campbell argues, "Without some personal and temporal aspect, a statement such as *ezōn* and *apethanon,* not to mention the dramatic cry of verse 24, become meaningless and unreal."[68] Packer argues likewise.[69] Gundry is right in asserting the forcefulness of that "I myself" in verse 25:

> Surely Paul puts forward his experience as typical — otherwise it would fail to carry the argument — but it remains. What could be plainer than the *autos egō* (I myself) of emphatic self-reference in verse 25?[70]

But Gundry misses the point when he speaks of Paul's experience as his sexual-psychological conflict at his bar mitzvah. What is more realistic and theologically sound is Paul's struggle with the Torah in relation to the Gentile issue. In short, the "I" represents both Paul and those Jewish Christians who are unconvinced or unaware of the new act of God's righteousness in Christ bringing Gentiles into the covenant of God. Because of the devotion of those Jewish Christians to the Torah, their mission to "Judaize" the Gentiles is described by Paul as having "a zeal for God, but it is not enlightened . . . [for they are] ignorant of the righteousness that comes from God" (Rom 10:2).

Gentile Christians are not excluded from this pericope. In Romans 1–2 the Gentiles are said to have the law though they do not have the Torah; that is, the Gentiles are not better than the Jews. Considering themselves as the strong who do not need to observe the Torah, and considering themselves now as in Christ in whom they take pride, the Gentile Christians have missed the new act of God, the righteousness of God in Christ. Having received the righteousness of God, the Gentile Christians suppose themselves to be

68. Campbell, "The Identity of *egō* in Romans 7:7–25."
69. Packer, "The 'Wretched Man' of Romans 7," 623.
70. Gundry, "The Moral Frustration of Paul before His Conversion," 229.

thankful and merciful; instead, they have taken pride in their identity in Christ and sought to convert the Jews and "Christianize" them to be Gentile. They have pressured the Jewish Christians not to observe the Torah, such as the food laws and Sabbath.

3. The Present and Past Tense

The use of the present tense in verses 14–25 indicates the struggle Paul has as a Pharisee with both sin and the Torah. His past action (zealous with the Torah and persecuting the church) is congruent with the present struggle of the Roman Christians, both Jews and Gentiles. Rom 7:7–13 was written in the past tense.[71] But in verses 14–25 Paul uses the present tense.[72] These present tenses are used to describe not his present struggle with sin as a believer, but his past struggle seen from the perspective of the present.[73] Phil 3:3–6 gives us the perfect example of Paul's use of the present tense to describe his Judaistic past.[74] This use of the historical present not only portrays the vividness of Paul's past experience viewed in the present reality, it also depicts the current behavior of the Jewish Christians in Rome who use the Torah to exert superiority (righteousness) over others. It also depicts the current behavior of the Gentile Christians in Rome who use the name of Christ to exert superiority over Jewish Christians.

The "I" in Rom 7:14–25 is then to be understood as referring not only to Paul's former life, but also to those who seek self-righteousness rather than submission to God's righteousness. The

---

71. Note for example: "I should not have known" (v. 7); "sin…wrought in me" (v. 8); "I was once alive…I died" (v. 9); "sin…deceived and killed me" (v. 11); "It was sin working death in me…" (v. 13).

72. Note for example: "I am carnal" (v. 14); "I do not understand my own actions…I do…I do" (v. 15); "I do…I agree" (v. 16); "it is no longer I that do it" (v. 17); "I can will…but I cannot do it" (v. 18); etc. Also note vv. 19, 20, 21, 22, 23.

73. Steele and Thomas (*Romans: An Interpretive Outline,* 126) say that "Paul is writing out of his experience as a mature Christian." Packer ("The 'Wretched Man' of Romans 7," 624) rightly maintains that "the only natural way for Paul's readers to interpret the present tenses of verses 14ff. is as having a present reference [since] there is no recognized linguistic idiom which will account for the change of tense."

74. See Alexander, "Sanctification Reconsidered," 6, and Martin, "Some Reflections on the Identity of *EGŌ* in Rom 7:14–25," 40–46.

fundamental human sin conceived by Paul is similar to Paul's former sin. The corollary of that sin is the sin of achieving one's
righteousness by means of a religious or cultural system without
accepting or trusting in the righteousness of God in Christ. Such
an interpretation universalizes the experience of the "I" and makes
the present tense here into the "customary present."[75] The Jewish
Christians seek righteousness by upholding the Torah; the Gentile
Christians seek righteousness by upholding Christ.

4. The "Torah of the Spirit"

The "Torah of the Spirit" mentioned in Rom 8:2 is the answer to
Paul's concern for bringing Gentiles into the people of God. What
Paul is trying to show by using his own experience with regard to
the Torah is that, no matter how holy one's tradition may be, that
tradition often presents hindrances to and creates tensions in our
relationships with other people and with God, particularly when
one insists on conformity to the tradition. The reason for the frustration of the "I" is not due to the psychological peculiarity of the
"I";[76] nor is it due to the fact that Paul is living in "the interim
period [between the two ages of Adam and Christ when] the believer's loyalties are bound to be torn between the demands of the
two ages to which he belongs. . . . Hence the cry of 7:24 is one of
frustration that the process of salvation still has to work through
the body of death."[77] Nor is the reason for the frustration to be
understood in terms of the salvation history of God, that covenantal nomism in the age of Christ is no longer the valid way to define
one's access to the righteousness of God. The frustration stems
rather from the seeming contradiction between one's intention and
one's actions, between fulfilling the Torah and performance that
contradicts the intent of the Torah.

  Daniel Patte is right at this point in saying that Paul's faith is
"a charismatic, eschatological, typological faith in the Gospel as

---

75. That is, the present tense that is used to denote that which habitually occurs;
the act is assumed to be true in the past, future, or present.

76. Theissen, *Psychological Aspects of Pauline Theology*, chap. 13.

77. Dunn, *Romans 1–8*, 377.

power of God for salvation,"[78] that is, a faith that is a dynamically open set of convictions in contrast to the closed system of Pharisaic Judaism. The human predicament, as portrayed by the experience of the "I," is the bondage of the will under sin and the Torah.[79] It is the tendency to absolutize a system of convictions and to make an idol of them, and that is sin. A charismatic, eschatological, typological faith in the gospel of Jesus Christ compels one to destroy all idolatrous systems. It is charismatic because God is at work in the present moment through the Spirit,[80] eschatological because final truth is available at the end time (not now);[81] truth is never complete, because it is revealed in the next evolving moment. Jews and Greeks should have open and tolerant minds and attitudes. They should conform to Christ, the "normative type,"[82] who is the lawbreaker of the Pharisaic system in order to shatter its idolatry. According to Patte, the Pauline gospel does not destroy completely a system of belief or conviction[83] but reinterprets it, relativizes it, and sees it anew in light of Jesus the Christ.

The Torah is good, spiritual, and perfect; but, says Paul, when Pharisaic Jews or Gentile Christians exert a prideful control over themselves and others by means of the Torah or by means of their own Christian experience, they experience frustration — as Paul himself did. To live a life of righteousness is *not* to ask whether one has fulfilled the requirement of the law, but how one must relate to others and to God in a way that manifests God's grace and love. A life of righteousness, which is new life in Christ, is not to be understood simply as a transcendent source of life poured into humans from outside, but as a process which is directed toward the ultimate goal of the realization of the image (glory) of God in

---

78. Daniel Patte, *Paul's Faith and the Power of the Gospel: A Structural Introduction to the Pauline Letters* (Philadelphia: Fortress, 1983), 350.

79. Patte, *Paul's Faith and the Power of the Gospel*, 275–76.

80. Patte, *Paul's Faith and the Power of the Gospel*, 324.

81. Patte, *Paul's Faith and the Power of the Gospel*, 238.

82. Patte, *Paul's Faith and the Power of the Gospel*, 240.

83. Patte says that the gospel is "a system of convictions which is open-ended in that it can incorporate parts of the system of convictions, whatever it might be, from which the believers converted, and conversely that conversion to the Gospel demands that only a part of one's old system of convictions be rejected..." (*Paul's Faith and the Power of the Gospel*, 72).

humans, initiated in this life as a life of faith and love. This life of faith and love toward neighbors is an expression of a life of faith and love of God.

Finally, the contrast between the "I" in Rom 7:14–25 and the plural pronoun in chapter 8 seems to suggest that the reason for the frustrated "I" *may be* because of the "I's" unawareness of others in the life of righteousness toward which the Spirit is consciously moving it. Paul reminds his readers that they are not under the Torah but under grace (v. 14). They are not under the demand of the Torah, but they are under the provision of the Torah to love one another, which is the fulfillment of the Torah.

The Pauline "Torah and Spirit" Compared with Confucian *Li* and *Jen*

The Pauline discussion of Torah and Spirit in terms of Pharisaic and Christian perspectives for both Jewish and Gentile audiences is a cross-cultural endeavor. The law of the Spirit ushers in a divine energy for the cross-cultural enterprise, and the Christ event provides a hermeneutical paradigm for the Chinese-Pauline interaction below. The discussion below will avoid a systematic comparison between Pauline theology and Confucian thought; rather, it offers an intertextual reading back and forth between Romans and Confucian classics regarding five major themes: the Confucian "transcendence/immanence" *(T'ien)* and the Pauline "Spirit/God"; Confucius, the reformer of heavenly mandate, and Paul, the reinterpreter of the Torah; *li* and the Torah and *jen* and the work of Spirit in love; cultivating selfhood in *jen* and living in the Spirit of love; and human nature as individuation and socialization.

Confucian "Transcendence/Immanence" (T'ien) and Pauline "Spirit/God"

The concept of transcendent and immanent Being is present in both Paul and Confucius's thinking. The book Confucius (551–479 B.C.E.) admired, *The Book of Odes,* says: "*T'ien* [Heaven] gave birth to the multitude of people, where there is a thing, there is a principle; that is why people hold to rightness and like this natural, beautiful virtue."[84] This religio-philosophical understanding of human life assumes that all human beings come from *T'ien*, the Creator, and that morality is endowed with *T'ien*. Confucius does not mention this poem in the *Analects*, but a concept similar to the "transcendence/immanence" of *T'ien* is expressed in the *Analects*. According to the Confucian scholar Donald L. Alexander, Confucius's religious-metaphysical understanding of ultimate reality is couched in the bipolar conception of *T'ien*. He writes:

> *T'ien* is the symbol[85] of the universal creative life-principle inherent in the universe whereby the world of all living things comes into being.... The second dimension will be called the temporal pole; that is, *T'ien* is the symbolic expression of the concrete function of the universal principle of creativity. In other words, Confucius recognized the intrinsic value of human nature in congruence with the creative power of the universe.[86]

The "creativity" aspect of *T'ien* is transcendence, yet the all-pervading and all-integrating spontaneous life force is immanence.[87]

The transcendent and immanent notions are similar to God the Creator (or Father) and the Holy Spirit, respectively, in Christian theology. The immanence of *T'ien* is the closest Confucian thought gets to the idea of the Holy Spirit in Christianity. The Tao of

---

84. Ta-ya, III: 3, 6; 505 and 541.

85. According to Donald Alexander, the word "symbol" means "any object, act, event, quality, or relation which serves as a vehicle for conception — the conception is the symbol's meaning. A symbol, then, is a form in which reality discloses itself to our consciousness. The symbol is not itself reality but its manifestation; and yet the symbol is not another thing but the epiphany of that thing which is not without some symbol. Hence, the symbol encompasses and unites both the symbolized thing and the consciousness of it" ("The Concept of *T'ien* in Early Confucian Thought," *His Dominion* [1985]: 12–13). See Liu Shu-hsien, "The Use of Analogy and Symbolism in Traditional Chinese Philosophy," *Journal of Chinese Philosophy* 1 (1974): 313–38, and Clifford Geertz, "Religion as a Cultural System," in *A Reader in Comparative Religion: An Anthropological Approach*, ed. William A. Lessa and Evon Z. Vogt (New York: Harper & Row, 1965), 168.

86. Alexander, "The Concept of *T'ien*," 11.

87. Alexander, "The Concept of *T'ien*," 14. See Mencius 5.A.6.2.

Heaven is the way of the Spirit, which not only gives birth to people but continues to regenerate and sustain them.[88] In this eschatological age, the Spirit being the Creative Force binds believers in the confession that they are the children of God. For this reason, one stands in awe of the greatness and creativity of *T'ien*.[89]

The creative force of *T'ien* has many elements corresponding to the Pauline understanding of the working of the Holy Spirit in the lives of the believers. For example, both *T'ien* and the Holy Spirit are the symbols of the creative and mysterious presence of God. Both dwell in persons, not just to present them with descriptive truth but to convey to them the vision of reality which is embodied in the concept of creativity and continuous regenerativity. Both seek to establish a wholeness of life for all.

The creative force of the Spirit may be seen in how Confucius remolds the idea of *T'ien*. From this starting point, we can understand why Confucius is the reformer and not the mere preserver of the ancestral tradition of *li* ("propriety"), just as Paul was with respect to the Torah.

Confucius the Reformer of T'ien Ming and Paul the Reinterpreter of the Torah

Confucius wants to preserve the traditional value and culture of knowing and doing the *T'ien Ming;* on the other hand, he wants each person to be renewed by the power of that mandate which had been long established by the sages in past dynasties. In the *Analects, T'ien* is mentioned directly seventeen times, of which ten are spoken by Confucius and seven by others. Interestingly enough, in his ten uses of *T'ien,* Confucius employs the familiar personal term of "I" in relation to *T'ien.* An analysis of this usage by Sung-Hae Kim reveals that what Confucius is doing here is transferring the *Ming* of *T'ien* ("mandate of Heaven") from a highly political claim of the ruling family to a universally appropriated claim for all. That is, Confucius seeks to popularize that same mandate

---

88. See *Shih-Ching: The Chinese Classics,* trans. James Legge, 4:352, 505, and 552.

89. Chung Yung 33, *Analects* 16:8, and Alexander, "The Concept of *T'ien,*" 15.

of Heaven so that everyone can cultivate selfhood and attain the wholeness of life.[90]

Confucius could not have been a mere transmitter of tradition in its outer form, for that would never have sustained and forged a way of life which has exerted its influence on the Chinese society for the last two millennia — and likely for more to come. Fung Yu-lan argues that "Confucius was in fact a great reformist thinker who instilled a new spirit into the traditional forms."[91] What Confucius intended was to reinterpret his ancestral tradition in light of its meanings and moral principles for the sake of creative and lively appropriation.[92]

Paul, too, is interested in reinterpreting tradition. In Romans, Paul is not seeking to eliminate the Torah. In fact, he affirms that the Torah is holy and good. But Paul's interpretation of the Torah in the light of the Spirit and the Christ event in Romans 7–8 does not merely accept the Torah as it is. Certainly, his view of Torah is not the same as that of his contemporary Jewish friends. More important, the age of the Spirit and *T'ien* compels one not to absolutize his beliefs (culturally or religiously) and to create an idol of them, but to examine the truth afresh always as the creative One reveals and intervenes in the eschatological moment.

Li *and* Torah; Jen *and* Work *of* Spirit *in* Love

In terms of the Pauline language of the Torah and Love (as fulfillment of Torah), perhaps we can supply the equivalent Confucian language of *li* and *jen,* respectively. To Jews such as Paul, the tradition is no doubt the Torah, that which is divine and upheld by Jews as covenantal with God. Jews consider the Torah as a divine gift

---

90. Sung-Hae Kim, "Silent Heaven Giving Birth to the Multitude of People," *Ching Feng* 31, no. 4 (1988): 195–96.

91. Quoted by Alexander, "The Concept of *T'ien*," 10. Fung Yu-lan observes that "Confucius took the principles underlying the writings of the Ch'un Ch'iu and of the other early histories, and drew from them the doctrine of the Rectification of Names, thus rationalizing the Ch'un Ch'iu. The great contribution of Confucius to Chinese civilization, indeed, has been the rationalization he has given to the originally existing social institutions" (*A History of Chinese Philosophy,* trans. Derk Bodde [Princeton: Princeton University Press, 1952], 1:36).

92. See Alexander, "The Concept of *T'ien*," 10–11.

unique to Jews, for it marks them as Jewish, both religiously and culturally. The Chinese consider their tradition as best couched in the word *li*, the proper and holy way of doing things (thus propriety also). Etymologically, the ideograph *li* symbolizes a sacrificial act. Wing-tsit Chan points out that it originally meant "a religious sacrifice."[93] However, the earliest available dictionary meaning of *li* is "treading" or "following." Specifically, it indicates the act or ritual whereby spiritual beings are properly served and human happiness obtained.[94] Neither Paul nor Confucius wishes to discard traditions altogether. What they are advocating is to let *jen* ("love") be the fundamental motive of our action and relationship while respecting the revelatory nature of the Torah and *li*. To live a life of *li*, a cultured yet natural pattern of interpersonal relationship that "works through spontaneous coordination rooted in reverent dignity,"[95] is the same as using the Torah (and *li*) but not imposing it on others. Paul's ethic is neither legalistic nor antinomistic; it is love, empowered and guided by the Spirit. And love is the fulfillment of the Torah.

Paul pinpoints the greatest danger of religious people. It is that those who inherit long-standing and sacred religious traditions often through their piety and religiosity hurt and persecute people in the name of the very God they seek to please. Paul recognizes that it is possible to love God and yet not to love people; it is possible to be set right with God and not be right with people. Similarly, in Confucian thought, *li* is good and perfect and holy. Confucius says, "Merely to feed one's parents well...even dogs and horses are fed" (*Analects* 2:7). In other words, merely doing the expectation of *li* is not sufficient; what is essential is a higher principle than that structure, and that is *jen*. So *li* without *jen* can degenerate into formalism or insensitivity (see *Analects* 3:3). Therefore, *li* must be grounded in *jen*.[96]

---

93. See Chu Hsi, *Reflections on Things at Hand*, trans. Wing-tsit Chan (New York: Columbia University Press, 1967), 367.

94. *K'ang-hsi tzu-tien* (Taipei: I-wen Book Co., 1957), 1920.

95. Herbert Fingarette, *Confucius — The Secular as Sacred* (New York: Harper & Row, 1972), 8. Cf. *Analects* 2:3, 13:3.

96. This is what Tu Wei-ming means by "the primacy of *jen* over *li* and the inseparability of *li* from *jen*." See "*Li* as Process of Humanization," *Philosophy East and West* 22 (April 1972): 188.

Cultivating Selfhood in Jen and Living in the Spirit of Love

Confucius is deeply concerned that humans live in *jen*, for *jen* is more basic and crucial than the rule of propriety. He insists that each human being is to actualize the mandate of Heaven by committing him/herself to *jen*.[97] *Jen* is what makes human beings human.[98]

In Chinese, the word *jen* is composed of two ideograms: "person" connotes self, and "two" connotes relation.[99] Peter Boodberg renders *jen* as "co-humanity."[100] *Jen* connotes all the moral qualities which govern the relationships between two human beings. Etymologically, it is to be translated simply as human-relatedness, but philosophically, the human-relatedness should be defined specifically as love, which is the cardinal principle of human relationships.[101] This is even more vividly expressed by Fang Ying-hsien when he says that, in light of the term's "two semiotic foci, *jen* is the tender aspect of human feelings, namely, love as well as an altruistic concern for others...."[102]

In other words, to be a *jen jen* ("a loving person") is to express and to participate in the holy as a dimension of all truly human

---

97. Milton M. Chiu, *The Tao of Chinese Religion* (Washington, D.C.: University Press of America, 1984), 191–92.

98. The word *jen* appears in the *Analects* over 105 times. It is translated variously as human-heartedness (E. R. Hughes), benevolence, love (Derk Bodde), benevolent Love (H. H. Dubs), humaneness, humanity-at-its-best, goodness (A. Waley), humanity, virtue (H. G. Creel), human-relatedness, charity, humanity (W. T. Chan), morality, etc. See Fung, *A History of Chinese Philosophy*, 69–73; Wing-tsit Chan, "Chinese and Western Interpretations of *Jen* (Humanity)," *Journal of Chinese Philosophy* 2 (1975): 107.

99. Tu Wei-ming says, "Etymologically *jen* consists of two parts, one a simple ideogram of a human figure, meaning the self, and the other with two horizontal strokes, suggesting human relations" (*Confucian Thought: Selfhood as Creative Transformation* [New York: State University Press, 1985], 84). See Chan, "Chinese and Western Interpretations of *Jen* (Humanity)," 108–9.

100. Peter Boodberg, "The Semasiology of Some Primary Confucian Concepts," *Philosophy East and West* 2 (October 1953): 317–32.

101. Fung, *A History of Chinese Philosophy*, 69–73, and Chan, "Chinese and Western Interpretations of *Jen* (Humanity)," 109.

102. Tu, *Confucian Thought*, 84. See the original by Fang Ying-hsien, "Yüan-jen lun-tzu shih Shu chih K'ung Tzu shih-tai kuan-nien chih yen-pien" (*Ta-lu tsa-chih* 52 [March 1976]: 22–34).

existence. Fingarette writes, "Human life in its entirety finally appears as one vast, spontaneous and Holy Rite: the community of man [humanity]."[103] As we have already seen, to be a *jen jen* is to be courteous, diligent, loyal, brave, broad-minded, and kind (*Analects* 13:19, 14:5, 17:6), as actualized in public.

Human Nature Is Individuation and Socialization

Paul and Confucius understand human nature not in terms of intrapersonal conflict between flesh and spirit, but in terms of interpersonal socialization between self and group. Tu Wei-ming has used Wayne C. Booth's "rhetoric of assent"[104] to interpret the *Analects* and has come to perceive the "commonality, communicability, and community of the human situation."[105] What he means is that Confucian ontology is not based on an atomic-mechanistic split of and conflict between flesh and spirit, but a more holistic understanding that through symbolic interchange, human beings are called into the "fiduciary community" of sharing intentions, values, and meanings. Tu Wei-ming offers a perceptive observation here: "The symbolic exchange wherein self-identification and group awareness in both cognitive and affective senses take place thus becomes the primary milieu. [Hence, we must have] a willingness to participate in the creation of sharable values."[106] This "fiduciary community" of "sharable values" is the "beloved of God" community in Christ to whom the Jewish and Gentile Christians in Roman house churches belong.

The fiduciary community advocated in the *Analects* does not have the notion that all persons will always finally agree. On the contrary, it is natural that diverse personalities will have differing visions of the Way.[107] Even among Confucius's disciples, for

---

103. Fingarette, *Confucius,* 17. See *Analects* 3:17, 4:5, 6, 8. For different interpretations of *jen* and *li* in Confucius's thought, see Fung, *A History of Chinese Philosophy,* 72–82, 94, and Tu, *Confucian Thought,* 81–92.

104. Wayne C. Booth, *Modern Dogma and the Rhetoric of Assent* (Chicago: University of Chicago Press, 1974).

105. Tu, *Confucian Thought,* 82.

106. Tu, *Confucian Thought,* 83.

107. See Tu, *Confucian Thought,* 83.

example, the paths of self-realization are varied.[108] Similarly, the "strong" and the "weak" in Romans are not encouraged to be other than themselves as they must hold true to their own "measuring rod of faith."[109] The singularly crucial point for both groups is "the continuous process of symbolic exchange through the sharing of communally cherished values with other selves."[110] This similar Pauline and Confucian emphasis is presupposed by their understanding of human nature. In the *Analects,* for example, the self is a center of relationships rather than the center of an isolatable individual. In other words, the self is a dynamic, open organism which actively seeks human community for wholeness of life and is transformed through the person of the Spirit. Tu Wei-ming puts it this way: "It [self-transformation] is not a quest for pure spirituality nor is it a liberation from the flesh, the mundane, or the profane."[111] The task of that transformation, as seen in Romans 7, is to accept vulnerability and to support one's fellow beings. Living a life free from the bondage of sin and death does *not* move us nearer to God while simultaneously moving us further away from our neighbors; it moves us toward God *and* one another.

One must be careful, however, not to speak of the Confucian notion of the human as only a social being without any personal selfhood or identity. Confucius sees both processes of becoming human (socialization and individuation) as equally essential and mutually supportive. Zehua Liu and Quan Ge have observed, "The former means that the development of the individual is impossible unless there is a process of social adaptation; the latter indicates that the individual is the entity in which the process of socialization is to be incarnated — otherwise, there would be no meaning to 'socialization.' "[112] Paul does not advocate different factions to dissolve their uniqueness or particularity; Paul is asking them

---

108. See Tu Wei-ming, "The Confucian Perception of Adulthood," *Daedalus* 105, no. 2 (1976): 110.

109. Robert Jewett, *Christian Tolerance* (Philadelphia: Westminster Press, 1982), 62.

110. Tu, *Confucian Thought,* 83.

111. Tu, *Confucian Thought,* 133.

112. Zehua Liu and Quan Ge, "On the 'Human' in Confucianism," *Journal of Ecumenical Studies* 26 (Spring 1989): 319.

to "greet one another with a holy kiss" (16:1–16) despite their differences.

Confucius's understanding of the socialization process is that one authenticates one's being not by detaching from the world of human relations but by making sincere attempts to harmonize one's relationship with others. Confucius says, "Virtue does not exist in isolation; there must be neighbors" (*Analects* 4:25).[113] "In order to establish oneself, one helps others to establish themselves; in order to enlarge oneself, one helps others to enlarge themselves" (*Analects* 6:28). The process of learning to be a sage does not take the form of linear progression but that of gradual integration. The human is transformed by participation with others in communal ceremony. And that is the mandate of Heaven, that all may live in righteousness and orderliness in relation to others as a society of sacredness.

Toward a Fruitful and Loving Community

The will of God for the Jewish and Gentile Christians in Rome is the righteousness of God. It is a way to life and freedom graced by the Christ event, sustained through the Spirit and *jen* ("love") within the faithful community. *Jen,* the way to being human, is neither theocentric nor anthropocentric; it is a mutuality of the human and the heavenly.[114] As such, human responsibility has its transcendent anchorage and, at the same time, that transcendent anchorage always seeks its expression in the immanent reality of human affairs. How can the Jew and the Gentile and the many factions within the Roman house churches live in harmony? This question which was Paul's was also Confucius's concern in the splintered society of his time. Confucius says, "The person of humanity is naturally at ease with humanity" (*Analects* 4:2). In Christian ter-

---

113. In the first instance, this link is to the general reciprocal good faith and respect among men (*shu* and *chung*); in the second instance this reciprocal good faith is given a specific content: it is that set of specific social relationships articulated in detail by *li*. In short, where reciprocal good faith and respect are expressed through the specific forms defined in *li,* there is *jen*'s way. See Fingarette, *Confucius,* 42.

114. Fingarette, *Confucius,* 60.

minology, the answer is that the Spirit wills the faithful to become fully human in loving relationship with others. The Torah is not abrogated but fulfilled through a lifestyle guided and controlled by the Spirit (see Rom 13:8). The power of the Pauline gospel is that which grants righteousness to all who place their faith (trust) in Christ. That faith and grace must be concretely expressed in our "faith" (trust) and "grace" toward one another so that all might come to worship the One God, "for from him and through him and to him are all things. To him be glory for ever, amen" (Rom 16:27).

Part III

Biblical Messages for the Current Chinese Situation

Chapter 7

Jerusalem, Athens, and Beijing in Acts

Just a survey of scholars and the exegetical methodologies used to study Acts 17 is enough to deter one from stirring the already muddy water.[1] Nonetheless, another look may prove useful, since the passage at hand has not yet been rhetorically analyzed. Furthermore, the implications of rhetorical analysis for a Chinese hermeneutic is too great a challenge to forgo.

The Rhetorical Analysis of Acts 17:22-31

The rhetorical analysis pursued below follows George Kennedy's reconstruction of the classical rhetorical model.[2]

---

1. For a bibliography of textual criticisms, philological, stylistic, historical, archaeological, theological, and exegetical studies, see A. J. Mattill, *A Classified Bibliography of Literature on the Acts of the Apostles* (Leiden: E. J. Brill, 1966), #2767–73 and 6029–6179. For source criticism of this pericope, see H. Hommel, "Neue Forschungen zur Areopagrede Acts 17," *Zeitschrift für die Neutestamentliche Wissenschaft* 46 (1955): 145–78, and Colin J. Hemer, *The Book of Acts in the Setting of Hellenistic History* (Tübingen: J. C. B. Mohr, 1989). A good bibliography is Watson E. Mills, *A Bibliography of the Periodical Literature on the Acts of the Apostles* (Leiden: E. J. Brill, 1986).

2. See George Kennedy, *New Testament Interpretation through Rhetorical Criticism* (Chapel Hill: University of North Carolina Press, 1984). The five-stage approach is further outlined by Wilhelm Wuellner, "Where Is Rhetorical Criticism Taking Us?" *Catholic Biblical Quarterly* 49 (1987): 448–63.

The Rhetorical Unit

Acts 17:22b–31 is an integrated unit of speech which is persuasive in its argumentation. The unit is set within the context of a larger unit, that is, Acts 17:15–32, which tells of Paul traveling between Beroea and Corinth, waiting in Athens for Silas and Timothy. This context-unit is set within the larger unit of Acts 13:1–21:14, which narrates Paul's missionary journey to the Gentile world and which portrays Athens as one of its most important cities. The ministry of Paul at Athens represents the pivotal point of his ministry in the whole Gentile world, as Luke tells it.[3] The larger unit is Luke's

---

3. The question is whether Acts 13:22–31 is the speech given by the historical Paul, or is it merely a creation of Luke, or a mixture of both? Norden argues that the speech is based on the one given by Apollonius of Tyana at Athens. Nock, Macgregor, Dibelius, Haenchen, and Conzelmann deny the Pauline authenticity of the Areopagus speech; they propose that the speech is a literary work of Luke. Calvin, Hackett, Mare, Bahnsen, Bruce, and Hemer, however, argue for the authenticity of at least the setting of the speech by Paul, i.e., it could have been delivered by Paul. See Eduard Norden, *Agnostos Theos: Untersuchungen zur Formengeschichte Religioser* (Leipzig and Berlin: B. G. Teubner, 1929), 24; his thesis later was accepted by Wendt, Preuschen, Reitzenstein, and Wellhausen, but opposed by A. von Harnack. See J. T. Townsend, "The Speeches of Acts," *Anglican Theological Review* 42 (1960): 150–59; A. D. Nock, review of *Aufsätze zur Apostelgeschichte,* by M. Dibelius, *Gnomon* 25 (1953): 497–99; G. H. C. Macgregor, "The Acts of the Apostles," *Interpreter's Bible* (1955), 2:232; Martin Dibelius, *Studies in the Acts of the Apostles,* ed. Heinrich Greeven, trans. Mary Ling (New York: Charles Scribner's Sons, 1956), 71–73; Hans Conzelmann, "The Address of Paul on the Areopagus," in *Studies in Luke-Acts: Essays Presented in Honor of Paul Schubert,* ed. Leander E. Keck and J. Louis Martyn (Nashville: Abingdon, 1966), 218–27; H. B. Hackett, "The Discourse of Paul at Athens: A Commentary on Acts 17:16–34," *Bibliotheca Sacra* 6 (1849): 338–56; Bertil Gärtner, *The Areopagus Speech and Natural Revelation* (Uppsala: C. W. K. Gleerup, 1955), 52; Edward Fudge, "Paul's Apostolic Self-Consciousness at Athens," *Journal of the Evangelical Theological Society* 14, no. 3 (1971): 193–98; W. Harold Mare, "Pauline Appeals to Historical Evidence," *Bulletin of the Evangelical Theological Society* 11, no. 3 (1968): 121–30; G. L. Bahnsen, "The Encounter of Jerusalem with Athens," *Ashland Theological Bulletin* 31, no. 1 (1980): 4–40; C. J. Hemer, "Paul at Athens: A Topographical Note," *New Testament Studies* 20 (1974): 341–50; W. Schmid, "Die Rede des Apostels Paulus vor den Philosophen und Areopagiten in Athen," *Philologus* 95 (1942/43): 79–120. This paper takes the position that the speech is not the exact wording of Paul's preaching at Athens; rather it largely reflects Luke's own theological interest rather than that of the historical Paul. This understanding will be made clear as we analyze the theology of the speech in contrast to the theology of Paul. "Paul" in this chapter means Lukan Paul. See Dibelius, *Studies in the Acts of the Apostles,* 82; Conzelmann, "The Address of Paul on the Areopagus," 218. On the historicity of

conscious portrayal of the movement of the gospel from Jerusalem to Rome as the gospel of Christ is preached so that "all flesh shall see the salvation of God" (Lk 3:6).

The Rhetorical Situation

The issues that are relevant for the rhetorical analysis of this pericope, relative to the so-called *Situationsfrage*[4] or the "status/stasis" (the basic issue),[5] accord with the setting which gives rise to the speech. The basic issue is recounted in verses 16 and 19. Paul (the Lukan Paul) did not plan to stay and preach at Athens. He was waiting for Silas and Timothy, and he was probably touring and sightseeing in the city. But then he saw the city full of idols, and his spirit was provoked (v. 16). Luke tells us that Paul went to the synagogue (v. 17) and argued with the Jews. Some Epicurean and Stoic philosophers met him and were puzzled that he was babbling on about the new gods called Jesus and Resurrection. Intrigued by new teachings, these philosophers brought Paul to the Areopagus to hear his teaching.

Paul was provoked when he saw the city was full of idols (v. 16). Athens was the center of Greek intellectual life and piety,[6] an important city representing the best of the Gentile intellectual world. The Roman satirist Petronius once said that it was easier to find a god in Athens than a man. The religiosity of the Athenians is evident in the altars of Eumenides (goddesses), Hermes, the twelve Gods, the Temple of Ares, the Temple of Apollo Patroos, Zeus, Mercury, Hercules, Isis, Serapis, Cybele, Fortune, Necessity, Victory, the image of Neptune on horseback, and the sanctuary of

---

Paul at Athens, see Otto F. A. Meinardus, "An Athenian Tradition: St. Paul's Refuge in the Well," *Ostkirchliche Studien* 21, nos. 2-3 (1972): 181–86; on the historicity of the speeches of Acts, see J. A. Fitzmyer, "Acts of the Apostles" in *Jerome Biblical Commentary*, ed. R. E. Brown, J. A. Fitzmyer, and R. E. Murphy (Bangalore: TPI, 1980), 2:200.

4. Heinrich Lausberg, *Elemente der literarischen Rhetorik,* 3d ed. (Munich: Max Heuber, 1967), 21–23.

5. Kennedy, *New Testament Interpretation,* 18–19; Heinrich Lausberg, *Handbuch der literarischen Rhetorik: Eine Grundlegung der Literaturwissenschaft,* 2d ed., 2 vols. (Munich: Max Hueber, 1973), vol. 1, §§79–138.

6. Conzelmann, "The Address of Paul on the Areopagus," 218.

Bacchus.[7] Wycherley keenly observes that "full of idols" (v. 16) gives the sense of "luxuriant with idols" or "veritable forest of idols."[8] The ethos of the time and the pathos of the Athenians are one and the same in the sense that a religious quest is evidenced everywhere, including the marketplace.

The Rhetorical Disposition or Arrangement (taxis, dispositio)

The genre of Acts 17 is deliberative[9] with the following rhetorical structure:[10] (*a*) the *exordium* (or *proem*) of verses 22–23a in which (i) the speaker praises the audience's religiosity in verse 22, and (ii) the *narratio* in verse 23a describes the basic issue which will lead to the thesis; (*b*) the *propositio* (or *thesis*) of verse 23b, in which the rhetor states the desired goal of the discourse or the fact he desires to prove, which is to make known what they worship as unknown; (*c*) the proof (or *pistis* or *confirmatio*) of verses 24–29, in which the rhetor advances his argument regarding what is right; and (*d*) the *peroratio* (or *conclusio*) of verses 30–31, in which he dissuades the audience from a wrong course of action and persuades them into the right course. Then he states, as adduced or

---

7. As described by Sophocles, Livy, Pausanias, Strabo, and Josephus. See Oscar Broneer, "Athens: City of Idol Worship," *Biblical Archaeologist* 21, no. 1 (1958): 4–6. For archaeological evidence, see J. Marcus, "Paul at the Areopagus: Window on the Hellenistic World," *Biblical Theological Bulletin* 18, no. 4 (1988): 143–48; S. Johnson Samuel, "Paul on the Areopagus: A Mission Perspective," *Bangalore Theological Forum* 18, no. 1 (1986): 21; Mare, "Pauline Appeals to Historical Evidence," 122–23; W. A. McDonald, "Archaeology and St. Paul's Journeys in Greek Lands: Part II, Athens," *Biblical Archaeologist* 4, no. 1 (1941): 1–10; Pausanias, *Description of Greece*; Colin J. Hemer, "The Speeches of Acts II: The Areopagus Address," *Tyndale Bulletin* 40, no. 2 (1989): 239–43; P. M. Fraser, "Archaeology in Greece, 1969–1970," *Archaeological Reports* 16 (1969–70): 3–4; R. E. Wycherly, "St. Paul at Athens," *Journal of Theological Studies* 19 (1968): 619–20.

8. Wycherley, "St. Paul at Athens," 619.

9. For a full discussion on this genre, see Aristotle *Rhet.* 1.4–8; *Rhet. ad Alex.* 1–2, 29–34; Cicero *De Or.* 2.81.333–83.340; *Inv.* 2.51.155–58.176; *Part. Or.* 24–37; *Her.* 3.2–5; *Quint.* 3.8; Lausberg, *Handbuch*, 1:123–29; and Josef Martin, *Antike Rhetorik* (Munich: C. H. Beck, 1974), 167–76.

10. See Dibelius, "Paul on the Areopagus," 27; D. W. Zweck, "The Exordium of the Aeropagus Speech, Acts 17:22, 23," *New Testament Studies* 35, no. 1 (1989): 97.

developed in the proof, what is required of them: to repent and to believe.

Thus, the disposition of argumentation in Paul's Areopagus speech is (in my translation):[11]

Exordium or *proem* (v. 22):

- **address:**   "Men of Athens,"
- *captatio benevolentiae:*   "in every way I perceive (how) very religious you are."

Narratio (v. 23):

- *narratio* proper: "For as I was passing through and observing the objects of your worship, I found even an altar with this inscription, 'TO AN UNKNOWN GOD.'"
- *propositio:*   "What therefore you worship in ignorance, this I proclaim to you."

Probatio or *pistis* (vv. 24–29):

- **First Proof:** Nature of God in relation to the world:
      Creator and creation/creature (vv. 24–25)

    a. maker of the   "The God who made the world and all in it, this
       universe and Lord: one, being Lord of heaven and earth, does not dwell
                             in handmade temples;"
    b. Sustainer of life: "neither is he served by hands of men, as though he
                             needed anything, since he himself gives to all men
                             life and breath and all things."

- **Second Proof:** Providence of God to human race (vv. 26–27a)

    a. Maker of human   "And from one he made every nation of men to
       race: dwell on all the face of the earth,"
    b. determiner of their "having determined their appointed periods, and
       time and space: the boundaries of their habitation;"
    c. purposes of creating
       them:
       i.   "[that] they are to seek God,"
       ii.   "in the hope that they might feel him and find him,"

---

11. See M. Dibelius's outlines (literary rather than rhetorical): Introduction (v. 23); I. God as creator (vv. 24–25); II. Men should seek God (vv. 26–27); III. Relationship of men with God as offspring (vv. 28–29); Conclusion (vv. 30–31). See Dibelius, *Studies in Acts of the Apostles*, 27.

- **Third Proof:** Affinity of humans to God as immanence of God (vv. 27b–29)

  a. immanence of God: "indeed he is not far from each one of us,"

  b. *chreia* or *iudicatum:*

      i.   "for 'in him we live and move and have our being';
                  as also some of your poets have said,"

      ii.   " 'For we are indeed his offspring.' "

  c. first *adfectus* (appeal)   "Being then the offspring of God, we ought not to
     with *comminatio:*   think that the Deity is like gold, or silver, or stone, a
                         representation by the art and imagination of man."

Peroratio (vv. 30–31):

- *recapitulatio* **with first**   "The times of ignorance therefore God over-
  adfectus **in** *expositio:*   looked;"
- **second** *adfectus:*   "but now he commands all men everywhere to
                         repent,"
- **rationale for appeal:**   "because he has appointed a day in which he will
                         judge the world in righteousness by the man whom
                         he has appointed, and of this he has given assurance
                         to all men by raising him from the dead."

In the *Rhetorica* Aristotle recognizes three genres of rhetoric: deliberative, judicial, and epideictic.[12] Every speech may be divided into exordium, statement of thesis, proof, and *peroratio*.[13] The genre of this speech can be judicial or deliberative, depending on how one reads the arguments therein. There is no unanimity in this regard. Zweck says that "the closest parallel to the Areopagus speech is the Olympic Discourse of Dio Chrysostom."[14] But the Olympic Discourse is an epideictic and not a deliberative piece. Some scholars and translators consider Paul's speech as a trial[15] (thus making the speech a judicial piece) because of the words *Areiospagos* and "arrest." Fred Veltman suggests it is

---

12. Aristotle *Rhet.* 1.3.3 (1357b.7–8).

13. Aristotle *Rhet.* 3.13.3 (1414b.8–9).

14. Zweck, "Exordium of the Aeropagus Speech," 99.

15. As Timothy D. Barnes ("An Apostle on Trial," *Journal of Theological Studies* 20, no. 2 [1969]: 407–19); Conzelmann ("The Address of Paul on the Areopagus," 219), and Bahnsen ("Encounter of Jerusalem," 19) claim. Also, see the New English Bible: "So they took him and brought him before the Court of Areopagus" or "brought him to Mars' Hill" in the footnote. A still more vague translation appears in the Authorized Version: "Mars' hill," a Latin equivalent of "hill of Ares."

a defensive speech based on the *Gattung* (genre) studies of the speech in comparison with ancient literature, but he subsequently declines an analysis of the speech "because of the clear reference to a trial."[16]

The term *Areiospagos* can refer to Mars Hill (the rocky spur west of the Acropolis) and the court which met on the hill.[17] It was similar to London's Hyde Park, an open-air forum.[18] *Areiospagos* is near the Stoa Basileios and the Stoa Poikila (Painted Colonnade), the place where Zeno and other philosophers argued and taught.[19] *Epilambanomai* (v. 19) means "take hold of" and does not necessarily mean "arrest."[20] *Agō* (in v. 19) means "lead" and not "bring to a trial." *Symballō* (in v. 18) can mean "to converse with" or "to argue with,"[21] but not in a legal sense. R. Pervo may be correct in interpreting the speech as a "trial of the faith."[22] It is a trial only in the sense that Paul is asked to explain his teaching for an audience that wishes to know more (vv. 19–20). Paul is never asked to defend the gospel. And no verdict is ever rendered. The Areopagus speech is best categorized as a deliberative oratory.[23] This is because it aims to convince and not to defend or appraise. Quintilian

16. Fred Veltman, "The Defense Speeches of Paul in Acts," in *Perspectives on Luke-Acts,* ed. Charles H. Talbert (Danville, Va.: Association of Baptist Professors of Religion, 1978), 253, and see 243–56.

17. See Athenagoras *Pol.* 47.2 and 60.2; Barnes, "An Apostle on Trial," 407–19. F. F. Bruce, however, argues that the construction with *en mesō* indicates the court and not the hill. See Bruce, *The Acts of the Apostles: The Greek Text with Introduction and Commentary,* 3d revised and enlarged edition (Grand Rapids, Mich.: Eerdmans, 1990), 379.

18. E. Haenchen, *The Acts of the Apostles* (Philadelphia: Westminster, 1971), 519; W. G. Morrice, "Where Did Paul Speak in Athens — On Mars' Hill or before the Court of the Areopagus? (Acts 17:19)," *Expository Times* 83 (1972): 377.

19. Cicero *Acad.* (Priora) 2.24.75; Horace *Sat.* 2.3.44; Plutarch *Mor.* 1058D.

20. Morrice, "Where Did Paul Speak in Athens," 377. The same meaning appears in Acts 9:27 (Barnabas brings or leads Paul to the apostles) and Mt 14:31 (Jesus keeps Peter from sinking into the water). Richard I. Pervo prefers the meaning "arrest" (see *Profit with Delight: The Literary Genre of the Acts of the Apostles* [Philadelphia: Fortress, 1987], 154, n. 148).

21. See Walter Bauer et al., *A Greek-English Lexicon of the New Testament and Other Early Christian Literature* (Chicago: University of Chicago Press, 1979 [henceforth BAGD]), 46; Norden, *Agnostos Theos,* 333; Haenchen, *Acts,* 517.

22. Pervo, *Profit with Delight,* 44.

23. So Zweck, "Exordium of the Aeropagus," 95.

sees the deliberative genus as "a more varied field for eloquence, since those who ask for advice and the answers given to them may easily present the greatest diversity.... religion, too, has its place in the discussion."[24]

Paul's "speech may be understood as apologetic dialogue directed successively to the classes of interlocutors represented among the hearers, the representatives of Stoicism, Epicureanism and Athenian religion."[25] "May we know what this new teaching is which you present?" is an invitation to a scholarly discourse.[26] The nature of the dialogue is seen most forcefully in Paul's use of the audience's arguments, in this case, the words of philosophers. The most obvious reference is the citation of the Stoic poet Aratus of Soli (*Phaenomena* 7) in verse 28. We should also note Cicero's *De natura decorum* (Book 2), where Balbus gives a deliberation on Stoic theology which seems to have a division similar to that of the Areopagus speech, except for the last few verses: "[T]he topic of the immortal gods which you raise is divided by our school into four parts: first they prove that gods exist [2.4–44]; next they explain their nature [2.45–72]; then they show that the world is governed by them [2.73–153]; and finally they state that they care for the fortunes of mankind [2.154–67]."[27]

Paul was thought to be preaching two foreign deities to the philosophers: *anastasis* (resurrection) and Jesus.[28] The two deities were understood to be the subject matter of Paul's speech. Paul's speech is "a hellenistic speech about the true knowledge of God."[29] However, the motif of worship[30] is not central in the text. More plausible is Nauck's discovery that there are three motives in the speech regarding the two deities: creation (vv. 24–26a, 27–28), preservation (v. 26b), and redemption (v. 31), which, he says, are

---

24. Quintilian *Inst.* 3.8.15; 3.8.29.

25. Hemer, "Speeches of Acts II," 243.

26. On arguments against trial, see Haenchen, *Acts,* 519, n. 1, and Conzelmann, "The Address of Paul on the Areopagus," 219.

27. Cicero *Nat. D.* 2.4.

28. See Haenchen, *Acts,* 518, n. 1.

29. Dibelius, "Paul on the Areopagus," 57. So Bruce, *Acts: Greek Text,* 379.

30. As argued by R. F. O'Toole, "Paul at Athens," *Revue Biblique* 89, no. 2 (1982): 185–97.

similar to the missionary literature of Hellenistic Judaism.[31] These religious motives constitute a deliberative oratory according to the *Rhetorica ad Alexandrum*.[32] This speech is deliberative because of the appeal the rhetor puts forward (v. 30) in order to change the course of action of the audience.[33] Second, the time referent is predominantly future.[34] Third, the *topoi* are concerned with what is advantageous and expedient to the audience.[35]

What Has Jerusalem to Do with Athens?

The Jewish Christian and Greco-Roman Rhetorical Techniques

We now turn to analyze the rhetorical techniques used in this pericope. The Jewish Christian and Greco-Roman rhetorical skills and competence of Luke is most evident from the varied rhetorical techniques he uses: imitation (Athens as a philosophical center, Paul as Socrates), parallelism, assonance of *parechesis* (*heuron kai bōmon* of v. 23; *zōēn kai pnoēn* of v. 25; *cheirōn anthrōpinōn... prosdeomenos tinos, autos* of v. 25), alliteration (*andres Athēnaioi* of v. 22; *pantos prosōpou* of v. 26; *pistin paraschōn pasin* of v. 31), *paronomasia* (*theōrō, anatheōrōn* of vv. 22, 23; *Agnōstō... agnoountes* of v. 23; *pantas pantachou* of v. 30), particle groupings (*monon de, de kai, alla kai*), and so forth. F. Danker is right in describing Luke as an author of "broadly ranging rhetorical competence."[36]

---

31. That is, the Sibylline Oracles, fragments I and III. W. Nauck, "Die Tradition und Komposition der Areopagrede," *Zeitschrift für Theologie und Kirche* 53 (1956): 26–43.

32. *Rhet. ad Alex.* 1423a.22–26.

33. Aristotle *Rhet.* 1.3.1358b.3; *Rhet. ad Alex.* 1.142b.17ff.; Cicero *Inv.* 1.5.7; *Part. Or.* 24.83ff.; *Her.* 1.2.2; *Quint.* 3.4.6, 9; 3.8.67–70.

34. Aristotle *Rhet.* 1.3.1358b.4; 1.4.1359a.1–2; 2.18.1392a.5; *Quint.* 3.4.7; 3.8.6; cf. Cic. *Part. Or.* 3.10; 20.69.

35. Aristotle *Rhet.* 1.3.1358b.5; *Rhet. ad Alex.* 1.1421b.21ff.; 6.1.1427b.39ff.; Cic. *Inv.* 2.4.2; 2.51.155–58.176; *Part. Or.* 24; *Top.* 24.91; *Her.* 3.2.3–5.9; *Quint.* 3.8.1–6, 22–35. Cf. Cicero *De Or.* 2.82.333–6; *Quint.* 3.4.16.

36. F. W. Danker, *Benefactor: Epigraphic Study of a Graeco-Roman and New Testament Semantic Field* (St. Louis: Clayton, 1982), 28.

Exordium to Religious Athenians

The exordium of the speech (v. 22) is comprised of an address and a *captatio benevolentiae*. The word "standing" may indicate that Paul is assuming the common posture of an orator (see 2:14, 5:20, 27:21). The address "men of Athens" is a common rhetorical convention by which the orator begins the speech with the vocative address: "Men of Athens."[37] We see this in the exordia collected by Demosthenes, one of which fits our interest in religious oratory: "It is just and right and important, men of Athens, that we should exercise care, as you are accustomed, that our relations with the gods shall be piously maintained...."[38] In using an accepted and traditional way of addressing the audience, Paul speaks the language of the people and portrays himself as one of their teachers or philosophers.

The extraordinarily gracious and gentle exordium of the speech is seen again in the *captatio benevolentiae* of verse 22: "You are very religious."[39] The orator is using the *principium* or *prooimion* instead of the *insinuatio* or *ephodos*, for he appeals to their goodwill and attention immediately.[40] The word "religious" can have both positive and negative meaning depending on the context.[41] Negatively, it means superstitious, as for example in Epicurean literature.[42] Literally the word *deisidaimonesterous* (v. 22) means "very demon-fearing." This goes along with verse 16, where "Paul's spirit was provoked,... because he saw the town full of idols." However, in light of the *captatio benevolentiae*, it is better to render the word as "very religious" (RSV) — "a flattering term."[43] Taking the speech as a whole, one wonders if this is not

---

37. See Aristotle *Pan. Or.* 1.

38. Demosthenes *Exordia* 54.

39. See Xenophon *Cyr.* 3.3.58; Aristotle *Pol.* 5.11.1315a.1.

40. The *insinuatio* or *ephodos* is a subtle and gradual attempt to ingratiate a hostile or disinterested audience to the case. See Cicero *Inv.* 1.15–17; *Her.* 1.4–7; *Quint.* 4.1.42; cf. *Rhet. ad. Alex.* 29.1437b.33ff.

41. *"Deisidaimōn,"* BAGD, 173.

42. E.g., Plutarch *Mor.* (*De superst.*) 164E–171F. See A. J. Festugière, *Epicurus and His Gods* (Oxford: Blackwell, 1955), 54.

43. L. Legrand, "The Unknown God of Athens: Acts 17 and the Religion of the Gentiles," *Indian Journal of Theology* 30 (1981): 165. However Bruce (*The Acts of the Apostles* [London: Tyndale Press, 1952], 350) cites Lucian, *De Gymn.* 19, as

used as an ironic rhetorical device.[44] In verse 16, Paul seems to be angry, but in verse 22 he praises the religiosity of the Athenians. The contrast in mood is undoubtedly a favorite Lukan technique.[45]

In any case, the audience would obviously have thought of themselves as religious rather than superstitious. The use of a "laudatory introduction" may not be exclusively positive or negative. It should be seen as a rhetorical technique whereby the "preacher" establishes rapport with the audience by means of a *captatio benevolentiae* (currying favor).[46] Zweck rightly points out the threefold function of *captatio benevolentiae:* "It gains their good will in that they are praised for being 'very religious,' it removes the dangerous suspicion that the speaker has been trying to introduce new deities to Athens; and it introduces the motif of 'unknown god.' "[47]

Narratio *of the* Unknown God

The "unknown god" motif becomes the turning point of Paul's proclamation message. The motif of proclamation is given in the *narratio* (v. 23) in which (23a) the *narratio* proper accounts for the cause of the speech, and (23b) the *propositio* previews and hints at the main theme of the speech. In the *probatio* (vv. 24–29), the speaker then begins with this motif and gives the Christian view of God using the conventional Stoic argumentation.[48] The *narra-*

---

saying that complimentary exordia to secure the goodwill of the Areopagus were forbidden.

44. Hemer, "Speeches of Acts II," 245.

45. Zweck ("Exordium of the Aeropagus," 101) says that the contrast is literary rather than psychological. See Conzelmann, "The Address of Paul on the Areopagus," 219.

46. Paul in the exordium is eliciting audience attention, receptivity, and goodwill toward him and the message through the vocative address, *narratio,* and *propositio.* See Aristotle *Rhet.* 3.14.1415a.7; *Rhet. ad Alex.* 29.1436a.33ff.; Cicero *Inv.* 1.15.20; *Or.* 14.122; *Part. Or.* 8.28; *Top.* 26.97; *Her.* 1.34; 1.4.6; *Quint.* 4.1.5, 41, 50–51.

47. Zweck, "Exordium of the Aeropagus," 100. The *Rhetorica ad Alexandrum* says that the exordium of a speech is " ... to make them well-disposed toward us" (1436a). Aristotle *Rhet.* 3.15.1 (1416a) says, "One way of removing prejudice is to make use of the arguments by which one may clear oneself from disagreeable suspicion."

48. See Zweck, "Exordium of the Aeropagus," 100.

tio has the three virtues of brevity, clarity, and plausibility.[49] The smooth transition from the exordium proper to the *narratio* is indicated by the "for and." Watson observes, "Being future oriented, deliberative speech does not really need a *narratio* unless it contributes to decision making about the future."[50] Here the *narratio* is crucial, because the speech is aimed toward leading the audience to repentance in verse 30. The *narratio* gives the account which will lead to the *propositio* (thesis) and the *probatio* (vv. 24–29). In this case, the *narratio* states the *stasis* of how the speech is caused and is needed — the issue of ignorance on the one hand and knowledge of God on the other.

As Paul was observing the objects of the Athenians' worship, he found the altar where heathen sacrifices took place. On it was an inscription, "To an unknown god."[51] This inscription was an old one as the pluperfect *epegegrapto* ("inscription") indicates. There is no archaeological evidence of the inscription,[52] but in literature there is.[53] Pausanias and Diogenes Laertius indicate there were a number of cults of indeterminate and unnamed deities[54] (that is, plural and not singular). Altars dedicated to "unknown gods" existed in Olympia, Pergamum, and Phalerum near Athens.[55] Marcus humorously but accurately paraphrases "to an unknown god" as "To whatever god we might have forgotten to honor: sorry about that!"[56] This Hellenistic tolerance for other gods is "based on their respect for their antiquity."[57] Idolatry is seldom monotheistic; ignorance breeds polytheism.

---

49. For full discussion of the *narratio*, see Lausberg, *Handbuch*, 1.163–90, §§289–347.

50. Duane Watson, "A Rhetorical Analysis of 2 John," *New Testament Studies* 35 (1989): 116. See Aristotle *Rhet.* 3.16.1417b.11; Cicero *Part. Or.* 4.13.

51. For various parallels of "unknown god" in Greek literature, see Pausanias 1.1.4, Diogenes Laertius (*Vit. Philos.* 1.110), Plato *Leg.* 1.642D; Plutarch *Solon* 12; and Philostratus (*Vit. Apoll. Tyan.* 6.3.5). Cf. Bruce, *Acts: Greek Text,* 380–81.

52. Oscar Broneer, "Athens," *Biblical Archaeologist* 21, no. 1 (1958): 20.

53. See Philostratus, *Vit. Apoll. Tyan.* 6.3.5; *Pausanias* 1.1.4.

54. *Pausanias,* 1.1.4; Diogenes Laertius, *Vit. Philos.* 1.110; Philostratus, *Vit. Apoll.* 6.3.5.

55. Norden, *Agnostos Theos*, 53ff.; M. P. Nilsson, *Geschichte der griechischen Religion* (Munich: Beck, 1955–61), 2:338, 355, 357.

56. Marcus, "Paul at the Areopagus," 145.

57. Marcus, "Paul at the Areopagus," 145.

The audience has polytheistic belief. "Unknown" is an attributive adjective "to a god." The devotee (audience) ascribes and acknowledges the unknown quality of the god they worship. Semantically, however, the description of the god as unknown seems to imply that the devotee is worshiping out of ignorance. The practice of offering to unknown gods is occasioned by the fear that through ignorance a god may be denied the respect which was due.[58] Not offending the gods was considered a virtue by the Greeks. Paul disagrees.

Paul is determined not to preach a foreign god. Paul's purpose then is to share the specific knowledge concerning the only true and real God so that his audience would turn to God. This he did by beginning with the gods familiar to the audience. Some of the gods they are familiar with have no names; they are acknowledged as unknown by the audience members themselves. The stupidity of their religious practice is indicated in this contradiction of not knowing what they are worshiping. Paul uses this contradiction as a springboard to share the Christian message. The rhetoric is effective in that at least some in the audience do recognize the inconsistency of their faith and piety.

Paul also starts with his hearers' belief in an impersonal god (which is indicated by *ho...touto*), then he moves to the Living God who is the Judge and Creator.[59] Paul's technique here is to claim that the Athenians already have altars to the God he is proclaiming; therefore, he is not introducing a new religion. Unlike Socrates, he is not "guilty of rejecting the gods acknowledged by the state and of bringing in strange deities."[60] He is too shrewd for that, as evidenced by his rhetorical skill. He first praises the Athenians for being religious. He acknowledges the god they worship — the "unknown god." He then proclaims as known that which the Athenians have long been worshiping but have not known. So there is only one God, but the knowledge of that God may not be the same for the worshipers. Idolatry is not so much worshiping a false god per se, but not knowing the identity, nature, and at-

58. Samuel, "Paul on the Areopagus," 21.
59. Bruce, *Acts: Greek Text,* 381.
60. The accusation is stated in Xenophon *Mem.* 1.1.1.

tributes of the true God or not knowing the purpose that the true God has for creation and humanity. Paul, therefore, is not preaching a new God, but a new knowledge concerning the One they worship. Lacking true knowledge they practice idolatry by their polytheism. Worshiping a false god has its roots in false epistemology. Haenchen says, "Paul concludes from this devotion that the heathens live at one and the same time in a positive and negative relationship with the right God: they worship him and do not know him — they worship him indeed, but along with many other gods!"[61] In other words, Paul uses both techniques, affirmation and refutation, effectively side by side.[62] After referring to the religious mind-set of his audience, Paul shows that their belief system has broken down. This technique is strong rhetorically without an imperialistic tendency. Its value as a technique lies in the rhetor's extreme care to convey to the audience his positive pathos so that his deliberation of the *topoi* may be heard.

At the close of the *narratio* is found the *propositio* (v. 23b),[63] which contains the basic proposition to be developed in the *probatio*. The *propositio* serves to outline what the *probatio* will expound. In the *probatio*,[64] verses 24–29, there are three proofs or *topoi* (places where arguments can be found)[65] concerning God. Each proof is expanded and qualified by means of various devices. It is important to note that the language used in verses 24–29 resembles that of the Greek philosophers, but the content does not.[66]

---

61. Haenchen, *Acts,* 521.

62. See Zweck, "Exordium of the Aeropagus," 103.

63. The element of arrangement which contains the proposition to be developed in the *probatio*. See Cicero *Inv.* 1.22–23; *Quint.* 3.9.1–5; 4.4–5.

64. Cicero *De Or.* 2.80.325; *Quint.* 4.1.23–27; see Cicero *De Or.* 2.79.320.

65. See Lausberg, *Handbuch,* 1.201–20, #373–99. See John C. Brunt, "More on the *Topos* as a New Testament Form," *Journal of Biblical Literature* 104 (1985): 495–500.

66. M. Dibelius consistently proposes Stoic philosophy as Paul's speech framework (Dibelius, *Studies in the Acts of the Apostles,* 26–27); B. Gärtner argues for OT or Judaism as its background (Gärtner, *Areopagus Speech,* 14–15. R. P. C. Hanson, *The Acts in the Revised Standard Version,* with introduction and commentary (repr. Oxford: Clarendon Press, 1974), 176–77, and E. Norden suggest a combination of both but with prominent Jewish Christian and secondary Stoic thought (Norden, *Agnostos Theos,* 3–83; cf. Haenchen, *Acts,* 454–55).

We see this in verse 24, which begins with the creatorship and lordship of God over the cosmos. *To theion* ("the Divine," "the Godhead"; v. 29) is philosophical language referring to the Absolute. It was used especially by the Stoics, for example, by Epictetus (2.20.22).[67] Whenever Paul talks about the Christian God, however, he uses the definite article (vv. 24, 26, 29, 30), indicating a contrast to the anarthrous "unknown god" which he has seen on an altar.

Jewish and Christian Probatio of God

Paul further proclaims that God is the Maker of the world. The word "cosmos" is found widely in the writings of Hellenistic philosophers.[68] Chrysippus, an early Stoic, argues that the perpetual and orderly universe could not have been created by man, but by one who is superior to man: "What better name is there for this than 'God'?"[69] Paul also says that God is the Lord of heaven and earth. "Heaven" and "earth" are terms used both in the OT and in Hellenism. Philo, Plato, and Aristotle use "cosmos" for the universe or heaven.[70] The convergence of both the OT and the Hellenistic tradition is also apparent in the term. Paul says that such a God does not live in shrines made by humans. Epicureans and Stoics too had problems with shrines and altars (see Lucretius 5.1198–1203). The belief that Deity is not in need of being "served by human hands" is well attested in Hellenism.[71] Euripides says, "God wants for nothing, if he is truly God."[72] Seneca also says that "God seeks no servants. Of course not; he himself does service to mankind. . . . "[73] It is a doctrine of Zeno also that "one should not build temples for gods!" (*Moralia* 1034b). Popular religion, however, was something else, as the shrines and altars prove. Practical

---

67. Hemer, "Speeches of Acts II," 244.
68. For example, Epictetus 4.7.6.
69. Cicero *Nat. D.* 2.16.
70. H. Sasse, *"Kosmos," TDNT* 3:871.
71. D. W. Zweck, "The Areopagus Speech of Acts 17," *Lutheran Theological Journal* 21, no. 3 (1987): 114.
72. Euripides *HF* 1345f. See also Plato *Ti.* 34B, and Xenophon *Mem.* 1.4.10.
73. Seneca *Ep.* 95.47; also Lucretius 2.646.

belief did not concur with the intellectual teaching of philosophers. In verse 24c Paul therefore refutes this popular practice.

Paul's first argument appeals to the cosmological evidence of the existence and lordship of God. The argument is plain and probably familiar to the audience, since it is the same as that used by Greek philosophers. The inconsistency and insufficiency of the belief system of the audience is their notion that the gods they worship live in shrines or altars, implying that the people themselves are the makers of gods.[74]

The second point of the first proof relates to the sustaining power of God. Paul shows that God is the Creator and Sustainer of all that is and therefore is in need of nothing. The audience's view on this issue is that of the Stoic rather than the Epicurean understanding of the gods. As seen in Lucretius, the gods of the Epicureans are indifferent to humans, because they are "part of the cosmos engendered by the fortuitous collision of atoms."[75] On the other hand, the Stoic concept of gods as seen in the *De natura deorum* of Cicero is that all things in this world have been created and provided for the sake of mankind.[76] The Stoic understanding is more compatible with Paul's view; this divergence of thought may explain why some in the audience believed, while others mocked him (v. 32).

In any case, Paul seems to rely on the OT tradition of divine providence as found in Is 42:5 to prove his point.[77] The words "the God who made...everything in it, and...he gives...and breath" are quoted verbatim from Isaiah. Paul replaces "the people" with "to all," and "all things" is added for emphasis. He shortens "to the people who are upon it, and life to those who walk on it" to a simple "all," and says that God gives "life" where the LXX has the word "breath."[78] Why would Paul use the OT in his address to

---

74. S. G. Wilson, however, sees verse 24b as Jewish polemic against the Jews, and not against Greeks; see his *The Gentiles and Gentile Mission in Luke-Acts* (Cambridge: Cambridge University Press, 1973), 199.

75. Hemer, "Speeches of Acts II," 244.

76. Cicero *Nat. D.* 2.154 and 2.154–67.

77. Is 42:5: "This is what God the Lord says — he who created the heavens and stretched them out, who spread out the earth and all that comes out of it, who gives breath to its people, and life to those who walk on it."

78. Fudge, "Paul's Apostolic Self-Consciousness at Athens," 195.

Athenian philosophers and intellectuals? Of course we may assume that this usage reflects Luke's special interest in imitating the Old Testament as a way of narrating the story, rather than an effort to cite the historic Paul's actual argument.[79]

From a rhetorical point of view, Paul is trying to convince the audience of the "reverse logic" of their idolatry. Paul points to the fact that God sustains his creatures and not vice versa. Granted, the rhetoric is gentle and the concept itself is subtle. According to Paul, the rightful relationship of humans to God is that of creature-Creator, consumer-Provider.

The second proof of the *probatio* (vv. 26–27a) concerns the theme of the providence of God toward humankind. The anthropological concern for habitation and welfare is also a concern of the Stoics.[80] "From one" probably means "from Adam,"[81] but it could have been left intentionally unclear in order to allude to the Hellenistic idea of the unity of the human race.[82] The verb "make" is used by two Stoics, Musonius Rufus (18b) and Epictetus (2.8.19), in explaining the creation of the human race.[83] "He made from one..." (v. 26) probably comes from the Stoic understanding that the *logos* is the one principle underlying all realities, the principle of order and harmony.[84] But the latter verses (vv. 30–31) suggest an Old Testament background, namely, Adam.[85] "That they should inhabit the entire face of the earth" alludes to Gn 1:28 ("Be fruitful and multiply, and fill the earth and subdue it") and Gn 10:32 ("the nations spread abroad on the earth").

This understanding of a single origin of the human race im-

---

79. See n. 3 in this chapter.

80. Cicero *Nat. D.* 2.154–67.

81. So H. P. Owen, "The Scope of Natural Revelation in Romans 1 and Acts 17," *New Testament Studies* 5 (1958–59): 135; Helmut Flender, *St. Luke, Theologian of Redemptive History*, trans. Reginald H. Fuller and Ilse Fuller (London: SPCK, 1967): 68.

82. As Dibelius, *Studies in the Acts of the Apostles*, 36–37, and M. Pohlenz, "Paulus und die Stoa," *Zeitschrift für die Neutestamentliche Wissenschaft* 42 (1949): 85, argued. See Haenchen, *Acts,* 523, n. 2.

83. See Legrand, "Unknown God of Athens," 164.

84. Legrand, "Unknown God of Athens," 164.

85. Gärtner, *Areopagus Speech*, 129, and Fitzmyer, "Acts of the Apostles," 200.

plies no superiority of the Greeks as the autochthonous people of Athens. More pertinently, the single source speaks to the universal providence of God, not only to Jews, but also to Greeks and barbarians. Unity does not mean uniformity. The creativity of God is manifested in his diversified creation of the human race (Acts 17:26b). This verse (Acts 17:26) alludes to Ps 74:17 ("You made all the boundaries of the earth, summer and spring, you formed them"). Similarly, Hellenistic thought has this same understanding; Dio Chrysostom (Or. 12.32), for example, says that "experiencing all these things . . . men could not help admiring and loving the divinity, also because they observed seasons. . . . "[86] This verse conveys the idea that God is the maker of the human race and the determiner of its time and space. The purpose of this creation and determination is given in verse 27.

God's purpose in creating the human race is so that people would seek God, in the hope that they might "feel after" him and find him. "To seek" is an epexegetical (purpose) infinitive complementing "he made," and so is the infinitive "to live." Reiteration of the word "to seek" in a synonym "to find" constitutes the figure of speech known as transplacement or traductio.[87] This transplacement serves to amplify the topos, which in turn serves to heighten the argument.[88] "Feel after" has the idea of human groping for God in the darkness when the special revelation in Christ has yet to be fully revealed. It shows the insufficiency of general revelation. "Seeking God" is an OT concept denoting serving God piously and uprightly.[89] Philo speaks of seeking God as apprehension or grasping: "Nothing is better than to seek the true God even if his discovery eludes man's capacity."[90] According to Paul, it is possible to seek and find God because God is indeed (kai ge) near each one of us. This is not a spatial nearness of God, as Haenchen

---

86. For technical analysis and interpretations of kairous and horothesias, see Wilson, Gentiles, 201–6, and Bruce, Acts: Greek Text, 382–83.

87. Traductio is either the frequent reintroduction of the same word or a word used in various functions: Her. 4.14.20–21; Quint. 9.3.41–42; Lausberg, Handbuch, 1:333, #658–59.

88. Her. 4.28.38. Cf. Quint. 9.3.28–29; Lausberg, Handbuch, 1.314–15, #619–22.

89. Hanson, Acts in the Revised Standard Version, 180.

90. Dibelius, Studies in the Acts of the Apostles, 32.

points out, but God's relationship to humans in the sense that God created them.[91]

The third proof begins with verse 27b (to v. 29) and concerns the affinity of humans to God. Verse 27b speaks of the immanence of God. The idea of the nearness of God is also found in both Hebrew religion and Greek philosophy.[92] The motif of seeking God is prominent in the LXX (Dt 4:29, Am 5:6, Is 55:6, 1 Chr 22:19, 28:9) and Hellenistic thought (especially Stoic but not Epicurean).[93] In verse 28, the orator uses a *chreia* or *iudicatum*,[94] namely, "one of your poets," in order to make his point more convincing by claiming the authority of the audience. The idea of the proximity ("not far") of God to human beings, defined in terms of God's offspring, is foreign to the OT though popular in Greek philosophy.[95] For example, Aratus in his *Phaenomena 5* wrote how Zeus is praised: "For we are also his offspring." Likewise, Cleanthes in his Hymn to Zeus wrote: "For we are offspring from you."[96]

Again the orator, Paul is using an indigenous concept to make his point for the sake of the audience. Cleanthes further described Zeus in Stoic terms as "the general law, which is logos, pervading everything, the supreme head of the government of the universe." So Zeus is this logos, the cosmic force of rationality. Cleanthes, like other Stoics, believed that each human is a spark or the offspring of this logos: "To call upon you is proper for all mortals, for we are your offspring."[97] Clement of Alexandria is the first to identify the

---

91. Haenchen, *Acts,* 525.

92. Dio Chrysostom 10.11.28: "Since they were neither far from nor outside of the divine, but by nature in the midst of it, or rather, with a like nature and in every way bound up with it, they could not long remain in ignorance." Quoted by E. Haenchen, *Acts,* 524, n. 2.

93. Dibelius, *Studies in the Acts of the Apostles,* 32, with ancient witnesses.

94. Quintilian says that *iudicatum* is "...whatever may be regarded as expressing the opinion of nations, peoples, philosophers, distinguished citizens, or illustrious poets..." (*Quint.* 5.11.36; see also Cicero *Inv.* 1.30 for similar definition).

95. Haenchen, *Acts,* 524, n. 2. See Dio Chrysostom *Or.* 12.28; Cicero *Nat. D.* 2.164; Seneca *Ep.* 41.1.

96. Stobaeus *Ecl.* 1.1.12.

97. *Hymn to Zeus* by the Stoic Cleanthes (*Fragment 537*).

Phaenomena of Aratus of Soli[98] as the source text for Paul's phrase "we are indeed his offspring."[99] Eduard Norden believes the source of "in him we live and move and have our being" to be Stoic;[100] but M. Dibelius and K. Lake surmise that it is derived from a poem on Minos of Epimenides.[101] "In him we live and move and exist" is thought to be taken from Epimenides the Cretan, but Max Pohlenz has proved that wrong.[102] Pohlenz and Hildebrecht Hommel argue against the Epimenides hypothesis[103] and suggest a quote from Plutarch (*De tranq. animi* 20, 1477 CD), which he derived from Posidonius.[104] Peter Colaclides argues this is a trinomial[105] "synonymic formula amplifying the concept of life."[106] Rhetorically it means that God is not just our Creator but Creator-Parent who wills the prodigal children to return to the Abba's Love. Paul's argument is that, being offspring of God, human beings are not to create an idol (*charagma* means "man-made image") of God, but to know God as Creator-Parent. Verse 29 uses the figure of thought called *comminatio,* which warns the audience to guard against

---

98. Born c. 310 B.C.E., a friend of Zeno the Stoic. *Phaenomena* is a treatise on astronomy.

99. Clement of Alexandria, *Strom.* 1.19; 94.4f. See K. Lake, "Your Own Poets," in F. J. Foakes Jackson and K. Lake, *The Beginnings of Christianity,* pt. 1: *The Acts of the Apostles,* vol. 5: *Additional Notes* (London: Macmillan, 1932), 246–51.

100. Norden, *Agnostos Theos,* 22: "So werden wir in *zōmen, kinoumetha, esmen* stoische Begriffe zu erkennen haben, die aber vielleicht erst der Verf. der Acta zu einer formelhaften, feierlich klingenden Trias verbunden hat."

101. Dibelius, *Studies in the Acts of the Apostles,* 48–50; Lake, *Beginnings of Christianity,* 5:246–51. So does Hemer, "Speeches of Acts II," 245–46.

102. For the hypothesis, see K. Lake, "Your Own Poets," in *Beginnings of Christianity,* 5:246–51. For critique, see Pohlenz, "Paulus und die Stoa," 101–4.

103. Pohlenz, "Paulus und die Stoa," 101–4; and Hildebrecht Hommel, "Neue Forschungen zur Areopagrede Acta 17," *Zeitschrift für die Neutestamentliche Wissenschaft* 46 (1955): 145–78.

104. Hommel writes: "Hier wird der Fundort Poseidonios deutlich nicht nur für die Formulierung des Gedankens von Leben und Bewegung und Sein des Kosmos, also auch des Menschen, in Gott, sondern auch für den ursprünglichen Zusammenhang mit einer wohlbegründeten Ablehnung des Bilderdienstes, wie sie in der Areopagrede sich ebenfalls gleich darauf findet (v. 29)" ("Neue Forschungen zur Areopagrede Acta 17," 166).

105. Lausberg, *Handbuch,* 330.

106. Peter Colaclides, "Acts 17:28A and Bacchae 506," *Vigiliae Christianae* 27, no. 3 (1973): 162. Colaclides alludes to passages such as Homer *Il.* 17.447; Cleanthes *In Iovem* 5; Aristotle *Phys.* 8.4; Homer *Od.* 4.540; and above all else Euripides' *Bacchae* 506.

worshiping an idol.[107] The *probatio* ends with the first appeal to the audience (and the rhetor himself), which says in effect that we ought not to think of the Deity in perishable material forms.

In the *probatio*, the true nature and providence of God is affirmed; consequently, idolatry is proved to derive from ignorance. Verses 30–31 are the *peroratio*.[108] The *peroratio* is the last element of the arrangement, having the twofold division of recapitulation (*repetitio*) and emotional appeal (*adfectus*). The recapitulation acts as a review so that the appeal may be effective. The *adfectus* is to attain the final goal of the speech: repentance and belief. "Therefore" (v. 30) seems to mark the beginning of a new train of thought, which says that the time of ignorance has passed. Yet this new thought is not altogether new, because verse 30 can be seen as a *recapitulatio* of the first appeal in verse 29 not to worship God with images and material things. Verse 30 uses a form called *expolitio*, or refining, which "consists in dwelling on the same topic and yet seeming to say something ever new."[109] In this case, the *expolitio* is achieved by repeating the thought in a different form. As such, the *peroratio* (vv. 30–31) calls for repentance to the true God as the rationale of the appeal, and states that ignorance is culpable and the period of ignorance is past. This appeal is a call to turn to Yahweh[110] from the unknown gods, which the audience has been worshiping.

Peroratio *on Resurrection and Judgment*

The speech ends with a "plea for the Jewish doctrine of God, and for the specifically Christian emphasis on a 'Son of Man' doctrine of judgment."[111] The indirect introduction of Jesus as "by the man whom he has appointed" is rhetorically powerful. An outright statement of the name of Jesus may be too blunt and therefore not effective. An introduction of Jesus without mentioning his name, but referring to him as "the man whom he has appointed," is

---

107. Aristotle *Poet.* 19.1456b.7–9; Cicero *Or.* 40.1.138.
108. See Lausberg, *Handbuch,* 1:236–40, #431–42.
109. *Her.* 4.42.54.
110. E. Würthwein, "*Metanoeō,*" *TDNT* 4:985.
111. See Lake and Jackson, *Beginnings of Christianity,* 4:208–9.

subtle and effective. Rhetorically, this subtle approach draws the mind of the audience to focus on the mission of Jesus: to judge the world in righteousness.

Paul the orator begins respectfully and gently;[112] only at the end does he state the basic difference between their philosophical worldviews, which was to be found in the issues of judgment and resurrection. The audience asks specifically about resurrection, but Paul does not give a direct answer; instead he presents his points slowly but surely. The audience context calls for Paul to mention resurrection; the fact of the resurrection is the highlight of Paul's speech. Without the proper context, the mentioning of resurrection to a monistic, deterministic, and materialistic audience would mean the monstrous resuscitation of a corpse.[113] Marcus rightly points out that the Hellenistic world did not have a developed idea of the afterlife; what concept they did have "was a rather vague one of mystical absorption into the cosmos, becoming one with the cosmic logos."[114] The Stoic school (e.g., Zeno) postulated sensation as the sole origin of knowledge. It held reason (logos) to be the integrative principle governing both human beings and the universe. Such a pantheistic thrust (living in harmony with nature) and a cyclic view of history, moving through a conflagration-regeneration sequence, has no place for immortality or resurrection.[115] This is true also in the atomistic view of Epicureanism. For example, Democritus taught that the universe consists of eternal atoms of matter, and the changing combination of the configuration of atoms gives birth to chance. Such naturalistic epistemology maintains that all knowledge stems from sense perception. Therefore, the Epicureans had no view of life after death, since what is lasting is pleasure. Similarly, Philodemus wrote: "There is nothing about god. There is nothing to be alarmed at in death." That may be the reason why some of them mocked Paul's mention of resurrection, because what Paul preached was absurd in their eyes.[116] In short, "by present-

---

112. See Bahnsen, "Encounter of Jerusalem," 19.
113. Bahnsen, "Encounter of Jerusalem," 19.
114. Marcus, "Paul at the Areopagus," 148.
115. See Chrysostom (*Hom. in Act.* 38.1).
116. Marcus, "Paul at the Areopagus," 148.

ing God as Creator and Judge, Paul emphasizes his Personality in contrast to the motivating pantheism of the Stoics."[117]

A Synchronic View of Paul's Rhetoric in Acts 17

We have already noted that the argumentation is not just on the level of pure intellectual knowledge; it is knowledge that impinges on the moral and religious aspect of the audience's responsibility before the Creator God. The missionary and conversion motivations of the speech are clear; the last two verses appeal to the audience to act.[118]

We shall trace Paul's argumentation as a whole and see how he handles his subject matter freely and skillfully to make his point. The rhetorical method is purposely chosen to enhance the discourse deliberated. Athenagoras of Athens drew a distinction between two kinds of theological discourse or argument: one on behalf of the truth and one concerning the truth. The former is a method that opens the way for argumentation by disposing of falsehood; the latter, which is primary here, provides content for the subject matter.[119] In his own case, Paul is not simply constructing a theology on the philosophical platform of the audience. Paul has his own understanding of God. But Paul is sensitive to the contextual needs of the audience. The Epicureans believed that the gods are materialistic in nature and far removed from, and unconcerned about, humankind. They believed pleasure to be the goal of life. The Stoics were pantheists, believing that God is pantheistically the soul of the universe and the universe is the body of God. The Areopagus speech in Acts 17 provides an alternate picture of God as eternal, knowing, and loving, in contrast to the impersonal Stoic God, who is incapable of knowledge, love, or providential acts.

---

117. Bruce, *Acts of the Apostles,* 338–39.

118. Munck mistakenly argues that the speech and "its doctrine is a reworking of thoughts in Romans transformed into missionary impulse." It is hard to see how Paul could be so negative in Romans 1 and how the Lukan Paul could be so positive in Acts (Johannes Munck, *The Anchor Bible: The Acts of the Apostles,* revised by W. F. Albright and C. S. Mann [Garden City, N.Y.: Doubleday, 1967], 173).

119. Athenagoras, *Peri anastaseos,* 1.3; 11.3; cf. *Presbeia,* 9.1, and T. F. Torrance, "*Phusikos kai Theologikos Logos,*" *Scottish Journal of Theology* 41 (1988): 11.

The genius of Paul (or the Lukan Paul, rather) is his ability to use the language of Greek philosophy and yet to be able to communicate the stereotypical meaning contained in the language. As Krodel writes, "The whole speech is carefully balanced and its parts interrelated."[120] The similarities between Paul's and the Greek philosopher's language is not a coincidence; Paul intentionally creates similarities. Even though Paul uses the audience's imagery and language, he has transformed their worldview by giving it new meaning and significance.[121] In Stoicism God is Nature, Fate, Fortune, and the all-pervading Mind. But the God Paul proclaims is personal and immanent, the Creator and Sustainer of all.

The cosmological argument in verses 24–29 seeks to prove the existence and the providence of God by reference to natural revelation. The natural revelation of God is recognizable to the human mind and senses. Because of human manipulation, ignorance, distortion, and the suppression of truth, human beings have created idols for worship instead of worshiping God. Paul is working out of a framework of special revelation without doing away with general revelation. Paul uses natural revelation but not natural theology, natural theology being that natural revelation which is sufficient for redemption. The revelation of God in Christ, which is a special revelation, is more decisive and final than revelation in nature and history.[122] In this regard, T. F. Torrance has skillfully analyzed the method and content of Paul's theology. He says that Paul is preaching the gospel on behalf of the truth and concerning the truth.[123] Torrance views the resurrection motif as the primary and central motif. He writes: "[W]hile he [Paul] certainly linked his address with Greek ideas, he deliberately gave them a Christian sense.... St. Paul was not trying to commend the Gospel to the Greeks from within the frame of their religious thought, but bringing the Gospel to bear upon it in such a way as to expose

---

120. G. Krodel, *Acts* (Minneapolis: Augsburg, 1986), 329.

121. See Ronald H. Nash's discussion, *Christianity and the Hellenistic World* (Grand Rapids, Mich.: Zondervan, 1984), 263–70.

122. B. Shields ("The Areopagus Sermon and Romans 1:18ff: A Study in Creation Theology," *Restoration Quarterly* 20 [1977]: 23–30) also works along this line.

123. Torrance, *"Phusikos kai Theologikos Logos,"* 11–26.

its anthropomorphic and idolatrous distortion of the truth about God."[124] Torrance is correct except when he says, "Paul was not trying to commend the Gospel to the Greeks from within the frame of their religious thought." It is accurate to say that Paul intended to let the gospel critique Greek thought and that the resurrection and the coming judgment are distinctively Christian. But Paul does begin from the audience's perspective and then works forward to the gospel. He shares the gospel with the purpose of aiming toward belief and trust in the Lord Jesus Christ.[125] The beliefs and practices in Greek culture, Paul was convinced, were inconsistent and idolatrous. How Paul sought to motivate his audience to move from idolatry to faith is instructive. An insight from Martin Buber may be helpful here. Buber distinguishes between two types of faith: faith built on trust (Jewish) and faith based on belief (Greek).[126] Here we see how the argumentation of Paul's speech motivates the audience to believe. The consequent belief becomes a logical understanding of reality on which the audience can then build a trustful relationship with God. What is being suggested here is that Paul is working out of the combination of both Jewish and Greek notions of faith. In Greek rhetoric, "proof" or "belief" is a persuasion which aims to change one's mind because one is convinced, assured, and confident of the rhetor's argument.[127] Acts

---

124. Torrance, *"Phusikos kai Theologikos Logos,"* 13.

125. See Acts 2:44; 4:4, 32; 5:14; 8:12, 13, 37 (2x); 9:26, 42; 10:43; 11:17, 21; 13:12, 39, 41, 48; 14:1, 23; 15:5, 7, 11; 16:31, 34; 17:12, 34; 18:8 (2x), 27; 19:2, 4, 18; 21:20, 25; 22:19; 24:14; 26:27 (2x); 27:25.

126. Martin Buber, *Two Types of Faith,* trans. Norman P. Goldhawk (New York: Macmillan, 1951), 7. Buber agrees with other scholars such as D. M. Baillie (*Faith in God and Its Christian Consummation: The Kerr Lectures for 1926* [Edinburgh: T. & T. Clark, 1927], 5–19); William Henry Paine Hatch (*The Pauline Idea of Faith in Its Relation to Jewish and Hellenistic Religion,* Harvard Theological Studies 2 [Cambridge: Harvard University Press, 1917], 1–20); and Edward D. O'Connor (*Faith in Synoptic Gospels: A Problem in the Correlation of Scripture and Theology* [South Bend, Ind.: University of Notre Dame Press, 1961], 11–18). Kinneavy adds the rhetorical component of persuasion to the Greek notion of faith and argues that New Testament faith is more Greek than Jewish. James L. Kinneavy, *Greek Rhetorical Origins of Christian Faith: An Inquiry* (Oxford: Oxford University Press, 1987), 15–21.

127. Henry G. Liddell and Robert Scott (*A Greek-English Lexicon* [Oxford: Clarendon Press, 1968], 1408) give the first definition of faith as "trust in others, faith . . . persuasion of a thing, confidence, assurance."

17 discusses this in terms of belief in the Lord Jesus Christ or conversion. The Areopagus speech is persuasive in its logical, ethical,
and pathetic argumentation.[128]

To summarize this section, we may ask the question again:
"What has Jerusalem to do with Athens?" Jerusalem offers Athens
the prospect of transformation. According to Paul in Acts 17, the
Athenian understanding of God is not totally removed from that
of the Jewish Christian notion of the One True God. The bulk
of Paul's speech in the pericope is not Christocentric but theocentric, ending with the Christ event, and the proofs are taken not
so much from Scripture as from the audience's sources.[129] Nor is
the speech an "unfinished symphony,"[130] because both the structure and content suggest its compactness and fullness. The essential
essence of the gospel is presented: Jesus' death, resurrection, and
eschatological role, and an appeal for a response.[131]

What Has Jerusalem to Do with Beijing?

The Areopagus speech represents Paul's cross-cultural preaching of
the Jewish Christian gospel to the Athenian philosophers. Paul's
approach is different from that of Tertullian, who in his *Prescription against Heretics* (VII) argues, "What indeed has Athens
to do with Jerusalem? What concord is there between the Academy and the Church? . . . Our instructions come from 'the porch of
Solomon.' . . . Away with all attempts to produce a mottled Chris-

---

128. Just as Kinneavy writes regarding persuasiveness in Greek rhetoric: "It [per-
suasive rhetoric] elicits a strong trust in the credibility of the speaker (the ethical
argument); it elicits a free assent from the recipient of the message who must believe
that it is to his or her good to assent (this is the essence of the pathetic argument);
and it passes on information and some knowledge about the subject matter involved
(the logical argument)" (*Greek Rhetorical Origins*, 51).

129. So E. Schweizer, "Concerning the Speeches of Acts" in *Studies in Luke-Acts*,
208–14; and Legrand, "Unknown God of Athens," 159.

130. As L. Legrand would argue, calling the speech an *opus infinitum*, "Unknown God of Athens," 159.

131. See W. Barclay, *Turning to God: A Study of Conversion in the Book of Acts
and Today* (Philadelphia: Westminster Press, 1964); U. Wilchens, *Die Missionsreden
der Apostelgeschichte* (Neukirchener, 1974), 178–86.

tianity of Stoic, Platonic, and dialectic composition!"[132] Tertullian used the terms "Athens" and "Jerusalem" to mean "reason" and "faith"; that is, Christian faith and Greek philosophy should not be synthesized. Though this chapter has broadened Tertullian's use of terms to mean "Christian faith" (Jerusalem) and "culture" (Athens or Beijing), his paradigm is still helpful to the cross-cultural hermeneutic we seek. Many modern scholars are less critical than Tertullian in his understanding of faith and reason. Hemer, for example, argues that "[t]he paradigmatic character of the speech, as a classic of intercultural communication applicable to our own increasingly pluralistic world, is indeed inseparable from the appreciation of the 'reality' of its original context."[133] Likewise, L. Legrand says that "Acts 17 represents a positive stance towards the surrounding religious world."[134] And S. Johnson Samuel claims, "The Areopagus speech serves as a paradigm in sharing the Christian faith with people of other faiths."[135] Conzelmann and Samuel rightly exhort Christians to avoid a rigid strategy when sharing the gospel cross-culturally.[136]

The Rhetorical Relationship between Jerusalem and Beijing

The perennial issue is how to proclaim Jesus Christ in a secular and philosophical world, how to relate reason and faith, natural revelation and special revelation. In applying the rhetoric of Acts 17, there are a few approaches one may take: (*a*) Athens is actually another form of Jerusalem; (*b*) Jerusalem is against Athens; (*c*) Jerusalem is integrated with Athens; (*d*) Jerusalem is segregated from Athens; (*e*) Jerusalem is the capital of Athens.[137]

---

132. A quote used by Dibelius, *Studies in the Acts of the Apostles*, 32.
133. Hemer, "Speeches of Acts II," 255.
134. L. Legrand, "Unknown God of Athens," 230.
135. Samuel, "Paul on the Areopagus," 29.
136. Samuel, "Paul on the Areopagus," 29; Conzelmann, "The Address of Paul on the Areopagus," 227.
137. See Bahnsen, "Encounter of Jerusalem," 5. Samuel further lists three approaches out of his study of the Areopagus speech for missiology consideration. The first is the positive approach which does not condemn idolatry out front. The second is the continuity approach which seeks to lead the audience to the fuller

Given the five approaches above, Paul's approach is perhaps closer to (c) than any other, but only with clear differentiation between Christian monotheism and Greek pantheism. He neither disguises Christian faith in the form of Greek philosophy as (*a*) does, nor condemns idolatry out front as (*b*) does. Unlike (*d*) Paul intentionally brings Christian monotheism into dialogue with Greek belief; unlike (*e*) Paul does not wish Christian monotheism to replace Greek culture altogether. Instead, Paul seeks to lead the audience to the fuller knowledge of monotheism, that is, faith in Jesus and the power of Christ's resurrection. This he does from the audience's vantage point and in the audience's language. And that constitutes the relationship between Jerusalem and Athens.

The relationship between Jerusalem and Beijing can likewise be construed when we imitate the approach of Paul in the Areopagus speech. I wish to extend the classical, rhetorical approach, drawing insights from the modern theories of rhetoric, so as to relive the message of Acts 17 for a Chinese Taoist audience. I have chosen the Taoist context of Beijing in order to apply Paul's rhetorical moves concretely to a particular audience, rather than vaguely deducing his rhetorical principles for a mixed audience of all Chinese religions. This hermeneutical dialogue between Paul and the Taoists is experimental and paradigmatic in that the rhetorical interaction can also be extended to other religions. But for illustrative purposes, I will limit my task to Taoism. Another reason for choosing Taoism as a conversation partner is because of the similarity between Stoicism and Taoism. This similarity will make it easier to apply rhetorical criticism from the Pauline context to that of Beijing.

Rhetorical criticism is not just a theoretical criticism; it is also a practical criticism that rereads and reinterprets texts in the ever widening "social relations between writers and readers."[138] C. W.

---

knowledge of the truth from their vantage point. The third is the inclusive approach of sharing a testimonial of one's belief and sharing God's eternal life through Christ. See Samuel, "Paul on the Areopagus," 30–32.

138. Terry Eagleton, *Literary Theory: An Introduction* (Minneapolis: University of Minnesota Press, 1983), 205–6.

Perelman's "new rhetoric,"[139] Bakhtin's "dialogic imagination,"[140] and K. Burke's notion of social identification and transformation[141] may prove to be helpful in relating Acts 17:22–31 to the religious context of Chinese Taoism. Three points will be suggested below for consideration for a cross-cultural, hermeneutical reading of Acts 17.

The Rhetoric of Dialogic Imagination between Jerusalem and Beijing

First, the rhetoric of dialogic imagination is not imperialistic but open to effect change. In the Areopagus speech Paul is not presenting a monologue. That he uses much of the cultural, social, and literary material of the audience indicates the forum or dialogue in progress between rhetor and audience. Through dialogue the gospel is indigenized by the use of native words, concepts, and expressions.

Affirming the religious value and the insights of Taoism in the context of the Chinese audience may be the best way to approach dialogue. Only after or through that affirmation can and should one point out the insufficiency and weakness of the other's belief system. Rhetorical theory and practice has its effectiveness in dialogue and community discourse, rather than in monologue. Dialogue should be used in the preaching and sharing of the gospel. Even Taoism affirms that kind of rhetoric. *Tao Te Ching* says: "The Tao that can be told of is not the Eternal Tao; The name that can be named is not the Eternal Name.... The Nameless is the origin of Heaven and Earth; The Named is the mother of all things" (chap. 1). The religiosity of Taoism is seen in its genuineness and its openness to encounter the Tao through inclusion and pluralism. A Taoist master named Chuang Tzu (369–295 B.C.E.) said: "There are presently [namely, the Warring States Period, 403–221 B.C.E.] many masters in the schools of philosophy, and each of them has claimed to possess the correct solution to the problems of

---

139. Chaïm Perelman, *The Realm of Rhetoric,* trans. William Kluback (Notre Dame, Ind.: University of Notre Dame Press, 1982), 8.

140. Or E. Black's imaginative criticism; see his *Rhetorical Criticism: A Study in Method* (New York: Macmillan, 1965), 177.

141. K. Burke, *Rhetoric of Motives* (Berkeley: University of California Press, 1969), 49–59.

our chaotic society. We may ask what happened to the philosophy of ancient Tao. I would say that it must have been diversified into each and every system."[142] Here we see that the rhetoric of Tao is characterized by its openness to conversation and by argument free from supposition.

The openness and the syncretistic tendency of Chinese religions, including Taoism, suggest that Chinese people are religious, and that they do worship a multitude of gods, either from fear or from respect for all gods.[143] There are discrepancies between the religious beliefs and the practices of the Chinese, just as there were among the Greeks. The gospel, as Paul proclaimed it, however, calls persons and their cultures to see the weakness and inconsistency of their belief system and to trust in nothing else but God alone.

Dialogue between the gospel and Taoism may focus on the understanding of God, the Creator-Sustainer-Parent. Lao Tze says in *Tao Te Ching:*

> There is Something undifferentiated, and yet complete in Itself. Soundless and Formless; Independent and Unchanging; Pervasive and Inclusive. It can be regarded as the Mother of the Universe. I do not know Its name. I named It "Tao." Only I was forced to give It a name. I regard It simply "Great." For in greatness, It produces. In producing, It expands. In expanding, It regenerates. (Chap. 24)

Tao, then, is the creative universal principle or reality. Lao Tze continues, "The great Tao flows everywhere.... All things depend on It for life. And It does not turn away from them. It accomplished Its tasks, but claims no credit. It clothes and feeds all things, but does not overlord." And again, in chapter 51: "It is Tao that gives them life. It is Virtue that nurses them, grows them, fosters them, shelters them, comforts them, nourishes them and protects them. To give life but not to be possessive, to care for life but expect no reward, to guide them but control them not, this is called the

---

142. Chuang Tzu, chap. 33.
143. For a discussion of Taoist polytheistic belief and cultic practice, see Henri Maspero, *Taoism and Chinese Religion*, trans. Frank A. Kierman, Jr. (Amherst: University of Massachusetts Press, 1981).

Primordial Virtue." Tao is the primordial principle of all creativity and materiality. The Taoist idea of the providence of God, seen here, is closer to Stoicism than to Epicureanism. From the Taoist notions of greatness, emptiness, and silence comes the idea that Tao is possibility or perpetual creativity.[144] Paul would say, as seen in Acts 17, that the God he believes in is the God of which the *Tao Te Ching* speaks. For God does not dwell in shrines or temples and does not need the service of human hands. Of course, if Paul were to preach to the Chinese, he would say that the God he trusts in is a personal God who cares for humanity.[145]

The Rhetoric of Identification between Jerusalem and Beijing

Second, the rhetoric of identification is necessary if one has to make the message relevant and applicable to the needs of the audience. In the speech Paul is not speaking above his audience; he speaks to them at their level and need. Paul is also extremely careful in the exordium to gain the attention and goodwill of the audience. Some believe, and others wish to hear more. The rhetoric had an effect on the audience. The *principium* or *prooimion* of the exordium and the *captatio benevolentiae* of verse 22 serve as good models to begin an interfaith dialogue. Their purpose is to establish a rapport which gains the audience's goodwill and which helps remove suspicion and distrust.

In the *probatio* (vv. 24–29), Paul begins to give a Christian view of God which he places in the context of conventional Stoic argumentation. This model can be understood in the following example. In the cultural context of Chinese Taoism, the distinctive human being is seen as obtaining virtue/morality (Te) from the Tao:

> The things they obtained by which they came into existence,
> it was called their Te.... Form without Tao cannot have ex-

144. Yieh Siew Shan, "Few Thoughts after Reading the Book of 'Lao Tze,'" in *Research on Taoism Culture*, vol. 2, ed. Chen Gu-Ing (Shanghai: Gu Chik Publisher, 1990), 133–51 (Chinese).

145. The anthropological concern for habitation and welfare to which Paul refers in v. 26 is also a Stoic concern. Similarly, Taoism understands the logos as the one principle underlying all realities, the principle of order and harmony.

istence. Existence without Te cannot have manifestation.... Tao is what all things (including human) follow. Te is what things individually obtain from it.[146]

Had the audience of the Areopagus speech been Chinese, I surmise that Paul would have said, "People of the Dragon, I perceive that in every way you are very religious and virtuous...." Such an exordium would help to identify the audience with the rhetor and the message that he is going to communicate. Paul would also have used the interpersonal Tao to clarify the interpersonal relationship, which human beings as creatures should have with God the Creator. And of course, the mystical understanding of God in Taoism lends itself nicely to the Christian understanding of God. Indeed, the *probatio* of verses 24–29 fits very well with the Taoist understanding of Tao. But transformation will not occur until the gospel actually encounters another culture. That is the concern of the next point.

The Rhetoric of Transformation between Jerusalem and Beijing

Third, the power of transformation will come only after the audience has identified with, and been convinced by, the "proof" of the speech. The greatest challenge to the Chinese Taoist is the proclamation of Christ in verses 30–31. The cyclical worldview of Taoism can be transformed, Paul would say. History has an end and purpose. Paul proclaims that God and humans interact in time and space: God *did* work in this world in the past (vv. 24, 26, 30), he *is* existing (v. 27) and acting (v. 30). God *is* not being served (v. 25), but *is* giving (v. 25) to humanity's needs, and he *will* execute his plan and judge the world (v. 31). Taoism by contrast regards history as cyclical and believes that all will be dissolved into the logos, the Source of all. Similar to Hellenistic philosophy, Taoism does not have a developed idea of an afterlife but a vague mystical notion of absorption into the universe in unity with the cosmic logos. By presenting God as Creator and Judge, Paul

---

146. Chuang Tzu, chap. 12.

emphasizes God's Personhood. This contrasts with the pantheistic view of God held by the Taoist.

Many Chinese who are steeped in Taoism are aware that their lifestyles and religious practices are not often congruent with their philosophy. Some live in fear, others in uncertainty of life after death. Idolatry is practiced through ignorance, out of fear that a god may be angered if not revered. To avoid that problem, they practice polytheism so that all the gods — wherever and whatever they may be — are appeased and delighted. The question arises, if Tao is one, why worship many gods? And even worse, why worship out of fear? This was a problem faced by the Stoics and the Epicureans, and it is one faced by the Taoists. Paul's speech on the Areopagus is a refutation of such practices (v. 24c). The message of the creation of the human race (v. 27) can be proclaimed to contemporary Chinese audiences so that they may seek God. Groping after God in the dark is no longer necessary, because now it is possible to seek and to know God, that is, to serve God piously and uprightly in light of the Christ event.

Toward Resurrection and Hope

Because Christ's resurrection has confirmed that history has an end, and that the future is proleptically present in the now, life is hopeful! Another aspect which is lacking in the Tao but which is revealed in the Christ event is resurrection and hope. Human beings are neither destined nor created to be caught in the web of unending conflagration. Applying Paul's rhetoric to Beijing would suggest that Taoism has created an idolatrous situation in which polytheism, the worship of "unknown gods," is prevalent. Paul's rhetoric suggests a way of approaching Taoists with the gospel so that they gradually see the logic of turning to Christ, whom God, the one we can know, has raised from death.

Chapter 8

Christology and Suffering in the Book of Revelation and in China

Although the book of Revelation has been subjected to many abuses over the centuries, one fact remains true: Revelation continues to be meaningful to Christians all over the world who live in the grim reality of overt and covert persecution and suffering. The abundant esoteric imagery found in Revelation has not deterred Christians from tapping the power of its faith and finding comfort in it. This chapter will conclude with the experience of Chinese Christians during the Cultural Revolution. It will not focus exclusively on their situation but on the power of biblical utterance in Revelation; that is the reason for the great length devoted to biblical analysis. It is hoped that the process will enable readers to know of the living hope portrayed in Revelation 5.

The intent of this chapter is, therefore, not to give the psychological, but the biblical and theological reasons for the communicative and pastoral power of Revelation for both its ancient and modern audiences. The argument presented here follows closely Pannenberg's interpretation of Christology in his book, *Jesus — God and Man,* but to it is added an exegesis of Revelation 5, focusing on the central imagery of its Christology: the lion and the lamb. At the end of the chapter, we shall turn to the model of the Three-Self Patriotic Movement, which is a Chinese church movement with different ideological assumptions than those of the author of Revelation. However, before outlining Pannenberg's position regarding history and Christology, which this chapter will use as a framework for interpreting Revelation 5, it may be helpful to review some of the major historical methodologies used in the study of Revelation.

The Methods in the Studies of Revelation

The bewildering array of interpretations are often summarized into four main schools: preterist, historicist, futurist, and idealist.[1] The preterist's interpretation is a contemporary historical approach which sees the applicability of Revelation to the original audience alone. The historicist understands Revelation as covering history from the original audience up to the eschaton. The futurist projects the history which Revelation covers entirely into the future eschaton. A moderate futurist interpretation of Revelation (offered by G. Ladd) sees the seven seals as "the forces in history...by which God works out his redemptive and judicial purposes in history leading up to the end."[2] And the idealist employs a symbolic approach which sees time as cyclical rather than linear. The stance taken here incorporates elements of both the historicist and the idealist, one which views history as having a spiral movement.

The book of Revelation does not set forth stages of world history, but a Christian philosophy of history with heavy orientation on eschatology.[3] Schüssler Fiorenza's survey of various

---

1. These interpretations are found, for example, in C. Brütsch, *Die Offenbarung Jesu Christi: Johannes-Apokalypse,* 2d ed., 3 vols. (Zurich: Zwingli Verlag, 1970), 1:179–95; A. Feuillet, *The Apocalypse* (Staten Island, N.Y.: Alba House, 1965), 2–7; E. F. Harrison, *Introduction to the New Testament* (Grand Rapids, Mich.: Eerdmans, 1964), 435–38; G. E. Ladd, *A Commentary on the Revelation of John* (Grand Rapids, Mich.: Eerdmans, 1972), 10–14; L. Morris, *The Book of Revelation* (Grand Rapids, Mich.: Eerdmans, 1987), 17–24; R. H. Mounce, *The Book of Revelation* (Grand Rapids, Mich.: Eerdmans, 1977), 39–45; M. C. Tenney, *Interpreting Revelation* (Grand Rapids, Mich.: Eerdmans, 1957), 135–46; A. Wikenhauser, *New Testament Introduction,* trans. J. Cunningham (New York: Herder & Herder, 1958), 558–62, and his *Die Offenbarung des Johannes: Übersetzt und erklärt* (Regensburg: Verlag Friedrich Pustet, 1959), 18–22; F. D. Mazzaferri, *The Genre of the Book of Revelation from a Source-Critical Perspective* (Berlin and New York: de Gruyter, 1989), 33–34, and others.

2. G. E. Ladd, "The Theology of the Apocalypse," *Gordon Review* 7, no. 2–3 (1963–64): 73–86.

3. I. A. Feuillet, "Les diverses méthodes d'interprétation de l'Apocalypse et les

approaches from the philosophy of history is helpful to our understanding of Revelation's philosophy of history. She uses three
narrow categories: the history of the church (*Kirchengeschichte*),[4]
the history contemporary to the author (*Zeitgeschichte*),[5] and final
history (*Endgeschichte*). Schüssler Fiorenza points out that interpretations from both the *geschichtstheologische* (theology of
history) approaches and the *heilsgeschichtliche* (salvation history)[6]
approaches emphasize eschatology as the fundamental principle
of interpretation.[7] Similarly, the *endgeschichtliche* approach also
uses the "eschaton" as the principle for interpretation of history. Schüssler Fiorenza is critical of the preterist and *geschichts-
philosophische* (historical-philosophical) interpretations of Revelation (history as the fundamental), preferring the eschatological
interpretation as the proper horizon for the understanding of
Revelation.[8] She contends that

> the main concern of Revelation is not (salvation) history, but
> eschatology, that is, the breaking-in of God's kingdom and
> the destruction of the hostile godless powers. The author of
> Revelation is, indeed, aware of time, but he knows only a
> "short time" before the eschaton. The eschatology of Rev-
> elation is, therefore, not dependent on or legitimated by a
> certain course of historical events. Rather, time and history
> have significance only insofar as they constitute the "little

commentaires récents," *American Clergy* 71 (27 April 1961): 257–70. But whether
John is rereading the OT in the light of the Christ event, as Feuillet contends, is
debatable. A. Feuillet distinguishes the many types of philosophy used, such as
millenarianism, recapitulation, universal history, eschatology, contemporary history,
and comparative religion.

4. Revelation presents "a picture of the things that are to come until the end
of history from the viewpoint of the Church of Christ." See J. Michl, "Die Deutung
der apokalyptischen Frau in der Gegenwart," *Biblische Zeitschrift* 3, no. 2 (1959):
301.

5. See M. Hopkins, "The Historical Perspective of Apocalypse 1–11," *Catholic
Biblical Quarterly* 27, no. 1 (1965): 42–47.

6. See A. Feuillet's comment: "history as a closed and divided totality and
presented in mythological images" ("Les diverses méthodes d'interprétation de
l'Apocalypse et les commentaires récents," 260).

7. See Elisabeth Schüssler Fiorenza, *The Book of Revelation: Justice and
Judgment* (Philadelphia: Fortress, 1985), 37. See her n. 23 on salvation history.

8. Schüssler Fiorenza, *The Book of Revelation*, 36–51.

while" before the end. This means that in Revelation "history" is completely subordinated to eschatology and receives its significance from the future.[9]

Schüssler Fiorenza, therefore, argues that eschatology, and not history, is the interpretive key to Revelation.[10] Her thesis is correct but needs modification. Eschatology involves "future history." The breaking-in of God's kingdom and the destruction of evil forces at the end time have confirmed for believers their present reality. The present is subordinated to the future and confirmed partially by the past. The present receives its significance from the future. The Book of Revelation is a Christian theology of history in terms of the Christ event that defines the meaning of history in terms of eschatology.[11]

The concern of this chapter is not with the chronological sequence of events in world history that coincide with history in Revelation. Instead, the focus is on a particular view of history that gives birth to the rhetorical effect and imagery of the apocalypse, which in turn evokes hope and faith. To understand that view, we need first to call on Pannenberg's understanding of history and Christology.

Christ the End of History and Christ the Hope of the World

There are two basic interrelated points in Pannenberg's *Jesus — God and Man* which are indispensable for this chapter: one is his view of history, the other is his understanding of Christology. His interpretation can be outlined in four subpoints.

---

9. Schüssler Fiorenza, *The Book of Revelation*, 46.

10. See Elisabeth Schüssler Fiorenza, "The Eschatology and Composition of the Apocalypse," *Catholic Biblical Quarterly* 30, no. 4 (1968): 537–69. A. J. Bandstra gives a good critique to Schüssler Fiorenza's main thesis. See his "History and Eschatology in the Apocalypse," *Calvin Theological Journal* 5, no. 2 (1970): 180–83.

11. See B. Marconcini, "Differenti metodi dell'interpretazione dell'Apocalisse," *Biblica et Orientalia* 18, no. 3–4 (1976): 121–31. Marconcini also mentions that the yearning "Come, Lord Jesus" is an assured timely victory of Christ's intervention in history.

First, like most systematic theologians, Pannenberg uses a unifying principle to construct a coherent, systematic Christology. His understanding of history is grounded in the historical Jesus and his Jewish apocalyptic context. This methodology is a reaction to both existentialist (Bultmannian) and dialectic (Barthian) theology and to the dichotomy drawn by M. Kähler between kerygma and history (*Historie* and *Geschichte*).[12] In other words, Pannenberg does not choose to make a distinction between the fact and the meaning of history, between the Christ of proclamation and the Jesus of history. Also, he does not choose to begin an investigation of Jesus "from above" as the Barthian approach does, nor from the "below" of human experience like Bultmann. He approaches Christology from below only in the sense that he begins with the historical Jesus, whose context is the Jewish apocalyptic expectation of the imminence of the Kingdom of God. For Pannenberg, revelation is not to be found in the ghetto of salvation history or in the dogmatic authority of the revealed Word, but in history.[13]

Pannenberg believes that the Jesus of history is the basis and source of Christian faith.[14] The Jesus of history gives subjective faith an objective base (27, 47), for without that verification or confirmation faith may be illusory or demonic. He believes that Jesus is present with us now, not in the kerygma, but as the exalted hidden One waiting to be fully revealed in glory in His final return (21, 28, 371). This approach has its emphasis on the past reality and final return of Jesus.[15]

---

12. See W. Pannenberg, *Jesus — God and Man,* trans. Lewis L. Wilkins (Philadelphia: Westminster Press, 1977), 33–37. M. Kähler, *The So-Called Historical Jesus and the Historic Biblical Christ,* translated, edited, and with an introduction by Carl E. Braaten (Philadelphia: Fortress, 1964), 5.

13. Note that the first disclosure of Pannenberg's methodology is not found in his book *Jesus — God and Man,* but in the 1961 book he edited, *Offenbarung als Geschichte* (Eng. trans.: *Revelation as History,* trans. David Granskou [New York: Macmillan, 1968]).

14. Pannenberg, *Jesus — God and Man,* 22, 49. (Subsequent page references in text and notes are to this volume.) His argument is that since we are not God, we cannot begin with the perspective of God; we can begin from the context of a historically determined human situation.

15. Pannenberg advocates that "the past reality of Jesus did not consist of brute facts in the positivistic sense, to which arbitrary interpretations, one as good as another, could be added. Rather, meaning already belongs to the activity and

Second, Pannenberg affirms that God's self-revelation can be understood as the identity, and thus the unity, of the revealer and the revealed one in the totality of Jesus' history (128). Pannenberg's Christology begins with Jesus' unity with God, that is, the union of Jesus with God in the revelatory event of his resurrection from the dead — an event which can be understood only as the union of Jesus with the eternal being of God. Jesus' unity with God is related to the preexistent Sonship of Jesus;[16] yet, it is a unity which can be understood only in the resurrection (65). The deeds and words of Jesus are not proofs of Jesus' Sonship; only the resurrection confirms and consummates Jesus' Sonship. Resurrection is "the ground of his unity with God" (chap. 3). "Jesus appeared at the beginning not as a God-man but as a man, and as a man he knew himself to be under a mission, an office, an assignment from Israel's God. Jesus was the bearer of an office from God first as simply man. Precisely the confirmation of Jesus in his earthly mission through his resurrection was the basis for the confession of his divinity" (223). The resurrection of Jesus has a "retroactive force" (*rückwirkende Kraft*). Just as importantly, the metaphor of resurrection, which is grounded in the apocalyptic expectation, is absolutely essential to Christian faith and its vision of the future (82–96). Here Pannenberg is influenced by Hegel's understanding of history, namely, the notion that the truth of history lies at the end of history.[17] The resurrection of Jesus, seen within its Jewish apocalyptic context as Pannenberg sees it, means that the end of the world has begun. It means that God has confirmed the divinity and life of Jesus, and that God is revealed in him, because the end of history has happened proleptically in the resurrection of Jesus

---

fate of Jesus in the original context in the history of traditions within which it occurred . . . " (49).

16. Jesus is one with God before his earthy life (see Pannenberg, *Jesus — God and Man,* 150); the essential union of the risen one with God leads by intrinsic logic to the thought of preexistence (153). Therefore, "the revelatory union of Jesus with God, who is from eternity to eternity, brings in the ideal that Jesus as Son of God is pre-existent" (150).

17. According to Pannenberg, "The ultimate divine confirmation of Jesus will take place only in the occurrence of his return. Only then will the revelation of God in Jesus become manifest in its ultimate, irresistible glory" (128).

(71–73). God is revealed at the end of history and in "Jesus the End."[18]

Third, Jesus' dedication to God is what mediates (*vermittelt*) and establishes (*begründet*) his divinity (336). It is in the Triune God that personal community is seen; although Jesus is not identical to God the Father (334, 339), the two are in a reciprocal relationship of self-surrender and self-dedication,[19] the purpose of which is to establish God's Kingdom (334–35). According to Pannenberg, Jesus the Son of God is not the preexistent *persona*, nor is he of the divine substance/nature; he is Jesus the obedient One in unity with God. Jesus the human is not the human substance/nature; he is the One self-dedicated to the Father, a self-dedication confirmed by the resurrection. "Trinity has to do with the participation of a plurality of persons in a single nature, Christology has to do with a unification of several natures through a single person" (343). Through this "openness-relationship" (344) Jesus becomes the Son of God. The two natures of Jesus are not a mixing, union, or compound (*Zusammensetzung*) of divine-human substance, but the personal-relational (*Persongemeinschaft*) in functional unity: Jesus' filial humanity, the perfect dedication (*Hingabe*) and obedience of sonship to God the Father, even to the point of self-surrender (*Selbstpreisgabe*). Again Pannenberg derives this interpretation from the Hegelian understanding of personhood as one who "relinquishes one's particularity to extend it to universality."[20]

Finally, soteriology, in the language of death and hope, is dealt with under the "office" of Jesus (38, 48–49). Jesus' historical words and deeds, says Pannenberg, cannot give meaning to Jesus' divinity (i.e., his unity with God), but Jesus' human life is of so-

---

18. This is Snook's term; see Lee E. Snook, *The Anonymous Christ* (Minneapolis: Augsburg Publishing House, 1986), 30.

19. Pannenberg, *Jesus — God and Man*, 181–83. "Jesus is one with God through his dedication to the Father that is confirmed as a true dedication by the Father's acknowledgment of him through Jesus' resurrection. Such personal community is at the same time essential community.... Thus the divinity of Jesus as Son is mediated, established through his dedication to the Father. In the execution of this dedication, Jesus is the Son... whose characteristic it is not to exist on the basis of his own resources but wholly from the Father" (336).

20. G. W. F. Hegel, *Lectures on the Philosophy of Religion* (London: Routledge and Kegan Paul, 1962), 3:24. See Pannenberg, *Jesus — God and Man*, 182, 336.

teriological importance: he calls people into the kingdom of God through openness to God and the future (190). The human condition is one of lostness, which for Pannenberg is hopelessness and death. He maintains that Jesus' message on the imminent Kingdom of God speaks to the human condition in terms of its perspective of hope and its openness to the future and to the world: "[R]adical hopelessness has death as its consequence.... The phenomenology of hope indicates that it belongs to the essence of conscious human existence to hope beyond death" (84–85). Pannenberg adds, "This opening-up of human beings for God's future, through which man's destiny to openness toward the future — even in his relationships to the world — is realized, is independent of particular apocalyptic deadlines" (226; also see 193, 199).

Salvation then means, according to Pannenberg, fulfillment of one's openness in unity with God.[21] The delay of the parousia is not a refutation of Christian hope as long as one maintains the unity between what happens in Jesus and the eschatological future: openness to the world (108). Jesus is "the eschatological judge" (191), "the executor of the end" (192) who grants us eschatological salvation. "Salvation is the wholeness of one's life for which one longs but never finally achieves in the course of one's earthly existence" (192). But through Jesus' life and work, God reveals that human essence is granted community with God and participation in eschatological salvation; human fate is not death but life resurrected from the dead (see 193–95).

A Thematic Interpretation of Revelation 5

The four subpoints of Pannenberg's interpretation on history and Christology provide a handy structural framework for this section,

---

21. Pannenberg adopted this idea from Wilhelm Dilthey, K. Rahner, and B. Welte (Pannenberg, *Jesus — God and Man*, 204, 357): (*a*) Meaning in existence is dependent on the relation between the parts and the whole, thus the meaning of human life is determined by the end of life correlated with the Resurrection; (*b*) Human beings are not bound to the earth, but unfulfilled in this finite earthly existence; they are open for meaning and fulfillment beyond the world and the presence of death. Only the future will decide the essence of human being, the world, and the context of our life situation (136).

in which we develop four "thematic" interpretations of Revelation 5. The first will examine historical issues of the book and the pericope's genre and context in terms of a philosophy of history. The second will deal with the identity of the Lamb in the throne room, and the imagery of hope. The third will consider worship and liturgy in Revelation 5 as communion and union with the Divine. The fourth will provide a theological summary of the rhetorical effect of the above three interpretations — the effect of an apocalyptic salvation in the conquering death of Jesus and in the notion of surrender or openness to the future.

The Genre and Philosophy of History and Social Context, and the Final Meaning of the Scroll

The identification of the genre[22] of Revelation as apocalyptic literature or otherwise will shape and inform one's interpretation of Revelation. While scholars such as A. Y. Collins,[23] H. D. Betz,[24] Karrer,[25] Lohse,[26] and H. Moore,[27] consider the book of Revelation to be apocalyptic literature, many do not. For example, Corsini contends that "[a]pocalyptic literature is closely associated with an 'endtime' messianism . . . [but the] Apocalypse is concerned

---

22. The Apocalypse Group of the Society of Biblical Literature has worked collaboratively on this issue over the past twelve years or so and has published the results in *Semeia* 14 (1979) and 36 (1986).

23. A. Y. Collins, "Early Christian Apocalypses," in *The Combat Myth in the Book of Revelation* (Missoula, Mont.: Scholars Press, 1976), 61ff.

24. H. D. Betz argues that Jewish and Christian apocalyptic writing is not a further development of OT prophecy but a specific phenomenon influenced by Hellenistic syncretism. See H. D. Betz, "Zum Problem des religionsgeschichtlichen Verständnisses der Apokalyptik," *Zeitschrift für Theologie und Kirche* 63, no. 4 (1966): 391–409.

25. Karrer adds that Revelation is thoroughly epistolary and not simply an epistolary framework within the Jewish apocalyptic or Christian epistolary framework. See M. Karrer, *Die Johannesoffenbarung als Brief* (Göttingen: Vandenhoeck & Ruprecht, 1986): 2–7.

26. Lohse sees some links between Revelation and Jewish apocalyptic writings, but clarifies that Revelation has its Christian character because of the centrality of Christ. See E. Lohse, "Wie christlich ist die Offenbarung des Johannes?" *New Testament Studies* 34, no. 3 (1988): 321–38.

27. H. Moore sees Revelation as having combined elements of apocalypse, prophecy, and epistle. See H. Moore, "The Book of Revelation," *Irish Biblical Studies* 9, no. 4 (1987): 155–74.

with the *first coming,* and especially in the climatic and culminating event of his [Jesus'] death and resurrection."[28] While Revelation does deal with the first coming of Christ, the second coming is clearly indicated. Corsini also argues that when John[29] speaks of his work as "prophecy" (1:3, 22; 7:18) and of himself as a "prophet" (19:10; 22:9), John is speaking in line with Old Testament prophets.[30] Corsini argues that Revelation is not apocalyptic but prophetic because (*a*) it calls itself prophecy (1:3 and 22:7) and

---

28. Eugenio Corsini, *The Apocalypse,* translated and edited by F. J. Moloney (Wilmington, Del.: Michael Glazier, 1983), 24. Italics his.

29. Papias and Justin Martyr in Eusebius point to the apostolic authorship. The *Apocryphon of John* discovered at Chenoboskion also identified John the Apostle as the author (A. Helmbold, "A Note on the Authorship of the Apocalypse," *New Testament Studies* 8, no. 1 [1961]: 77–79). The *Apocryphon* is from the fourth and/or early fifth century; the original composition goes back to the second and possibly to the end of the first century. S. S. Smalley ("John's Revelation and John's Community," *Bulletin of the John Rylands University Library of Manchester* 69, no. 2 [1987]: 549–71) says that Revelation was composed by John the apostle in the 70s with the same ethos, theology, tradition, language, and structure as the Fourth Gospel. Gunther ("The Elder John, Author of Revelation," *Journal for the Study of the New Testament* 11 [1981]: 3–20) proposes that the Elder John is the author. J. N. Sanders ("St. John on Patmos," *New Testament Studies* 9, no. 2 [1963]: 75–85) advances his hypothesis that "John of Ephesus, the seer and exile of Patmos, was a Sadducean aristocrat, a Jerusalem disciple of Jesus, the last survivor of the eye-witnesses of the incarnate Logos, but not the son of Zebedee, and that he wrote down in his own hand the visions he had seen as he received them, and in response to requests dictated a new version, perhaps a translation or rearrangement, of an earlier Gospel by another eye-witness, a man he must have known and trusted" (85). A. Y. Collins (*Crisis and Catharsis* [Philadelphia: Westminster Press, 1984], 25–53) proposes that this John cannot be identified with a historical person but is an itinerant prophet speaking the message on behalf of God to Christians; he is probably a native of Palestine.

30. This can be substantiated by John's uses of the OT (out of 404 verses in Revelation, 278 were composed with OT material). Whether John used the LXX (so G. K. Beale, "A Reconsideration of the Text of Daniel in the Apocalypse," *Biblica* 67, no. 4 [1986]: 539–43), or the LXX for the first seven chapters and the MT for the remaining chapters (so H. R. Swete, H. von Soden, and E. Lohmeyer), or the MT (so R. H. Charles) is not clear (so Vanhoye). Most probably the writer used the MT and thought in Hebrew, but wrote in Greek (so A. Lancellotti, "L'Antico Testamento nell'Apocalisse," *Rivista Biblica* 14, no. 4 [1966]: 369–84). Other scholars propose that John is translating from Aramaic (C. C. Torrey, *The Apocalypse of John* [New Haven: Yale University Press, 1958], 13–48) or Jewish-Greek, a unique dialect used by Jews in Palestine (so Stanley E. Porter, "The Language of the Apocalypse in Recent Discussion," *New Testament Studies* 35, no. 4 [1989]: 582–603).

not apocalypse; and (*b*) apocalyptic writing tends to neglect contemporary events, portrays a rigid determinism and a false dualism, and fosters a passivity that awaits divine intervention on the part of the reader, whereas Revelation speaks of contemporary events, speaks of Satan as having power only as God allows it (6:1–2; 13:7), and portrays the faithful as actively conquering (2:6; 3:21) through the blood of the Lamb (12:11). In the Old Testament, prophets are God's spokespersons seeking to bring the people of God back to a holy and living covenant; they are not prophesying in the sense of predicting future events.[31] F. D. Mazzaferri also argues along the same line as Corsini but from a source-critical perspective. Mazzaferri concludes that "Revelation cannot be equated with apocalyptic in form. It lacks pseudonymity.... Its eschatology is Christian.... John dips his hands freely into classical apocalyptic, the synoptic tradition, pagan mythology, and even astral symbols. But he bathes himself in one corpus alone, classical OT prophecy."[32] J. Kallas believes that Revelation is not an apocalyptic book because the imagery and symbolism is not the essence of Revelation, but merely a literary device. He further argues that the attitude toward suffering in Revelation is not apocalyptic, but Platonic: the view is that cosmic forces oppose God and result in the suffering of humankind.[33] Prigent also argues against the view that the genre of Revelation is apocalyptic, both because the images are perfectly understandable to first-century Christians and because the writer is not pessimistic about the present, but confident of assured victory.[34]

In the midst of this conversation it has been accepted that " 'apocalypse' is a genre of revelatory literature with a narrative framework, in which a revelation is mediated by an otherworldly being to a human recipient, disclosing a transcendent reality which

---

31. Corsini, *Apocalypse,* 21–22.

32. Mazzaferri, *Genre of the Book of Revelation,* 377–78.

33. J. Kallas, "The Apocalypse — An Apocalyptic Book?" *Journal of Biblical Literature* 86, no. 1 (1967): 69–80. See a critique of this position by B. W. Jones, "More about the Apocalypse as Apocalyptic," *Journal of Biblical Literature* 87, no. 3 (1968): 325–27. Jones argues that the suffering theme is too inconsistent to be a useful criterion.

34. P. Prigent, "Apocalypse et apocalyptique," *Revue des sciences religieuses* 47, no. 2–4 (1973): 280–99.

is both temporal, insofar as it envisages eschatological salvation, and spatial, insofar as it involves another, supernatural world."[35] The Book of Revelation fits this definition. For example, in Revelation 5, the "I saw" (vv. 1, 2, 6, 11) introduces the revelatory vision John saw. The mediator is the "angel" (v. 2) who discloses the transcendent reality that is fully manifested later by "the lion who is from the tribe of Judah, the root of David," that is, the *arnion* ("lamb"; vv. 5–6). Since all except one of the characteristics of apocalyptic literature, such as pseudonymity, esotericism and symbolism, dualism, supernaturalism, and a particular understanding of history,[36] fit the genre of Revelation, the argument of a whole host of scholars that Revelation is an apocalyptic book seems much more persuasive.

Here we focus on the two main characteristics of apocalyptic literature which are interrelated and relevant to the present thesis, namely, that apocalyptic literature presents a philosophy of history and is itself literature created in the midst of crisis with the "purpose of exhortation and/or consolation by means of divine authority."[37] Concerning the latter, Schüssler Fiorenza is right in observing, "In contrast to some Jewish apocalyptic writings, Revelation attempts to give meaning to the present suffering of the community not with reference to a divine plan of history, but with an understanding of the present from the horizon of the future, that is, from the coming kingdom of God."[38] John is presenting a philosophy of history in which the historical process is completely under the control of God.[39] For John, both the present and the final period (*Endgeschichte*) are under the lordship of the glorified Christ.[40] In other words, the present belongs to the future, and the latter is experienced now. The fulfillment of the promise in the

---

35. John J. Collins, "Introduction: Towards the Morphology of a Genre," *Semeia* 14 (1979): 9.

36. See H. Giesen, "Christusbotschaft in apokalyptischer Sprache: Zugang zur Offenbarung des Johannes," *Bibel und Kirche* 39, no. 2 (1984): 42–53.

37. David Hellholm, "The Problem of Apocalyptic Genre and the Apocalypse of John," *Semeia* 36 (1986): 27.

38. Schüssler Fiorenza, *The Book of Revelation*, 50.

39. See P. Fannon, "The Apocalypse," *Scripture* 14 (1962): 33–43.

40. K. Karner, "Gegenwart und Endgeschichte in der Offenbarung des Johannes," *Theologische Literaturzeitung* 93, no. 9 (1968): 641–52.

future can be seen and experienced now as John unveils for the audience the eschatological reality.

The question that troubles the writer and the audience is not so much the meaning of history (though that is partially the issue), but the meaning and termination of suffering in history. To convey a response to the meaning in suffering, John offers a particular view of history.[41] He does not narrate the *whole* of world history from the beginning to the eschatological end. Rather, as Schüssler Fiorenza points out, "Revelation consists of pieces or mosaic stones arranged in a certain design, which climaxes in a description of the final eschatological event. The goal and high point of the composition of the whole book, as of the individual 'little apocalypses,' is the final judgment and the eschatological salvation."[42] If our interpretation here is correct then we can say that John and Pannenberg are kindred spirits in that both attempt to stretch human finitude beyond the present to the historical past (Jesus' death and resurrection) and to the futuristic end of time (eschatological hope), thus granting humanity a vision of the past, present, and future.[43] The future and present overwhelm John's concern for the past. That is, the reality of the future can envelop (extend) backward to the past and the present and save them from being lost or ambiguous, thereby

---

41. Orna argues that John's concepts of time and history are different from the Greek *chronos* concept and also the Jewish *kairos* concept. John's view does not take a "celestial vantage point" of the old creation, but elevates the whole creation (including the beginning, the center, and the end of history) to a new creation of time and space. See M. v. Orna, "Time and History in the Apocalypse," *Cross Crown* 20, no. 2 (1968): 184–200. Orna cites 2:17; 3:12; 5:9; 14:3; 21:1; and 21:4–5, "...for the former things have passed away. And he who sat upon the throne said: 'Behold, I make all things new.'" My critique is that first, the *kairos* concept is in Revelation, and this concept is both Greek and Jewish; second, Orna seems to have an extreme view of history in terms of space and time, whereas John seems to be advocating a directional understanding of history and God's creation, i.e., viewed from the end to the beginning to the center.

42. Schüssler Fiorenza, *The Book of Revelation*, 47.

43. Pannenberg says, "Man as man is always something more than and extending beyond his present situation; his destiny is not fulfilled in any given framework of his life. God's reality is not only the ultimate source and guarantee of a present form of life, but points beyond every presently given or possible security and fulfillment of existence" (*Jesus — God and Man*, 226).

claiming them as belonging to the absolute future of history,[44] which is God.

Social-Historical Context. From a literary point of view, we would say that the genre of Revelation falls within the scope of Jewish apocalyptic, but from a theological point of view it is a Christian apocalyptic. Revelation depicts the religious, cultural, economic, and political struggles of Christians at the end of the first century,[45] probably during the reign of the Roman emperor Domitian.[46] While one would generally agree with Collins's social description of the "perceived crisis" the Christians are experiencing, it should certainly be pointed out that the "perceived crisis" is real, near, personal, and objective as far as Christians in the seven churches are concerned.[47]

The perceived crisis is political, social, and religious in nature. Barclay views the background of Revelation as that of Caesar worship. He sees the Roman Empire as the earthly body of Satan through which Satan exercises his power.[48] For example, in Pergamum at the time of John's writing there were many temples and

---

44. This is a suggestive notion made by B. O. McDermott, "Pannenberg's Resurrection Christology: A Critique," *Texts and Studies* 35 (1974): 716–17.

45. This date is found in Irenaeus, *Adv. Haer.* 5.30.3, and Eusebius, *EH* 3, 18. See W. G. Kümmel, *Introduction to the New Testament,* trans. A. J. Mattill (London: SCM Press, 1966), 327–29. My reconstruction basically agrees with Collins's and Thompson's research that Irenaeus's dating of Revelation to the reign of Domitian (ca. 90–95 C.E.) does not seem to rest on the tradition that Domitian was the second great persecutor of Christians. Furthermore, though internal evidence in Revelation is consistent with Irenaeus's dating, there is no reliable external evidence that Domitian systematically persecuted Christians — the first two centuries witnessed only sporadic repression of Christians. See Collins, *Crisis and Catharsis,* 54–140; and Leonard Thompson, "A Sociological Analysis of Tribulation in the Apocalypse of John," *Semeia* 36 (1986): 147–74.

46. Most commentaries hold this view: e.g., Swete, Charles, Loisy, Beckwith, Allo, Carrington, Wilkenhauser, Bonsirven, Behm, Brütsch, Féret, Boismard, Lohse, Cerflaux-Cambier, Caird, Visser, Kiddle-Ross, etc. However, Barclay Neuman challenges the Domitian hypothesis. See his "The Fallacy of the Domitian Hypothesis: Critique of the Irenaeus Source as a Witness for the Contemporary-historical Approach to the Interpretation of the Apocalypse," *New Testament Studies* 10, no. 1 (1963): 133–39.

47. See Collins, *Crisis and Catharsis,* 84–110.

48. The power culminated in the return of Nero Redivivus. See W. Barclay, "Great Themes of the New Testament: v. Revelation xiii," *Expository Times* 70, no. 9 (1959): 260–64; 292–96.

public buildings that honored Zeus with great altars. Pausanias in his account of Pergamum described the thronelike altar to Zeus the Savior on the top of the crag above the city. In the Roman period, the first provincial temple of the imperial cult in Asia was built at Pergamum in honor of Rome and Augustus (29 B.C.E. probably). The imperial cult, the worship of the spirit of Rome and of the emperor, was found at the center of the city. The one and only criterion recognized as loyalty to the country was a citizen's willingness to perform the ritual of the state religion, and to make an offering to the imperial God, the Divine Emperor. This Augustan temple is perhaps "Satan's throne" of Rv 2:13. The worship of Dionysus, the god of vegetation, Asklepios, the god of healing, and Athena were also practiced widely. Snakes and the handling of reptiles were associated, as the *Bacchae* of Euripides shows, with the cult of Dionysus. Snakes were the symbol of Asklepios. The four patron deities of Pergamum were Zeus, Athena, Dionysus, and Asklepios. Revelation was written in a time of sporadic persecution and tribulation in order to strengthen the faith, endurance, and hope of the Christians in Asia Minor.[49] During the reign of Domitian (81–96 C.E.), for example, Christian martyrs emerged as victors in Roman persecution. "Throne" in Revelation is a political term. The usage perhaps indicates the political polemic in light of the Caesar cult. The repeated "Worthy art thou" (4:11; 5:9, 12) reflects the acclamation used to greet the emperor during his triumphal entrance.[50] The title "Lord and God" (4:8) is paralleled by the claims of Domitian and other emperors. It is even surmised that the twenty-four elders may be the twenty-four lictors who surrounded Domitian.[51]

There are of course a number of references to suffering. John describes "the souls of those who had been slain for the word of God and for the witness they had borne" (6:9). And in Reve-

---

49. Pliny's letter to Trajan indicates that Christians in Asia Minor soon lived up to John's worst expectation of martyrdom. See W. H. C. Frend, *Martyrdom and Persecution in the Early Church* (Oxford: Blackwell, 1967); Howard Clark Kee, *Origins of Christianity* (Englewood Cliffs, N.J.: Prentice-Hall), 51–53.

50. M. E. Boring, *Revelation* (Louisville: John Knox Press, 1989), 103.

51. D. E. Aune, "The Influence of Roman Imperial Court Ceremonial on the Apocalypse of John," *Biblical Research* 28 (1983): 13.

lation 7 the crowd is identified as those "who have come out of the great tribulation; they have washed their robes and made them white in the blood of the Lamb" (7:14). Among these Christian victims was Antipas, described in 2:13 as "my [Jesus'] witness." Those at Pergamum are urged to "hold fast my [Jesus'] name" and "not deny my faith." And John himself is banished for life to an island, probably because of a specific offense against public interest.[52] Socially and economically Christians who were determined to hold fast their faith would suffer through denial of membership in the trade guilds. Collins describes a few ways Christians' social status was threatened: "Christians were being ostracized and sometimes accused before the authorities by their Jewish neighbors. Local Gentiles despised and were suspicious of them and were also inclined to accuse them before the magistrates."[53]

The problems faced by the audience of Revelation do not occur on one front, though it is difficult to delineate the full complexity of their situation. C. van der Waal takes the position that Revelation is not anti-Roman but anti-Jewish, that it depicts the fall of Jerusalem as the center of the Jewish world, not the fall of Rome.[54] Schüssler Fiorenza has shown that being anti-Roman and anti-Gnostic are not mutually exclusive.[55] From the writings of the church fathers, we know that Gnostics were able to adapt to the syncretistic Roman culture and religion, whereas the more orthodox Christians refused to accept any idolatrous practice even if that meant death and persecution. The conflict of orthodox Christians with Jewish synagogues and Jewish communities is seen in the letters to Smyrna and Philadelphia, where similar words are found — "those who say that they are Jews and are not, but are the synagogue of Satan" (2:9; cf. 3:9). Thompson observes that the "conflict with the synagogue probably arises for John because, on the one hand, Christians had lost their 'Jewish shelter' in dealing

---

52. Collins, *Crisis and Catharsis*, 102.

53. Collins, *Crisis and Catharsis*, 98.

54. C. van der Waal, "The Last Book of the Bible and the Jewish Apocalypses," *Neotestamentica* 12 (1978): 111–32. Revelation used Jewish symbols against the synagogue. The "great city" in 11:8 refers to Jerusalem, and "Babylon" too was the old city of the covenant — Jerusalem.

55. Elisabeth Schüssler Fiorenza, "Apocalyptic and Gnosis in the Book of Revelation," *Journal of Biblical Literature* 92, no. 4 (1973): 565–81.

with the Romans, and on the other hand, Asian Jews participated fully in the social and political structures of Roman life."[56] The status of Christians in Asia had clearly become distinct from that of Jews, and Jewish hostility to the early Christians is attested.[57] It is likely that Roman authorities were pressed by local Jews to take action against those Christians. If one takes the view that John sees the destruction of Jerusalem as punishment and judgment on the Jews for not believing in the Messiah (Christ), then the polemic against the Jews can be interpreted in the light that they are eventually to come to salvation (3:12; 21:2, 10).

Against that complex content and audience, John claims that history is under the control of God, and that the end of history is the defining point of both the past and the present. John conceives history as God's revelational activity. Jesus is the real anticipation of the final end of universal history; Jesus is, in Pannenberg's understanding, the "proleptic presence of the eschatological future of all history."[58] According to John, revelation from God takes place not just in the sacred word or tradition, but in history.

The Scroll That Revealed the Finality of History. If the whole book of Revelation provides the readers a view of history (past and present in terms of the future), Revelation 5 speaks directly to that point through one word: *biblion* ("book/scroll").[59] The context of

---

56. Thompson, "Sociological Analysis of Tribulation," 149.

57. Collins, *Crisis and Catharsis,* 85.

58. Carl E. Braaten, "Wolfhart Pannenberg," in *A Handbook of Christian Theologians,* ed. Martin E. Marty and Dean G. Peerman (Nashville: Abingdon, 1984), 643.

59. The scroll is unlikely to be the book of life (3:5; 13:8; 17:8; 20:12, 15; 21:27) containing the names of the redeemed (Pss 69:28; 139:16; Dn 12:1; *1 Enoch* 104:1; Lk 10:20; Phil 4:3; Heb 12:23; Jn 3:5; 13:8; 17:8; 20:15; and 21:27), nor the contract deed (Beasley-Murray, *The Book of Revelation* [London: Marshall, Morgan & Scott, 1981], 120–22). See Emmet Russell, "A Roman Law Parallel to Revelation Five," *Bibliotheca Sacra* 115 (1958): 258–64. J. Massingberd Ford's theory that the scroll has the connotation of the nuptial document, either of the *ketubah* or a bill of divorce or a command of jealousy (*get mekushshar*), is an interesting interpretation because the symbolism in chapter 5 lies embedded in the Sinai-Exodus motif. Ford's theory of detailed correspondence is not correct, but the idea of faithfulness in relationship to God is worth pondering. See J. Massingberd Ford, "The Divorce Bill of the Lamb and the Scroll of the Suspected Adulteress: A Note on Apoc. 5, 1 and 10, 8–11," *Journal for the Study of Judaism in the Persian, Hellenistic, and Roman Period* 2, no. 2 (1971): 136–43. Corsini interprets the

the scroll should be found in chapter five, which is set in the midst of a three-part outline: (*a*) vision of the past glorified Christ (chap. 1); (*b*) present condition of the church (chaps. 2–3); and (*c*) revelation of the future concerning Jesus, the church, and the world (chaps. 4–22).[60] The text of chapter 5 has a clear structure,[61] and its outline has been noted by William H. Shea.[62] First comes the appearance of Christ (vv. 1–3), followed by the prophet's interjection (vv. 4–5). Next is the appearance of Christ who comes to the Father as Redeeming Lamb (vv. 6–7). The chapter concludes with a heavenly interjection in four hymns of four substrata, sung by the four living creatures and twenty-four elders (vv. 8–10), angels (vv. 11–12), the entire universe (v. 13), and again the elders (v. 14). The setting for the appearance of Christ is related to the sealed scroll (v. 1), the angel's question for the one worthy to open the scroll (v. 2), and the cosmic silence indicating the paramount importance of the quest (v. 3). The prophet's interjection is seen in the weeping of the seer (v. 4) and the consolation by the elder (v. 5). The appearance of the Lamb (vv. 6–7) is in some sense parallel to the appearance of Christ (vv. 1–3), but his appearance now is a climactic turning point of the destiny of the world. What follows then is the cosmic response to the lordship of Christ by the four living creatures and the elders (v. 8); the new song (vv. 9–10) in contrast to the weeping (v. 5); the hymn of the angels (vv. 11–12; cf. v. 4); the praise of the whole universe (v. 13; cf. v. 3); and the affirmative amen of the four living creatures and the adoration of the elders (v. 14; cf. v. 2).[63]

The opening of the "scroll" is one of the major issues in

---

scroll not as the book of future events but the word of God or revelation (see 1:3 and 10:9ff.). See Corsini, *Apocalypse,* 132.

60. R. L. Thomas, "John's Apocalyptic Outline," *Bibliotheca Sacra* 123 (196): 334–41.

61. William H. Shea (in his "Revelation 5 and 19 as Literary Reciprocals," *Andrews University Seminary Studies* 22, no. 2 [1984]: 249–53) proposes a chiastic structure for chapter 5 with chapter 19; see also K. A. Strand, "Chiastic Structure and Some Motifs in the Book of Revelation," *Andrews University Seminary Studies* 16, no. 2 (1978): 401–8; and W. H. Shea, "Chiasm in Theme and by Form in Revelation 18," *Andrews University Seminary Studies* 20, no. 3 (1982): 249–56.

62. See Shea "Revelation 5 and 19," 257.

63. See Elisabeth Schüssler Fiorenza, *Invitation to the Book of Revelation: A Commentary on the Apocalypse with Complete Text from the Jerusalem Bible* (Garden City, N.Y.: Image Books, 1981), 77.

chapter 5. The notion of the scroll may have been familiar to first-century Christians, because many religious and cultural traditions of the time have similar motifs. In ancient mythology the highest God possesses plates or scrolls which contain the destiny of the whole world, just as here Jesus is depicted as the eschatological ruler of the world and its destiny.[64] The scroll in Revelation 5 is similar to the scroll of the law which contains God's will or God's judgment on the future day (Is 8:16; 29:1; Dn 12:4). The scroll is also similar to the heavenly tablets of destiny containing the gods' decisions about the future (1 Enoch 81:1–3).[65] Pertinent here as well is that, according to Roman law, certain documents were required to be sealed by seven witnesses.[66] John was surely aware of this Roman legal tradition. Sealing, too, has its significance. In Daniel 8:26 the prophet is told to "seal up the vision, for it pertains to many days hence" (see Is 29:11), the idea being, as Mounce points out, that "when the time has fully come, the seals will be removed and history will move swiftly to its consummation."[67] Again, the "heavenly tablets" of Jewish apocalyptic contain "all the deeds of men...that will be upon the earth to the remotest generations."[68]

Clearly John is concerned to show that the faith of his audience depends on holding a particular view of history, namely, knowing the end. Present faith is objectified when it is linked to the end of history. That faith is assured when it is connected to the christological definition of the end. Revelation of the yet-to-come Hidden One in the present defined for present faith the ultimate purpose and victory of God's activities in history.

---

64. Schüssler Fiorenza, *Invitation to the Book of Revelation*, 78. Also Mounce, *Revelation*, 142. Bergmeier says that the *biblion* ("scroll") in v. 2 refers to the scroll of the end-time prophecy. R. Bergmeier, "Die Buchrolle und das Lamm (Apk 5 und 10)," *Zeitschrift für die neutestamentliche Wissenschaft* 76, no. 3–4 (1985): 225–42.

65. This is taken from Babylonian religion, which adopted Jewish apocalyptic (Schüssler Fiorenza, *Invitation to the Book of Revelation*, 77).

66. E. Stauffer, *Christ and the Caesars*, trans. K. and R. Gregor Smith (London: SCM Press, 1955), 182–83.

67. Mounce, *Revelation*, 142.

68. See 1 Enoch 81:1–2; cf. also 47:3; 106:19; 107:1. Cf. also Ex 25:9–10 and Eph 2:10.

The Lion/Lamb Imagery of Hope:
Conquer through Sacrifice

The christological definition of the end grants the believer assurance of victory and hope in the midst of suffering; the portrayal of Christ in the imagery of the lion/lamb also grants the readers strength in times of weakness. In the pericope, the angel's concern is to have someone worthy to bring history to its foreordained consummation.[69] The seer (i.e., John) weeps at the prospect of an indefinite postponement of God's final and decisive act setting the course of future history.[70] But one of the elders says to John: "Weep not; lo, the Lion of the tribe of Judah, the Root of David, has conquered, so that he can open the scroll and its seven seals" (v. 5). Then the stage of the throne room is set and the curtain drawn. John's description of the heavenly ceremony in the throne room of God bears such a striking resemblance to the ceremonial of the imperial court and cult that the former (i.e., John's description of God's throne room) can only be a parody of the latter (the imperial court and cult).[71] The imagery of the throne room in chapters 4–5 and the heavenly liturgy are probably borrowed from the OT prophets to describe the power and glory of God. Similarly, Christ is portrayed here with OT titles: Lion of the tribe of Judah,[72] and the root of David.[73] Both these terms carry messianic implications and are used in Judaism.[74] The lion image for Judah is found in Gn 49:9, and again in Ez 19:1–9, where the last rulers of the Da-

---

69. Mounce, *Revelation,* 143. Morris comments that the angel's concern "is with worthiness, not naked power" (94).

70. Morris is wrong in saying that the weeping of John is related to the content of the scroll (Morris, *Revelation,* 95). It is related to the fact that no one can open the scroll which contains the destiny of the future. If the future, especially the end of history, is sealed, then existence in the present is hopeless. No wonder that John wept.

71. D. E. Aune, "Influence of Roman Imperial," 5–26.

72. Gn 49:9f. Judah is called a lion's whelp in Gn 49:9 (see Ez 19:2, 3, 5, 6). Israel as a whole is referred to as the lion also (Nm 23:24, 24:9), as is the tribe of Gad (Dt 33:20). It may even be used of heathen, as in Pharaoh's opinion of himself (Ez 32:2). The lion is the symbol of the Messiah in 2 Esdras 12:31f. See Morris, *Revelation,* 95.

73. Is 11:10.

74. E.g., 4QPatr 3 and 2 Esdras 12:31f. See I. T. Beckwith, *The Apocalypse of John* (New York: Macmillan, 1919), 509.

vidic line in the house of Judah are depicted as lions (cf. Mi 5:8). "Root of David" is derived from Is 11:1, which announces the appearance of a branch from the root of David — the David-like warrior-Messiah who will fight God's enemies. This "root" imagery is, paradoxically, congruent with the violent image of the lion (Gn 49:9–10).[75] How? Although the Lion of Judah in Rv 5:5 grants readers a sense of victory and hope in the conquest, what follow are the words that John "saw a Lamb standing, as though it had been slain, with seven horns and with seven eyes, which are the seven spirits of God ... " (v. 6). "A lion" is supposed to appear but instead "a slaughtered lamb" appears. Boring calls this change of imagery a "rebirth of images";[76] Rist calls the juxtaposition of the Lion (5:5) and the Lamb (5:6) "a quick incongruous shift and incompatible collocation";[77] Mounce suggests that the seeming contradiction disappears if the Lamb is seen as a triumphant leader.[78] Admittedly, the juxtaposition of lion and lamb does call for an explanation.[79]

What is indisputable is that the lion is the lamb, representing the ultimate power of God.[80] The Lamb is powerful in that he represents God as God's Messiah, as the sacrifice and cosmic Judge. In these respects, the lamb is as powerful as the lion. The words *ho arnion* ("the lamb") appear twenty-eight times in Revelation,[81] and only once elsewhere in the New Testament (Jn 21:15).[82] The lamb evokes the Old Testament notions of paschal lamb, servant of Yahweh, and Davidic shepherd-king. This cultic and sacrificial imagery

---

75. So Mounce, *Revelation*, 144. The *Testament of Judah* (24:5) understood the lion of Gn 49:10 to be the Messiah; so does 2 Esdras 12:31–32: "the lion ... is the Messiah." Morris contends that the "root of David" is not found in the OT and that the reference in Isaiah is a shoot (later generation) and not the root (ancestor). See Morris, *Revelation*, 95–96.

76. Boring, *Revelation*, 108.

77. Martin Rist, "The Revelation of St. John the Divine," in *The Interpreter's Bible* (New York: Abingdon, 1957), 1:407.

78. Mounce, "The Christology of the Apocalypse," *Foundations* 11 (1969): 44.

79. See Boring, *Revelation*, 109–11, for a summary of interpretations.

80. So Boring, *Revelation*, 110–11.

81. Rv 5:6, 8, 12, 13; 6:1, 16; 7:9, 10, 14, 17; 12:11; 13:8; 14:1, 4 (twice), 10; 15:3; 17:14 (twice); 19:7, 9; 21:9, 14, 22, 23, 27; 22:1, 3. See 13:11, a satanic counterfeit.

82. "Lamb" in Jn 1:29, 36; Acts 8:32; and 1 Pt 1:19 is *amnos* and not *arnion*.

is seen in the Passover sacrifice of the daily Tamid offering or in the rites of the Day of Atonement (see Is 53:7).[83] The imagery may also recall the astrological sign of Aries.[84] "The lamb" is also the apocalyptic horned lamb,[85] the bellwether of God's flock, the Messiah, who will take away the sins of his people and will triumph over evil; that is, "the lamb" is a messianic title.[86] The lamb is also to be understood as the cosmic judge,[87] who is the victorious and resurrected Christ. It is an image taken from Jewish apocalyptic literature.[88] F. C. Grant rightly says that "lamb" in Revelation is a "mystic, apocalyptic designation of the glorified Christ, enthroned with God and destined to be victorious over all the opposing forces in the universe, both human and demonic."[89]

The lamb is no symbol of weakness, but of strength through suffering, of redemption through self-sacrifice, because "the sevenfold ascription of power, wealth, wisdom, might, honor, glory and blessing (5:12) are intended to set the slain lamb in right perspective."[90] The word *arnion*, the diminutive form of *arēn*, seems to have no diminutive connotation of weakness.[91] Barr speaks of

---

83. Norman Hillyer, " 'The Lamb' in the Apocalypse," *Evangelical Quarterly* 39, no. 4 (1967): 228. The lamb here refers to the paschal lamb, rather than the daily sacrifice, so Mounce, "Christology," 43: the writer takes the imagery from Jewish apocalyptic literature; so also Morris, *Revelation,* 96. Swete postulates the apocalyptist gets the word from a non-Septuagint text of OT (*Apocalypse,* 76). Moffatt, however, suspects that the lamb symbol may have had an astral origin in the Persian zodiac; see James Moffatt "The Revelation of St. John the Divine," *The Expositor's Greek Testament* (Grand Rapids, Mich.: Eerdmans, n.d.), 5:384.

84. Schüssler Fiorenza, *Invitation to the Book of Revelation,* 77.

85. R. H. Charles says the concept of lamb comes from the apocalyptic tradition; in *1 Enoch* 90:9 the Maccabees are symbolized as "horned lambs." See his *A Critical and Exegetical Commentary on the Revelation of St. John* (New York: Scribner, 1920), 1:141.

86. See C. K. Barrett's critique, "Lamb of God," 210ff.

87. As Collins and Mounce observe. See A. Y. Collins, *Apocalypse,* 40.

88. Mounce, "Christology," 43.

89. Frederick C. Grant, "Lamb of God," in *Dictionary of the Bible,* ed. James Hastings (New York: Charles Scribner Sons, 1962), 562. F. C. Grant argues that *arnion* is used here as a cryptogram for "Jesus the Nazarene will conquer with a rod," to fulfill the prophecy of Ps 2:9.

90. Donald Guthrie, "The Lamb in the Structure of the Book of Revelation," *Vox Evangelica* (London) 12 (1981): 65.

91. "Arnion," in Bauer et al., eds., *A Greek-English Lexicon of the NT,* 108; and Mounce, "Christology," 42.

"transvaluation" in Revelation 5; the lamb is the lion, a complete reversal of value. His death is not defeat but victory through conquest of supernatural power. Likewise, the faithful will bring salvation and judgment through their suffering. They are decisively changed as they are brought to a new understanding of existence in the world through the paradigmatic suffering of Christ. The lamb is a sign, not of weakness, as we have noted, but of vulnerability. Victims become the victors. Mounce is right in arguing that the Lamb as the messianic leader "has not achieved his position by force but by sacrifice.... This concept of victory through sacrifice is the underlying philosophy of the entire Apocalypse."[92] This is affirmed also by Charles who speaks of the Lamb as symbolizing "love going forth in sacrifice."[93]

The self-sacrificing Lamb is the conquering One, who is "slain from the foundation of the world" (13:8). God Himself, with regard to the slaying of the Lamb, has this "end"-perspective of history, even at the creation of the world. As Hillyer states, "The Cross was no afterthought, but was predetermined before all ages in the comprehensive and loving purpose of God, and that same Lamb who was slain has invaded and conquered history."[94] Christ has conquered once and for all — the aorist "conquered" stands unqualified and in an emphatic position. The Lamb "conquered/overcame."[95] The word "conquer" (also translated as "overcome, prevail, win the victory, triumph"), is a christological verb. It occurs twenty-three times in the book of Revelation, twice as often as in all other New Testament books combined. A. Collins has identified it as a legal word connoting "being acquitted in a court of law." She continues, "The acquittal of the faithful is paradoxical. It is expected that they will be found guilty in the local Roman courts and executed. But the testimony [*martyria*] they give and their acceptance of death will win them the acquittal that counts — in the heavenly court, in the eyes of eternity."[96]

The omnipotence and omniscience of the lamb are seen in the

---

92. Mounce, "Christology," 45.
93. Charles, *Revelation*, cxiv.
94. Hillyer, "Lamb," 231.
95. Rv 3:21; 5:5; 17:14.
96. Collins, *Apocalypse*, 14.

imagery of the "seven horns and seven eyes." The symbolism of the "eyes" comes from the ancient world, in which a ruler would need constant and accurate information about everything going on in his realm.[97] The "horn" is an ancient Jewish symbol for strength or power.[98] The seven horns and seven eyes therefore are identified as the seven spirits sent out into all the earth, symbolizing the fullness of power and omniscient control over the world.[99] The apparently helpless lamb, in fact, has great power. Its weakness lies in its surrender rather than in its own incapacity. Since seven is the symbol of perfection, the lamb is all-powerful and all-knowing.

Because of what the lamb has done, believers "shall reign on earth" (v. 10). Christians will exercise their kingship over the earth. The future tense *basileusousin* is attested by most of the manuscripts, the present tense being found only in Codex Alexandrinus. Even when *basileuousin* is read instead of *basileusousin,* the verb serves as a futuristic present and imparts a tone of assurance.[100] Only those Christians who have been faithful and taken part in the final salvation will reign eschatologically with Christ. Likewise, the throne of God in Revelation is not grounded in the present, but in the future, though it is assured in the present.[101] As the future is proleptically present, the past traditions of the Lion of Judah, the Root of David, and the Lamb of God are brought meaningfully into the audience's present experience of hardship. The future or, more specifically, the end of history enlightens the past and the present. This is the "retroactive force" of the future which gives birth to hope. In faith, the new age has begun.

To summarize, the lion/lamb christological imagery seeks to provide hope through Christ's self-sacrifice and provide strength

---

97. Moffatt, "The Revelation of St. John the Divine," 384. Eyes stand for the seven spirits of God sent out into all the earth. See Zec 4:10 where the seven lamps are interpreted as "the eyes of the Lord, which range through the whole earth." In Rv 5:6 the eyes are attributed to the lamb; in Zechariah they are God's.

98. See Dt 33:17. In Dn 7:7, 20, the fourth beast had ten horns; the ram of Dn 8:3 had two great horns. See Rv 12:3; 13:1, 11; 17:3ff.

99. Schüssler Fiorenza, *Invitation to the Book of Revelation,* 78.

100. James Hope Moulton, W. F. Howard, and Nigel Turner, *Grammar of the New Testament Greek* (Edinburgh: T. & T. Clark, 1908–76), 1:120.

101. O. Schmitz, *"Thronos," TDNT* 3:165–66.

through the retroactive force of the end. If human lostness is hopelessness, then the theology of hope[102] appeals to readers ancient and modern. This theology is not a dualistic, apocalyptic teaching, but a message set forth in the historical future. Rubem Alves puts it well: "Visions of the future not extracted from history cannot be called hope; they are forms of alienation."[103] In an age of crisis and uncertainty, this message helps readers see how Christ fulfills and saves human destiny from ambiguity and lostness in the concreteness of human experience.

It is worth noting that in verses 9, 12, and 13 Christ and God are one. This is to stress John's conviction that the revealed and the revealer are one and the same. In chapter 4, worship is rendered to God alone; in 5:1–12, worship is rendered to the Lamb alone; and in 5:13ff., worship is rendered to both God and the Lamb. "To him who sits upon the throne and to the Lamb" are one in receiving blessing, honor, glory, and might forever and ever (v. 13).

Worship as Communion with the Divine

This chapter has so far spelled out the christological definition of the end of history through Christ's conquering death. The question arises of how the writer and the audience internalized that vision of Christ and history. The answer lies in the setting of the pericope: worship. John is called up into the heavenly throne room (4:1), where he beholds "the One who is seated on the throne." It is the splendid worship scene which comforts and assures both John and readers of their release from all struggles, of their liberation from all bondage and conflict, and of their redemption from all the evils of the world. God is in control despite circumstances which seem to indicate otherwise. The universe may be in chaos, but the throne is not empty.

The throne of God is a venerable place in OT tradition.[104] The

---

102. Among the many theologians who propose this theology are J. Moltmann (*Theology of Hope*); Johannes B. Metz (*Theology of the World*); Carl E. Braaten (*Future of God* and "Toward a Theology of Hope," 208–27); and Rubem M. Alves (*Theology of Human Hope* [Corpus Books, 1969]).

103. Alves, *Theology of Human Hope,* 102.

104. E.g., Ex 24:9–18; 1 Kgs 22:19–22; Jer 23:16–22; Is 6:1–13; Ez 1:1–28; 10:1–22; and Dn 7:9–10.

liturgy imbedded in chapters 4–5 may be Jewish. It is possible that some kind of Jewish mystical tendency was also present in some of the audience, such as Hekalot or Merkabah mysticism, which claimed access to God through human manipulation.[105] In Revelation 4–5, the multilayer structure of heaven reflects not so much the inaccessibility, but the sophistication of the heavenly realities;[106] emphasis on the number and kinds of heavenly creatures also has the effect of emphasizing the awesomeness and formidability of God. The Jewish liturgical order follows the pattern of praise of God the Creator, then celebration of the Torah the scroll, then thanksgiving for God's redemption. The worship of God together with the Lamb in Revelation 5 is distinctively Christian, not Jewish, though the Apocalypse adapts the Jewish imagery in the context of the early church. The setting seems to reflect the worship of the early church in Asia.[107] "The throne" derives from the *cathedra* of the bishop, with the elders seated on either side, and the deacons (the seven spirits) standing before the throne and the scriptural scroll on the holy table (see 6:9).[108]

Here John is saying that the triumph of the sacrificed lamb alone can implement God's eschatological plan; thus he deserves all worship. He offers two reasons for the eschatological reign of the lamb and for worship of the lamb. First, "he was slain" (vv. 6, 9) refers to the violent death of the lamb, following typologically the fate of the paschal lamb of the Exodus tradition.[109] Second, "he ransomed" with his blood people from every tribe, tongue, and nation.

---

105. Gershom Gerhard Scholem, *Jewish Gnostic Man* (Dallas: Spring Publications, 1986), 1–8; and I. Greunwald, *Apocalyptic and Merkavah Mysticism* (Leiden: E. J. Brill, 1980).

106. L. W. Hurtado, "Revelation 4–5 in the Light of Jewish Apocalyptic Analogies," *Journal for the Study of the New Testament* 25 (1985): 107.

107. See Massey H. Shepherd, Jr., *The Paschal Liturgy and the Apocalypse* (Richmond: John Knox Press, 1960), 77–78.

108. See Ward Ewing, *The Power of the Lamb* (Cambridge, Mass.: Cowley Publications, 1990), 71.

109. O. Michel, *"Sphazō,"* TDNT 7:925–35. An early tradition used to refer to Christ's death, see 1 Cor 5:7 and 1 Pt 1:18. Schüssler Fiorenza says, "This image evokes the memory of Israel's exodus and liberation, which was considered in Judaism as a prototype for the final eschatological salvation" ("Redemption as Liberation: Apoc. 1:5f. and 5:9f.," *Catholic Biblical Quarterly* 36 [1974]: 228).

The verb "he ransomed" comes from business life and denotes a commercial transaction, but in this case it refers to the ransom of prisoners of war in general.[110] This image again alludes to the Exodus tradition, which speaks of liberation. The image declares: He has liberated[111] and made the redeemed into a kingdom and priests to our God.

The relation between liturgy and narrative, between cult and eschatology, provides the kind of communion and union the audience needs in time of crisis. As far as form is concerned, we may differentiate between "dramatic narratives" and "heavenly liturgies" as two types of visions in Revelation. The former is the literary form by which John presents the eschatological program. The latter serves as the context by which the program unfolds.[112] G. Delling's form-critical study of Revelation has shown that the unity and meaning of Revelation come through this doxological pericope. God and the Lamb are ascribed worth *(Würdig-Rufe)*, which is actualized and consummated in the eschatological end, in the power of God and the lordship of Christ.[113]

The doxological celebration is evidenced in the "new song" which denotes the eschatological praise of the redeemed.[114] "New" is the expression of eschatological perfection and redemption (2:17; 3:12; 21:1, 2, 5).[115] This new song evokes the "new song" of Ps 98:1, "Oh sing to the Lord a new song, for he has done marvelous things!" (see 33:3; 40:3; 96:1; etc.). Every new act of mercy calls for a new song of praise. In Is 42:5–17 we find the same injunction to sing to the victorious One who created the heavens. In

---

110. Schüssler Fiorenza, "Redemption," 228.

111. Schüssler Fiorenza argues that the new song in 5:9–10 reveals that redemption and salvation as conceived in Revelation are political-social rather than individualistic, spiritualistic categories. "[F]ully realized redemption and salvation presupposes not only the liberating and dignifying of individual persons, but also the creating of a new world" (see Schüssler Fiorenza, "Redemption," 220–32).

112. L. Thompson, "Cult and Eschatology in the Apocalypse of John," *The Journal of Religion* 49, no. 4 (1969): 330–50.

113. G. Delling, "Zum Gottesdienstlichen Stil der Johannes-Apokalypse," *Novum Testamentum* 3, no. 1–2 (1959): 107–37.

114. This expression is often found in the Psalms (33:3; 96:1; 98:1; 149:1).

115. See J. Behm, *"Kainos,"* TDNT 3:447–50; R. H. Harrisville, "Concept of Newness in the NT," *Journal of Biblical Literature* 74 (1955): 69–79.

spite of these reminiscences, however, we can affirm with Mounce that, "The song to the Lamb is a new song because the covenant established through his death is a new covenant. It is not simply new in point of time, but more important, it is new and distinctive in quality."[116] The first of the four hymns in chapter 5 is sung by the four living creatures and the twenty-four elders (vv. 8–10). The next hymn is sung by the heavenly host of angels in infinite number[117] (vv. 11–12). Then all of the animate universe joins in on a grand chorus of praise: every creature in heaven, on earth, under the earth, and in the sea (v. 13). Finally, the four living creatures and the twenty-four elders harmonize with the finale, "Amen!" (v. 14).

If the lion imagery speaks of conquering and the lamb imagery speaks of sacrifice, the message to sing indicates trust in and thanksgiving to God. The relational exhortation of trust and obedience of faith is portrayed most beautifully in the worship scene. For in such worship, one communes and encounters the Almighty, who reigns in and beyond history. It is in such a worshipful attitude that Christians gain vision, strength, faith, endurance, and hope. In worship, past, present, and future collapse into one. The hymn of all creation to the Creator and Redeemer has a proleptic dimension to it. The strong liturgical character shows that hope and faith are best nurtured in worship amid sin, evil, and suffering.

Apocalyptic Salvation and Openness to the Future

Let us now summarize the effect of the imagery and rhetoric of chapter 5 on its readers in terms of apocalyptic salvation. The power of apocalyptic rhetoric, as A. Y. Collins has pointed out, resides in the power of catharsis in crisis. Often two sets of symbols are used in apocalyptic rhetoric: one describes what ought to be

---

116. Mounce, *Revelation*, 147. That *kainos* and not *neos* is used is significant. Behm notes that *neos* is new in time or origin while *kainos* is "what is new in nature, different from the usual, impressive, better than the old, superior in value or attraction.... Theologically *kainos* is the epitome of the wholly different and miraculous thing which is brought about by the time of salvation" (H. Schlier, "*Ekkenteō,*" *TDNT* 2:447, 449).

117. "Myriads of myriads and thousands of thousands" represents an infinite number (10,000 x 10,000 x 1,000 x 1,000 = 100,000,000,000,000).

and the other describes what is. The "ought to be" portrays hope, the other reality. The language is primarily "commissive language" which calls "for commitment to the actions, attitudes and feelings uttered."[118] This expressive and evocative language is powerful. As expressive language, Revelation creates a virtual experience for the hearers; it expresses a perspectival view of history, suffering, and reality. As evocative language, it elicits a response from the hearers in terms of thoughts, attitudes, and feelings through the use of effective symbols and dramatic plot, inviting imaginative participation.[119] As E. Schüssler Fiorenza has observed,

> Revelation is a poetic-rhetorical work [which] . . . seeks to persuade and motivate by constructing a "symbolic universe" that invites imaginative participation. The strength of its persuasion for action lies not in the theological reasoning or historical argument of Revelation but in the "evocative" power of its symbols as well as in its hortatory, imaginative, emotional language, and dramatic movement, which engage the hearer by eliciting reactions, emotions, convictions, and identifications.[120]

The rhetorical effect of the imagery of Christ in Revelation 5 is intended to give hope and assurance (confident faith) to Christians under persecution. The self-surrender of Jesus is a sacrifice of self for humanity and serves as an example, albeit a divine and inimitable one, to empower believers through persecution. The community is called to believe that it has access to the celebration of the saving work of God by sharing in the present suffering of Christ and participating in the fullness of Christ's glory in the future. The death of the hero thus becomes a victory and not a defeat, because the death is a sacrificial death "which makes him worthy to set in motion the foreordained events of the endtime."[121] Antipas, the martyr of Pergamum, is mentioned because he had chosen to give his life rather than to deny his faith (2:13),

---

118. Collins, *Crisis and Catharsis*, 144.

119. See Collins, *Crisis and Catharsis*, 144–45; and Boring, *Revelation*, 12.

120. Elisabeth Schüssler Fiorenza, "The Followers of the Lamb: Visionary Rhetoric and Social-Political Situation," *Semeia* 36 (1986): 187.

121. Collins, *Apocalypse*, 40.

the end to which the rhetoric is aimed. Countless other martyrs will be crying out to God for vindication (6:9f.). The beast will arise to deceive all who dwell on the earth, and those who refuse to worship the beast will be slain (13:11ff.). The challenge for the faithful, says John, is not to compromise, but to overcome and conquer (2:7, 11, 17, 26; 3:5, 12, 21). The victorious power of faith is the apocalyptic salvation the audience gains in reading or hearing the Apocalypse.

Since the end of history has now been revealed and is known, the audience is invited to participate in that future by anticipation. God, who alone has the power to bring history to its unification and dynamic consummation, "incorporating each temporal present as it occurs,"[122] is the end of time. It is for this reason that one can anticipate with assurance that God the Almighty reigns. That is the central message and purpose of the Apocalypse.

The Suffering of Chinese Christians in the Cultural Revolution

The persecution of Christians in the book of Revelation arose from their resistance to emperor worship,[123] their exclusive loyalty to Christ without compromising with the synagogue, and their persistent adherence to a faith at odds with the syncretistic practices of pagan religions. The historical context of the Apocalypse can be inferred from the situation of the seven churches (Revelation 2–3). In a narrow sense, the reading audience of the book is composed of the Christians of the seven churches. The opponents are specifically named in the letters to the churches in Ephesus (2:1–7), Pergamum (2:12–17), and Thyatira (2:18–29): the Nicolaitans. These are presumably the "apostles" (2:2), that is, the itinerant missionaries.[124] In the letter to Pergamum (2:15) the church is reproached for tol-

---

122. Lewis S. Ford, "God as the Subjectivity of the Future," *Encounter* 41 (1980): 292.

123. S. MacL. Gilmour, "Use and Abuse of the Book of Revelation," *Andover Newton Quarterly* 7, no. 1 (1966): 15–18.

124. W. Bousset, *Offenbarung Johannis* (Göttingen: Vandenhoeck & Ruprecht, 1906), 204–6.

erating them. Those who hold the teaching of Balaam (2:14) may
also be the same group of people who hold to the teaching of the
Nicolaitans, because of the etymological equivalence of Balaamites
and Nicolaitans.[125] Later in church history, Ignatius praised the
church in Ephesus for rejecting heretical teachers who passed by
on their way (Ign. *Eph.* 9:1; cf. 6:2; 7:1; 8:1).[126] Both the phrases
"to eat food sacrificed to idols" and "to practice immorality" are
references to syncretistic tendencies of the people toward pagan and
gnostic practices.[127] The message to Thyatira accuses the prophetess
Jezebel of the same vices: eating idol meat and practicing fornica-
tion. Schüssler Fiorenza suspects the Thyatiran opponents to be of
the same group of Nicolaitans.[128] Revelation 2:24 explicitly spells
out their teaching as "knowing the deep things of Satan." Schüssler
Fiorenza concludes that the Nicolaitans are those who claimed to
have knowledge of demonic realities, which granted them both the
freedom to live in peaceful coexistence with pagan society, without
sacrificing their faith in God and Jesus Christ, and the license to
engage in libertine behavior.[129]

The Chinese Context of Suffering

The persecution experienced by Chinese Christians during the
Cultural Revolution had its ideological-political and religious-

---

125. Nikolaos (*nika laon*) is equivalent to the Hebrew *bl'a 'am* = "he has
consumed the people."

126. See also R. H. Charles, *A Critical and Exegetical Commentary on the
Revelation of St. John* (New York: Scribner, 1920), 1:52–53.

127. See Nm 25:1–18; 1 Corinthians 8 and 10; R. H. Charles, *Revelation*, 1:63;
A. T. Ehrhardt "Social Problems in the Early Church," in *The Framework of
the New Testament Stories* (Cambridge: Harvard University Press, 1964): 276–90;
E. Lohmeyer, *Die Offenbarung des Johannes* (Tübingen: Mohr, 1953), 31; Elisabeth
Schüssler Fiorenza, "Apocalyptic and Gnosis in the Book of Revelation," *Journal of
Biblical Literature* 92, no. 4 (1973): 567–68; and G. B. Caird, *A Commentary on
the Revelation of St. John the Divine* (London: Black, 1966), 39.

128. H. Zimmermann also contends that the Nicolaitans had a prominent role
in these churches. H. Zimmermann, "Christus und die Kirche in den Sendschreiben
der Apokalypse," in *Unio Christianorum: Festschrift Jaeger* (Paderborn: Schöningh,
1962), 176–97. See also E. Lohse, *Die Offenbarung* (Göttingen: Vandenhoeck &
Ruprecht, 1966), 27–28.

129. Schüssler Fiorenza, "Apocalyptic," 569–71. Boring also suspects gnostic
influence on the opponents. Boring, *Revelation*, 107.

philosophical cause, as did the persecution suffered by Christians in Roman times. In Communist China, religious freedom was guaranteed in Article 88 of the 1954 constitution ("Citizens of the People's Republic of China enjoy freedom of religious belief")[130] and was in line with the Marxist dogma. According to this dogma, religion originated in primitive society as a way of dealing with the unexplainable forces of nature and with human tragedy. But as society developed, religion had become a tool of the upper class to exploit and control the lower class by taking "the minds of the exploited off their present condition of misery."[131] The Chinese constitutional idea that religion must not become an exploiter of the people was thus in agreement with Marx's famous dictum that "religion is the opiate of the people."[132]

Marx's understanding of religion largely echoed Feuerbach's view that "religion in general, and Christianity in particular is a conceptual manifestation of man's projection of his own understanding, will and especially feelings."[133] Marx viewed religion as the human protest against social alienation through the offering of imaginary, otherworldly consolation, which would doom one's destiny. How Chinese Communists adapted Marx's and Feuerbach's ideas to the Chinese scene has been outlined by Donald MacInnis in his book *Religious Policy and Practice in Communist China:*

> Religion is a social ideology, "the fantastic reflection in men's minds of those external forces which control their daily life." The fantastic interpretations by religion of natural phenomena, social phenomena, and especially of oppression and class exploitation play the role of paralyzing the minds of the working people, and disintegrating their combat will.[134]

---

130. For more, see G. Thompson Brown, *Christianity in the People's Republic of China* (Atlanta: John Knox Press, 1986), 76–77.

131. Brown, *Christianity,* 76–77.

132. Robert C. Tucker, *Philosophy and Myth in Karl Marx* (Cambridge: Cambridge University Press, 1972), 105.

133. Julia Ching, "Faith and Ideology in the Light of the New China," in *Christianity and the New China* (South Pasadena, Calif.: Ecclesia Publications, 1976), 18.

134. Donald MacInnis, *Religious Policy and Practice in Communist China* (New York: Macmillan, 1973), 60.

The Chinese communist has viewed religion (especially Christianity) as a foreign imperialist's ideological tool for the exploitation of common people.[135] Mao Tse-tung himself considered Christian missionary work in China to be a form of foreign cultural aggression. Seen through the eyes of the Chinese, the eight-year Treaty of Nanking (1842)[136] and that of Tientsin (1858)[137] were both totally unjust and acts of blatant imperialism, exploiting China's resources and forcing its people to accept opium grown in India in exchange for tea and silk. The Boxer Rebellion of 1900 was the culmination of sixty years of antagonism toward all foreigners.[138] It may be correct that some missionaries had condemned the opium traffic, and that they had never been part of imperialist or colonialist activity against China.[139] But the facts were that imperialists had often used the name of Christianity to conquer, that the preaching of Christianity had often been dominated by Western culture, and that the native churches had always been tied to the leadership and control of overseas mission boards. Julia Ching explains:

---

135. That view is understandable if one views Chinese history (prior to the communist regime) through the eyes of the Chinese. See Leslie Lyall, *God Reigns in China* (London: Hodder and Stoughton, 1985), 126, which elaborates this point.

136. Various unfair terms were included in this treaty with the British: Hong Kong was ceded to the British; Canton (now Guangzhou), Amoy (now Xiamen), Foochow (now Fuzhou), Ningpo, and Shanghai opened to British residence and trade; China had to pay for the confiscated opium and the cost of the war; and Britain gained the extraterritorial right to reside in the treaty ports (that is, they were not subject to Chinese law and trial).

137. Various unfair terms were included in this treaty with the French and British: additional ports in China were opened for trade; foreigners received privileges to travel throughout China and the right to reside in certain cities without being subject to local laws; and China was to pay indemnity to cover the loss in the war. The treaty also called for religious tolerance and the protection of foreign missionaries entering the interior of China.

138. MacInnis in *Religious Policy and Practice* explains how the Chinese Communist Party viewed Christianity: "The imperialist powers have never slackened their efforts to poison the minds of the Chinese people. This is their policy of cultural aggression. And it is carried out through missionary work" (12).

139. MacInnis, *Religious Policy and Practice*, 126. See *Documents of the Three-Self Movement* (hereafter *Documents;*), ed. Wallace C. Merwin and Francis P. Jones (New York: National Council of the Churches of Christ, 1963), 172.

The reliance of the 19th century Christian missionary bodies on Western political power for rights and privileges secured by invasions and unequal treaties, compromised their presence and activities in China. It was a result of Western triumphalism: at once racial, political, religious and cultural. ...Christian missions could continue their work only with the help of foreign funds, contributed generously by believers overseas for the cause of saving the souls of Chinese pagans. ...Frequently, the need of overseas funding also favoured the continuation of such foreign leadership.[140]

It is understandable that the Christian Manifesto[141] would agree with the Communist Party's view. As such, the Christian Manifesto states that "missionaries who brought Christianity to China all came themselves from these imperialistic countries, [and] Christianity consciously or unconsciously, directly or indirectly, became related with imperialism."[142] It is not surprising, then, that although religious freedom was guaranteed in Article 88 of the 1954 constitution, under the banner of Mao after 1949 pastors and Christians were harassed and placed under constant surveillance and suspicion. Many were persecuted, imprisoned, and killed.[143] Many had to go through "accusation meetings" and were suspected of "counter-revolutionary" activities. Few Christians escaped trial and death after being accused of subscribing to, and being brainwashed by, the foreigner's religion.

In 1966 Mao approved the organizing of the Red Guards (1966–67). Millions of teenagers indoctrinated with fanaticism ravaged the country and wrecked structures of orderly society, in-

---

140. Ching, "Faith and Ideology," 23.

141. In 1950 nineteen Protestant leaders, led by Y. T. Wu, met with Zhou Enlai to prepare a statement called the Christian Manifesto, which would address the difficulties the churches faced in New China. The controversial document states specifically the political viewpoints of the Christian church. It is therefore not a theological document. The full text of the document is published in *Tien Fung* 233–34 (September 1950): 146–47. See Philip L. Wickeri, *Seeking the Common Ground: Protestant Christianity, the Three-Self Movement, and China's United Front* (Maryknoll, N.Y.: Orbis Books, 1988), 127–33.

142. *Documents,* 19–20.

143. See C. Jones, *The Church in Communist China: A Protestant Appraisal* (New York: Friendship Press, 1962).

cluding religious institutions. Churches were closed and Christians suffered greatly.[144] A correspondent describes what happened in Shanghai on 24 August 1966:

> On that day all the churches, active and inactive, whether conducted by their meager congregations or preserved by the Shanghai Municipal Bureau of Religious Cults, were stripped of the crosses, statues, icons, decorations and all church paraphernalia by the revolutionary students, wearing Red Guard armbands and determined to eradicate all traces of imperialist, colonial and feudal regimes.[145]

Again,

> Throughout the Guangxi region, the ranks of open believers were decimated by these early persecutions. In 1949 in the provincial capital of Guilin were four Protestant churches, ... but as this wave of persecutions took its toll, attendance dwindled. Finally all churches were combined into one.... In 1966 that church was closed by the Red Guards of the Cultural Revolution.[146]

Many churches installed a large white statue of Mao at the center. Posters such as this one were common:

> There is no God; there is no Spirit; there is no Jesus;... How can adults believe in these things?... Protestantism is a reactionary feudal ideology, the opium of the people.... We are atheists; we believe only in Mao Tsu-tung. We call on all people to burn Bibles, destroy images, and disperse religious associations.[147]

In the midst of the Great Leap Forward (1958–60), the consolidation of churches and worship services was required and monitored by the Religious Affairs Bureau. All pastors were told

---

144. W. Dehoney, *The Dragon and the Lamb* (Nashville: Broadman Press, 1988), 22.

145. *South China Morning Post,* quoted in George N. Patterson, *Christianity in Communist China* (Waco, Tex.: Word, 196), 139.

146. Dehoney, *Dragon and the Lamb,* 47.

147. Brown, *Christianity,* 125.

to align themselves with the socialist reconstruction of the mother land. Biblical teaching concerning the Last Day was prohibited for preaching, as it was considered a poisonous thought.

The Thriving of Chinese Christians

However, during the ten catastrophic years of the Cultural Revolution (1966–76), when all the churches were closed, house churches kept functioning and blossoming. These "underground" Christians kept meeting, praying, witnessing, and studying in family and close-knit groups. In the 1970s and 1980s these house congregations became the mainstream of New China's Christianity.

Most of these groups have loved to study the book of Revelation, from which they derive strength, faith, and hope. They hold to this apocalyptic hope in the midst of turmoil and danger. A high view of Christology helps them to hold fast to their faith. The worship experiences and preaching of such groups are often charismatic. The important doctrines they hold dear center around the sacrificial death, resurrection, and second coming of Christ. All these doctrines grant hope and assurance to these Christians.

The Book of Revelation did not give Chinese Christians during the Cultural Revolution merely existential strength; the book also infused them with a view of history which differed from that of the communists. Unlike the communists, Chinese Christians are able to see the world from the transcendent perspective in the apocalyptic visions of Revelation. Chinese Christians counter the communist, socialist, and human construction of utopian society by opening the world to divine transcendence and the New Heaven. By means of the motifs of visionary transportation to heaven, visions of God's throne room in heaven, angelic mediators of revelation, symbolic visions of political powers, coming judgment, and new creation, Chinese Christians see the final destiny of this despaired world in the transcendent divine purpose.

The achievement of God's righteous rule over his world encourages Chinese Christians to counter the communist worldview, which is anti-divine. The righteous suffer, the wicked flourish: the world seems to be ruled by evil, not by God. But that is only part of the picture then! The apocalyptic worldview assures Chinese Christians that God's kingdom is about to reign, and that they should maintain their faith in the one, all-powerful, and righteous God in the face of the harsh realities of evil in the world, especially the political evil of the oppression of God's faithful people by the pagan regime. God rules his creation, and the time is coming soon when he will overthrow the evil empire and establish his kingdom. The theology of the Lamb as One who suffers and the One who controls history speaks to the Chinese Christians the assured victory of the faithful despite the apparent domination of the evil power. It is the hope portrayed in the Book of Revelation that sustains Chinese Christians to endure to the end.

History has proved that such hope has worked miracles among Chinese Christians for the past forty years. The number and faith of these Christians have not declined, but increased. Chinese Christians have seen the whole picture of God's revelation working itself out in history. For they have seen the end of history; and that grants them assurance of victory, comfort in suffering, and hope in the midst of dismay. They have learned to be open to God and to the future in an attitude of obedience and surrender. As a people oppressed, they have seen salvation emerge from hopelessness and death, for they have seen Christ as the end and the hope in history.

The Three-Self Patriotic Movement and Anti-Roman Ideology

Despite the fact that the Christians of Revelation and of China both suffered for their faith because of political-religious causes, there is one church movement in China that is different from what we can find in the Book of Revelation. Unlike the stance taken by the Book of Revelation, in which separationists were commended and accommodationists accused, the TSPM (Three-Self Patriotic Movement)[148] held to political accommodation. The TSPM thrived despite its position.

---

148. Richard X. Y. Zhang, "The Origin of the 'Three Self,'" *Jian Dao* 5 (1996): 175–202.

Separation Strategy and Independent Results

Separation was ordered by the Communist Party, which stated that Chinese churches had to be loyal to none other than the Chinese government. The Religious Affairs Bureau was set up in Peking in 1950 and was commissioned to cut off all Christian bodies in China from their overseas ties, to expel foreign missionaries, and to promote an autonomous church movement.[149] In the mid-1950s, Chou En-lai met separately with Protestant and Catholic leaders, assuring them of the government's intention to protect freedom of religious belief, but requesting them to separate themselves from overseas imperialist control and to express their patriotic sentiments by adapting to the new political situation in the New China.[150] The new government officially launched the TSPM in 1951, calling for self-support, self-government, and self-propagation by the Protestant Christian bodies in China.[151] However, this separation from outside contact provided a nursing bed for the healthy growth of the Chinese churches.

The three-self concept had originally been the idea of two American missionaries, S. L. Baldwin and V. Talmage, in the 1800s.[152] In the 1890 and the 1907 missionary conferences, the thematic emphasis of the Chinese churches was on self-support, leadership, and evangelism.[153] When the communist government came to power,

---

149. Brown, *Christianity,* 84–85. See also a few documents in *Documents:* "Message from Chinese Christians to Mission Boards Abroad" (14–18); "Church of Christ in China Report to Mission Boards Abroad" (24–25); "Methodist Patriotic Covenant" (26–27); and "Methods for Dealing with Christian Bodies" (27–28).

150. See Ching, "Faith and Ideology," 24.

151. Lyall (*God Reigns,* 129) notes, "The three-self slogan adopted in the 1920s by missionaries and the national church as a guide to the indigenisation of the church was now given an entirely new twist by making it mean the total severance of the relationship between the church in China and the church universal; the slogan was thus given a political connotation totally absent from the original concept." See *Documents,* 44, 121–32.

152. S. L. Baldwin, "Self-Support of the Native Church," and J. V. N. Talmage, "Should the Native Churches in China Be United Ecclesiastically and Independent of Foreign Churches and Societies?" in *Records of the General Conference of the Protestant Missionaries of China Held at Shanghai, May 10–20, 1877* (Shanghai: Presbyterian Mission Press, 1878), 283ff., 429ff.

153. G. L. Mason "Methods of Developing Self-Support and Voluntary Effort," in *Records of the General Conference of the Protestant Missionaries of China Held at Shanghai, May 7–20, 1890* (Shanghai: American Presbyterian Mission Press,

they seriously adopted this policy and added a political twist. C. M. Chen, an official of the Religious Affairs Bureau, once said that the purpose of the government was not outright extermination but restriction, reformation, and control. Chen pointed out that the TSPM had been created to make religion serve politics and to make the church politically harmless.[154]

The separation strategy of the communists has also meant that the Chinese churches have had to work closer with the communist leadership. Wu Yao-tsung, a visionary and first president of TSPM, was influenced by the worldwide Christian socialist movement of the 1930s and became more and more sympathetic to Chinese Communist ideas.[155] He saw a crucial task neglected by Christians and the churches but fulfilled by communists. He commented that the Chinese Christian church was tragic, because

> China is today face to face with the greatest change in its history, and in this period of great change the Christian church, beside the negative reactions of feeling sorry for itself, and trying to escape reality, has nothing to say or to do.[156]

The uniqueness of the TSPM is its willingness and courage to co-operate with the Communist Party at least on the common ground of social issues. It is little wonder that the Christian Manifesto was prepared by Wu Yao-tsung and premier Chou En-lai.[157] By that time (1950) war had broken out in Korea, anti-American sentiment was high, and patriotic fervor was rampant. A massive campaign was launched to get Christians all over China to sign the manifesto.[158] The manifesto called on Chinese Christians to heighten their "vigilance against imperialism, to make known the clear political stand of Christians in New China, to hasten the building of a Chinese Church whose affairs are managed by

---

1890), 415ff. See also J. C. Gibson, "The Chinese Church," in *Records: China Centenary Missionary Conference, Held at Shanghai, April 25 to May 8, 1907* (Shanghai: Centenary Conference Committee, 1907), 1ff.

154. Lyall, *God Reigns*, 129.

155. *Documents*, 184–91. See Brown, *Christianity*, 81.

156. Brown, *Christianity*, 82.

157. *Documents*, 19–21.

158. By 1952, at least 400,000 Christians had signed it. See Brown, *Christianity*, 83; *Tien Fung*, 233–34 (30 September 1950): 2–3.

the Chinese themselves." It stated further that Christians should support the "common political platform under the leadership of the government."[159] It called on churches relying on foreign personnel and financial aid to discontinue these relations and work toward self-reliance.[160] In October 1950, the biannual meeting of the Chinese National Christian Council was held for the purpose of adopting the manifesto and implementing means to bring about the "three-self reform."[161] In April 1951, the newly organized Religious Affairs Bureau of the government invited 151 Protestant leaders to a conference in Peking. There, they voted

> to thoroughly, permanently and completely sever all relations with American missions and all other missions, thus realizing self-government, self-support and self-propagation in the Chinese church.[162]

In order to carry out this policy, the Protestant TSRM (Three-Self Reform Movement)[163] was officially established.[164] In 1958 Wu wrote in *Tien Fung (Heavenly Wind)* that "without the Communist Party there would not have been the TSPM or the Christian Church....I love the Communist Party."[165] At that time, TSPM drafted a "message of respect" to Chairman Mao which had four main points: (1) to promote the greater unity of all Christian churches by carrying out the three-self policy in response to their love for both the country and the Christian religion; (2) to support the draft constitution of the People's Republic of China and to strive with the people of the whole nation to construct a socialist society; (3) to oppose imperialist aggression in order to safeguard

---

159. *Tien Fung* 423 (7 July 1954): 1, and 425–27 (3 September 1954): 3–10.

160. Brown, *Christianity*, 84, and *Documents*, 177–86.

161. MacInnis, *Religious Policy*, 99.

162. MacInnis, *Religious Policy*, 99.

163. In 1954 the name was changed to the Protestant Three-Self Patriotic Movement for the sake of unity. See *Documents*, 4.

164. Lyall critically observes that TSPM is not a spontaneous, free independent body of the Chinese church, but an organization created by the Communist Party to carry out party policy. Lyall's point is that the late Wu Yao-tsung was pro-communist and a serious student of Marxism.

165. Lyall, *God Reigns*, 131; *Documents*, 184–91.

the peace of the world; and, (4) to encourage all Christians of the nation to seriously learn patriotism.[166] Most of the resistance to TSPM came from conservative preachers like Wang Ming-dao[167] and Watchman Nee,[168] some underground house churches, and the Roman Catholic Church,[169] who were reacting against the more "liberal" theology of TSPM and its cooperation with the Communist Party.[170] Obviously, the Roman Catholic Church in China could not break its ties to Rome.

Chinese Christianity in the Communist Context

A brief survey of the rise of TSPM within the context of the complex historical development of communist ideology will suffice to raise some crucial issues related to the Christian church in the New China,[171] even though these issues may raise more questions than answers. The issues are interrelated and must be thought through before one can talk about Chinese Christianity as a Westernized or as an indigenous faith in China.

Chinese Christians within New China struggle with the issue of

---

166. Patterson, *Christianity in Communist China*, 88–89.

167. Wang Ming-dao (1900–88) was a militant preacher who independently organized his own church, the Christian Tabernacle, in Beijing. He distributed *The Spiritual Food Quarterly*. See his two articles, "We, Because of Faith" and "Self-Examination," in *Documents*, 99–113, 117–20, criticizing TSPM in the light of the Bible. See Ng Lee Ming, "Christianity and Social Change: The Case of China" (diss., Princeton Theological Seminary, 1970).

168. Watchman Nee (1903–72) was a prolific author and charismatic speaker who founded "Little Flock" (see Lk 12:32) or "Christian Assembly" in Fuzhou. He opposed denominational structure, which he believed to be a human construction. He preached the message of personal salvation and sanctification. He was arrested and charged with "counter-revolutionary activity" many times; even TSM and Protestant leaders denounced him. See *Tien Fung* 498 (6 February 1956): 9–10; Brown, *Christianity*, 82–85; Patterson, *Christianity in Communist China*, 91–93; Wickeri, *Seeking the Common Ground*, 162–64.

169. See Brown, *Christianity*, 86–88, for details.

170. This chapter has no intention of examining the theological views of TSPM. If interested, see *Zhouggua Yu Jiaohui* 3 (April–May 1986): 21–24, and 4 (June–July 1986): 21–27, for the systematic theology of TSPM.

171. This chapter has no intention of commenting on the critical issue of the changing/shifting concept of "three-self" principle and movement from the 1920s to the 1980s. But see *Zhouggua Yu Jiaohui* 1 (January 1986): 7–9.

the basis of governmental authority.[172] Is it divine or human? Some Chinese Christians

> consider the state as a part of God's creation, and...men should obey it; others consider that the government and spiritual life are two separate categories...without conflict; still others think that the state is the result of Adam's sin, that God's redemption only becomes effective through the Church, and therefore [Christians] have no interest in the state, and finally, some consider that the state is also under the rule of God, that believers...should take part in the state.[173]

However, TSPM believes that the state is under the rule of God and that therefore believers should take part in the state.[174] This is not to imply that the state is perfect but that the communist state in New China is sincere and earnest in its attempt to reconstruct and improve China and in its desire to attack poverty and exploitation. The communist may be an atheist, but this does not mean that God cannot work through unbelievers; ultimately God is the ruler of the nation and of the universe.

Chinese Christians struggled with the issue of the Christian's ultimate loyalty, whether it should be to God or to the state. TSPM Christians declare, "We love our country, the People's Government and socialism.... The communists are atheistic, but they respect our faith.... [175] ...Although we and the communists differ in faith, we are all Chinese, and are one in our desire for the increasing prosperity and...building up of our country."[176] That Chinese Christians love their country does not mean that they have

---

172. *Documents,* 171.
173. *Documents,* 171.
174. *Documents,* 169, 184.
175. Zhou En-lai once remarked to a Christian delegation during a conference, "So we are going to go on letting you teach, trying to convert the people. After all we both believe that truth will prevail; we think your beliefs untrue and false, therefore if we are right, the people will reject them, and your church will decay. If you are right, then the people will believe you, but as we are sure that you are wrong, we are prepared for that risk." See MacInnis, *Religious Policy,* 24.
176. *Documents,* 172.

ceased to love God or that they love God less. Like John's attitude toward the Roman government, Western Christians often have a deep prejudice or unjustified fear that because communism allows less freedom than democracy, to cooperate with the Communist Party is to ally with the devil. The question becomes, can Christianity survive only in a capitalistic society? Or, is one form of government more divinely ordained than another? In fact, the three-self principles should mean that the church is independent of foreign churches and also of the Communist Party within China. Brown rightly points out that TSPM is not China's "official church."[177] China has no official church. The Chinese church is run by Chinese Christians.

Chinese Christians also struggled with the relation between God's creative work and God's redemptive work.[178] Is the gospel of Christ concerned only with the reconciliation of people to God, or does it also have meaning for the state and society? After years of breaking off all relations with imperialism and gradually learning to rule, to support, and to propagate, the Chinese Christian church has come to recognize communist government leadership as sincere in its policy of freedom of religious belief, and in its willingness to help the church in any difficulties it may meet. It has also come to recognize that to participate in the government is one way to bear witness for the Lord.[179] Bishop Ting, for example, has commented that Christians must learn to live with atheists in New China, not being seduced by them but learning how to present the gospel to them.[180] In his article "A Call for Clarity: Fourteen Points from Christians in the People's Republic of China to Christians Abroad," K. H. Ting affirms the positive attitude TSPM has toward the New China. His point is that Chinese Christians' patriotism is "not without a prophetic and critical character."

By supporting the TSPM, the Chinese Christians have chosen

---

177. Brown, Christianity, 213. See K. H. Ting, "A Call for Clarity: Fourteen Points from Christians in the People's Republic of China to Christians Abroad," China Notes 19 (Winter 1980–81): 145–49.

178. Documents, 171.

179. Documents, 172.

180. Documents, 156.

the common ground between Christianity and communism instead of magnifying their difference. This does not compromise the Christian truth. No doubt these two competing "ideologies," each supremely sure of its own understanding of reality, have "compatible and partly convergent positions regarding the dignity and destiny of man and his call to transform the world."[181] Julia Ching calls this alternative way "that of collaboration in the humanist cause,... a faith in man which can be acceptable to Christians, in so far as it is open to God."[182] TSPM regards the policy of religious freedom to be "a reasonable one" but has no illusions about communism's atheist views.[183] TSPM therefore can and must work with the state on the "common ground" explained above for the sake of Christ and the benefit of the people.

Many Protestant churches have long been guilty of using religion as opium or as escapism. They are guilty of neglecting social reform, and are only interested in saving pagan souls. TSPM has striven to maintain the more holistic approach of combining the social gospel and the personal gospel. TSPM has pointed out the root problem which has existed in missionary strategy in the proclamation of the gospel for centuries. The old way to evangelize was to convert a pagan into a Westerner with Western ideas, cultural values, and ways of practicing Christian faith. Julia Ching says it well: "Faith is directed toward that which is beyond history, dogma or myth, to a God who Himself transcends theism, since, if He exists, it will be so independently of men's affirmations and negations."[184] Chinese Christians have reacted against becoming Westernized Christians. Easterners never bow down to the god of logic, dogma, or creeds. Religion to them has always been a way of life. Eastern peoples are puzzled by the freedom they hear in the gospel and by the dogmatic formulae of the church.

---

181. Ching, "Faith and Ideology," 26.
182. Ching, "Faith and Ideology," 26.
183. Ting, "A Call for Clarity," 145–49.
184. Ching, "Faith and Ideology," 31; and see Franklin J. Woo, "Another China Visit: Religion, the Religious Dimension, and Religious Surrogates," *LWF Marxism and China Study Document* No. 4, 1, 2, 11, 2.

Toward an Indigenous Chinese Faith

Chinese Christianity must be a product of reflection on the Chinese experience and culture as lived by the Chinese themselves, neither as interpreted by Westerners, nor by a simple and linear application of the message of Revelation. Christians, wherever they live, ought not abandon their traditions.[185] In fact, adding another "self," that is, "self-expression," to the three-self principle is appropriate in the context of the Chinese experience.

The hermeneutical implications of the whole chapter do not call for a simple application of the message of Revelation to the situation of the Chinese Christians. If they did, the Three-Self Movement would have to be deemed heretical according to the standard of Revelation. We have already pointed out the similarity of the Christians in both the book of Revelation and in China going through suffering because of their faith. We have also seen a unique church movement in China that is unparalleled in Revelation.

As a historic movement the TSPM represents postdenominational unity in an unprecedented manner for the Chinese people.[186] The divisions and denominations of Christianity in the West have long confused Chinese Christians. Ecumenical concern for unity in variety and for a pluralism of self-expression is characteristic of TSPM. During the last thirty years or so, it has held dialogues between the church and the state and between Christians and non-Christians. Today the vast majority of Chinese Christians are patriotic citizens and support the three-self principles.[187]

The three-self principles should not be perceived as totally nationalistic, or as a Chinese-culture Christianity which has adopted a "closed-door policy." During the formative period of TSPM, it may have been necessary to be completely independent of foreign influence or assistance. However, TSPM has always said, "The church is not only local and indigenous, it is also ecumenical and

---

185. Robert Jewett in his book *Christian Tolerance* ([Philadelphia: Westminster Press, 1982], 43–67) expounds carefully the issue of Christians keeping their tradition and relating it to Christian truth.

186. Brown, *Christianity,* 213.

187. Brown, *Christianity,* 213.

catholic. Not only must it relate to a particular nation and culture, it is transnational and transcultural. Not only is it independent, it is interdependent with every other part of the Body of Christ."[188]

This chapter does not seek to give the impression that TSPM is a perfect movement; it has its shortcomings and weaknesses. The chapter merely tries to point out that Christ, the end of history, gives hope for the Chinese Christians under persecution, but that they seek in their own context to live the biblical message, in some ways quite different from the intention of the writer of Revelation. TSPM is not a "communist" Christianity but a Chinese Christianity in the New Communist China. TSPM may be "the result of the leading of the Holy Spirit" in light of the complex historical and ideological situation of New China from which it has emerged, but without believing in Christ as its hope, TSPM will not thrive.

188. Brown, *Christianity*, 216.

Chapter 9

Rejection and Restoration in Isaiah and Tienanmen Square

Two Chinese words transliterated as "six, four" may not mean anything to Westerners. To the Chinese, however, these two words represent the military crackdown on the democratic movement at Tienanmen Square on June the Fourth 1989. The so-called Beijing massacre means national shame and disgrace to many Chinese. To many Chinese Christians as well, the event triggered the question of whether God had forsaken them — if not allowed judgment to fall on them. June Fourth still shocks their conscience; it causes them to wonder whether human sinfulness has terminated the faithfulness of God. This chapter does not seek to answer the "why" and "how" of the event itself. It only intends to know the divine utterance many Chinese Christians seek as they deal with the emotional despair caused by the tragedy.

Despite the fact that answers to the question of the tragic event are not explicitly and readily available, Scripture does offer a timely and paradigmatic message. The Word of God as found in Isaiah speaks to the June Fourth event in reading and hearing, when readers are conscious of their own hermeneutical horizon as well as the horizon of the text. Is 5:1–7 and 27:2–6 are texts that speak not only to the original audience concerning divine providence and promise, but also to modern Chinese Christians.[1]

---

1. See the initial response of some Hong Kong Christians to the event. Helena P. W. Wong edited *Some Christian Reflections on the June 4 Massacre and the Democratic Movement* (Hong Kong: Hong Kong Christian Institute, 1990); the collection of essays mentions events in the books of Jeremiah and Isaiah, but not Is 5:1–7 and 27:2–6.

Three Hermeneutical Hearings

To understand the meaning of the text, we shall first provide a translation of the pericopae from the Masoretic Text, and then look at Is 5:1–7 and 27:2–6 (not 27:2–9)[2] within the overall conceptualization of 5:1–27:13, so that the message of judgment and the message of restoration can be held in juxtaposition. Both are important to us here. The overwhelming message of June Fourth is one of national affliction. What is needed is hope in national restoration. From the standpoint of the person of faith, the question is whether the latter message is found in Scripture, and specifically in the text at hand, Isaiah — or is such hope present only in the heart of the reader? The selected pericopae are explicit in providing an answer. The following analysis will argue that Isaiah 5 and 27 cannot be heard apart from one another.

I render the English translation of the pericopae as:

> [5:1] Now let me sing[3] for my beloved [friend]
>   a song of my beloved about his vineyard.
> There was a vineyard (of) my beloved
>   on a fertile hill.[4]

---

2. All commentators agree that 27:2–6 is modeled on 5:1–7, but there is no consensus on whether this unit should end in verse 5, 6, 9, or 11. Verses 2–5 are strictly a unit, with verse 6 as the important annotation. Note the differences between vv. 2–6 and vv. 7–13: (a) the change in theme from the vineyard to the slaying of peoples; (b) the change of perspective from future to past; (c) the interrogative beginning v. 7, indicating a new subunit; (d) the ending in v. 6, seeming to correspond with the song in 5:1–7; and (e) the positive subject matter of vv. 2–6 and the negative subject matter in vv. 7–11. (See D. G. Johnson, *From Chaos to Restoration* [Sheffield: JSOT, 1988], 85.) I see the shortest intact unit as vv. 2–6, in view of the theme of the restored vineyard, the time perspective, and grammatical-literary considerations.

3. "Let me sing" is an "emphatic statement of a fixed determination" of a cohortative strengthened by the particle (*Gesenius' Hebrew Grammar,* ed. E. Kautzsch and A. E. Cowley, 2d ed. [Oxford: Clarendon, 1910], §108b, 319). (Hereafter GKC.) So "I will sing" or "let me sing." G. R. Williams ("Frustrated Expectations in Isaiah V 1–7: A Literary Interpretation," *Vetus Testamentum* 35 [1985]: 459–60) interprets as a "song in praise of."

4. *Qrn* means a "horn" in OT, but here it is used to describe a piece of land. *Hebrew and English Lexicon of the Old Testament* (London: Oxford University Press, 1907), 901–2 (hereafter BDB), lists this word in Is 5:1 under both meanings of "horn" and "hill." The Hebrew *ben* "is used poetically of things without life" (GKC, §128v, 418).

[2]He dug it up and cleared it of stones,
    he planted it (with) choice vines.[5]
Then he built a watchtower in the midst of it,
    and also a winepress he cut out in it.
Then he waited for (it) to yield grapes,
    but it yielded wild grapes.
[3]Now inhabitants of Jerusalem
    and people of Judah,
Judge, I pray you, between me
    and my vineyard.
[4]What (was there) more to do for my vineyard
    that I did not do to it?
Why did I long for (it) to yield grapes?
    But it yielded wild grapes![6]
[5]And now let me tell you
    what I am going to do with my vineyard:
I will take away its hedge and it will be destroyed;
    break up its wall and it will be trampled.
[6]So I will make it a wasteland;
    it will not be pruned nor hoed,
    it will grow briar and thorn.
And to the clouds I will command
    from raining rain upon it.
[7]For the vineyard of the Lord of Hosts is the house of Israel,
    and the people of Judah are the garden of his delight;
he longed for justice but beheld bloodshed;[7]
    for righteousness but beheld a cry of distress....

---

5. *Šrq* is used in the OT for places (Jgs 16:4; Gn 36:36; 1 Chr 1:47). See J. D. W. Watts, *Isaiah 1–33*, Word Biblical Commentary (Waco, Tex.: Word, 1985), 55.

6. The Hebrew word is obscure. LXX has "thorn, thistles"; the Vulgate has *labruscas*, "wild vines"; BDB relates it to "have a bad smell, stink"; *Gesenius' Hebräisches und Aramäisches Handwörterbuch*, ed. F. P. W. Buhl (Berlin: Springer Verlag, 1915), notes a Coptic word *bees*, "unripe fruit," and conjectures with the Vulgate, "grapes with a bitter, sour taste"; G. R. Driver (*Studies in Old Testament Prophecy* [Edinburgh: T. & T. Clark, 1950], 53, n. 6) suggests "spoiled by anthracnosa" following "decayed, rotten." See Watts, *Isaiah 1–33*, 55, and E. J. Young, *The Book of Isaiah 1–18* (Grand Rapids, Mich.: Eerdmans, 1972), 199, n. 4.

7. The Hebrew word is an obscure one. LXX translates "lawlessness"; the Vulgate has *iniquitas*, "iniquity," while BDB (973) has "bloodshed."

[27:2] In that day
     a vineyard of wine, sing[8] of her.
[3]I the Lord am watching over her;
     every moment I water her.
Night and day I guard her
     lest she is harmed.
[4]I have no wrath;
     who would give me briar and thorn,
     in the battle[9] I would march against them.
I would burn them up[10] altogether.
[5]Or (rather)[11] let him take hold of my protection,
     let him make peace with me[12]
     let him make peace with me.
[6]In days to come Jacob shall take root,
     Israel will bud and blossom,
     and fill the whole world with fruit.[13]

Why place Isaiah 27 alongside Isaiah 5? The answer is, the context and the conceptual literary matrix of Isaiah demand such a reading. Concerning the context, W. Roth rightly argues that the

---

8. Young (*Isaiah 19–39*, 237–8) follows Alexander's and Gray's arguments to translate the word *'nh* as "afflict": "The thought is that through the prophet God commands those who are hostile to His people to afflict Jerusalem. They may do their worst, but because God is with His people, He will triumph." But this meaning seems to be inconsistent with the context. BDB has "sing" (772–77.)

9. "In the battle" is placed in the first line by MT; *BHS* finds it obscure and wants to eliminate it altogether or draw it into the second line. See Watts, *Isaiah 1–33*, 347; O. Kaiser, *Isaiah 13–39*, 2d ed., trans. R. A. Wilson (Philadelphia: Westminster Press, 1983), 225.

10. *'Aṣîtenah* is to be read *'aṣî tenah* as *BHS* and GKC (§71, 193) suggest, because of the *y* being assimilated into the *ṣ*.

11. "Rather" or "or" is an emphatic adversative conjunction. GKC (§162a, 500) seems to suggest an introduction of another case unlike that mentioned before. Young (*Isaiah 19–39*, 241) translates "unless." Note the transition of *hiphil jussive* to two imperfects in the circumstantial clauses. Here, repetition gives emphasis; the object placed first in the second clause gives extra emphasis on "peace."

12. LXX has "let us make peace with him." But note MT has the speaker as Yahweh. My translation follows the MT.

13. R. E. Clements (*Isaiah 1–39*, New Century Bible Commentary [Grand Rapids, Mich.: Eerdmans, 1980], 220) sees v. 6 as a later interpolation. Kaiser (*Isaiah 1–12*, 224) sees vv. 2–6 as a later addition which is "badly preserved." Verses 2–6 are taken here as an authentic unit.

Isaiah scroll must be seen in its integrated "conceptual literary matrix": the Lord's deliverance of Jerusalem.[14] This matrix moves through the scroll and holds the prologue (1:2–4:6), the main body of three parts (5:1–55:13), and the epilogue (56:1–66:24) together.[15] In the first part (5:1–27:13), the song of the vineyard is set in the context of the six reproaches (5:8–23) for Israel's failure to be faithful to the word of the Lord and to cultic and social righteousness. On the other hand, 27:2–6 is set in the context of the Syrian-Ephraimite attack on Judah,[16] and contains a sure and glorious promise for the future of Israel.[17] What frames the first part (5:1–27:13) then is precisely this highly poetic-prophetic song of the vineyard (which also appears in the prologue [1:2–9] and the epilogue [65:21–23]).

Thus, it is the intent of this chapter to show the coherence of the message of 5:1–7 and 27:2–6 and the dynamic between them when seen in relationship to one another.[18] In the first part of the song (5:1–7), the vineyard is destroyed by the faithless keepers who lack loyalty in cultic and social life; in the counterpart (27:2–6), we see a restored vineyard which is "purified of idolatry and divinely protected, its vines deeply rooted and abundantly watered. At peace

---

14. Wolfgang Roth, *Isaiah* (Atlanta: John Knox Press, 1988), 4, 7, 17. For example, the scroll points out the deliverance of Jerusalem from the Aramean-Ephramite coalition in 733 B.C.E. (7:1–17), from the siege of Sennacherib, King of Assyria (36:1–37:38) (see also the deliverance of Hezekiah from illness [38:9–20]), and from the Babylonians (see 13:2–14:23, 21:1–10).

15. Many commentators do not see the whole picture of the scroll as Roth does. At this point, I am following Roth's overall argument quite closely. Roth summarizes on page 9 of his commentary that Isaiah 1–66 is, to a large extent, in its longer and shorter text units, molded by the pattern "from threat and castigation to deliverance and assurance."

16. In 734/733 B.C.E., when Ahaz sought help from Assyria instead of the Holy One of Israel. Whether chaps. 5–27 were written then (so Clements, *Isaiah,* 57–58) or composed later (e.g., Roth's view) varies in the opinions of scholars.

17. Roth also mentions at least three ways the promise is couched: "in the celebration of King Hezekiah's birth (9:1–6), in the vision of King Josiah's exemplary loyalty to the Lord's law (11:1–6), and in an announcement of a future banquet on Mount Zion for all peoples (25:6–8)" (Roth, *Isaiah,* 39).

18. The argument here is not that these two pericopae were originally found in a single song. Rather, it is being suggested that when we look at these pericopae (which are intentionally placed where they are) as a whole, then we discover why they are placed where they are. Then we begin to appreciate the dynamics at work in the first part of the scroll (5:1–27:13).

with its divine master and with itself, it reaches out and covers the world with its tendrils and its fruit."[19]

To explicate this thesis, we shall "hear" the whole song; not just the first part, but also the counterpart. We shall attempt to hear the whole song in three "voices,"[20] that is, in three layers of interlocking meanings: from the standpoint of the vineyard owner, from the bridegroom, and the Lord (though at times not as distinct as we would like them to be). More precisely, we shall hear the whole song in three rounds (perspectives), form-contextual, poetic-structural, and literary-analytical so that the central message of the pericopae concerning God's enduring love for his people will not be missed.

First Round: *Form (Genre)-Contextual Reading*

This first round of hearing the song in terms of its form-contextual setting will help us determine the number of "voices" (or layers of meaning) within it. The song contains a brief introduction (v. 1a), the song proper in three stanzas (vv. 1b–2, 3–4, 5–6), and an interpretation (v. 7).[21] The poet-prophet-singer recalls the events (for his bridegroom-friend or beloved,[22] possibly at a vintage festival[23]) which led up to this song (vv. 1b–2). The song contains

---

19. Roth, *Isaiah*, 18.

20. One could have used the three voices of the poet-prophet, the vineyard owner, and the lord of the song as three perspectives. But "voices" is used here to refer to three layers of meaning within the pericopae. In this chapter, where the word *voice* is used it refers to the person in the pericope and appears without quotation marks; where it is used to mean "layer of meaning," "voice" (with quotation marks) is used.

21. Kaiser, *Isaiah 1–12*, 59.

22. There are at least three translations of the word *dod*: bridegroom-friend, or bride or fertility deity. For more, see William Lee Holladay, *Isaiah: Scroll of Prophetic Heritage* (Grand Rapids, Mich.: Eerdmans, 1978), 62; Kaiser, *Isaiah 1–12*, 60; and Watts, *Isaiah 1–33*, 54–56.

23. The context in which the song is sung is difficult to construct. Kaiser however argues that "the choice of the material for comparison and the presence of the inhabitants of Jerusalem assumed in v. 3 suggests that the universally observed harvest and vintage festival was the actual occasion on which this prophecy was uttered (cf. Lev 23:34–43; Deut 16:13–15)" (*Isaiah 1–12*, 59). So also O. Eissfeldt (*The Old Testament: An Introduction* [New York: Harper, 1965], 88–89). However, Adrian Graffy ("The Literary Genre of Isaiah 5:1–7," *Biblica* 60 [1979]: 409) disagrees.

an accusation against the bride. The vineyard's owner, who is the bridegroom,[24] then recites his response demanding a judgment (vv. 3–4) before the Judahites and Jerusalemites. At verse 3 one hears Yahweh's voice emerging. It becomes clearer in verses 5–6 as Yahweh's voice, by means of a hermeneutical bridge, uses the vineyard song to accuse and castigate unfaithful Judah. In verses 5–6 the bridegroom's voice and Yahweh's voice (commanding the clouds)[25] are intermingled with harsh announcements of rejection. The plaintiff here becomes the judge as well. The poet-prophet concludes the song in verse 7 with a crescendo that reinforces the lesson of the whole song and that identifies the roles of the person in the song.[26] The whole song does not really end here, for after a long interval (5:8–27:1), it reappears in 27:2–6 when the Lord himself rounds it up with the sure and sharp note of restoration.

In terms of its literary context, one observes that the sixfold "woe" (5:8–23) sets the song into the larger setting of lament and judgment. Is it a love song with a funereal mood? Yes, for the first part of the song is a love story that ends in death. The whole song begins with a song of lamentation using a vineyard as its image. The imagery of 27:12–13 then ends the song with triumph, hope, and celebration.

"Song" is the intentional form of the pericopae. It is used perhaps as a means of catching the attention of the audience with a familiar motif and joyful tone. The song here works itself out in its literary-dramatic function as it begins with a familiar, innocent, joyful, and romantic note. The image of a vineyard would have been a familiar image to all Isaianic contemporary audiences. The love-song theme would also mean that it was meant to be entertaining. But the song moves into an incisive indictment of Israel.[27]

---

24. Note that *dod* in Song of Songs is used only by the young woman in speaking of the man she loves. There is no suggestion here, however, that the vineyard is the bride, because vv. 3–6 seem to suggest that it is the bride (it cannot be the bridegroom) who is barren and unfaithful.

25. Command of the clouds can only be done by a divine being. The poet is using metaphorical language here.

26. See Watts, *Isaiah 1–33*, 53–54; Clements, *Isaiah*, 58; and Kaiser, *Isaiah 1–12*, 58, who also see the same subdivisions in the song.

27. This is not a song of the poet's beloved but of the poet's friend concerning

In verse 3 the song shifts its thematic expectation.[28] That is, it turns into a "lawsuit." Verse 4a gives the judgment, namely, rejection. The matter becomes worse still in verse 7, in which accusation is pointedly turned against Israel. So the effect of the song at this point is to disappoint and frustrate the listeners as much as the vineyard-Israel disappoints and frustrates the Lord. Another subtle point is that the audience is asked to judge (v. 3) and to accept the judgment and God's rejection (vv. 5–7). No doubt, the woes (vv. 8–25) that follow are most fitting.

Are these pericopae songs and/or poetry? Not all scholars have considered them to belong to the song or poetry genre.[29] Clements, Kaiser, Yee, Williams, Sheppard, and Fohrer speak of 5:1–7 as a "legal indictment parable" or "lawsuit."[30] Graffy calls it a "self-condemnation parable."[31] Roth calls it a "parable."[32] Willis identifies it as a "parable ... [with its] contents as a parabolic song of a disappointed husbandman."[33] The Targum, Roche, and Korpel put this unit in the category of "allegory."[34] However, we miss

---

his friend's love affair. See Watts, *Isaiah 1–33*, 55; and R. E. Murphy, *Wisdom Literature* (Grand Rapids, Mich.: Eerdmans, 1981), 177.

28. The shifting of a positive theme into a negative theme is a poetic device commonly used by Isaiah (5:1–7), Jeremiah (2:2–3, 4:29–31, 6:1–5, 11:16, 12:13, 13:12–14, etc.), and Hosea (9:14). See Louis Dorn, "The Unexpected as a Speech Device: Shifts of Thematic Expectancy in Jeremiah," *The Bible Translator* 37 (1986): 216–22.

29. With the exception of Watts who seems to use "requiem ... love-song" (*Isaiah 1–33*, 55).

30. Clements, *Isaiah*, 57–59; Kaiser, *Isaiah 1–12*, 59; G. A. Yee, "A Form-Critical Study of Isaiah 5:1–7 as a Song and a Juridical Parable," *Catholic Biblical Quarterly* 43 (1981): 37–38; G. R. Williams, "Frustrated Expectations in Isaiah V 1–7," 462; Gerald T. Sheppard, "More on Isaiah 5:1–7 as a Juridical Parable," *Catholic Biblical Quarterly* 44 (1982): 45–47; G. Fohrer, *Das Buch Jesaja*, vol. 1, Zürcher Bibelkommentäre (Zurich: Zwingli, 1960), 75; Michael de Roche ("Yahweh's *rib* against Israel: A Reassessment of the So-Called 'Prophetic Lawsuit' in the Pre-exilic Prophets," *Journal of Biblical Literature* 102 [1983]: 563–74) argues that *rib* should not be translated as "lawsuit" because most prophetic *rib* are simple complaints and not lawsuits involving a third party.

31. Graffy, "The Literary Genre of Isaiah 5:1–7," 400–409; see John T. Willis, "The Genre of Isaiah 5:1–7," *Journal of Biblical Literature* 96 (1977): 351–52.

32. Roth, *Isaiah*, 39.

33. Willis, "The Genre of Isaiah 5:1–7," 337–62. Willis takes the most natural interpretation of the vineyard as a piece of land, not as the bride in a love song.

34. J. F. Stenning, *The Targum of Isaiah* (Oxford: Clarendon, 1949), 16; M. C. J. Korpel, "The Literary Genre of the Song of the Vineyard (Is. 5:1–7)," in

the point by using Western and modern self-defined terminology to characterize the Hebraic understanding of *mashal* (literally "to be like"),[35] which can refer to allegory, parable, or fable. *Mashal* is inclusive of all the above genres.[36] In other words, the ancient Hebrew writers did not have these literary-compositional categories (e.g., parable, fable, allegory, etc.) to limit them. Therefore, scholars should be cautious when importing modern categories lest they force the ancient text into inappropriate molds.[37] Clearly, Is 5:1–7 as a *mashal* has some affinities with almost all of the above. In short we can say that the genre of 5:1–7 is a *mashal,* which in this instance is poetry-song.

As poetry-song, 5:1–7 has at least three layers of meaning: one literal (referring to a vineyard — at least up to v. 6) and two metaphorical meanings, the precise identification of which is disputed, though commonly understood as a beloved bride and the people of God.[38] Whether the relationship between the vineyard

---

The Structural Analysis of Biblical and Canaanite Poetry, ed. Willen van der Meer and Johannes C. de Moor, Journal for the Study of the Old Testament Supplement Series 74 (Sheffield: JSOT Press, 1988), 155.

35. *Mashal* can refer to a variety of verbal figures, including proverbs (1 Sm 24:13; Ez 18:2–3), riddles (Ps 78:2; Ez 17:2–3), taunts (Is 14:4; Ez 16:44), wisdom sayings (Prv 10:1, 26), allegories (Ez 17:2–3), oracles (Nm 23:7; 24:3), and others, like metaphors and similes. See Otto Eissfeldt, *Der Maschal im Alten Testament,* Beihefte zur Zeitschrift für die alttestamentliche Wissenschaft 24 (Giefzen, 1913).

36. The Greek word *parabolē* means "to place beside" or "compare"; it is an extended metaphor or simile. Modern scholars differentiate precisely the meaning of allegory from parable: (*a*) allegory differs from a parable in that each metaphorical element of the allegory represents a corresponding reality, whereas the parable conveys a single truth; (*b*) allegory reads into or finds in an ancient historical event, story, or literary production meanings that were not originally intended. See F. Büchsel, *"Allēgoreō,"* TDNT 1:260–61; J. D. Crossan, "The Parable of the Wicked Husbandmen," *Journal of Biblical Literature* 90 (1971): 462; Willis, "The Genre of Isaiah 5:1–7," 353–62; E. E. Nourse, "Parable (Introductory and Biblical)," *Encyclopaedia of Religion and Ethics IX,* ed. James Hastings (New York: Scribner's, 1922), 630; Hauck, *"Parabolē,"* TDNT 5: 746; and most importantly, J. D. Crossan ("Parables as Religious and Poetic Experience," *Journal of Religion* 53 [1973]: 334), who criticizes the distinction between allegory and parable on philosophical grounds.

37. For example, M. C. A. Korpel ("The Literary Genre of the Song of the Vineyard [Is. 5:1–7]," 119) immediately dismisses 5:1–7 as a parable because his definition of parable only allows one point of comparison.

38. Since it is poetry, the metaphorical meaning is emphasized for the following reasons: (*a*) nobody is asked to judge a literal vineyard; and (*b*) the OT sees the rela-

and the owner here is that of "friends" or "erotic lovers" or "uncle-nephew" may seem difficult to judge at first.[39] But it is very likely the intended audience would understand the song as a love song concerning a bridegroom (the singer's friend) and a bride (vineyard).[40] Because (a) the word *dod* is not used as a divine name in the OT, and (b) the most natural meaning is that of friend or beloved one, we accept the one literal and the two metaphorical meanings and reject the notion that this song is a "satirical polemic against Palestinian fertility cults."[41]

Second Round: Poetic-Structural Hearing

The literary style is so poetic that the pericopae can be heard as song. The effect of the song is achieved most powerfully here through a poetic-rhetorical device in that the indictment couched in the song is passed onto the accused, not by a third party, but by the audience itself, because the accused and the judge are one and the same.[42]

---

tionship between the people of Israel and the Lord as precisely that of the marriage covenant. See Hos 1:9–2:4; Ez 16:8, 59–60; Mal 2:14; Jer 2:2.

39. This has to do with the translation of "vineyard." Williams says the uses of "vineyard" are "metaphors for love making and the female sexual partner" ("Frustrated Expectations in Isaiah V 1–7," 460, n. 7). B. Z. Luria ("What Is the Vineyard in Isaiah's Parable?" *Beth Mikra* 31 [1985/86]: 289–92]) interprets the literal meaning of "vineyard" as "worked land."

40. Often "vineyard" refers to the bride (see Song 2:15, 4:16f., 6:1f., 8:11f.). Perhaps this song, which uses the vineyard motif, is similar to that in Song of Songs. Ugaritic, Egyptian, and Akkadian literature also use the vineyard as a metaphor of sexual love. See Williams, "Frustrated Expectations in Isaiah V 1–7," 460; Willis, "The Genre of Isaiah 5:1–7," 345–46.

41. Willis lists various commentators who advocate this interpretation, and delineates their reasoning, namely, that: (a) *dod* is a divine name on the Moabite Stone (Mesha inscription); (b) Akkadian divine names of *Dadi-ilu, Abu-dadi, Dadiya,* and OT proper names like *Dodai* (1 Chr 27:4) and *Dodo* (Jgs 10:1; 2 Sm 23:9 [Qere], 24; 1 Chr 11:12, 26) are related to the Palestinian fertility deities; (c) Is 5:1–7 is modeled after Song 8:11–12, with Isaiah satirizing the potentially harlotrous Yahwism which they were practicing by using the divine name *Dod* for Yahweh; and, (d) the reference to "pruning" the vines in v. 6 betrays fertility cult language. See Willis, "The Genre of Isaiah 5:1–7," 338–40; W. C. Graham, "Notes on the Interpretation of Isaiah 5:1–12," *American Journal of Semitic Languages and Literature* 45 (1928/29): 167–68.

42. A. Graffy makes the point forcefully, and calls it a "self-condemnation parable." See Graffy, "The Literary Genre of Isaiah 5:1–7," 408.

Referring to the aesthetic composition of the song, especially its first part, Delitzsch aptly writes: "The winged rhythm, the euphonic music, the sweet assonance of this appeal cannot be reproduced."[43] In 5:1 alone, we have the assonance of Hebrew words; we have the repetitive parallelism and alliterative parallelism.[44] Concerning verse 2a, Korpel remarks that "the verse is marked by repetitive parallelism creating assonance and striking rhyme."[45] In verse 2b, we have the end rhyme and repetitive parallelism. In verse 3a, there is parallelism but without any rhythm. What happens at this point? Korpel rightly observes that the song "strikes a false note"[46] to indicate the seriousness of the appeal. That is, what begins as an entertaining piece has turned into a harsh indictment that demands judgment. The indictment resumes the rhyme in 3b. Verse 4 shows again the assonance and the rhyme of the song. The repetitive use of "to do" expects the listeners to know how to respond to Yahweh's covenantal love. In verse 5, Yahweh says what he is going "to do" with the Israel-vineyard. Throughout verse 7 end-rhymes are still maintained.[47] Then in verse 7a, chiastic parallelism is seen in

For <u>the vineyard of the Lord of Hosts</u> is *the house of Israel*

and *the people of Judah* are <u>the garden of his delight</u>

---

43. Franz J. Delitzsch, *Biblical Commentaries on the Prophecies of Isaiah*, trans. J. Martin (Edinburgh: T. & T. Clark, 1910), 120.

44. For more on ancient Hebrew poetry, see Hans Kosmala, "Form and Structure in Ancient Hebrew Poetry: A New Approach," *Vetus Testamentum* 14 (1964): 423–45, and *Vetus Testamentum* 16 (1966): 152–80; S. A. Geller, *Parallelism in Early Biblical Poetry* (Missoula, Mont.: Scholars, 1979); Y. Avishur, *Stylistic Studies on Word-Pairs in Biblical and Ancient Semitic Literatures* (Neukirchen-Vluyn: Neukirchener, 1984); W. G. E. Watson, *Classical Hebrew Poetry: A Guide to Its Techniques* (Sheffield: JSOT, 1984); A. Berlin, *The Dynamics of Biblical Parallelism* (Bloomington: Indiana University Press, 1985).

45. Korpel, "The Literary Genre of the Song of the Vineyard (Is. 5:1–7)," 126.

46. Korpel, "The Literary Genre of the Song of the Vineyard (Is. 5:1–7)," 130.

47. E.g., the assonance and rhyme in verses 5 and 6.

This chiastic structure shows that (*a*) the house of Israel is not contrasted but equated with the people of Judah; (*b*) the vineyard is equated with the Lord's planting; and, (*c*) a is equated with b. In verse 7b, what Israel is doing and what is expected of them is contrasted in a poetic pun of alliterative assonance:

> He longed for *justice* but beheld *bloodshed;*
> for *righteousness* but beheld a *cry of distress.*

This verse is not only the finale of this song, but also its crescendo as the word play between *mishpāṭ* ("justice") and *miśpāḥ* ("bloodshed") and *ṣedāqāh* ("righteousness") and *ṣeʿāqāh* ("cry of distress") so poetically grasp the attention of the audience. The Hebrew poetic pun is beautiful; this English rendition tries to convey that characteristic: "For measures he looked, but lo massacres! For right, but riot."[48] Here, the first part of the song reaches its crescendo. But in the midst of this poetic beauty there lies both harsh judgment and great comfort. Comfort? Yes, because despite what Israel (Judah) has done, Israel is still "the garden of his [Yahweh's] delight." This high note of the song entices the listener into listening for more. Sure enough, as we hear its counterpart in 27:2–6, it becomes clearer that the critical song of 5:1–7 also speaks about Yahweh's gift of hope, promise, and deliverance to Israel.

Because we are dealing with poetry and not prose, we must move from the literal meaning to the metaphorical meanings of the song. In other words, we have to focus on the two layers of metaphorical meaning: marriage on the human level (bridegroom-bride) and covenant on the divine level (Yahweh-Israel).[49] We can infer then from 5:1–7, as Williams does, the first metaphorical meaning, namely, that

> the removal of the hedge and/or wall and the destruction of
> the vineyard through the grazing and trampling of animals

48. Holladay, *Isaiah: Scroll of Prophetic Heritage,* 64. *Ṣeʿāqāh* is used elsewhere in the OT as the cry of those afflicted by political and social violence (see Gn 27:34; Ex 3:7, 9; 11:6; Ps 9:13). See Watts, *Isaiah 1–33,* 56.

49. Here allegorical meanings are visible. No precise distinction is made here between parable and allegory (see nn. 37–38). We cannot assign meaning to all details in an allegorical sense. The interest here is in reconstructing, if possible, how images in the pericope are received by the listeners or readers. And of course, imagination and creativity were at work in the ancient listeners' minds as well as in our own.

suggest that the poet will cease to help his wife. More specifically, he will cease to protect her from those who might take advantage of her. The chaos in the vineyard (v. 6a) perhaps represents the problems which will engulf her. The curse of drought (v. 6b; see 2 Sam 1:21) may represent a curse of barrenness, the opposite of the wedding blessing of Gen 24:60.[50]

By the time we come to verse 7, the first layer of interpretation proves inadequate. The friend of the poet is not just a human friend but his best friend — Yahweh. In the second layer, a fertile hill can be a reference to the land of Canaan, flowing with milk and honey. The plowing up of the ground and the clearing of stones (v. 2a) perhaps represents the expulsion of the Canaanites (see Ps 80:9–10). The planting of the choice vines recalls the noble generation of Joshua (see Jer 2:21; Dt 32:23; Ez 19:10; Hos 10:1, 14:8). The removal of the wall (v. 5) may imply that Judah would no longer enjoy divine protection. The devouring and trampling can refer to enemy invasions, and the infinitive "to destroy" suggests a similar effect.[51] The growth of thorns and thistles, resulting from discontinued hoeing (v. 6), suggests long-term desolation after military destruction.[52] "He/she/it is/will be pruned or cultivated" means Judah will neither be protected nor praised in song.[53] Both readers and listeners might immediately call to mind the covenant curses on Israel, for here they are being reminded of military threat and drought.[54] This interpretation is consistent with the counterpart of the song, in which we are told clearly that the Lord "redeems" and restores his "bride" Israel, even filling the whole world with Israel's "fruit."

---

50. Williams, "Frustrated Expectations in Isaiah V 1–7," 461–62; and so Korpel, "The Literary Genre of the Song of the Vineyard (Is. 5:1–7)," 125–27. See also Willis, "The Genre of Isaiah 5:1–7," 355, for his critique of this interpretation.

51. For more detailed uses of this word, see H. Ringgren, "*B'r*," *TDOT* 1:201–5.

52. See Is 1:7, 7:23–25, 32:12–14, 34:13. For a technical understanding of this problematic phrase see Korpel, "The Literary Genre of the Song of the Vineyard (Is. 5:1–7)," 136–38.

53. For various uses of this word, see C. Barth, "*Zmr*," *TDOT* 4:91–98.

54. Both military threat and drought are covenant curses found in the Mosaic Law: Lv 26:16–36; Dt 28:23–42.

Third Round: Literary-Analytical Hearing

The first two rounds give us the overall picture of the song. The third round will help us probe deeper into the text, in which the covenantal love between Israel and God is examined. Their relationship is characterized by the word *dod,* which is used almost exclusively in the OT as "friend" or "beloved" of God.[55] In this pericope (5:1–7), this word represents first the owner of the vineyard, then Yahweh himself. "Vineyard" is a common metaphor for a beloved woman in the ancient Near East.[56] The relationship between Israel and the Lord is portrayed in this song as a "marriage-love" relationship, as the ancient writer clarifies for the readers in verse 7. In verse 1, the poetic and creative play on the word "fertile" is used to describe the "hill" of Canaan and the perfumed oil used in sacred marriage.[57] The vineyard owner's preparation of the ground is thorough, so he has high expectations for good fruit. He has worked wholeheartedly at his vineyard to ensure the best harvest of fruit — justice and righteousness. First he chose the most fertile site on a hillside.[58] Then he loosened the ground by plowing it.[59] He then cleared it of all stones, lest the

---

55. See Dt 33:12; Jer 11:15; Pss 60:5; 108:5; 127:2. Clements (*Isaiah,* 58) and Watts (*Isaiah 1–33,* 55) prefer the translation "friend" rather than "beloved." The Vulgate translated "uncle" (*patruelis mei*) and was followed by Luther. See Young, *Isaiah 1–18,* 193; Willis, "The Genre of Isaiah 5:1–7," 337. Whether this word has sexual connotation (as in Jer 11:15; Ps 65:1) or not (as in Dt 33:12; Pss 60:7, 127:2) is difficult to determine here. But the most natural meaning of *dod* here seems to be "beloved, darling, friend" as most biblical and Canticle passages tend to suggest. For more on these three meanings ("uncle," "friend," "beloved" with erotic sense) in the OT and other Near Eastern sources, see Williams, "Frustrated Expectations in Isaiah V 1–7," 460, n. 6. I tend to see the relationship between the singer and the vineyard's owner as "intimate friends" and not as lovers.

56. See Song 1:6; 2:15; 8:11, 12. For evidence in Sumerian, Egyptian, and Ugaritic texts of this similar usage of "vineyard," see S. N. Kramer, *The Sacred Marriage Rite* (Bloomington: Indiana University Press, 1969), 81, 100; J. B. White, *A Study of the Language of Love in the Song of Songs and Ancient Egyptian Poetry* (Missoula, Mont.: Scholars Press, 1978), 176–77.

57. Korpel, "The Literary Genre of the Song of the Vineyard (Is. 5:1–7)," 125–26.

58. The hill is described literally as "son of fat (oil)" to show its fertility.

59. "Dig" or "plow" appears only here in OT. The LXX's rendering of "put around it a fence" and the Vulgate *saepivit* ("enclose") do not do justice to the meaning. See Watts, *Isaiah 1–33,* 55; Kaiser, *Isaiah 1–12,* 60.

stones hinder the growth of the vine. He used the choicest vine, built a watchtower[60] and a wine vat. The owner rightfully expected good grapes. Instead, the fruit it produced was a terrible disappointment — "wild grapes," "rotten grapes," "grapes with bitter taste."

In verses 3–4 the listeners from Judah and Jerusalem are asked to judge the case because the owner is utterly disappointed by his vineyard: it yielded wild grapes! Of course, the guilty ones serve as judge. They are the very ones called to offer judgment, as the verdict makes obvious in verse 7 (see 2 Sm 12:1–6; David, called to be the judge, is the guilty one). The case is clear. There is nothing else the owner could have done for the vineyard. The same is true of the Lord with Israel, whom he has elected, formed, and protected like a choice vine (see Jer 2:1–2). But the result is most disappointing. So in verses 5–6 the owner is determined to dismantle the protective walls and to abandon all care. The vineyard will be trampled, dried up, and burned, to be overgrown with thorns and briers, to become a wasteland (literally "end" or "desolation"). The owner wants the listeners to know (as the causative cohortative with the precative particle shows clearly): "I pray you, let me cause you to know." Who is the owner? Watts says, "The owner is unmasked in this speech. He is Yahweh."[61] In case the reader or listener misses the point, it is made clear in verse 7. The chiastic arrangement of verse 7 shows that Yahweh is the owner; Israel is the vineyard; justice and righteousness are the best grapes; bloodshed and the cry of distress are the wild grapes. Note that three times (vv. 2, 4, 7) "wait/long" is used to stress God's patience. But Israel, the favorite garden of Yahweh, has broken the covenantal love relationship.[62] This is not, however, the abrupt end of the song of accusation, nor is it the end of Israel. In 5:7, despite the harsh indictment, Israel is still being portrayed as the "garden of [Yahweh's] delight." Whatever happens, Israel remains Yahweh's vineyard. In 27:2–6,

---

60. A watchtower is needed for the protection of the vineyard. The owner is so anxious for a good harvest that the final preparation is to build a winepress.

61. Watts, *Isaiah 1–33*, 56.

62. Refer to "Second Round" above for the artistic indictment of Yahweh through the use of wordplay and poetic devices.

we hear again the final note of the song, which reverses the verdict given in the first half.

The song of the vineyard reappears in 27:2–6. It is now more than a counterpart to the previous song (5:1–7), but a new version of the old. The subject matter is the same, but the musical notes and mood are all rewritten. God will be watching over his vineyard (Israel) because she will be a fruitful vineyard and a delight.[63] In fact, Israel will be gathered from exile[64] to worship the Lord in Zion. Israel will be restored. Israel will be protected and cared for personally by the Lord. Israel will even be a worldwide community. Most precious about this part of the song is that it is sung by Yahweh throughout, untainted by the voice of the poet-prophet or the bridegroom. It is Yahweh's song for the people!

By juxtaposing these two pericopae and seeing them as one song, we discover that 27:2–6 is a counterpart to 5:1–7. Both parts are poetry-song about Israel as God's fertile vineyard ("fertile hill" of 5:1 and "vineyard of wine" of 27:2). Seeing both pericopae as a whole illustrates a thematic movement: from Yahweh's wrath in 5:5–6 to delight in 27:4; from briars and thorns replacing the vineyard in 5:6 to briars and thorns burned up in 27:4; from Yahweh's forbidding the cloud to rain on the vineyard in 5:6 to Yahweh's own regular watering of the vineyard in 27:3; from the unfaithful vineyard in 5:7 to the restored one in 27:5; from Yahweh's destroying the vineyard in 5:5, 6 to Yahweh's personal watch over the vineyard, night and day, in 27:3; from the malevolent yield of wild grapes in 5:7 to the abundant yield throughout the world in 27:6.

A Hermeneutical Voice to My People

We need to hear the whole song in order to perceive the love of God for the chosen people of Israel as well as for the Chinese

---

63. "A vineyard of delight (wine?)" is clearly a counterpart of 5:1, "a vineyard on the fertile hill." MT (the Leningradensis text) and texts from Qumran have "vineyard of wine." *BHS,* the Targum, and the Syriac read "delight"; LXX has "good." I prefer "delight." See Watts, *Isaiah 1–33,* 346; Young, *Isaiah 19–39,* 237.

64. The context from 5:1–27:13 seems to tell us that in 5:1–7 the vineyard "Israel" is not in exile, whereas in 27:2–6, Israel is. See 27:12.

people. For too long the Old Testament has been in captivity to Jerusalem. Indeed what has Beijing to do with Jerusalem (see chapter 7 of this book)? What has Tienanmen Square to do with the Jewish Temple? Probably nothing, except for the embracing and enduring love of God for all people. Assumptions regarding the chosenness of the people of God (Israel) have often led to the view that the Old Testament is for the Jewish people only. But is God partial in his salvation? Is God biased in his love for all people? Has God chosen the Jewish people only?

More pertinently, we who are Chinese are uncertain as to whether God continues to judge us or whether God's judgment should be seen in the light of His restoring love for us. Looking at the success of the movements for democracy in Poland and Czechoslovakia, the tearing down of the Berlin Wall, and the fall of Ceausescu in Romania, we are still puzzling over why we had to face the bloodstained reality of Tienanmen Square.

The June Fourth event has had a worldwide impact on all Chinese, not because it is a tragic event, but also because it is the pivotal event serving as a strong reminder of all the tragic events in Chinese history. We have experienced civil strife throughout our rich cultural history — a history marked by the invention of silk, writing, porcelain, and paper; and by the creation of great philosophical and ethical works (e.g., Confucianism, Taoism). The Great Wall may have been able to keep out nomadic invasions and "barbarian" encroachments, but it could not keep millions of diaspora Chinese from leaving the motherland to inhabit every corner of the world. As a self-proclaimed cultured nation, China has persecuted and killed many of the Nestorian, Franciscan, Jesuit, and Protestant missionaries and rejected the message they brought. As the Chinese watched the June Fourth event telecast live, many relived the tragic experience of the opium wars and the unequal treaties of 1839–60, the Taiping Rebellion in 1860, the Sino-French War in 1883–85, the Sino-Japanese War in 1894–95, the Boxer Rebellion in 1900, the antiforeign riots by students on 4 May 1919, the Sino-Japanese War in 1937, the civil war, the political corruption of 1946–49, and other tragic events.

The vineyard pericopae in Isaiah are especially relevant because the Chinese have come to a point in present Chinese history where they need to reassess their identity and to refine their vision of the future, just as the Israelites were required to do at crucial times in their history. Though the sonship, the glory, the covenants, and the giving of the Torah do not belong to us, through Christ we can have a similar relationship with God. Indeed, God is not the God of Jews alone, but God is the God of all.

To divide the two parts of the song and to see them as unrelated is a mistake. These vineyard pericopae serve as the opening and the closure of the first main part of the Isaiah scroll. The scroll's theme progresses "from warning of castigation to promise of restoration"[65] of Israel. By comparing and contrasting these two texts (Isaiah 5 and 27), and by understanding them from three perspectives with their three layers of meaning, we can hear clearly the message of Yahweh, the Most High God. This message recalls and interprets our history (and Israel's too) in terms of our faithfulness to God. This message also consoles us, the weary, afflicted, threatened, and hopeless community; we will be restored and even transformed into a worldwide community.[66] The final mood of the song is not doom, despair, desolation, and disappointment (see also Is 62:2–4a), but promise, pleasantness, and prosperity. That is the whole song we have heard, the whole song of the Lord for the people of God.

As the Chinese Christians find hope and identity by recalling their traditions and listening to God's message, may they find "the vision of the whole" (29:11). That vision will grant them new insight into our past, present, and even future, because history is determined by the coherent pattern of divine purpose explicit in the lyric of the whole song we have just heard.

---

65. Roth, *Isaiah*, 85.

66. Roth, *Isaiah*, 85–87. Roth relates 27:2–6 within the context of the "apocalypse" transformation of heaven and earth (24:1–23), of Mount Zion (25:1–26:6), and of Israel (26:7–27:13).

Chapter 10

The Role of Women in 1 Corinthians and "Vision 2020"

This chapter seeks to bring together the Malaysian "Vision 2020"[1] with Paul's understanding of gender relations as found in 1 Corinthians 11 and 14. We shall begin with a rhetorical-literary analysis of these texts and seek a critical appraisal of the role of women in the Malaysian Vision 2020, with the last part of the essay responding to the feminist waves already sweeping through this "global village." It is hoped that Vision 2020 can be articulated in such a way that, even as the nation pursues radical technological advances, both men and women, now so deeply affected by complex social changes, may continue to find meaning and value in their lives rather than finding themselves controlled by machines or relegated to the world of data and statistics.

---

1. "Vision 2020" is a program advocated by Malaysian Prime Minister Yang Amat Berhormat Dato' Seri Dr. Mahathir Mohamad. Its goal is to enable Malaysia to attain the rank of an industrialized nation by 2020. On 28 February 1991, the prime minister presented a working paper at the inaugural meeting of the Malaysia Business Council in which WAWASAN 2020 (Vision 2020) was outlined. It contained nine strategic goals: (1) a united Malaysian nation which is territorially and ethnically integrated; (2) a psychologically liberated and secure society that is self-confident; (3) a mature democratic society; (4) a moral and ethical society imbued with religious and spiritual values; (5) a liberal and tolerant society in which Malaysians respect each other's creeds and customs; (6) a scientific and progressive society that is innovative and forward-looking; (7) a caring society in which the welfare of people revolves around the family and not the individual or state; (8) an economically just society; and (9) a prosperous society with a competitive, dynamic, robust, and resilient economy.

The Biblical Traditions on Gender Relations

The Bible does provide a rich resource for Christians to consult as they wrestle with gender relations in the modern world. Admittedly, biblical views of male and female relations are diverse. Some scholars have argued that gender subordination was first taught in Judaism,[2] though in the OT radical departure from the prevailing norm is evident, such as the case of the prophetess Deborah (Jgs 4:4). Equality between male and female is seen more in the New Testament, as in 1 Pt 3:7, where both husband and wife are "joint heirs of the grace of life." The case of Paul, however, is difficult to sort out, that is, whether he is chauvinistic or egalitarian. His earlier writing, Gal 3:28, a pre-Pauline baptismal formula — though it may be a Pauline formula from his early missionary work[3] — seems to suggest an egalitarian theology: "There is neither Jew nor Greek, there is neither slave nor free, there is neither male nor female; for you are all one in Christ Jesus." It is baptism which brings about oneness in Christ. As Scroggs points out, "Any value judgments based on the distinctions in human society are nullified by baptism."[4] In her book *In Memory of Her*, Schüssler Fiorenza develops the equality effected by baptism even further: through baptism, she writes,

---

2. See Elizabeth MacDonald, *The Position of Women as Reflected in Semitic Codes of Law* (Toronto: University of Toronto Press, 1931); S. W. Baron, *A Social and Religious History of the Jews,* 2d ed. (New York and London: Columbia University Press, 1952), 1:111–14; R. de Vaux, *Ancient Israel: Its Life and Institutions* (New York, Toronto, and London: McGraw-Hill, 1961), 24–40; and R. Loewe, *The Position of Women in Judaism* (London: SPCK, 1966).

3. See H. D. Betz, "Spirit, Freedom, and Law: Paul's Message to the Galatian Churches," *Svensk exegetisk arsbok* 39 (1974): 145–60; M. Boutier, "Complexio Oppositorum: Sur les formules de I Cor xii.13; Gal iii.26–28; Col iii.10.11," *New Testament Studies* 23 (1976): 1–19. See also Robbin Scroggs, "Paul and the Eschatological Woman," *Journal of the American Academy of Religion* 40 (1972): 291–93; Wayne Meeks, "The Image of the Androgyne: Some Uses of a Symbol in Earliest Christianity," *History of Religion* 13 (1973–74): 181; Elisabeth Schüssler Fiorenza, "Women in the Pre-Pauline and Pauline Communities," *Union Seminary Quarterly Review* 33 (1978): 158, and idem, *In Memory of Her: A Feminist Theological Reconstruction of Christian Origins* (New York: Crossroad, 1983), 208ff.; and H. D. Betz, *Galatians: A Commentary on Paul's Letter to the Churches in Galatia,* Hermeneia (Philadelphia: Fortress, 1979), 184.

4. Scroggs, "Paul and the Eschatological Woman," 293.

women became full members of the people of God with
the same rights and duties. This generated a fundamental
change, not only in their standing before God but also in their
ecclesial-social status and function. ... In baptism Christians
entered into a kinship relationship with people coming from
very different racial, cultural, and national backgrounds.[5]

Baptism into Christ constitutes a liberation from the bondage of
sin and death — including gender relationships. Christian freedom
is the result of spiritual justification and the reversal of the Fall.
It is noteworthy that the phrase "male and female" follows the
technical formula in the creation account. The first pair (Galatians)
is joined with "nor" but this pair (Genesis) is joined with "and,"
indicating the dependence of male and female.[6] The Christ event
into which the Christian is incorporated by faith through baptism brings radical change to the old order of race, social status,
and sexual relationships, as D. Williams has written: "Redemption
brings into being a whole new world, a whole new order. Male
dominance, egotism, patriarchal power and preferential priority
is at an end. No longer can Genesis 2–3 be employed to reduce
women to an inferior position or state."[7] We may tentatively conclude that Paul is an egalitarian theologian whose feminist theology
is different from that of Genesis.

When we turn to Ephesians, 1 Timothy, and Titus for a discussion of gender relationship the situation changes. Here, neither
the word "obedience" nor the word "submission" is found. Ephesians 5:21 speaks of the mutuality of husband and wife. In 1 Cor
9:5 Paul maintains that he, like other apostles, has the right to
be supported financially and the right to be accompanied by female co-missionaries, because other apostles, the brothers of the
Lord and Cephas, were entitled to take with them a "sister" as
"woman/wife." The double accusative object "sister woman" is

---

5. Schüssler Fiorenza, *In Memory of Her,* 210–11.

6. Richard and Joyce Boldrey, *Chauvinist or Feminist? Paul's View of Women*
(Grand Rapids, Mich.: Baker, 1976), 33.

7. Don Williams, *The Apostle Paul and Women in the Church* (Van Nuys,
Calif.: BIM, 1977), 70.

best understood as a missionary coworker.[8] Even in 1 Corinthians 7, the mutuality of husband and wife is obvious.[9] In 1 Corinthians, the two most difficult passages to deal with from the standpoint of gender relations are 1 Corinthians 11 and 14, to which we will now turn our attention.

1 Corinthians 11: Differentiation and Mutuality of Male-Female Relations

The history of research[10] on this pericope has revealed its "notorious exegetical difficulties," namely, its uncertain logic, its imprecise

---

8. Elisabeth Schüssler Fiorenza, "Missionaries, Apostles, Co-workers: Romans 16 and the Reconstruction of Women's Early Christian History," in *Feminist Theology: A Reader*, ed. Ann Loades (London: SPCK, 1990), 69. Note Clement of Alexandria, *Stromateis* 3.6.53.3f.: "[The early apostles] took their wives with them not as women with whom they had marriage relations but as sisters that they might be their co-missionaries (*syndiakonous*) in dealing with housewives" (Schüssler Fiorenza, "Missionaries, Apostles, Co-workers," 291, n. 28).

9. The three big questions of race, freedom, and sexes are dealt with in 1 Cor 7:17–39 (Was anyone at the time of his call already circumcised?...Was anyone at the time of his call uncircumcised? [v.18]; Were you a slave when called? [v.21]; Are you bound legally or morally to a woman?...Are you free from a woman? [v.27]). On the sex issue, equality and mutuality in marital obligation and relationship is stressed. So also R. Scroggs, "Paul and the Eschatological Woman," 294–95; G. B. Caird, "Paul and Women's Liberty," *Bulletin of the John Rylands University Library of Manchester* 54 (1972): 276: "The remarkable thing about this chapter is that Paul from the start to finish treats husband and wife as equals. Whatever is said of the one is equally said of the other." Meeks, "The Image of the Androgyne," 199, argues: "Formally, the striking thing about that chapter is the number of monotonously parallel statements made about the obligations, respectively, of men and women: verses 2, 3, 4, 10, 11, 12, 13, 14, 15, 16, 28, 32, 34. It looks as though Paul were laboring to express the male and female roles in almost precisely the same language." E. H. Pagels, "Paul and Women: A Response to Recent Discussion," *Journal of the American Academy of Religion* 42 (1974): 541, was surprised that "Paul does advocate an astonishingly egalitarian view of marriage — especially astonishing in view of his own background." Elisabeth Schüssler Fiorenza, "Women in the Pre-Pauline and Pauline Churches," 161, notes that Paul "acknowledges the equality and reciprocity of husband and wife," though his "preference for the unmarried state is plain."

10. For the history of research on this pericope, from John Calvin up to 1970s, see Linda Mercadante, *From Hierarchy to Equality: A Comparison of Past and Present Interpretations of 1 Cor 11:2–16* (Vancouver: Regent College, GMH Books, 1978). Material on this pericope dated after 1970 appears sporadically in the footnotes of this chapter.

terminology, and its underlying customs.[11] The difficulties are compounded by the question of the overall literary unity of 1 Corinthians. Is the text as we have it the work of a redactor?[12] Walker argues that the pericope at hand is inauthentic,[13] that it is to be judged an interpolation because the passage "so obviously breaks the context of the letter at this point."[14] He also argues on the basis of the vocabulary that the pericope is un-Pauline.[15] Responding to this argument, however, Murphy-O'Connor contends that the "praying and prophesying" motif of the pericope is related to the overall theme of worship found in chapters 8–11 and therefore should be considered authentic.[16] Whether Murphy-O'Connor's

---

11. Problems include the question of authenticity, of hairstyle or head covering, the meaning of "head," the context of this pericope, and the logic of Paul's argument. For details, see Gordon Fee, *The First Epistle to the Corinthians* (Grand Rapids, Mich.: Eerdmans, 1987), 492.

12. Johannes Weiss, *Der erste Korintherbrief* (Göttingen: Vandenhoeck & Ruprecht, 1910), xi–xliii; Walter Schmithals, *Gnosticism in Corinth: An Investigation of the Letters to the Corinthians* (Nashville: Abingdon, 1971), 87–96, 224–29; Jean Héring, *The First Epistle of Saint Paul to the Corinthians* (London: Epworth, 1962), xii–xiv; Robert Jewett, *Paul's Anthropological Terms: A Study of Their Use in Conflict Settings* (Leiden: E. J. Brill, 1971), 23–25. For other scholars' views, see John C. Hurd, *The Origin of 1 Corinthians* (New York: Seabury, 1965), 43–47, 131–42, which has a tabular presentation; and W. Schenk, "Der 1. Korintherbrief als Briefsammlung," *Zeitschrift für die Neutestamentliche Wissenschaft und die Kunde der älteren Kirche* 60 (1969): 219–43. Gerhard Sellin, "Hauptprobleme des Ersten Korintherbriefes," *Aufstieg und Niedergang der römischen Welt* 2.25.4 (1987): 2964–86, provides a summary of most scholars' views. See Khiok-Khng Yeo, *Rhetorical Interaction in 1 Corinthians 8 and 10: A Formal Analysis with Preliminary Suggestions for a Chinese, Cross-Cultural Hermeneutic* (Leiden: E. J. Brill, 1995), chap. 5, and Martinus C. de Boer, "The Composition of 1 Corinthians," *New Testament Studies* 40 (1994): 229–45.

13. O. Walker, "1 Corinthians 11:2–16 and Paul's Views regarding Women," *Journal of Biblical Literature* 94 (1975): 94–110; reply by J. Murphy-O'Connor, "The Non-Pauline Character of 1 Corinthians 11:2–16?" *Journal of Biblical Literature* 95 (1976): 615–17; J. P. Meier, "On the Veiling of Hermeneutics (1 Cor 11:2–16)," *Catholic Biblical Quarterly* 40 (1978): 212–22; and recently Walker's new response: "The Vocabulary of 1 Corinthians 11:3–16: Pauline or Non-Pauline?" *Journal for the Study of the New Testament* 35 (1989): 75–88.

14. Walker, "1 Corinthians 11:2–16 and Paul's Views regarding Women," 99.

15. Walker, "1 Corinthians 11:2–16 and Paul's Views regarding Women," 94–110, and "The Vocabulary of 1 Corinthians 11:3–16: Pauline or Non-Pauline?" 75–88.

16. Murphy-O'Connor, "The Non-Pauline Character of 1 Corinthians 11:2–16?" 616.

argument that 10:14–11:1 is connected to 11:2–16 is plausible requires further study. The disjuncture between the two pericopae, which Walker notes, can be explained by the redaction process. According to the most convincing redaction theory of 1 Corinthians, this pericope is a part of *Letter A* ("Sexual Roles and the Eucharist"), which consists of 1 Cor 11:2–34.[17] Walker argues that 11:2–16 is composed of three distinct pericopae: *A* (vv. 3, 8–9, 11–12), *B* (4, 5, 7, 10), and *C* (14–15). *A* deals with the relationship between men and women; *B* deals with the issue of head covering; and *C* addresses the question of the proper length of hair.[18] Walker also contends that the theological position of the pericope contradicts other Pauline passages, such as Gal 3:28. The argument presented here will show that this is one the most revolutionary of Pauline passages because it interprets male-female relationships in terms of mutuality.

The Context and Audience

The audience situation will reveal the problem of gender identification, differentiation, and mutuality in the Corinthian church. There are explicit references to women leaders and patrons in Corinth, such as Prisca, Chloe,[19] and Phoebe.[20] The references to the

---

17. See Yeo, *Rhetorical Interaction in 1 Corinthians 8 and 10,* chap. 5; also, Robert Jewett, "The Redaction of 1 Corinthians and the Trajectory of the Pauline School," *Journal of the American Academy of Religion Supplements* 46 (1978): 389–444. Jewett argues that 10:14–11:1 is "advocating the freedom position" (408) while 11:2–16 is "advocating the institutions of apostolic legitimacy" (405). My interpretation will show that Paul is reinterpreting the apostolic tradition in a new light.

18. Walker, "1 Corinthians 11:2–16 and Paul's Views regarding Women," 102–3.

19. Elisabeth Schüssler Fiorenza suggests that Chloe's people were not converts of Paul because they were not baptized by Paul ("Rhetorical Situation and Historical Reconstruction in 1 Corinthians," *New Testament Studies* 33 [1987]: 394).

20. Concerning the role of women in general, see Schüssler Fiorenza, *In Memory of Her;* Robert Jewett, "The Conflict over Sexual Roles in Pauline Churches," in *Wesleyan Theology Today: A Bicentennial Theological Consultation,* ed. T. Runyon (Nashville: United Methodist Publishing House, 1985), 151–60; the study of feminine power in Corinth by Kitty D. Bendixen-Park, "Freedom and Responsibility: Paul's Use of *Exousia* in 1 Corinthians 11:2–16" (MTS thesis, Garrett-Evangelical

patronage of Chloe in 1 Cor 1:11, Stephanus in 1 Cor 16:15, and Prisca and Aquila in 1 Cor 16:19 have led to the theory that conflict in Corinth, which is of such concern to Paul, is the result of competition between patrons sponsoring different apostles.[21] It is difficult to see the issue of hairstyle as the result of conflict among different house churches in Corinth. It is more probable that Paul has received information about the agitation of proto-Gnostics, who are challenging traditional sexual roles and definitions. In responding to these radical, eschatological feminists who use male hairstyles (not an issue of veils) and who cause disturbances in the celebration of the Lord's Supper, Paul writes a short letter A (1 Cor 11:2–34) to state the institutionalized apostolic and traditional position regarding the Eucharist (11:23–26), with an insistence on solidarity (vv. 27–34). Concerning hairdressing, Paul expounds his position in terms of male-female relationships. In this regard, the pericope tends to affirm sexual differentiation, though equality is stressed in the conflict over hairstyles (11:2–16). The insistence on traditional hairstyles is seen in verses 5–15, with qualifying insistence on equality and mutuality in verses 8 and 11. One has to bear in mind that the audience to whom Paul is writing consists of at least two groups: loose-hair feminists and a conservative group which holds to traditional teachings and cultural norms concerning hairstyles.

It has to be admitted that we hear only one side of the dialogue between Paul and the two groups in the audience. The other side of the argument (the audience's side) is not explicitly recorded. Concentrating only on Paul's utterance without reconstructing the situation of the audience may look safe, but it is in fact inadequate and often ends up in partial exegesis. Exegesis that does not consider the audience claims objectivity and truthfulness in the name

Theological Seminary, 1984); and Antoinette C. Wire, *The Corinthian Women Prophets: A Reconstruction through Paul's Rhetoric* (Minneapolis: Fortress, 1990).

21. The conflict over the Lord's Supper in 1 Cor 11:17–34 is the result perhaps of patrons and their upper-class friends eating one menu while slaves and workmen ate common food. Wire uses six factors (wisdom; power; family name or honor [see 1 Cor 1:26, 4:10]; ethnic group; servitude condition; and gender [see 7:17–24, 12:13; see also Gal 3:28]) to reconstruct the Corinthian situation. Wire concludes that women did acquire their increase in status by participating in the Corinthian church. See Wire, *The Corinthian Women Prophets*, 127.

of ignorance and subjectivity. The question has to be asked, why would anyone in the audience want to adopt male hairstyles? The conjecture can be made that the audience was most probably made up of protognostic women who perceived reality eschatologically. They assumed that they already reigned with Christ (see 4:8) and that their bodies had no part in the triumphant life (see 15:12). Paul had taught that there is no male and female in Christ; perhaps this group misunderstood Paul's conviction (which we find in Gal 3:28) to mean that in Christ there is only one sex; since Christ is male there was no doubt that females had to become male. It is safe to say the group suffered from considerable confusion with regard to marriage role and function. It believed that women had to become men in order to be saved.[22]

If the Pauline tradition was true to the Jesus tradition, it is likely that these liberated women may have been familiar with Jesus' saying that "in the resurrection they neither marry nor are given in marriage but are as the angels" (Mt 22:30). To demonstrate their new status in Christ, these women did not dress their hair as other women did. Spirit-filled feminists held to the gnostic conception of male identity (e.g., *Gospel of Thomas*, Saying 114) and sought evidence of rebirth by the application of male symbolism (i.e., hairdo). This is a misunderstanding of Paul's message of "being in Christ." Paul never intends to says that those who are in Christ are *male* heirs of God, except for the grammatical *huioi* ("sons"); even then, *huioi* is purely a conventional term that would have included both male and female. The most vivid proof of Paul's mind is contained in 2 Corinthians 6:17–18, where Paul quotes the oracle of Nathan (2 Sm 7:14) to explain the ministry of reconciliation: "Therefore come out from them, says the Lord, and touch nothing unclean and I will welcome you and I will be a father to you, and you shall be my sons *and daughters* [Paul adds to the OT text], says the Lord Almighty." There is another audience, which holds to the hierarchical teaching of Jewish tradition regarding male-female relationships. Paul has to respond to both groups: the loose-hair,

---

22. Naasene *Gospel of Thomas* (II, 2) Saying 114. Also, Zostrianos ([VIII, 1] 131) asks believers to "flee from the bondage of femininity and to choose for themselves the salvation of masculinity."

liberated protognostic women and a more traditional, conservative party. Paul's mixed response contained in 1 Corinthians 11 and the theological perspective behind it can be explained in this context.

Paul may be dealing not only with female issues but also with male issues,[23] since all occurrences of male/female in 1 Corinthians reflect concrete situations (see 7:2–4, 10–16; 11:7–14; 14:34–35). Oster, making use of Plutarch's work *Aetia Romana et Graeca,* argues that Paul is addressing the issue of men's devotional head apparel.[24] Oster notes that during Paul's time Corinth was a Roman city, and that the context of 11:4 is a Roman liturgical practice in which male covering and female noncovering of the head was a symbol of leadership.[25] The relationship between 1 Corinthians 11 and this Roman practice may point to the possibility that Paul in this pericope deals with both male and female issues. The structural and exegetical analyses below will show that Paul has that discussion in mind.

An Outline and Translation of the Pericope

From a literary-rhetorical analysis of the pericope, we can observe the argument and the intention of Paul. First, the chiastic structure of the pericope is obvious (translation mine):

---

23. So J. Murphy-O'Connor, "Sex and Logic in 1 Corinthians 11:2–16," *Catholic Biblical Quarterly* 42 (1980): 483, and R. E. Oster, "When Men Wore Veils to Worship: The Historical Context of 1 Corinthians 11.4," *New Testament Studies* 34 (1988): 483, contrary to Weiss, *Der erste Korintherbrief,* 271; Archibald Robertson and Alfred Plummer, *A Critical and Exegetical Commentary on the First Epistle of St. Paul to the Corinthians* (New York: Charles Scribner's Sons, 1925), 229; Hans Conzelmann, *1 Corinthians.* Hermeneia (Philadelphia: Fortress, 1975), 184, n. 35; J. B. Hurley, "Did Paul Require Veils or the Silence of Women? A Consideration of 1 Cor. 11:2–16 and 1 Cor 14:33b–36," *Westminster Theological Journal* 35 (1973): 190–220; idem, *Man and Woman in Biblical Perspective* (Grand Rapids, Mich.: Zondervan, 1981), 170; F. F. Bruce, *1 and 2 Corinthians* (Grand Rapids, Mich.: Eerdmans, 1971), 104; F. W. Grosheide, *A Commentary on the First Epistle to the Corinthians* (Grand Rapids, Mich.: Eerdmans, 1955), 253; Susan T. Foh, *Women and the Word of God: A Response to Biblical Feminism* (Grand Rapids, Mich.: Baker, 1980), 101.

24. Oster, "When Men Wore Veils to Worship," 485.

25. Oster, "When Men Wore Veils to Worship," 493–505.

A. *Verses 2–3: Introduction with affirmation of traditional Pauline teaching*

  2. "Now I commend you
       because you remember me in all things,
       and just as I handed them on to you, you hold fast to the
         traditions.[26]

  3. And I want you to know that:
       the head [authority and source or authority] of every man is
         Christ,
       and the head of a woman is the man,
       and the head of Christ is God [affirming a hierarchical
         authority structure]."

B. *Verses 4–7: Traditional teaching on hair which affirms the difference between men and women*

  4. "Every man shames his head
       praying or prophesying while having something on the head
         [unmasculine hairdo],

  5. and every woman dishonors her head
       praying or prophesying with an uncovered [undressed] head
         [unfeminine hairdo].
     For it is one and the same
       as being shaved.

  6. If, therefore, a woman will not be covered [dressed hairdo],
       let her be shorn;
     if it is disgraceful to a woman to be shorn or shaven,
       let her be covered [dressed]."

  7. *from Genesis narrative*
     "For a man ought not to cover the head,
       being the image and glory of God,
     but the woman
       is the glory of man."

C. *Verse 8a: Man not from woman*

  8. "For man was not made from woman,"

D. *Verse 8b: Woman from man*

     "but woman from man."

---

26. This sentence implies the continuity of the traditions Paul passed down to the Corinthians.

E. *Verse 9a: Man not for woman*

   "For also man was not created for woman's sake"

F. *Verse 9b: Woman for man*

   "but woman for man." [Here Paul is affirming tradition, affirming the original hierarchical relations of creation.]

X. *Verse 10: The center inaugurates a new interpretation* [it is the turning point in the argument: a new creation creates more mutual relations in the context of differences between male and female.]

   10. "This is why a woman ought to have authority over her head: because of the angels."

F′. *Verse 11a: Woman is neither independent of man* [in contrast to F)

   11. "Nevertheless, in the Lord woman is not independent of man"

E′. *Verse 11b: Nor is man independent of woman* [in contrast to E)

   "nor is man independent of woman;"

D′. *Verse 12a: Interdependence of man and woman*

   12. "for as [in the first creation] woman was made from man,"

C′. *Verse 12b: Thus also the man is through the woman*

   "so [thereafter] man is now born of woman.
   And all are from God [which is more important than the first two]."

B′. *Verses 13–15: Woman to pray with dressed hair; hair is her pride*

   13. "Judge for yourselves; is it proper for a woman to pray to God with her head uncovered?

   14. Does not nature itself teach you that for a man to wear long hair is a dishonor to him,

   15. but if a woman has long hair, it is her pride? For her hair is given to her instead of a covering."

A′. *Verse 16: Conclusion of a new hermeneutic*

   16. "If anyone thinks of being contentious,
       we recognize no other practice,
       nor do the churches of God."

An Interpretation, Rhetorically Understood

The Divine Model of Hierarchy. The outline above reveals the skillful rhetorical technique of Paul as he responds to the problems of sexual roles, differentiation, and interdependence with which the Corinthians are wrestling. Paul begins his argument with the traditional teaching of the hierarchy of relationships (God, Christ, man, and woman), which obviously aims at affirming the conservative group while clarifying the tradition for the "loose-hair" party. The point is made based on Paul's understanding of the relationship of God and Christ, of Christ to human beings, and of human beings to each other as male and female. Of course, what that relationship is has implications for questions of leadership (which is a question of authority) and of sex roles (whether one is subordinate to another). In any case these questions are open to interpretation since the relational realities involved are not explicitly stated. Even if one reads the text as pertaining to leadership roles and admits that a certain hierarchy is involved, the relationship is still not one of domination, since the God-Christ relationship is the model, and Christ is subordinate to God only in mission and not in essence.

Not only is Paul's teaching based on the divine model, it is also a tradition that he has taught the Corinthian church. Paul's praise for his readers' efforts to "hold fast to the traditions" which he delivered to them (v. 2) seems ironic because in the next verse (v. 3) he writes, "but I would have you know . . ."[27] and in verse 17 that he has no praise for them. The irony is caught by James B. Hurley who paraphrases verse 3 as: "You have utterly discarded that which I taught you?"[28] The tone of verse 16, which accuses the Corinthians of having abandoned the universal custom of the church of God, is clearly one of displeasure.[29] The commendation found in verse 2, however, is not ironic or sarcastic, as some have ar-

---

27. See E. Evans, *The Epistles of Paul the Apostle to the Corinthians* (Oxford: Clarendon Press, 1930), 117; Hurd, *The Origin of 1 Corinthians*, 182–84; J. Moffatt, *The First Epistle of Paul to the Corinthians* (New York: Harper & Brothers, n.d.), 149; and Hurley, "Did Paul Require Veils or the Silence of Women?" 191.

28. Hurley, "Did Paul Require Veils or the Silence of Women?" 191.

29. Jewett however see this as an interpolation of a later and more conservative Pauline school; see "The Redaction of 1 Corinthians and the Trajectory of the Pauline School," 389–440.

gued,[30] for it states clearly the traditional teaching of Paul, which extends through verse 9. Paul praises them for following the tradition but adds (vv. 10–16) that his own teaching will provide a certain nuance to the tradition. Not surprisingly, misunderstanding has arisen in the process of handing on the tradition. Communication has broken down. On the one hand, Paul needs to preach the liberation of women in contrast to the mores of the patriarchal culture in which they live; on the other hand, Paul needs to maintain sexual differentiation without going as far as the radical feminists.

If the problem here is one of miscommunication, as certainly it seems, it is best explained in terms of rhetorical hermeneutics, in which what is said has not been fully understood as the rhetor intends. There are two possible reasons for the misappropriation of Paul's traditional teaching: interception occurs in the communication process, or there is a shift in the circumstances of the audience. Interception may be due to the audience's inability to understand the message. The change in circumstances may be due to the difficulty of applying Paul's message to the new issue of liberated women. For example, the Pauline tradition is restated in verses 3–7, where it is said that "man is the head of woman," and that "God is the head of Christ"; Paul may mean by this a generative-relational rather than an ontological-hierarchical relation. That is, just as Christ is begotten and sent by the Father (see Rom 8:3), so woman in the first creation is born out of Adam's flesh (see Gn 2:21–22), and man and woman (believers) are born out of Christ (v. 3). Paul may here be explaining the difference between male and female, but the conservative group may have heard it as hierarchical. Paul may here be affirming the equality of men and women (as Christ and God are equal), but the liberated women may have heard equality as meaning uniformity in sex roles, an idea used as a springboard for unisex hairdos.

Hairstyle and Veiling Customs. Hairstyles, so deeply rooted in gender and sexual mores, had serious social implications, and a unisex hairstyle ran against the social norms of Greco-Roman

---

30. Hurd, *The Origin of 1 Corinthians,* 182; Evans, *The Epistles of Paul the Apostle to the Corinthians,* 117; Hurley, "Did Paul Require Veils or the Silence of Women?" 205.

society. A woman with a male hairdo was seen as a prostitute, a lesbian, or a cultic heretic.[31] Pauline Christianity sought to safeguard itself against this practice.

The two traditions which are fundamental to a proper understanding of the text are (a) the hairstyle or veiling of the head (the latter being the custom signified by the verb *katakalyptō*, a custom which has no relation to this text); and (b) the hermeneutical understanding of the creation narrative as significant for a hierarchical interpretation of the relations among God, Christ, man, and woman.

Are the Corinthians dealing with the issue of hairstyle or veiling? The earliest evidence of veiling as a Near Eastern custom is found in Assyrian law:[32] the use of the veil is a sign of ownership rights over a woman. Even though this custom was practiced in Greece at least four hundred years before Paul's day (Grecian pottery shows hairstyles and head coverings common to the Greeks),[33] Hurley concludes that pre-Christian Greeks were not veiled in public, a practice found only among Oriental women.[34] In the Christian era the scene is more complex. Though head coverings may differ radically with class and occupation, both Greeks and Romans generally kept their hair trimmed.[35] However, the intermingling of Jewish and Greco-Roman culture is evident during Paul's time, and the veiling custom in Jewish culture should be explored also. Hurley has noted that heroes at Dura wore *himation* (a long rectangular mantle) with broad purple stripes. This garment, called *tallith* in the Talmud and in modern Judaism, was a sign of reverence and was worn over the head by Jewish men

31. Scroggs, "Paul and the Eschatological Woman: Revisited," *Journal of the American Academy of Religion* 42 (1974): 536; Hurley, "Did Paul Require Veils or the Silence of Women?" 203, interprets Nm 5:18 (LXX) and its reference to the uncleanness of adultery as wearing a male hairstyle. Schüssler Fiorenza (*In Memory of Her,* 227) mentions that disheveled hair was typical of mystery cults. Short hair marked females as lesbians (see Apuleius, *Metamorphoses* 7.6; 11.10).

32. G. Driver and J. Miles, *The Assyrian Laws* (Oxford: Clarendon Press, 1935).

33. See Hurley, "Did Paul Require Veils or the Silence of Women?" 194.

34. Hurley, "Did Paul Require Veils or the Silence of Women?" 194.

35. Cynthia L. Thompson, "Hairstyles, Head-Coverings, and St. Paul Portraits from Roman Corinth," *Biblical Archaeologist* 51 (1988): 99–115, here 104.

when they prayed.[36] Samuel Krauss cites rabbinic sources which indicate that Jewish men were not required to cover their heads while praying in a synagogue. Krauss also indicates that "covered" and "uncovered" means "dress hair up" and "hang hair loose."[37]

What is the point of reviewing this veiling custom? From Assyrian times through the Talmudic period, Jewish and Oriental women were not veiled at home, in public, or at familiar gatherings.[38] If Paul is familiar with this veiling custom, as he surely was, then his discussion of a man "having...on the head" (11:4) must be interpreted as a rejection of the custom. In the Old Testament, the high priest is urged to come before God with elaborate headgear (Ex 36:35–37). Paul is not imposing this Jewish custom on the women.[39] Palestinian custom did allow women's heads to be covered. We cannot say here that Paul is applying his principle of becoming "all things to all men," that is, of adapting mores to local practice; rather there is for Paul a normative rule applicable to the whole church of God concerning the custom of hair-covering. It is impossible to think that Jewish men converting to Christianity would abandon their custom so radically. The only conclusion open to us is that "having...on the head" refers not to hair-covering or to custom regarding veils, but most probably to hairstyle.

Similar evidence for this interpretation is evident in other verses. In verse 5 the preposition *kata* (on) with the genitive may refer to "covering on head," as Oster argues.[40] The phrase "having...on the head" (v. 4) cannot refer to the Jewish *tallith* or prayer shawl worn by the Jewish male,[41] because that practice was deemed a

---

36. Hurley, "Did Paul Require Veils or the Silence of Women?" 195.

37. Samuel Krauss, "The Jewish Rite of Covering the Head," *Hebrew Union College Annual* 19 (1945–46): 121–68.

38. We must not read the Muslim custom of veil into the Jewish and Christian traditions. In the OT we see that Rebecca traveled with a veil when with the servant of her betrothed and also put it on when she saw a strange man approaching (Gn 24:65). See Hurley, "Did Paul Require Veils or the Silence of Women?" 196, n. 16.

39. On the veiling of women in the ancient Near East, see A. Oepke, "*Kalyptō*," *TDNT* 3:556–58; R. de Vaux, "Sur le voile des femmes dans l'Orient ancien," *Revue Biblique* 44 (1935): 397–412.

40. Oster, "When Men Wore Veils to Worship," 486.

41. Fee, *The First Epistle to the Corinthians,* 508.

dishonor to God. Paul here is not ordering women to wear a veil or to let their hair loose. He is saying that they have to dress it up.[42] The object of "having" cannot be "veil" since "veil" is never mentioned in the text.[43] Verse 14 mentions "hair," suggesting that "hair" rather than "veil" is more in view.[44] If it were a veil issue, it would pertain to a practice that was anti-Jewish.[45] Again, the issue under discussion here is not that of wearing a shawl but the custom of wearing hair pinned up or folded into braids and placed on the top or at the back of the head, rather than hanging loose. The translation of *akatakalyptō* (v. 5) is disputed:[46] "with his head covered" supplies an object for the verb; "unveiled" is the most common translation. The subject of *akatakalyptō* should be "hair" rather than "veil" or "cover" to complete the phrase. Hurley's study has shown that the custom of Lv 13:45 was still valid in Paul's day and that Paul's word *akatakalyptos* is similar to the Hebrew word *paru'a*, rendered by the LXX as *akatakalyptos*, and signifies uncleanness and improper relationships within a community.[47] It would appear then that Paul is speaking here of "loose hair" (that is, "not dressed") rather than of "the lack of a shawl" when he writes of a woman being *akatakalyptos*.

---

42. Hurley, *Man and Woman in Biblical Perspective,* 169–71.

43. Murphy-O'Connor, "Sex and Logic in 1 Corinthians 11:2–16," 484.

44. In *Ep.* 1 and *Cor. hom.* 26, 1. See also Abel Isaksson, *Marriage and Ministry in the New Temple: A Study with Special Reference to Mt 19.13[sic]–12 and 1 Cor 11:3–16* (Lund, Glerup, and Copenhagen: Munksgaard, 1963), 166; William J. Martin, "1 Corinthians 11:2–16: An Interpretation," in *Apostolic History and the Gospel: Biblical and Historical Essays Presented to F. F. Bruce on His 60th Birthday,* ed. W. W. Gasque (Grand Rapids, Mich.: Eerdmans, 1970), 233; Hurley, "Did Paul Require Veils or the Silence of Women?" 199.

45. Thus argues Abel Isaksson, *Marriage and Ministry in the New Temple,* 165–86; Alan Padgett, "Paul on Women in the Church: The Contradictions of Coiffure in 1 Corinthians 11:2–16," *Journal for the Study of the New Testament* 20 (1984): 70; and Martin, "1 Corinthians 11:2–16: An Interpretation," 233.

46. Fee, *The First Epistle to the Corinthians,* 509; Hurley, *Man and Woman in Biblical Perspective,* 198.

47. Hurley, "Did Paul Require Veils or the Silence of Women?" 198. Also, in 1 Tm 2:9 the proper attire of women is discussed — "moderately and discreetly dressed, not with braided hair and gold or pearls or costly garment." Note that what is forbidden here is gold-braided hair rather than braids and gold ornaments. The first two items are joined by "and" and form a hendiadys. The image in mind is that of the dancing girl who puts gold bangles on her braided hair.

Male-Female Differentiation in the Order of Creation. According to Paul, hairstyle has the connotative meaning of differentiating human beings symbolically as male and female. In his understanding of human relationships, Paul uses the divine-human paradigm. 1 Cor 11:3 presents us not with a hierarchy but with the order of creation.[48] Paul uses "Christ," not "lord" or "master," in order to avoid any notion of subordination. In verse 8 Paul stresses that Eve derives her being from Adam (see Gn 2:18–22). And this seems to be the key to what he means in verse 3 by designating the male as "head"; that is, the male is "head" in the sense of "source" relative to the female.[49] The meaning of head should be seen in the context of the primordial reality of God and Christ, with God as Father (1 Cor 1:3; 8:6; 15:23–24) and Christ as Son (1 Cor 1:9; 15:28). The term *kephalē* thus becomes a christological hermeneutic used to infuse the creation account with new meaning, but in verses 2–9 this radical and transforming connotation is hidden. In any case, the relationship between man and woman is made to correspond to the relationship between the Father and the Son. Moreover, it is Christ who is responsible for the new creation (see 1 Cor 1:30).

Paul's concern in verses 3–4 is with distinction, not discrimination. The hairstyles of men and women are not to be the same. Meeks postulates that because of the audience's belief in realized eschatology, they thought that "the eschatological Spirit was already at work and functional distinctions which belong to that world may be disregarded."[50] In other words, Paul's use of the order of creation was intended to respond to the audience's misconception regarding the created order, a misconception which wanted to introduce similarity and dispense with hierarchy. The issue under discussion (hairdo and the created order) was not whether women should or should not pray and prophesy (that was assumed to be acceptable); the issue was how males and females should coexist in differentiation. It is for this reason that any notion of the woman's subordination to her "head," that is, her "lord" and "authority," is absent from Paul's argument.

---

48. So Scroggs, "Paul and the Eschatological Woman," 298.

49. S. Bedale, "The Meaning of *kephalē* in the Pauline Epistles," *Journal of Theological Studies* 5 (1954): 214.

50. Meeks, "The Image of the Androgyne," 202.

The Double Meanings of "Head". The meaning of the word *kephalē* in verse 5 and throughout the passage remains an exegetical problem.[51] The use of "head" as a metaphor for supremacy or authority is prominent in classical literature.[52] Wayne Grudem's analysis of 2,336 examples of the word *kephalē* in extrabiblical material is not very helpful since none of the biblical occurrences is taken into consideration.[53] The semantic range of the word is not taken seriously, nor is how Paul uses the term elsewhere. There is no denying that the word *kephalē* denotes "head" and connotes "authority and supremacy over." But what is being said here is that Paul's hermeneutic transforms the traditional understanding of the word to mean both head as "leader" and head as "source."

The use of *kephalē* ("head") as a metaphor for "source" is not impossible.[54] In the LXX (Paul's "Bible"), *kephalē* appears 281 times as the translation for *rosh* in the sense of chief or ruler, when used of an authoritative figure, an *archon* or *archegos*.[55] Looking through the LXX, Philo, and Josephus, Fitzmyer argues that "a Hellenistic Jewish writer such as Paul of Tarsus could well have

51. Bedale, "The Meaning of *kephalē* in the Pauline Epistles," 211–25; H. Schlier, *"Kephalē,"* TDNT 3:673–82; Kitty Diane Bendixen-Park, "Dramatism and Headship: A Survey of Text-Linguistic and Rhetorical Theory to Elucidate Paul's Use of KEPHALĒ in First Corinthians 11:2–16" (Ph.D. diss., Northwestern University, 1994), 484.

52. See commentaries of Weiss, *Der erste Korintherbrief;* Robertson and Plummer, *A Critical and Exegetical Commentary on the First Epistle of St. Paul to the Corinthians;* Héring, *The First Epistle of Saint Paul to the Corinthians;* and A. D. M. Derrett, "Religious Hair," in *Studies in the New Testament,* vol. 1: *Glimpses of the Legal and Social Presuppositions of the Authors* (Leiden: E. J. Brill, 1977), 172; Wayne Grudem, "Does *kephalē* ("Head") Mean "Source" or "Authority over" in Greek Literature? A Survey of 2,336 Examples," *Trinity Journal,* n.s., 6 (1985): 38–59; Joseph A. Fitzmyer, "Another Look at KEPHALĒ in 1 Corinthians 11:3," *New Testament Studies* 35 (1989): 503–11.

53. Grudem, "Does *kephalē* ("Head") Mean "Source" or "Authority over?" 38–59. See Fitzmyer, "Another Look at KEPHALĒ in 1 Corinthians 11:3," 503–11.

54. S. Bedale, "The Meaning of *kephalē* in the Pauline Epistles," 211–25; C. K. Barrett, *The First Epistle to the Corinthians,* Harper's New Testament Commentaries (New York: Harper & Row, 1968), 249; Scroggs, "Paul and the Eschatological Woman," 298–99; Murphy-O'Connor, "Sex and Logic in 1 Corinthians 11:2–16," 492–93; Fee, *The First Epistle to the Corinthians,* 503.

55. R. Scroggs, "Paul and the Eschatological Woman," 534, n. 8; also Murphy-O'Connor, "Sex and Logic in 1 Corinthians 11:2–16," 492.

intended that *kephalē* in 1 Cor 11:3 be understood as 'head' in the sense of authority or supremacy over someone else."[56] This is to assume that Paul's use of the word cannot exceed the semantic range of his contemporaries. But an analysis of Paul's exegesis of Genesis in 1 Cor 10:1–2 reveals that Paul is a creative thinker who often uses old patterns and concepts in a new way to prove his point.[57] Paul's rhetorical hermeneutic deserves a closer look. The attempt here is to show that Paul reinterprets the Genesis narrative to lay a basis for his understanding of the equality and mutual dependence of male and female while maintaining the differentiation of their roles.

In the passage at hand, contextual analysis indicates that Paul is shifting the word's metaphorical sense from "authoritative figure" to "source," as evidenced in "the head of a woman is the man" (v. 3b) and "woman from man" (v. 8). Man is the head of the woman because he is the source or the medium of her creation. This is no doubt implied in the creation account, but the second equally important creation is mentioned in verse 10.

The Image, Glory, and Authority of Woman. Let it be noted here again that the problem Paul is addressing arises from the desire of certain Corinthian women to be free from certain cultural rules and norms; specifically, they want to assume a masculine lifestyle, evidenced by the peculiar vocabulary and content of the letter — for example, in words and phrases such as "spiritual ones" (2:15), "possession of wisdom" (2:6), "mature" (2:6), "wise" (3:18), "already reigned in the new age" (4:8). Paul responds to the problem of the spirit-filled women by turning to Gn 2:21–22 (rather than Gn 1:26–28) in 1 Cor 11:7, which indicates that the male (the female is not mentioned) bears the image and likeness of God. The "image" language, if alluding to the Genesis creation accounts, no doubt comes from Gn 1:26–28. Yet Paul in verses 2–9 does not explicitly say that both male and female bear the image of God. Perhaps Paul is using the argument of the conservative group, but his seeming favoritism toward their argument is only

---

56. Fitzmyer, "Another Look at KEPHALĒ in 1 Corinthians 11:3," 510.
57. See Yeo, *Rhetorical Interaction in 1 Corinthians 8 and 10*, chapters 8 and 9.

short-lived. His allusion to their argument is significant for a later reversal of their traditional view of male-female relations.[58]

Why did not Paul use Genesis 1, so as to be inclusive of both male and female bearing the image of God? Genesis 1 narrates the story of God's creating humanity (Adam is a collective reference) in God's own image and likeness and commanding them (male and female) to have dominion over other parts of creation (v. 28). Perhaps the audience did not yet share Paul's conviction about Gn 1:26–28. Or perhaps the creation account of Gn 2:21–22 better differentiates the male-female relationship than Gn 1:26–28 does, though the word "image" is used in Genesis 1.

In 1 Corinthians 11 Paul affirms the order of the creation event. However, there is no indication whatsoever that Paul is using the dominion or subjugation theme found in Genesis 1 or 3. Had Paul intended to argue that man — but not woman — is created in the image of God, then he would *not* have used Genesis 2 and *not* have alluded to Genesis 1. But he alludes to it and he makes his argument clear by appealing to the "image" of male and the glory of male and female. "Image" has both relational and source connotations; Paul uses it to affirm both meanings. That is, male and female bear the glory of God, but the female also bears the glory of man; woman comes from man. Paul affirms the original hierarchical relations of creation. However, there is no indication whatsoever that Paul is using the dominion theme found in Genesis 1.[59] When referring to the Genesis account, Paul does not mention the divine decree of Gn 3:16 ("Your desire shall be for your husband, and he shall rule over you"). This omission is significant, because if Paul's intention were dominion and submission, then the divine decree of Gn 3:16 would be his strongest argument. The omission should not be understood as accidental; in other words,

---

58. A similar rhetorical technique is used in 1 Corinthians 8 as Paul deals with the issue of idol meat for the strong knowledgeable group and the weak-conscience group: first he cites the argument of the knowledgeable on monotheism, but at the end of Paul's interpretation he uses a christological hermeneutic to critique the knowledgeable group for being insensitive to the conscience of the weak, thus causing the weak to sin. For more, see Yeo, *Rhetorical Interaction in 1 Corinthians 8 and 10*, 180–98.

59. Hurley argues that Paul is using the theme of dominion here; see Hurley, "Did Paul Require Veils or the Silence of Women?" 205.

Paul intentionally avoids the meaning of the male ruling over the female.

The word "glory" is used by Paul in verse 7: "Man is the image and glory of God, and woman is the glory of man." Both man and woman lost the glory of God in their sin and wait to be restored in the eschaton. "Glory" means that woman is the glory and splendor of man (v. 7b). Paul has reinterpreted the phrase "man is the head of woman" (v. 3)! Why does being a woman honor or glorify a man? There are two reasons: the first one pertains to differentiation and the second pertains to order of creation. If a woman wants to be a man, then the difference between man and woman is eliminated. Woman is created last and is the acme of creation, more glorious and powerful than all creatures (see Psalm 8 on the last creation of humanity being the acme of creation). As the last part of creation and man (Adam) to be created, she thus bears the glory of man (Adam); that is, woman is the best part of humanity, the glory of her source (man/Adam) in first creation.

Paul affirms the distinctiveness of male and female in verses 8 and 9. In this regard he differs radically from other first-century writers. One compares, for example, the antiwoman bias in Philo's writing: "Why was not woman, like the other animals and man, also formed from earth, instead of the side of man? First, because woman is not equal in honor with man. Second, because she is not equal in age but younger. Wherefore those who take wives who have passed their prime are to be criticized for destroying the laws of nature. Third, he wishes that man should take care of woman as a very necessary part of him; but woman, in return, should serve him as a whole."[60] Paul's own positive affirmation of the distinctiveness of both men and women (verses 4–9) is his response to the feminists who seek to conform themselves to manhood. Paul encourages them to accept their womanhood.

Paul seeks to transform what is normally thought of as subordination, then as the glory, pride, and authority of the woman (from verse 10 onwards). The phrase "to have authority" in verse 10 is the Gnostic-Corinthian slogan connoting "having the right" or "liberty" rather than simply possessing power passively (9:4–6,

---

60. *Quaestiones et solutiones* in Genesis §27 (LCL).

7:37, 8:9, 9:18).[61] Fee gives several interpretations to the phrase "to have authority over her head": authority as under man's authority; authority as a metonym for veil; a sign of authority as a means of exercising authority; and freedom over her head to do as she wishes.[62] "Authority" has traditionally been translated as "a veil"! This translation is far from accurate in light of our discussion above. Cynthia Thompson argues that "authority" refers to the "freedom" or "right" of women to choose between two accepted hairstyles, though Paul prefers them to wrap their hair because of the observing angels who hover over the meetings to watch for order.[63]

The role of the angels is itself an exegetical problem. One must ask, are these fallen and therefore evil angels[64] or are they good angels? For some, the answer depends on speculation concerning Gn 6:2.[65] Angels can refer simply to human messengers.[66] Angels are mentioned in 1 Cor 4:9, in which Paul refers to the apostles as ones whom God has made a spectacle before people and the angels, suggesting that in contrast to the glorious reign the Corinthians assume for themselves the apostles are to suffer as part of the cosmic show. In 6:1ff. Paul points out the irony of the Corin-

---

61. R. A. Horsley, "Consciousness and Freedom among the Corinthians: 1 Corinthians 8–10," *Catholic Biblical Quarterly* 40 (1978): 574–75.

62. Fee, *The First Epistle to the Corinthians*, 519–21.

63. Cynthia L. Thompson, "Hairstyles, Head-Coverings, and St. Paul Portraits from Roman Corinth," 112. She mentions a parallel text from Tertullian who said that wearing veils was left to free choice (*arbitrio permissa res erat*), like the question of whether to marry (*On Veiling of Virgins*, sec. 3).

64. Philo sees angels as "the eyes and ears of the Great King, they watch and hear all" (*Som.* 1:140). They report on infringements of the Law: "We announce when we come before the Lord our God all the sin which is committed in heaven and on earth, and in light and in darkness and everywhere" (*Jub.* 4:6; cf. *1 Enoch* 99:3). See Héring, *The First Epistle of Saint Paul to the Corinthians*, 106–7; cf. Gn 6:4; *1 Enoch* 6–7; 67–68; 106–13; *2 Enoch* 7:18; *T. Reub.* 5:7; *Jub.* 5:1; *2 Apoc. Bar.* 56:8–13; Tob 6:10–18; 8:1–8; *Yoma* 67b; *Deut. Rab.* 11; *Beth ha-midrash* 4:127–28. See Trompf's reconstruction, G. W. Trompf, "On Attitudes toward Women in Paul and Paulinist Literature: 1 Corinthians 11:3–16 and Its Context," *Catholic Biblical Quarterly* 42 (1980): 207, nn. 34–36.

65. M. Hooker, "Authority on Her Head: An Examination of 1 Cor 11:1," *New Testament Studies* 10 (1963–64): 410–16; Weiss, *Der erste Korintherbrief*, 274; Héring, *The First Epistle of Saint Paul to the Corinthians*, 106–8. See Heb 12:22, Rv 5:11.

66. Padgett, "Paul on Women in the Church," 69–86.

thian "saints," who are supposed to judge the angels but cannot judge their own daily matters. In 13:1 and 3, Paul declares angelic speech and knowledge as nothing when pursued without love. In 11:10 Paul places woman in a hierarchy above all other things, even the angels. We may conclude that Paul does argue for the right of women to have authority on their heads as they maintain a feminine hairstyle. Paul also contends that a woman with an inappropriate hairstyle in worship will disrupt or dishonor the glory of God, because the angels present at the assembly are concerned with the created order of God.

Paul is admonishing women to accept the ontological character of their status within the cosmic design, of which hairstyle is a symbolic expression, a status which is by no means inferior to man's. The woman's hair functions as a sign of these ontological relationships to herself and to men. Bound hair is a sign of freedom. Not to bind or dress the hair, a symbol of her place in the cosmos, is a sign of rebellion and disgrace. As such, *her hair is indeed her glory* (v. 15). Paul's intention here is to express the new worldview. As Murphy-O'Connor puts it, "In Paul's view women have full authority (*exousian echein*) to act as they were doing, but they needed to convey their new status to the angels who watched for breaches of Law. The guardians of an outmoded tradition had to be shown that things had changed."[67]

Paul's Christological Hermeneutic of Mutuality. Paul's argument moves to a revolutionary perspective from verse 10 onwards. The change of course has been effected by the Christ event; it is the liberation which comes with a new creation. From Paul's point of view the female hairdo is a symbol of this newfound authority as well as being a glory to man. Scroggs is right when he writes, "In the eschatological community, where freedom reigns, woman no longer stands chained to the roles of the old creation. The days of Genesis 3 are gone forever!"[68] The new creation results in the

---

67. Murphy-O'Connor, "Sex and Logic in 1 Cor 11:2–16," 497. Also, Scroggs, "Paul and the Eschatological Woman," 300, n. 46; Hooker, "Authority on Her Head: An Examination of 1 Cor 11:1," 410–16; and Barrett, *The First Epistle to the Corinthians,* 255.

68. Robin Scroggs, "Paul: Chauvinist or Liberationist?" *The Christian Century* 89 (1972): 309.

mutual interrelatedness of man and woman (rather than subordination), which is spelled out in 11:11–12. The word "nevertheless" in verse 11 (used three times in Paul's letter to the Philippians [1:18; 3:16; 4:14]) serves as a pointer to the important statement to follow.[69] It introduces Paul's interpretation of Gn 2:18–22, in which he corrects a common misunderstanding and offers a new twist. Woman came from man, but now man comes through woman; *and both* are created by God (v. 12). Paul's argument is based on the christological insight that the mission of Christ was a *new* creation (through the re-creation of an old humanity).

This verse (v. 12) reveals Paul's christological hermeneutic. Paul notes the difference between man and woman by citing the different ways God created man and woman. Nevertheless, "woman neither is independent of man, nor is man independent of woman in the Lord." "In Christ" coupled with "neither...is independent" implies that the sexes are indispensable to each other. Whatever is true of the first creation needs now to be seen in light of the second creation in Christ. Though man and woman are in many respects different, it is precisely in those differences that man and woman need to relate to each other. Man cannot be independent of woman nor can woman be independent of man; both are *mutually inter*dependent. The key phrase here is "in the Lord." Verse 12 continues to underscore the interrelatedness and interdependence of man and woman. According to Genesis, woman was created from the body of man, but biologically speaking man(kind) is born through woman ("man comes from woman"). Only of the first creation is it true that "woman comes from man"; of all other births it is true that "man comes from woman." Woman was created "for man" (*dia* plus accusative), and he is born through her (*dia* plus genitive), showing the interrelatedness of male and female.[70]

---

69. Thomas P. Shoemaker, "Unveiling of Equality: 1 Corinthians 11:2–16," *Biblical Theological Bulletin* 17 (1987): 60–63.

70. A parallel to 1 Cor 11:11–12 is found in the *Genesis Rabbah* 8:9 (ascribed to R. Simlai, ca. 250 C.E.; in 22:2 ascribed to R. Akiba, ca. 135 C.E.): "In the past Adam was created from dust and Eve was created from Adam; but henceforth it shall be in our image, after our likeness [Gn 1:26]; neither man without woman nor woman without man, and neither without the Shekinah." See Madelein Doucher, "Some Unexplored Parallels to 1 Cor 11:11–12 and Gal 3:28: The New Testament on the Role of Women," *Catholic Biblical Quarterly* 31 (1969): 50–58.

From the rhetorical question in verse 13 and the argument concerning "nature" in verses 13–15, it is clear that Paul wishes to maintain both sexual differentiation and mutuality. "Nature" does not refer to the natural growth of hair — if a man does not trim his hair, it will be long as well. "Nature" refers to a culture's awareness of nature and its values rather than to natural law.[71] It includes a cultural perception of propriety. The notions of shame and glory are also culturally determined concepts which reflect those social relations in which propriety is the main concern. In this respect it is similar to the discussion of conscience in 1 Corinthians 8–10 involving the weak of conscience on one hand and Gnostics on the other. Here the argument about nature assumes that each group has a different perception into and valuation of a cultural practice. This is not to say Paul disallows innovative practices, but that Paul is concerned with renovation within an accepted structure. He is concerned that women dress their hair properly, but he is also concerned that they pray and prophesy. He wants women to affirm their uniqueness, rather than having to be like males. They can celebrate their equality with men in the Lord, but all — both men and women — have to learn to be interdependent.

It is interesting to observe that, if Paul did not explicitly base his argument on Gn 1:26–28 (*both* male and female *bear* the image of God), he seemingly concludes by affirming the mutuality and corporate identity of male and female (as we find in Genesis 1 rather than Genesis 2), but also maintains the differentiation between genders (as we find in Genesis 2). If this is so Paul's hermeneutics is not only contextually interactive with the argument of the audience, but also christologically creative as he rereads Genesis 2 (uniqueness) and Genesis 1 (commonality) into a theological anthropology of differentiation and mutuality.

Paul, a Christological and Mutual Egalitarian

It would be anachronistic to say that Paul was a feminist-liberationist. He was an eschatological, christological, and mutual

---

71. Fee, *The First Epistle to the Corinthians*, 526–27.

egalitarian advocate and practitioner. Scroggs is right in saying that "[i]n light of the passing away of the old world order, Paul envisages the church as a community with man and woman reunited in mutual dependence on each other and in mutual subjection to God.... In the eschatological community where liberation reigns, woman no longer stands chained to the subordinate roles of the old creation."[72] Paul's affirmation that there is "neither male nor female" in Christ does not mean that in Christ all are the same: one sex, one race, and one social status. Paul is affirming the common ground on which all stand before God, the communality of all races and of both sexes. In order to affirm the commonality and communality of sexes and races, Paul needs first to affirm the uniqueness and distinctiveness of each race and gender. In 1 Corinthians 11, Paul is doing precisely that. Man and woman have the same gifts of praying and prophesying; the question is how they are to maintain their own sexual identity and uniqueness while exercising a common ministry.

First Corinthians 11 suggests that both liberated women and male chauvinists have the same social consciousness of "honor and shame." A person's sense of honor and identity, then as well as now (as B. Malina points out),[73] hinges on one's ability to establish social worth in public. The liberated women of Corinth believed they were honored through obtaining a certain ascribed status: dressing as a male. Such a practice, however, only replaced the individual's true status and identity with a false one. Paul is not asking women to be inferior.[74] Rather Paul introduces a new paradigmatic understanding of "hierarchy" with his christological interpretation of the Genesis narrative. He does this, in this special case, to argue that "in the Lord" the liberated woman is unique, different

---

72. Scroggs, "Paul: Chauvinist or Liberationist?" 302. See Pagels, "Paul and Women: A Response to Recent Discussion," 538–49, and Scroggs, "Paul and the Eschatological Woman: Revisited," 532–37.

73. Bruce J. Malina, *The New Testament World: Insights from Cultural Anthropology* (Atlanta: John Knox Press, 1981), 5–9.

74. Julian Pitt-Rivers is correct in saying, "Where there is a hierarchy of honor, the person who submits to the precedence of others recognizes his inferior status." Julian Pitt-Rivers, "Honour and Social Status," in *Honour and Shame: The Values of Mediterranean Society,* ed. J. G. Peristiany (London: Weidenfeld & Nicolson, 1966), 23.

from the male, but interdependent in her relations with her male colleagues.

Paul's argument concerning the differentiation between males and females speaks to the fact that the woman does not have to be a man. Paul does not appeal to a teaching of Jesus, but his argument is christocentric, as is seen in his interpretation of Genesis. It is a clear and persuasive argument. One wonders then how Scroggs can say that "this is hardly one of Paul's happier compositions. The logic is obscure at best and contradictory at worst. The word choice is peculiar, the tone, peevish."[75]

Admittedly, Paul's argument in 1 Corinthians can easily be misunderstood. For example, the terms "male/female" in 1 Corinthians 11 refer not to husband and wife but man and woman, but it seems likely that the later Pauline school used 1 Corinthians 11 with that interpretation — perhaps in Ephesians 5:21–24, where we see the same hierarchy of God/Christ/Man/Woman found in 1 Cor 11:3. First Timothy 2:13–15 also appears to imitate 1 Corinthians 11 in its use of the Genesis material, but not with the same effect or theological thrust. In 1 Timothy the author expresses the desire for proper order and discusses the issues of dress and the role and place of women (vv. 9–11). Women are not allowed to teach or to have authority over men. First Timothy clearly has married women in mind, as is seen in the reference to childbearing. Both 1 Cor 11:8–9 and 1 Tm 2:13 appeal to the first human pair in Gn 2:7, 20–23, but with a different conclusion.

Another controversial passage in 1 Corinthians that discusses male-female relations is chapter 14. At the outset Paul here seems to be prohibiting women from being involved in the speaking ministry of the church because men and women are different. This view of male and female seems to contradict Paul's views in 1 Corinthians 11. We shall turn to 1 Corinthian 14 to understand the "Taceat" ("Let women be silent in church" is *Taceat mulier in ecclesia* in Latin).

---

75. Scroggs, "Paul and the Eschatological Woman," 297.

1 Corinthians 14: "Let the Women Be Silent"!?

The Scholarly Debate on the Pericope as a Unit, and on Authenticity

The interpretative controversy surrounding the "Taceat" of verse 33 remains unresolved in scholarly debate. One camp views the pericope in which it is located as authentically Pauline, the other does not. The passage is taken either to be consistent with the presupposed understanding requiring women to wear a sign of authority, as found in 1 Corinthians 11, or taken to be inconsistent with 1 Corinthians 11 because (*a*) Paul had changed his mind or (*b*) 1 Corinthians 14 has a different context than 1 Cor 11:3–16.[76] Accepting the Taceat as an authentic Pauline writing, Hurley offers a possible reconstruction of the situation:

> Women were among the prophets and it would seem that women entered into the judgment of the prophets as well, thereby assuming the anomalous role of judging men. It is to this situation that Paul addressed himself as he forbade the women to speak. Paul's wording shows that the antithesis in his mind was not simply that of silence or speaking but rather that of subjection to or violation of created authority structure.[77]

The problems with this view are many, some of which are pointed out by the other camp, which thinks that Paul would not have given such an absolute prohibition to women speaking in the church (particularly when 1 Cor 11:3–16 assumes that women prophesy).

Most scholars who believe that Paul is an egalitarian theologian argue that the Taceat is an interpolation by someone in

---

76. Hans Lietzmann, *An die Korinther I, II*, 4th ed. (Tübingen: Mohr [Siebeck], 1949), 2:75. Allison has given a review of various ways scholars in this camp attempt to qualify the words or particular context of this seemingly odd passage. R. W. Allison, "Let Women Be Silent in the Churches (1 Cor 14:33b–36): What Did Paul Really Say, and What Did It Mean?" *Journal for the Study of the New Testament* 32 (1988): 27–60.

77. Hurley, "Did Paul Require Veils or the Silence of Women?" 217.

the Paulinist school whose point of view is similar to the pastoral tradition of 1 Tm 2:11–15.[78] This camp argues that nowhere else in the genuine Pauline corpus can such theology be found.[79] Equally important, they contend, the theme of these few verses does not fit its literary context. Verses 26–33a talk about orderly worship in the exercising of spiritual gifts; verses 37–40 carry through the theme of verses 26–33, but verses 33b–36 deal with the theme of women in the church. The pericope simply lacks any genuine correspondence with either the overall argument of chapters 12–14 or with the immediate argument of verses 26–40. Verses 34–35 are found in all known manuscripts, but either after verse 33a or after verse 40. This suggests that it is an interpolation. Had it been original, it would not appear in two places in the manuscripts. Of the New Testament manuscripts extant, the earliest ones are from the third century, that is, the 200s; therefore interpolation could have taken place between Paul's time and the 200s.[80]

The interpretive impasse of the Taceat is complicated by the issues of redaction and rhetorical interaction, though when taken into consideration these questions nevertheless make the issue readily comprehensible. The first group of scholars we have looked at

---

78. Jewett, "The Redaction of 1 Corinthians and the Trajectory of the Pauline School," 420–21; Scroggs, "Paul and the Eschatological Woman," 284; Conzelmann, *1 Corinthians,* 290; Barrett, *The First Epistle to the Corinthians,* 330–33; J. Weiss, *Earliest Christianity: A History of the Period A.D. 30–150,* 2 vols. (New York: Harper Torchbooks, 1965), 1:456; C. T. Craig, "The First Epistle to the Corinthians: Exegesis," in *The Interpreter's Bible* (New York and Nashville: Abingdon, 1953), 10:213; Lietzmann, *An die Korinther I, II,* 2:75. On the possibility of vv. 33b–35 as an interpolation, see Hurley, "Did Paul Require Veils or the Silence of Women?" 218.

79. An argument for the egalitarian theology of Paul centers on: (*a*) Gal 3:28; (*b*) 1 Cor 11:2–16, where women pray and prophesy in the assembly, which is also assumed in the repeated "all" of 14:23–24 and 31 and the "each one" of 14:26; (*c*) 1 Cor 7:3–4, which speaks of mutual respect and mutual rights, and vv. 12–13 and 16, which addresses mutual relationships between husband and wife even when one of the partners is an unbeliever; and, (*d*) the fact that some of Paul's coworkers are female; see Philippians 4 and Romans 16: Euodia and Syntyche; Prisca and Aquila, Mary, etc.

80. That these verses are found in the Bible needs explanation. The phenomenon of glosses making their way into the biblical text is well documented elsewhere in the NT, e.g., in Jn 5:3b–4 and 1 Jn 5:7.

which attempts to clarify the words and their context is headed in the right direction, but this group ends up with the wrong conclusion. An analysis of 1 Corinthians 8 and 10 shows that Paul's argument is dialogical, containing many voices, sometimes quoting the audience, sometimes countering them.[81] Paul likes to underscore his own views by contrasting them with the audience's. The first group of scholars seems unaware of this rhetorical technique and makes Paul into an authoritarian chauvinist. Its desire to reconstruct the original context (e.g., Hurley) is commendable, but it is still unable to overcome and explain the so-called un-Pauline language and theology of the Taceat.

The argument that the language and the theology of the passage are un-Pauline does not necessarily lead to the conclusion that it is an interpolation. Only the language of verses 33b–35 looks un-Pauline, and this may in itself be the first indication that the verses are the interpolated words of the audience. This thesis can be substantiated through rhetorical and structural analysis, as seen below. The key to a thorough understanding of 1 Corinthians lies in untangling the redactional process of the letter. As I have tried to show elsewhere, the 1 Corinthians we now have is a highly redacted document, redacted by those whom we call the Paulinists.[82] In the Taceat we have evidence that the Paulinists, a group of Jewish Christians which held to a conservative Pauline theology, are at work.[83] They have drawn from the arsenal of Paul's writings to battle other Pauline factions. The double appearance of "in the churches" in verses 33b and 34a looks odd; Jewett's analysis and reconstruction of the text have shown that these are Paulinist interpolations introduced to catholicize Paul's words for other Pauline factions.[84] Instead of correcting the conservative Jewish faction, now Paul is being re-presented by a similar faction to appear to be on its side.

---

81. See Yeo, *Rhetorical Interaction in 1 Corinthians 8 and 10*, 209–11.

82. See Yeo, *Rhetorical Interaction in 1 Corinthians 8 and 10*, 78–83.

83. See Yeo Khiok-khng, *Feminist Hermeneutics and Theology* [in Chinese] (Hong Kong: Alliance Seminary, 1995), 101–12.

84. Jewett, "The Redaction of 1 Corinthians and the Trajectory of the Pauline School," 338–40.

The Unit and Location of the Taceat

The Taceat belongs to the redacted 1 Corinthians *Letter C* ("The Answer Letter," *Antwortbrief*), which is the mainframe of the letter, consisting of 1 Cor 1:1–6:11, 7:1–8:13, 9:19–23, 10:23–11:1, 12:1–31a, 14:1c–40, 12:31b–13:13, and 16:1–12. Paul has received a precise report from Chloe's people along with a letter requesting advice concerning the intensified conflicts which have arisen between the conservative factions and the proto-Gnostics.[85] Paul is now seriously concerned about factionalism in Corinth. *Letter C* deals with the multiple issues the Corinthians have raised: factions, idol food, worship, and so forth. The use of "concerning" in 7:1, 7:25, 8:1, 12:1, 16:1, and 16:12 is prominent and indicates the topics to which Paul is responding. While *Letter B* seems to be a response to a more general situation, *Letter C* deals with targeted issues.[86] First Corinthians 14:1c-40 deals with the issues of spiritual gifts and speaking in tongues in the Christian assembly.[87] It is here that the problem of silencing women appears.

The appeal to shame in verse 35 rather than to order or to edification constitutes a discrepancy, some argue, between the Taceat and the preceding passages. But that discrepancy can be explained

---

85. See my reconstruction of audience and redaction in Yeo, *Rhetorical Interaction in 1 Corinthians 8 and 10*, 76–83, 120–55.

86. First Corinthians 1:1–6:11 deals with the following issues: church divisions (1:1–17); the radical gospel versus the wisdom of the world (1:18–2:5); the cross as a "stumbling block" to Jews (1:23); the cross as "foolishness" to Greeks; Paul's preaching consistent with the irony of the cross (2:1–5); the cross of Christ and the falsity of the "wisdom and rulers of this age" (2:6–8); the spirit of God and the divine truth in the cross (2:9–10); the proper view of Paul as apostle (1 Cor 4:1–21); the apostle as a steward of the Lord, responsible to God rather than to human beings; the case of boastful incest (1 Cor 5:1–13); the demand to excommunicate the incestuous person from the congregation (5:1–5); and settling church disputes in secular courts (1 Cor 6:1–11). First Corinthians 7:1–40 deals with the following issues: marriage (1 Cor 7:1–16); the Christian's calling and social status (7:17–24); and advice to the unmarried during the end time (7:25–40). First Corinthians 9:19–23 deals with Paul's flexible missionary strategy. First Corinthians 8:1–13 and 10:23–11:1 deal with the issue of food offered to idols. First Corinthians 12:1–31a deals with spiritual gifts in a pagan environment, the mysteries of the charismatic power of speaking in tongues, the danger of spiritual superiority, and the democratic dispersion of the spirit in Christian congregations for the purpose of the "common good."

87. Note the contradiction in 14:22.

away *if* verses 33b–35 are taken not to be Paul's own thought but that of an opponent (perhaps conservative Jewish Christians). It is interesting to observe that codex D (Claromontanus), G, 88*, and others transpose verses 34–35 to follow verse 40, placing the pericope into a discussion of church order rather than prophecy. The Western text probably noticed the discrepancy between verses 34–35 and the discussion of orderly worship in verses 32 and before. John Chrysostom resolved the difficulty of the text's disjointed thought by suggesting that Paul was criticizing the conduct of disorderly women.[88] If Chrysostom's surmise is correct then verses 34–35 would equally fit the flow of thought (on orderly worship) if placed after verse 40.

However, the notion that the Taceat is a Pauline interpolation is to be rejected. Allison's proposal that this is a *fragment* of a "sarcastic rebuttal" by Paul inserted into its present place because of its verbal similarity with the context may be correct.[89] The theme of the Taceat does deal with the democratization of spiritual gifts, especially prophecy, and with orderly worship. Paul's response in verse 36 points to the fact that it is not just males who have been given the gift of prophecy: "What, did the word of God originate with you . . . ?" If the Taceat can be taken to explain Paul's response to the conservative Christians regarding the democratization of spiritual gifts between male and female, it can be seen as an authentic pericope of 1 Corinthians.

The Taceat is an intact unit, finding its place within the larger argument of chapter 14. Verse 33b does not go with 33a. These two juxtaposed verses are problematic because verse 33a focuses on the attribute of divine wholeness, and serves as a conclusion to Paul's response to the Corinthian proto-Gnostics concerning the exercise of spiritual gifts. Verse 33b ("as in all the churches of the saints") cannot be a conclusion but rather begins a new unit. This new unit concerns the right of women either to engage verbally in worship or to remain silent and participate passively. In other words, 33b–36 forms a basic unit within a larger discussion. Verses 37–40 then

---

88. *A Select Library of Nicene and Post-Nicene Fathers of the Christian Church,* trans. Philip Schaff (New York: The Christian Co., 1889), 12:222.
89. Allison, "Let Women Be Silent in the Churches (1 Cor 14:33b–36)," 44.

form the conclusion to 14:1–40. The Taceat constitutes Paul's response to a particular group. The dialogical feature of the verses and their context need to be taken into consideration.

The Audience and Rhetorical Context

The Taceat, both in rhetorical features and context, constitutes a discussion of the egalitarian and democratic nature of spiritual gifts, and it is plausible that it belongs where it is. It fits perfectly well with Paul's observation in verse 36 that the words of God are not limited to one group of people. The immediate context speaks of the need for orderly worship, but the Taceat's appeal to law and shame and not to order is simply the first indication that verses 33b–35 are not the words of Paul but those of the audience. Paul is *quoting the words of the audience.*

In the pericope Paul is vehemently reacting against an exclusively male group of leaders that wants women to be silent in church and to be subordinate to them. The strategy they use is to claim for themselves the exclusive authority to prophesy and to lead "Bible-study" sessions. Thus, a single group within the congregation (the women) is singled out to be silent.

Paul is responding to at least two groups of Christians: a conservative, Hellenistic Jewish group made up of authoritarian males, and a female, liberated, and spirit-filled group. The argument that subordination of women to men was first taught in Judaism is not accurate. In the Old Testament, the prophetess Deborah (Jgs 4:4) reveal the typical view of women. The male group in the Corinthian church is more aptly described as akin to the Hellenistic Jewish missionary tradition.[90] Silencing women through shame and by appealing to the Torah would be more characteristic of a conservative Jewish synagogue, which also may be present in Corinth. We can trace such antifemale bias in the Hellenistic Jewish writings of Sirach, Josephus, and Philo. For example, in the writing of Philo, *Spec. Leg.* 3:169–171:

---

90. Schüssler Fiorenza, *In Memory of Her,* 231; see S. Aalen, "A Rabbinic Formula in 1 Cor 14:34," in *Studia Evangelica,* vol. 2, pt. 1: *The New Testament Scriptures,* ed. F. L. Cross (Berlin: Akademie-Verlag, 1964), 517.

> Women...are best suited to domestic life and to devotion to the household....A woman, then, has no need to occupy herself with anything beyond her household concerns.

We find also in the writing of Josephus, *Ag. Ap.* 2.24, §201:

> The woman, says the Law, is in all things inferior to the man. Let her accordingly be submissive, not for her humiliation, but that she may be directed; for the authority has been given by God to the man.[91]

The appeal is to the law and to tradition. This attitude toward women suggests that the provenance of the Taceat was that of a Jewish Christian.

Having determined the audience and the context in which the response is given, we are ready to analyze the text in terms of its structure and in how the rhetorical interaction takes place.

Rhetorical Analysis: Outline, Technique, and Argumentation

The rhetorical disposition of the pericope can be outlined as below (translations mine). The phrase "As in all the churches of the saints" is an interpolation by a later redactor.[92] Verses 34–35 are a quotation from the audience, the recipients of the passage.

The rhetorical technique and argumentation of the pericope is mainly deliberated in simple dialogue. Verses 34–35 are absolute in tone and consist of two parallel articles. The genre of the pericope is judicial. The quoted material is harsh of tone, and Paul's rebuttal comes in the form of rhetorical questions.[93] The repetition of "in the churches" in verses 33b and 34 is awkward, while

---

91. See J. B. Segal, "The Jewish Attitude towards Women," *Journal of Jewish Studies* 30 (1979): 121–37.

92. Jewett, "The Redaction of 1 Corinthians and the Trajectory of the Pauline School," 421.

93. Similar to Allison's thesis: "Paul's rhetorical questions are his sarcastic rebuttal to his opponents' position which he has summarized in the authoritarian decree of vv. 33b–35. The decree that women should remain silent in church, then, must have been the assertion of an opposing group within the Corinthian church. The only words in the Taceat which express Paul's own views are the rhetorical questions following the disjunctive particle" (Allison, "Let Women Be Silent in the Churches [1 Cor 14:33b–36]," 47).

Conservative Audience:

First injunction:	"Let the women keep silence in the churches," (v. 34a)
Second injunction given as a rationale for the first injunction:	"for they are not permitted to speak." (v. 34b)
Third injunction and second reason:	"But they should be subordinate" (v. 34c)
Third reason:	"as even the law says." (v. 34d)
Fourth injunction:	"If there is anything they desire to know, let them ask their husbands at home." (v. 35a)
Fourth reason:	"For it is shameful for a woman to speak in church."

Paul:

One rebuttal in a double dose:	"What! Did the word of God originate with you (males)? Or are you the only ones (males) it has reached?" (v. 36)

verses 34–35 run in conflict with 1 Corinthians 11, the words "you [Corinthians]...only" contradict "in all the churches of the saints" (v. 33b). To say that verses 34–35 are the actual words and conviction of Paul is to contradict his theology in 1 Corinthians 11.

There are indications in verses 34–35 that the words are not Paul's. "To speak" in verses 34–35 may not be specifically referring to prophetic speech because the issue is one of raising questions for the sake of information. "To speak" may refer for example to women's "discernment," the discerning of prophetic oracles of 14:29.[94] One may assume that in the worship service the congregations were asking questions and giving answers.[95] Windisch, following Chrysostom's interpretation, thinks "to speak" refers to

---

94. So Hurley, "Did Paul Require Veils or the Silence of Women?" 217.

95. Nils Johansson, "1 Cor. XIII and 1 Cor. XIV," *New Testament Studies* 10 (1963/64): 391.

women's disruptive speaking.[96] This is unlikely because, had that been so, the male chauvinists would certainly have used that as a reason to forbid the women from speaking in church; second, Paul's response would also have clarified this crucial point for the conduct of orderly worship discussed in chapter 14. Of course, nothing like this appears. Allison also points out, "In the context Paul's principle is 'let everything be done for building up' (v. 27), 'for God is not a God of disorder, but of peace' (v. 33a). The Taceat, although 'verbally in complete harmony with that context,' stands 'outside the framework of normative principle (order) cited above (vv. 27, 33)...for *hypotassesthōsan* certainly means 'let them be subordinate,' not jut [*sic*] 'let them be orderly.' "[97]

One may explain verses 34–35 as Paul's words and explain the discrepancy between women prophesying in 1 Corinthians 11 and the silencing of women here by qualifying *gunaikes* to refer to married women.[98] There is however no social norm or practice known which singled out only married women to be reticent in public. Though the reasoning of the chauvinist males does appeal to wives to learn from husbands, the interpretation that the pericope speaks of relations between husband and wife is not well grounded. The pericope is discussing *women* in the church rather than *wives* exclusively.

Another reason to opt for "women" rather than "wives" in the interpretation is the extent of the prohibition found in the pericope, which reflects the dominion of the chauvinist males over women. The absolute language of "for they are not permitted to speak" has no qualification whatsoever. There is not a single absolute use (i.e., without qualification) of the verb "to speak" in its other twenty-one occurrences in 1 Corinthians 14, yet it is twice so used here. Similarly, the injunction "to silence" in verses 28 and 30 is absolute. C. K. Barrett's citation of Plutarch's *Conjugal Precepts* (31–32) is apt and illustrative of the chauvinist males: "Not only

---

96. See Allison, "Let Women Be Silent in the Churches (1 Cor 14:33b–36)," 36–37, for discussion on this word.

97. Allison, "Let Women Be Silent in the Churches (1 Cor 14:33b–36)," 38; see Meeks, "The Image of the Androgyne," 203–4.

98. For example, Robertson and Plummer, *A Critical and Exegetical Commentary on the First Epistle of St. Paul to the Corinthians,* 230.

the arm but the voice of a modest woman ought to be kept from the public, and she should feel shame at being heard, as at being stripped (31), and she should speak to, or through, her husband (32)."

Yet the chauvinist male appeal to the law ("just as the law says") is vague, if not without ground. Does the law here refer to Gn 3:16 where God decrees that the punishment for the woman's transgression is to be the pain of childbirth, and that her husband "shall rule over her"? This is pure speculation. Gn 3:16 is not a law, and was never perceived to be a law. Moreover, if Gn 3:16 is the allusion, then the explicit language of "ruling over you" would surely have been used. When Paul appeals to "the law" he always cites the text (as in 9:8, 14:21) to support the point he is making. Since nowhere does he appeal to the law as binding in this absolute way on Christian behavior, the Taceat here could not be Paul's prohibition. More difficult yet is that the law does not say any such thing. Perhaps the chauvinists made it up.

The vocabulary of verses 34–35 is un-Pauline also. The word "be permitted" occurs elsewhere only in 1 Tm 2:12, and the word has an authoritarian connotation. The formula "not permitted" is probably rabbinic in nature;[99] the prohibition cannot be from Paul. The gloss is obvious also in light of the redundant phrase "in the churches" in verses 33b and 34a. "As in all the churches of the saints" of verse 33a entails no qualification. Instead it is absolute and universal, a claim made by the conservative chauvinists. The argument of the chauvinists is hardly convincing without substantive support. Paul finds it quite unnecessary to refute their weak argument. But the intention implied within the argument needs to be rebutted. In short, Paul does not take the four *reasons* of the argument seriously, but he takes the *intention* of the four injunctions seriously.

To sort out the quotation from Paul's own words is our immediate task. Hurley thinks that verse 36 resumes Paul's argument on prophecy in verse 33. He thinks that the "command of the Lord" refers to his own words, so "you...only" in verse 36 stands in opposition to the "I" of verse 37, rather than to "all the churches

---

99. S. Aalen, "A Rabbinic Formula in 1 Cor 14:34," 513–25.

of the saints" in verse 33b.[100] But Hurley's logic is neither clear nor convincing, because this is not a pericope dealing with the polemic between who has the Lord's command or who has prophetic authority, namely, the congregation or Paul. The "command of the Lord" refers to the absolute prohibition pronounced by the conservative faction. The "you...only" refers to the conservative audience whose position regarding women Paul intends to correct.

The use of *ē*, a disjunctive particle, is used by Paul to set off his own view from that of the audience. One notices that the Western text cut out only verses 33b–35, perhaps sensing the gap between verses 35 and 36, which is the breaking point between Paul's quotation of the audience's argument and his own counterargument. Allison explains that

> Rhetorical questions introduced by the disjunctive *ē* are frequently used by Paul to counter opposing views.... This use of the disjunctive *ē* is a common grammatical feature of classical and Koiné Greek. It introduces a rebuttal against a point of view or corollary implicit *in the immediately preceding clause* which presumably is not perceived or recognized by its proponents.[101]

Examples of this contrastive or corrective usage is seen in 1 Cor 6:2f. and 6:8f., where Paul also contrasts his argument with that of the audience.

Paul's position is clear in his rhetorical question: "What! Did the word of God originate with you, or are you the only ones it has reached?" The negative answer is obvious and needs to be stated in the rhetorical force of the question raised. The divine distribution of the spiritual gifts of 1 Corinthians 12 and 14 has already given the answer: man and woman can speak and prophesy!

---

100. Hurley, "Did Paul Require Veils or the Silence of Women?" 218.

101. Allison, "Let Women Be Silent in the Churches (1 Cor 14:33b–36)," 46. See David W. Odell-Scott, "Let the Women Speak in Church: An Egalitarian Interpretation of 1 Cor 14:33b–36," *Biblical Theological Bulletin* 13 (1983): 90–93; H. W. Smyth, *Greek Grammar* (Cambridge: Harvard University Press, 1966), sec. 2861.

Paul, a Christological and Mutual Egalitarian

The interpretation of 1 Corinthians 11 and 14 causes us to raise the question of whether Paul was a male chauvinist, as most commentators think.[102] Blasi's conclusion that "the communion and egalitarianism of the Christian ideal clashed with the hierarchical reality of the household setting in which the churches were organized"[103] is neither a fair nor accurate description of the Pauline movement in Corinth. Paul worked hard at organizing an egalitarian setting for the Corinthian congregation so that all could participate in the church's life. Is Paul blatantly contradicting himself by affirming the women's right to speak (pray and prophesy) in 11:5–7 and by commanding women to be silent in 1 Corinthians 14?[104] Traditionally, scholars tend to reconcile the two texts by two efforts: the first approach is to bring 1 Corinthians 11 in line with 1 Corinthians 14, the latter being conceived as the normative Pauline view while chapter 11 is deemed Paul's response to the charismatic women in the Corinthian church;[105] the second approach is to domesticate the ultraconservative view in 14:34–35 to the normative view in 11:2–16 or simply to treat 14:34–35 as spurious.[106] The interpretation above has shown that Paul cannot be an anachronistic feminist-liberationist, but that he is an advocate and a practitioner of eschatological, christological, and mutual egalitarian theology.

---

102. Trompf, "On Attitudes toward Women in Paul and Paulinist Literature," 196–215; Weiss, *Earliest Christianity*, 452–584; idem, *Der erste Korintherbrief*; Pagels, "Paul and Women: A Response to Recent Discussion," 543–49.

103. A. J. Blasi, *Early Christianity as a Social Movement* (New York: P. Lang, 1988), 63. So Meeks, *First Urban Christians*, 75–77.

104. Scholars who detect such contradiction are R. St. J. Parry, *The First Epistle of Paul the Apostle to the Corinthians*, Cambridge Greek New Testament (Cambridge: Cambridge University Press, 1937), xlvi, and Moffatt, *The First Epistle of Paul to the Corinthians*, 152.

105. Scholars who tend toward this approach are Robertson and Plummer, *A Critical and Exegetical Commentary on the First Epistle of St. Paul to the Corinthians*, 232–33; Héring, *The First Epistle of Saint Paul to the Corinthians*, 154; and Leon Morris, *The First Epistle of Paul to the Corinthians: An Introduction and Commentary* (London: Tyndale Press, 1969), 201.

106. Scholars who tend toward this approach are Weiss, *Der erste Korintherbrief*; and R. Scroggs, "Paul: Chauvinist or Liberationist?" 307.

In Response to the Malaysian "Vision 2020"

The mutual, egalitarian, feminist theology of Paul in 1 Corinthians 11 and 14 has serious implications for the roles and spiritual gifts of women in the modern world, such as those in Malaysia. Paul's egalitarian view of the role of both women and men speaks to the conscience of the Malaysian nation as it seeks to bring women into the role of nation building.

The Place of Women in Malaysian History

The role of women in achieving national prosperity is not altogether a new agenda in Vision 2020. As early as 30 August 1975, Malaysian Prime Minister Tun Abdul Razak said, "Kerajaan yang saya pimpin hari ini sentiasa memberikan perhatian yang berat terhadap kemajuan kaum wanita supaya mereka dapat memainkan peranan serta mengambil bahagian yang sewajarnya dalam pembangunan negara." ("The government that I am leading today has always paid close attention to the *prosperity of women* so that they can *play a significant role* in the building of the nation.")[107] After going through the colonial, independent, and postcolonial periods, Malaysia now wants to be an industrialized nation, a technologically competent and prosperous country, and one of the Newly Industrialized Countries (NICs). In order to build up a mature, confident, democratic, and resilient nation, Malaysia will need rapid industrialization across all labor sectors, among all ethnicities, and between genders. The Sixth Malaysia Plan, 1991–95 (SMP6), and the Second Outline Perspective Plan, 1991–2000 (SOPP2), advocate a fair and equitable distribution of the nation's wealth among all groups and a wider participation by the society's women and disadvantaged members. This emphasis on the role of women is similar to Paul's intention to include women in the life of the church. The Sixth Malaysia Plan hoped to bring women into the mainstream of industrial development. Unfortunately, figures on poverty and the distribution of income from both the SMP6 and SOPP2 are not gender sensitive. As D. P. Abraham writes:

---

107. Taken from Nik Safiah Karim, *Wanita Malaysia: Harapan Dan Cabaran* (Kuala Lumpur: 'K' Publishing & Distributors, 1990), 117. Italics mine.

Of the households that are listed as existing below the poverty line there is no information on the situation of women as earners or owners of income in these households. While information on the employment distribution by occupation and sex for 1970–90 and by industry and sex is provided in the SMP (416–17) there is no information on the ownership of income of women who are wage earners. The contribution of women as unpaid workers in the home is not taken into account in the GNP as it is in some countries, and there is no information on the poverty level of housewives.[108]

During the precolonial and colonial periods, the role of women was defined functionally, according to ends: aristocratic women were to foster better political connections through international or tribal marriages, peasant women were to contribute to agricultural production, and prostitutes were to entertain when paid. The Pauline texts examined above provide a sharp critique of the attitude regarding women in the precolonial and colonial periods in Malaysia. The exclusion and abuse of women, which still continues, are social evils that need to be chastised, as Paul did in 1 Corinthians 14. The abuse of women belittles the gifts and talents of women and shows a disrespect for the image of God they bear.

There are glorious examples of women achieving great power and acclaim in Malaysia. In the absence of male heirs, Patani of the Tanah Melayu was once ruled by a queen. She was Raja Ijau. Kelantan was once ruled by Cik Siti Wan Kembang.[109] Can Vision 2020 supersede the precolonial acceptance of women's role in business, industry, and politics? From a Christian point of view, Vision 2020 will need to be sustained by the Pauline vision of male and female as found in 1 Corinthians.

Women in the Corinthian church were involved in the same ministries as men. Similarly, since precolonial times in Malaysia, women have played an active role in tin mining, trading, padi

---

108. Dulcie P. Abraham, "Malaysian Women and Vision 2020," in *A Christian Response to Vision 2020: Theoloji Wawasan 2020*, ed. Batumalai Sadayandy (Kuala Lumpur: S. Batumalai, 1992), 56–67.

109. Jamilah Ariffin, *Women and Development in Malaysia* (Kuala Lumpur: Pelanduk, 1992), 2.

planting, the fishing industry, the handloom sector, business enterprises, and various subsistence industries — in addition to being housewives and mothers. Ariffin writes,

> The reason for their active participation could be that they had the right to own land under customary laws or *adat*.... [I]n any patriarchal Malay community which practiced *Adat Temenggong,* women had an equal access to land, whereas in a matrilineal society which practiced *Adat Perpateh,* women had the exclusive right to land. However, the coming of Islam altered this right and women were only entitled to half the man's share.[110]

Today no one would call for a return to the feminist consciousness of the precolonial period, but a critical review of the history of women's roles in Malaysia requires us to question to what extent the nation is now heading toward an egalitarian, industrialized society in which a woman's worth is not reduced to her commercial value and the meaning of her existence to a mere statistic. Paul argues for the equality and mutuality of man and woman while maintaining the uniqueness of women, but he argues against women becoming men. Similarly, an egalitarian vision of women in Malaysia cannot result in the blind conformity of women with men.

Malaysia had taken various steps to protect the rights of women before Vision 2020. With the introduction of formal education for women by the British in the 1930s, women's active involvement in politics during the colonial period became evident in the first Malay women's organization, the Malay Women Teachers Union, with Hajah Zain Suleiman as its founder, in 1929. Subsequently, other women's organizations formed: Persatuan Kaum Ibu (formed in 1946 as auxiliary to the United Malay National Organization [UMNO]; it later became Wanita UMNO), Angkatan Wanita Sedar (AWAS), the Malayan Chinese Association (MCA; formed in 1949), Wanita MCA (formed in 1972),[111] the All Women's Action Movement (AWAM), the Association of Women Lawyers (AWL),

---

110. Ariffin, *Women and Development,* 3.
111. Ariffin, *Women and Development,* 20–21.

the National Council of Women's Organizations (NCWO), and the Women's Aid Organization.

The long and significant contribution of Malaysian women to education and to the caring services is evident in the St. Nicholas Home and School in Penang (set up by the Anglican Church), Malaysian Care, Bethany Home, the Little Sisters of the Poor, and other groups. A recent study by N. S. Karim shows that the role of women in education and social welfare has been visible and strong, but less so in the economic and political arenas.[112] However, Ariffin's study clearly shows that women in the precolonial, colonial, and postcolonial periods have been actively involved in almost all sectors of life.[113] Ariffin adds that "[p]erhaps the only position from which women are excluded are those related to the performance of religious functions, for example, leading the congregation in prayer, a position similar to that of the *Imam;* and the solemnization of marriages as in the case of the *kathi.*"[114] Can it be said that in Islam men and women are not equal? Could it be that the Islamic law permitting polygamy as an exclusive right of the male finds its rationale in the inequality of men and women? Some Christian denominations have the same challenge to face with regard to religious equality, such as the ordination of women.

Amid the challenges, the government has taken the necessary steps to ensure legal protection for women. The federal constitution guarantees the equality of men and women. The rights of women are also protected by such laws as the Law Reform Act of 1976 (Marriage and Divorce) and by the 1989 Rape Law.[115] Many laws have been enacted to protect the personal and labor rights of women, such as the Employment Act of 1955 (revised in 1981) and

---

112. See Karim, *Wanita Malaysia,* 99.

113. Ariffin, *Women and Development,* 1–29 and passim. On the history of women in the public life of Malaysia, see Karim, *Wanita Malaysia,* 1–43, and the more in-depth survey, including various statistics, of Ariffin, *Women and Development,* 1–29 (historical development), 30–53 (labor force), 54–72 (education), 73–105 (medicine and health), 106–23 (government), 124–70 (law).

114. Ariffin, *Women and Development,* 128.

115. The Law Reform (Marriage and Divorce) Act of 1976 prescribes compulsory registration of all marriages and prohibits polygamy in non-Muslims. The 1989 Rape Laws impose a 20-year sentence on those who rape women.

the Domestic Violence Act. Ariffin's study indicates that "at the outset, the labors laws in Malaysia do not reveal inequality or discrimination against women. These laws apply equally to both sexes although some provisions apply exclusively to women only under the guise of 'protecting' women workers."[116] For example, the maternity protection section gives a female employee 60 consecutive days off only if she has less than four children.[117]

The Malaysian government has also advocated and supported various institutions for the benefit of women. In 1975 the United Nations declared the period 1976–85 the Women's Decade, with the theme "Equality of Rights, Development, and Peace." In the same year, Malaysia set up the National Advisory Council on the Integration of Women in Development (NACIWID) to advise the government on women's issues. In 1983, the Secretariat for Women's Affairs (HAWA) was established to monitor and evaluate the services for women that were being provided by both the public and the private sectors. The government allocates funds for women who are housewives and mothers through the National Family Planning and Development Board, promotes educated and qualified women to high positions in government departments, and enacts laws to upgrade and protect the interests and status of women. Nongovernmental organizations, such as the National Council of Women's Organizations (NCWO), Women's Institute (WI), Islamic Women's Action Organization (PERTIWI), and Women's Aid Organization (WAO), provide and promote welfare services.[118] A National Policy for Women was created in December 1989, to be implemented in the Sixth Malaysia Plan (1991–95).[119]

In the Sixth Malaysia Plan, the government acknowledged the significant contribution of women in national development. The government actively and consistently promoted and facilitated the participation of women in the rapid economic and industrial de-

---

116. Ariffin, *Women and Development,* 133.

117. The International Labor Organization (ILO, ILO Convention Number 3) recommended maternity leave of twelve weeks as early as 1919.

118. Abraham, "Malaysian Women and Vision 2020," 55.

119. See Ariffin, *Women and Development,* 28.

velopment of the nation.[120] The government's National Policy for Women proposed two vague objectives: (*a*) to ensure equitable sharing in the acquisition of resources and information, and (*b*) to integrate women in all sectors of national development.[121]

The Challenge of Women's Issues in Vision 2020

The challenge of women's issues found in Vision 2020 is broad and complex. I will simply discuss a few for our reference.

1. The Malaysian Vision 2020 needs a sufficient balance between the Pauline vision of the uniqueness of the sexes (man being man, woman being woman) and of the mutuality of men and women. To protect the interests of women, the government must ensure that women are provided access to essential services, property ownership, substantial financial aid, housing and transportation facilities, and educational programs. The government should ensure a lower tax bracket for those in need.[122]

2. The process of industrialization may relegate women to the lowest-paying jobs and to some of the most tedious and abusive situations.[123] Being a part of the industrialization process does not necessarily mean equality for women, even though some jobs are better handled by women. Striking a balance between the needs of men and women will not come naturally. The answer lies in developing a cooperative process among all groups. Neither men nor women, of course, want low-paying, tedious, or abusive working conditions. While agreeing with both Abraham's and Karim's proposal that more women are needed in managerial and decision-making roles,[124] the crucial point is not whether women are given the decision-making role; rather, the crucial issue is how men and women are involved *together* in the decision-making process; the long discussion above on 1 Corinthians 11 speaks to this point.

---

120. "Sixth Malaysia Plan, 1991–1995" (Government of Malaysia, National Printing Department, Kuala Lumpur, 1991), 413.

121. "Sixth Malaysia Plan, 1991–1995," 413.

122. Abraham, "Malaysian Women and Vision 2020," 52–53.

123. Cecila Ng and Carol Young, *Malaysian Women at the Crossroads* (London: International Reports, Women and Society, n.d.).

124. Abraham, "Malaysian Women and Vision 2020," 56, and Karim, *Wanita Malaysia*, 81.

3. The feminist theological concern in Malaysia for gender issues needs to be broadened to include issues of race, nationality, and class. Such broadening will be crucial to the Malaysian setting in which race, national identity, and economic ability are at least as important as gender. The term "womanist theology" is more inclusive than "feminist theology" in that it seeks to make us aware of factors besides gender. An example of womanist theology is found in Phyllis Trible's interpretation of the story of Hagar in the Old Testament. Trible points out that Hagar is the embodiment of the oppressed because of her nationality, race, class, and sex. Trible explains that "[a]s a symbol of the oppressed... all sorts of rejected women find their stories in her. She is the faithful maid exploited, the black women used by the male and abused by the female of the ruling class... the resident alien without legal recourse... the pregnant young woman alone.... She is bruised for the iniquities of Sarah and Abraham; upon her is the chastisement that makes them whole."[125] She is the victim that makes others whole. Hagar is abused and rejected not just because she is a female but because she belongs to the wrong race. It is not uncommon even in the postcolonial period to see native women (and men) serving in subordinate positions, or worse still, in abusive situations in government offices and in major corporations. Malaysian womanist theology therefore has to break through the ethnically and socially insensitive position of much traditional feminist thought. Womanist theology for Malaysian Chinese needs to be sensitive not only to gender, but also to social, political, economic, and racial factors, just as Paul was sensitive to the situations, problems, and ideologies of his audiences.

4. A womanist concern in a Malaysia in the midst of industrialization is with the wholistic aspects of the role and participation of women in society. Nik Safiah Karim has already spelled out the identity and role conflicts which emerge from the full participation of women in national industrialization and in family relationships.[126] Building on technological concerns rather than on

---

125. Phyllis Trible, *Texts of Terror* (Philadelphia: Fortress, 1984), 27–28.

126. Karim, *Wanita Malaysia,* 72–74 and 77–86. Again, my critique of this book is that the author's concern for women's participation is too shallow, for she looks for equal participation of women in the public scene without considering

concern for human relationships (as does Paul), Vision 2020 may create inhuman, mechanical men and women, rather than a caring society based on ethnic and moral values. That is, rapid industrialization without a moral and human base is likely to create either a nation of robots or a nation in which the hurts and pains of those who have little power, such as women and non-Malays who are not in visible positions, are increased. A Malaysian womanist theology will need to be concerned with egalitarian instead of hierarchical relationships, sharing instead of domination, mutuality instead of subordination.

Toward Vision 20/20

We cannot just focus on the gender issue, especially on the feminine gender alone, when speaking of equality in a multifaceted social reality, be that in the Pauline churches or in Malaysian society. Paul worked hard at highlighting the image, glory, and status of women, and he also seeks to transform and point out the transformative mutuality which exists between female and male. Women do have freedom and authority, so do men. An individual's gender has to be integrated with one's race, age, social class, and religious faith. These qualifiers are not loosely independent but organically related. Nevertheless, the very nature of industrialization may impose on the worth and status of *women* an artificially mechanical and commercial value only. Insofar as this is true, great concern needs to be expressed about Vision 2020. It is suggested here that Paul's vision in 1 Corinthians provides a corrective lens for us as Malaysians so that our visions will truly be 20/20!

---

male-female relationships. The problem in the identity crisis experienced by contemporary women is that women are alone in their pursuit to become fully human, but that actualization cannot be achieved without relating to men.

A Chinese Conclusion

"What has Jerusalem to do with Beijing?" All the chapters in this volume attempt to answer this question from different biblical texts and with different perspectives. Part Two (Dialogue with Perennial Themes in Chinese Culture) and Part Three (Biblical Messages for the Current Chinese Situation) are experiments in theologizing the multidimensional grace and redemption of God from a Chinese perspective. The question, "What has Jerusalem to do with Beijing?" is meant not to seek a comprehensive answer; the intention of asking the question is to engender further experiment and dialogue.

This collection of ten essays represents my own experimental reading of the Bible over the past six years. After working through the material, I do find cross-cultural reading of the Bible a viable option. As the monograph has shown, a cross-cultural reading is also a contextual reading. A contextual reading of the Bible is difficult for me because "the historical tradition to which we all belong"[1] is predominantly a Western philosophical and theological tradition. I include myself in this tradition because my theological training occurred in the United States (1984–92). I have no pretense at all that the reading demonstrated in these essays is not "Westernized." Their use of biblical material, exegetical method, as well as thought forms is thoroughly "Westernized." Regarding exegetical method and the use of biblical research material, it is difficult to come up with a purely Chinese method or with purely Chinese research. The use of the English medium is an audience-oriented issue. If the monograph were written for those who can

---

1. H.-G. Gadamer, *Truth and Method*, trans. Garrett Borden John Cumming (New York: Seabury Press, 1975), xxv.

only read Chinese, the result would have been different if not totally new.

Although the medium of expression is indicative of one's cultural mind-set, it is not necessarily conditioned or limited by it. Just as Paul could convey Jewish thought through the medium of Greek, I have used English to express Chinese thought. What is intriguing and necessary is the transference of thought from one culture to another. In that sense, methods and material need to be multicultural. The cross-cultural reading done here is itself a Chinese perspective, with which I am experimenting. These are some of the factors that will increasingly shape and sharpen my critical reading of the Bible.

The urgent issue with which I am struggling is the metacritical principle within cross-cultural and critical readings of the Bible. What often occupies my mind as I reflect on my own cross-cultural reading is the question of a metacritical hermeneutic, one which involves not only a critical reading of the Bible but which also critiques the reader. As much as I would like for a mutual transformation between the biblical text and the context in which I live, I have to admit that I have no control over the transformative process. I do admit that if the formative powers of the tradition, the text, world history, and the pre-understanding I bring to the process are neither universal nor unified, neither Abraham-ically rooted nor historically oriented, then my cross-cultural and interreligious hermeneutic needs to be articulated and not left in silence. Furthermore, the hermeneutic has to be open to a genuine, ongoing community dialogue which is transcultural and free. Interpretation involves not only speaking but also listening, and transposing oneself "out of one's own frame of mind."[2] Such interpretation is not only dialogical in a social context but also critical in intentionality.

The sociocritical approach of Habermas's hermeneutics has increasingly gained my attention, though it is not prominent in this monograph. His approach is valuable to my own cross-cultural, hermeneutical considerations regarding the issue of metacritical

---

2. F. D. E. Schleiermacher, *Hermeneutics: The Handwritten Manuscripts,* trans. J. Duke and J. Forstman (Missoula, Mont.: Scholars Press, 1977), 109.

principles. Habermas rejects Gadamer's notions of "the ontological priority of linguistic tradition," the claim of universality, and the lack of social critique.[3] If I were to attempt to read the biblical text without a critical eye, I would end up agreeing with the claim of the universality of the biblical texts. To question the legitimacy of authority or tradition in the distorted communication process is what I need and have begun to do.[4] One cannot assume that one particular reading is the right one simply because it has been there for a long time. Neither can one assume that a particular person's reading is correct simply because of that person's authority within a community. One needs to assume that any reading is unavoidably a distorted process. Habermas's sociocritical hermeneutics aims toward the elimination of existing distorted communication.[5] In so doing he takes the communicative life-world seriously, but he also allows a *transcendental critique* of social interaction within social systems. The cross-cultural hermeneutic in this monograph constitutes a sociocritical enterprise which seeks to transform Chinese culture in the process of reading the biblical text from a Chinese context.

The cross-cultural reading in this monograph also faces the issue of my own ideological reading. If "ideological reading of the biblical text" means letting a "system of ideas [express] a particular point of view,"[6] then I must acknowledge my "ideology," which includes my cultural bias, certain ideological presuppositions, and a readerly orientation. However, if "ideological reading of the biblical text" means the rationalization of self-interest as well as the reinforcing of one's status quo, then I need to allow the ideological critique of a cross-cultural hermeneutic to challenge and transform my reading. Swartely argues correctly that "[b]iblical interpretation, if it is worthy to be so called, will challenge the ideology of

3. Jürgen Habermas, "The Hermeneutical Claim to Universality," in Josef Bleicher, *Contemporary Hermeneutics: Hermeneutics as Method, Philosophy, and Critique* (London: Routledge & Kegan Paul, 1980), 203–5.

4. Habermas, "The Hermeneutical Claim to Universality," 206–8.

5. Jürgen Habermas, *The Theory of Communicative Action: The Critique of Functionalist Reason,* 2 vols. (Cambridge: Polity Press, 1984, 1987).

6. Robert McAfee Brown, *Theology in a New Key* (Philadelphia: Westminster Press, 1978), 78–80.

the interpreter. It can and will lead to change."[7] For example, in the discussion of male-female relations in chapter 10, thorough-going and consistently hierarchical or egalitarian readings are less objective and more dangerous than ones that concede that "not all of the texts say the same thing."[8] "This vulnerability [of admitting not all texts say the same thing] becomes a strength because it shows that the projection of the interpreters' ideology onto the text has been broken. *They see something that doesn't say exactly what they would like the text to say.* This fact . . . represents breakthrough and hope because it witnesses to the possibility that interpreters can listen to the text carefully enough *not to like it.* . . . [For example, in texts dealing with women's roles,] the hierarchical position makes Genesis 1–2 mirror what 1 Corinthians 11 mixed with Ephesians 5:21–33 says. And then 1 Corinthians 11 is made to say exactly what Genesis 2 has been made to say."[9] One might cite the harmonization of Scripture as one of the best reading principles, but often such harmonization does not do justice to the cultural and authorial contexts. The biblical narratives of God's interaction with the people over the millennia, in different geographic, political, social, economic, and cultural settings, call for diversity in God's revelation and divine responses in the Bible. Biblical truth is transcendent only in the sense that it is from the divine (transcending the human realm and thought), but biblical truth is concretely and historically revealed for specific problems, needs, and opportunities in various contexts.

The cross-cultural reading of biblical texts in this volume has shown my concern for the way the biblical narratives help us to relate to our stories, diverse as they are in terms of racial, national, religious, educational, economic, and gender factors. The biblical texts point to a larger narrative in which the divine interacts with mankind's story to create meaningful and bountiful life. This is accomplished by the Messiah of Yahweh. How has the Messiah accomplished this? He has redeemed us from conflict and mistrust by exhorting us to love our neighbor as ourselves. He has redeemed

---

7. Willard M. Swartley, *Slavery, Sabbath, War, and Women: Case Issues in Biblical Interpretation* (Scottdale, Pa.: Herald Press, 1983), 185.

8. Swartley, *Slavery, Sabbath, War, and Women*, 185.

9. Swartley, *Slavery, Sabbath, War, and Women*, 185–86. Italics his.

us from ambiguity and meaninglessness by giving us hope and the promise of eternal life through the unveiling of the end by His resurrection. He has redeemed us from alienation and loneliness by incarnating God's presence both in the Word narrated (Scripture) and in the Word celebrated (sacrament). He has redeemed us from evil and suffering by his own passionate suffering on the cross, thus transforming evil into good (Rom 8:28). He has redeemed us from hubris and boasting by inviting all to come to him in faith as they accept the Abba's Love, a love which accepts all unconditionally. In short, the Messiah has accomplished this by disclosing "the presence of [the] Gratuitous Love"[10] of the Father, whose will is not to destroy each culture's story, but whose will frees all stories and incorporates them into "God's story." That is what the Good News is all about — Jesus is the story and symbol of the God whose love is redemptive, even of our stories!

---

10. David Buttrick, *Homiletic: Moves and Structures* (Philadelphia: Fortress, 1987), 15.

Index of Biblical References

Index of Modern Authors